To my family

FAMILY
POLICY

FAMILY POLICY

Constructed Solutions to Family Problems

Shirley L. Zimmerman

Sage Publications
International Educational and Professional Publisher
Thousand Oaks ▪ London ▪ New Delhi

For information:

Sage Publications, Inc.
2455 Teller Road
Thousand Oaks, California 91320
E-mail: order@sagepub.com

Sage Publications Ltd.
6 Bonhill Street
London EC2A 4PU
United Kingdom

Sage Publications India Pvt. Ltd.
M-32 Market
Greater Kailash I
New Delhi 110 048 India

Printed in the United States of America .

Library of Congress Cataloging-in-Publication Data

Zimmerman, Shirley.
   Family policy: Constructed solutions to family problems / by Shirley
L. Zimmerman.
      p. cm.
   Includes bibliographical references and index.
   ISBN 978-0-7619-2093-9
   1. Family policy—United States. 2. Family—United States. I. Title.
HQ535 .Z56 2001
306.85'0973—dc21   00-012630

09 8 7 6 5 4

Acquiring Editor:	Jim Brace-Thompson
Editorial Assistant:	Anna Howland
Production Editor:	Diane S. Foster
Editorial Assistant:	Kathryn Journey
Typesetter/Designer:	Tina Hill
Indexer:	Molly Hall
Cover Designer:	Michelle Lee

CONTENTS

There is no such thing as a fixed policy, because policy like all organic entities is always in the making.

Attributed to Lord Salisbury
—M. R. D. Foot (1956),
British Foreign Policy Since 1898–9

This book is about family policy, a topic that fascinates and has fascinated me for a very long time. Family policy is concerned with the problems of families in relation to society, and its goal is the advancement of family well-being. The book is divided into five parts. Part I lays the foundation for the discussion of family policy and is comprised of five chapters. The emergence of family policy discourse and knowledge-producing activities is the focus of Chapter 1. The chapter also includes definitions of family policy and a brief historical review of family policy developments in the United States. Chapter 2 discusses family policy discourse and how language is used in the construction (or the linkage of concepts and ideas) of family problems and their solutions. The problems of families are paramount themes in family policy discourse and are discussed in Chapter 3. Chapters 4 and 5 focus on the many and changing meanings of family; family values in family policy discourse in the context of family change; and attitudes toward government, families, and the economy as central to the construction of policy solutions to family problems.

Part II consists of three chapters and focuses on policy solutions actually constructed to address family problems at state and federal levels—mostly during the 1990s. Some constructions are included from the 1980s for comparison. Chapter 6 deals with family policies constructed at the federal level for selected years in the 1980s and 1990s. Chapter 7 focuses on the congressional debates of the 1996 Defense of Marriage Act (DOMA) (Defense of Marriage Act, 1996) that reveal the attitudes embedded in its construction as both problem and solution. Chapter 8 focuses on policy solutions constructed in the 1990s by six states with different political cultures (political culture refers to the attitudes held by a population toward government and other people). Data from the 1980s are included for three of the states for comparative purposes.

Part III, consisting of six chapters, focuses on policy frameworks or perspectives that readers can use as guides for policy practice. The different frameworks included in the discussion are the institutional framework (Chapter 9), the rational choice framework (Chapter 10), incremental theory and game theory (Chapter 11), political culture theory (Chapter 12), interest group theory and elite theory (Chapter 13), and systems theory (Chapter 14). My intent is to familiarize readers with a range of policy frameworks and theories that I have found useful in trying to understand how policy solutions are constructed and what may account for some constructions and not others. Please note that I use the words *conceptual frameworks, theoretical perspectives, theories,* and *models* interchangeably. A *model* is a pattern of conceptual relationships that in some way imitates, duplicates, or analogously illustrates a pattern of relationships observed in the empirical (real) world (Theodorson & Theodorson, 1969). Broadly, a *theory* consists of a set of interrelated propositions that provides a conceptual scheme for explaining human behavior and other phenomena. You, the readers, can pick and choose from among the frameworks presented here the one that best fits your questions about a given family policy, either as it is being formulated or constructed or after. You do not have to learn all the frameworks at once, but by knowing where to find them in this book, you can return to them when you want to use one of them to better understand a particular policy problem.

Throughout the book, I provide many examples from newspaper articles to show how the frameworks can be used to analyze the processes involved in constructing policy solutions to family problems. You can do the same thing. Having one or two frameworks in mind, as you are watching TV or attending public meetings or hearings or reading the newspaper, think about the concepts associated with that framework in relation to what you are observing and apply them to your observations, using the words—the concepts—associated with the framework so that they become easy for you to say. In class, I have four or five students break into groups to analyze news articles I have selected for analysis. Invariably, students find the exercise fun and enlightening. At the end of the sessions, the groups submit a summary of their analyses—based on the framework assigned for that day. Everyone is expected to participate in the discussions and to come prepared, having read the assigned framework chapter and accompanying article. Students take turns with various group roles: chair, recorder, observer, and so on. Because so many of the articles in the *New York Times* report on the processes involved in the construction of policy solutions to family problems as well as the substance of such solutions, I tend to rely on the *Times* for examples. Even if you are not a subscriber, you can access it via the Internet. But other news sources will do as well.

Part IV of the book focuses on family frameworks that can be used to assess the implications of constructed solutions to family problems for family wellbeing. It consists of three chapters that include family systems theory and exchange and choice theory (Chapter 15), symbolic interactionism and family stress theory (Chapter 16), and conflict, feminist, and cultural theories (Chapter

17). Each of these conceptual frameworks contains concepts—ideas, language, words—that you can use for thinking about the implications of constructed solutions to family problems. Again, you do not have to learn all the frameworks at first or all at once, but having a range of frameworks from which to choose and knowing where to find them when you want or need to use them will give you flexibility in assigning meaning to family problems and their solutions.

Again, I include many examples of the major concepts associated with the different family frameworks in the text. And as with the policy frameworks, I select news articles for students to analyze in small groups in class that are illustrative of the different family frameworks. Students break into small groups to analyze the news article that is illustrative of both a family problem and a policy solution or a family problem in need of a solution, find examples from the article that illustrate the concepts associated with the framework, and base their conclusions on evidence drawn from the news article. In other words, students are expected to assign meaning to the news article in terms of family well-being based on the framework in use for that day, drawing on the news article for evidence. The application of the frameworks to real life encourages students to think conceptually about family policy in relation to family problems and, at the same time, to learn about the issues that constitute and confront family policy. I design all assignments and exams to reinforce conceptual thinking about the policy/family connection and to transform students into a public interested in and informed about family policy and with an appreciation of the connections between family policies and their own lives.

Part V consists of just two chapters. Chapter 18 sums up the discussion in the context of postmodernism and the globalization of the economy, and Chapter 19 offers some suggestions for family policy practice, using the policy frameworks as guides. Here, much depends on your particular role and position in the policy structure, but at the very least, you as citizens have a role to play in this process if only by engaging in family policy discourse. Again, some of the policy frameworks can give you insights into that role—and the language for understanding and performing it. The same applies to the family frameworks, which provide the language for understanding the goal and substance of policy efforts.

Some of you may wonder about the inclusion of so many frameworks in the book, perhaps finding the range overwhelming. Speaking out of my own experience, when I was a student, I was not taught to think conceptually and therefore did not have the language for engaging in discourse about family problems and policies—at least not beyond the average layperson. Once I learned about the frameworks, my ability to analyze and interpret family policies from a family perspective increased enormously. The frameworks allowed me to not only place my observations in a larger context but also to assign meaning to my observations in ways I had not known before. Moreover, they heightened my interest in family policy—and in other subject matters as well. I hope they do the same for you.

I have placed the overall discussion in the context of postmodernism, because just as postmodernism emphasizes language and meaning, my discussion here does too. Some of you may find this material confusing or think it obscures more than it enlightens. The language of postmodernism *is* different, but like the frameworks that form a large part of the text, the language of postmodernism is sensitizing; it can sensitize you to developments that may be unsettling at worst or baffling at best. This is an exciting time to be thinking about family policy and engaged in its discourse. It is the beginning of a new decade, a new century, a new millennium—and also a new presidential era. There probably is no better time to learn about family policy and its goal of family well-being.

At this point, I would like to thank three anonymous reviewers, two of whom provided very detailed and helpful suggestions for clarifying what I am trying to communicate to you. I took their suggestions seriously and incorporated many of them. I do not know who they are, but I would like them to know how much I appreciate the time and thought they gave to their reviews of the draft they read of the book.

Thank you, again, Pete (my spouse), for your support and understanding of my single-mindedness in working to complete the project, especially in the face of time pressures for manuscript submission. Also thank you, Jim Brace-Thompson, editor, and Sage Publications for giving me a way of engaging in family policy discourse and sharing my ideas with others. And thank you to my colleagues in Family Social Science at the University of Minnesota for listening to my complaints and commiserating with me as I worked on the book. And of course, thank you to my family—my husband Pete, my children, children-in-law, grandchildren, extended family, and special friends who have made me appreciate what family and friends are all about.

Shirley L. Zimmerman

PART I

Laying the Foundations

In these beginning chapters, I lay the foundations for talking about family policy. In Chapter 1, I deal with definitions of family policy and talk about the historical developments related to families in the United States and those developments that have led to the emergence of family policy as a field of activity, study, discourse, research, and other knowledge-producing activity. The chapter provides the context for the discussion that follows. The term *family policy*, although not a common household phrase, probably is familiar to more people today than in the past (Al Gore even used the term on *The Oprah Winfrey Show* during the 2000 presidential campaign). The second chapter talks about family policy discourse within the context of postmodernism and the contested nature of the issues embedded in family policy and family policy discourse. It focuses on the role of language in the construction of policy solutions to family problems. It also talks about some of the risks that postmodern trends entail for family policy.

Chapter 3 focuses on the meaning of the term *family* and highlights its diversity and changing nature. The chapter also reviews some of the changes that have occurred in family life that underscore its dynamic nature for individual families and also for the family as an institution. Such changes are discussed in the context of larger societal changes. The term *family values* in family policy discourse forms the basis of Chapter 4. The discussion is placed in the context of a wider discussion of the meaning of *values* more generally, the role of language in the construction of values, and the meanings that people in nationally representative surveys assign to family values.

As more specific expressions of values or beliefs, the attitudes that people hold toward families, government, and the economy are the focus of Chapter 5. Because attitudes provide the impetus for action, attitudes toward family, government, and the economy are important for family policy—they are central to it. Again, data about attitudes presented in the chapter, like the data about family values, are based on nationally representative surveys.

I hope you find the discussion informative and interesting.

1

Family Policy

The Emergence of Its Discourse and Knowledge-Producing Activities

The discourse on family policy at the beginning of a new century is different from the discourse of the 1960s, when the term *family policy* was first introduced into the nation's policy vocabulary. *Discourse* refers to the expression of thoughts and ideas through words, written or oral. In terms of family policy, it is the expression of thoughts and ideas about families, their problems, the legislation that governments enact to address their problems, and related issues. The context of such discourse also is different from the 1960s. Although not necessarily couched in family terms in the 1960s, discourse at that time was about poverty as a problem that many families were experiencing and alternative ways of addressing it. It also was about making health care for the elderly and low-income individuals and families more affordable and the social sharing of its costs. Such discourse was premised on the belief that government not only had a responsibility to help individuals and families meet their needs, but that it had a positive role to play in this regard. During that period, Daniel Patrick Moynihan (1965), who later became a senator from New York, wrote one of the first American articles on family policy, warning of the negative consequences that emanated from the enactment of laws that neglected their family dimensions.

Since that time, the family dimensions of public policies have received much more attention from both academicians and politicians, so that the words *family policy* no longer sound as out of sync with policy discourse as when Moynihan first used them in 1965. However, with the increasing dominance of the markets in American society, the assumptions that gave rise to the idea of family policy have changed, eroding the belief that government is necessarily responsible for addressing the problems of individuals and families.

Indeed, given the country's political culture and value traditions of individualism, private property, and minimal government, the idea of family policy in the United States is almost counterintuitive. By its very nature, family policy implies government involvement in domains once considered private—the markets and family life. Then why are we talking about family policy here? In this chapter, I provide some of the historical background of the emergence of family policy as a domain of study, research, practice, political action, and discourse that I hope will answer that question. To make the task more manageable, I have largely confined the discussion to the role of government—at local, state, and federal levels—and thus do not focus on the very important contributions of nongovernmental organizations, sectarian and nonsectarian, to the development of family policy. Nor does the discussion in this chapter substitute for a history of social welfare and social policy in the United States. You are advised to read that history. A discussion of family policy developments in the 1990s follows in later chapters.

■ What Is Family Policy?

Family policy can be defined in many ways. It is ostensibly aimed at addressing the problems families are perceived as experiencing in society and is constituted of a series of separate but interrelated policy choices that address such problems as follows:

- Unwed parenthood
- Family breakup
- Poverty
- Suicide
- Unemployment
- Long-term care
- Lack of transportation
- Decline in family values
- Language barriers
- Mental illness
- Domestic violence
- Poor health

- Homelessness
- Drug/alcohol abuse
- Violence/crime
- Welfare dependency
- Absence/availability of abortion services
- Sex education in the schools
- Drunk driving
- Mental retardation
- Loss of parental authority
- Widened income disparities

- Lack of affordable health care
- Government too much, too little
- Sex/race discrimination
- Lack of affordable child care
- Work demands
- Parent involvement in children's schooling
- School safety
- Urban sprawl

Although not all family problems get on the policy agendas of local, state, and federal legislative bodies or result in policies that address them, the policies, when and if they do result, constitute agreed-upon courses of action for the achievement of some agreed-upon objective, such as reducing teen birthrates or poverty rates. The goal of family policy is to promote the well-being of families (Zimmerman, 1992a, 1995a), just as the goal of policy in general is to further the well-being of individuals (Lasswell, 1968), about which much more will be said in later chapters. Such policies, or courses of action, consist of a series of interrelated choices concerning what is to be done. For example, to reduce teen birthrates: Who is going to do it, where is it going to be done, under what circumstances is it to be done, to whom is it to be done, how is it to be financed, who is going to finance it, at what level? and so on. The phrases *agreed-upon courses of action* and *agreed-upon objective* indicate that in a democratic society, policy is not made by one person alone but by a majority of those who have been elected to consider and vote on such actions at whatever government level—federal, state, or local—such actions are pending. Such actions are what family policy is all about. Because society is dynamic and ever changing, and persons in governing positions are elected out of as well as in office, family policies are always subject to review and revision and hence are *temporarily* settled or agreed-upon courses of action. The rescinding of the 1988 Medicare Catastrophic Coverage Act, which provided catastrophic health insurance coverage for older persons, shortly after it was enacted is one example of a temporarily settled course of action. The Act was rescinded following the protests of seniors over the high cost of the insurance and the inadequacy of its coverage.

Representing sets of shifting, diverse, and contradictory responses to a range of political interests (Edelman, 1968), family policies also may be viewed as constructed solutions to family problems. The term *constructed solutions* refers to the connections that lawmakers and public opinion draw between family problems and their remedies. An example of such constructions are the different solutions that senatorial candidates in Minnesota proposed for dealing with the high cost of prescription drugs, especially for older persons. One candidate suggested that the federal government subsidize the costs of prescription drugs and that the charges accruing to the government, as a result of the subsidy, be offset by requiring drug companies that receive government grants for the development of new drugs to later return some of the grant monies to the government. Another candidate suggested that prescription drug retailers be allowed to buy drugs wholesale in Canada as a way of lowering their costs. Still another suggested that "to get better deals" on prescription drugs, the federal government should authorize volume buying programs with drug companies (Hopfensperger, 2000). Each solution, in effect, represented a different connection to the problem. Such connections, being neither preordained nor inevitable, are constructed through interactions that take place in the political process (Gergen, 1999).

Because some problems that families experience are the result of policy choices aimed at addressing other problems—such as job layoffs resulting from a decision by the Federal Reserve Board to raise interest rates to cool the economy—it also is useful to think of family policy as everything governments do that affects families. Such being the case, I tend to view family policy as a perspective—a lens, a prism—for looking at and thinking about policy in relation to families. Family policy also may be viewed as a field of activity that includes such programs as family life education, family planning, child care, adoption, homemaker services, Social Security, financial assistance, child development programs, fatherhood programs, and respite care, all of which are manifestations of individual family policies.

■ Language for Analyzing Family Policy

Family policy(ies) can be analyzed through the study of lawmakers' decisions and choices at various levels of government, especially the federal level, as expressed in budgetary expenditures, congressional appropriations, and approved programs (Morris, 1987) related to families. It also can be analyzed in terms of the *objectives* and *consequences* of individual family policies. The family *objectives* of individual family policies and programs can be *explicit* (that is, stated) or *implicit* (unstated but understood). They also can be *manifest* (that is, obvious), or *latent* (not evident). The *consequences* of such policies related to families (i.e., their family effects) can be *direct* or *indirect, intentional* or *unintentional* (Kanderman & Kahn, 1998).

Examples of explicit family policies include paternity establishment laws, child support laws, no-fault divorce laws, and child abuse laws. The family objectives of such policies are explicit with regard to the behaviors and role performance of family members. In the case of paternity establishment laws, for example, the objective is to establish the paternity of a child born to unmarried parents; in the case of child support laws, it is to ensure the financial support of children by their parents; in the case of child abuse laws, it is to protect children from abuse by their parents; and in the case of no-fault divorce, it is to avoid the assignment of spousal blame by divorcing partners.

Because most family policies in the United States are implicit rather than with respect to their family objectives, the goals and objectives of many implicit family policies often are hard to identify. For this reason thinking and talking about family policy in this country was delayed for a long time. Examples of implicit family policy(ies) include minimum wage laws, a $1,000,000 limit on corporate tax deductions for the salaries of corporate executives, and municipal zoning laws. Although unstated, a family objective of minimum wage laws might be to enable low-income parents to better support their families; limits on corporate deductions for executive salaries might be to ensure a fairer distribution of corporate profits between upper- and lower-level corporate employees and thereby protect the living standards of lower-level employees and their families; and municipal zoning laws might be to ensure the safety of the neighborhoods in which families live and raise their children. In none of these examples are family objectives actually stated. Rather, they are unstated; they are implicit.

Something that is manifest is that which is obvious or apparent. By extension, the family content and objectives of manifest family policies are obvious and apparent. This does not apply to latent family policies. Just as manifest family policies can be regarded as explicit family policies, many latent family policies can be viewed as implicit. The latter include any policy or program in which the family component is obscured by other emphases and objectives, such as school

finance reform to equalize state aid to school districts. Examples of both manifest and latent family policies include those cited above in the discussion of
explicit and implicit family policies.

Using terms like *direct* and *indirect* shifts attention to the immediacy of the
effects of different policies and programs on families. Social Security, for example, affects families directly by providing income for older family members.
Laws requiring the licensure of family counselors and therapists affect family
therapists directly but families receiving family therapy indirectly. The terms
intended and *unintended* focus attention on the consequences, effects, or outcomes of different policies and programs for families. Using these terms, it does
not matter much if policy objectives for families are explicit or implicit, manifest
or latent, direct or indirect. Only their outcomes for families are important.
Here, the Minnesota Family Investment Program (MFIP) is relevant. Intended to
encourage low-income families to work and improve their financial situation at
the same time, MFIP subsidizes the day care and medical costs of program participants and also allows them to retain part of their earnings while receiving
financial assistance from the government. As a consequence, many program
participants were working and living above the poverty line in 2000 ("Six
Month Study," 2000), as the program intended. Moreover, their family lives
were more stable, and rates of family breakup were lower among program participants than nonparticipants. Unintended consequences would have had the
opposite effects.

■ Why We Are Talking About Family Policy

From the above discussion, we can see that family policies can ameliorate—or
exacerbate—the problems of individual families and groups of families. In
effect, we are talking about family policy here because of the expansion of
knowledge about such problems and what governments can do to address them.
Problems refer to conditions that a sizable portion of the population deems
undesirable, as illustrated by the problems listed at the beginning of the chapter.
The view that such problems are treatable and solvable was fostered by the dramatic growth of technology and scientific knowledge over the last two centuries
(Dempsey, 1981). Replacing a theistic view of the world—a belief in the biblical
account of creation, human nature, destiny, and divine revelation that defined
right and wrong and pointed the way to heaven and hell (Leiby, 1987)—the new
technocracy of science and technology held out the possibility that many social
and other problems could be prevented or contained. The expansion of knowledge in the latter part of the 19th century about human needs and how to
address them spawned sociology and psychology as academic disciplines and
social work and home economics as professions with an interest in families.
These newer sciences—sociology and psychology—and professions—social
work and home economics—joined older, more established sciences and professions such as medicine and law that also had an interest in families.

Lending credibility to the sciences and professions was their research base (Dempsey, 1981). Indeed, science and technology account for many of the improvements often taken for granted today: indoor plumbing, refrigeration, telephones, central heating and air conditioning, subways, skyways, automobiles, airplanes, television, frozen foods, personal computers, the Internet. They also have helped to improve family living standards in other ways such as by making possible the control of family size. Also because of science and technology, the average life span at the beginning of the 21st century has been extended far beyond anyone's wildest dreams a century ago.

To better understand the emergence of family policy discourse in the United States in the latter part of the 20th century, however, and to answer the question of why we are talking about family policy here, given the value traditions of the country, it is useful to go back and look at some of the solutions that were constructed to family problems when the country was founded, as forerunners of many policy solutions today.

■ Looking Backward at Solutions Constructed to Family Problems

Mutual Aid and Local Responsibility

Although systems of help that were developed when the United States was founded clearly affected families, they were not viewed in family policy terms, as they are today. When the country was young, it offered conditions that contrasted sharply with those in Europe, especially England, from which most early settlers in this country came. It provided real opportunities for many people, most of whom were of modest means. Resources were abundant, unemployment was low, and a liberal system of land tenure enabled many without property to acquire it (Trattner, 1974). This was only part of the story, however, but it was the part that early promoters of settlement in America told and sold. Coming here under conditions that were less than desirable—people were packed into tiny ships where they lived in dirty quarters and were given inadequate food that was often contaminated, as was the water they drank—many never survived the ordeal. Those who did survive frequently reached shore sick or weak. Once here, life was so full of hardship and deprivation that many were forced to live in poverty. The English practice of shipping convicts, political prisoners, beggars, vagrants, orphans, unemployed laborers, and ne'er do wells to this country was not helpful in giving the country an auspicious start.

At the outset, the hardships of frontier life and the isolation and self-containment of early settlements fostered a strong sense of social responsibility and community solidarity among early settlers. When people needed help, their only recourse was a system of mutual aid they established with neighbors (Trattner, 1974). Such conditions also provided the rationale for local responsibility for people needing help, especially in New England, where a system of self-government prevailed. As the population grew and the social life of the colonies became more diverse, however, the need for a permanent, regulated poor relief policy and system of social provision became apparent, if not acute. The tradition of local responsibility for certain categories of persons—the aged, the physically helpless, widows, and orphans—became firmly entrenched about the middle of the 17th century. It was based, as one might expect, on the social and legal institutions the colonists had known in England and were a part of their cultural heritage—the English Poor Law of 1601.

English Poor Law

The English, or Elizabethan (as it also was called), Poor Law, which was hardly conceptualized in terms of family policy, was in fact one of the country's first family policies. It emphasized, among other things, local responsibility, the principle of least eligibility (which called for almost total destitution on the part of those seeking aid and levels of assistance below the wages of the lowest paid workers in the community), and relatives' responsibility for the material support of dependent family members (Kahn, 1969). At a time when most people were poor but not dependent, dependent destitution (which in 21st-century language is called welfare dependency) was the constructed problem, not destitution, and the English Poor Law was its solution, similar to today's Personal Responsibility and Work Opportunity Reconciliation Act (PRWORA). PRWORA, like the English Poor Law, constructs dependent destitution, not destitution, as the problem. As a solution to that problem, PRWORA requires low-income parents to work and, among other provisions, limits assistance to 2 years immediately upon its receipt and to 5 years over a lifetime.

Rooted in English Poor Law, early solutions to the problem of family destitution or poverty in the United States made a distinction between poor people deemed worthy and poor people deemed unworthy. The misfortunes of the worthy poor—widows, orphans, and the infirm—were seen as beyond their control and not their fault. The problems of the unworthy poor were seen as attributable to laziness, licentiousness, or other sinful lifestyles that *were* viewed as their fault. Although public solutions to the problems of the worthy poor were generally sufficient to sustain life, they were seldom generous or compassionate; solutions to the problems of the unworthy poor were consistently harsh, frequently involving imprisonment, corporal punishment, or forced labor (Trattner, 1974).

Worthy individuals and families who were destitute suffered poor law traditions in very personal ways. If their families could not or would not care for them, solutions to their problems were sought publicly—at town meetings. A destitute widow, for example, might be given a choice of firewood at the town square; a blind and ailing man might be boarded with a willing family that received small amounts of in-kind relief or cash subsidies as compensation. Less worthy types might be expelled or whipped and pressed into various forms of forced labor. The earliest legislation on destitution—the Virginia Poor Law Act in the early 1600s—attempted to "provide work for those who could work, relief for those who could not, and punishment for those who would not" (Jernegan, 1931, p. 177), very much in the manner of PRWORA today.

Almshouses and Poorhouses

As communities grew, and with them the problem of destitution, parish selectmen and, later, overseers of the poor handled individual cases according to what seemed best to them (Dempsey, 1981). Almshouses and poorhouses were established as institutions to serve diverse groups of destitute persons: debtors, beggars, vagabonds, loiterers, drunks, nuisances, and prostitutes (or ladies of the night, as they were called). With time, these all-purpose institutions evolved into specialized institutions that served specialized populations: criminals; persons who were physically handicapped, mentally ill, or mentally retarded; the elderly; orphans; and unwed mothers. With the later expansion of community-based services and the mainstreaming of special groups into the society, many of these specialized institutions—mental hospitals, orphanages, institutions for the deaf, blind, and retarded—gradually disappeared. To the extent these early institutions pertained to families, they too are a part of the history of family policy in the United States.

The Role of Municipal and State Governments

The first innovators of publicly supported service systems were municipalities, not surprisingly, given the emphasis placed on local responsibility for people's problems. Municipalities assumed responsibility for providing medical assistance to the sick and housing for tired travelers, orphans, the elderly, and in general, those in need, usually after problems had grown to such proportions that they could no longer be ignored (Trattner, 1974). In the 1790s, during a series of smallpox outbreaks, Baltimore established the first public health department in the United States to prevent travelers from entering the city and spreading the disease (Dempsey, 1981).

State systems of help developed more slowly than local systems and did not assume a dominant role vis-à-vis families until well into the 19th century. By the late 19th century, the commitment of state governments to meeting the needs of people had grown to encompass hospital care of the poor and mentally ill and emergency relief in times of economic crisis. By the early 20th century, several states also assumed responsibility for mothers' pensions, old age assistance, and workers' compensation (Morris, 1987).

Divorce as a Problem for States and
State Divorce Laws as Its Solution

States also were responsible for divorce petitions but delegated this responsibility to the courts early in the 19th century. State divorce laws were liberalized in the years before the Civil War to address the problem of intolerable marriages that unhappy couples resolved through formal separation rather than divorce (Mintz & Kellogg, 1988). Led by Indiana, the 1830s saw the adoption of more permissive divorce laws by a number of states, reflecting changing conceptions of family, marriage, and sex roles. As more and more people came to believe the primary objective of marriage was the promotion of personal happiness and ultimately the well-being of society, the revision of state divorce laws was more or less assured.

Such laws, however, generally did not permit injured spouses to remarry, even in states where divorce was allowed. Remarriage was allowed only where the first marriage could be annulled, mostly because of impotence or bigamy. Divorce was justified only for adultery, physical abuse, and the failure of marriage partners to fulfill their "proper" roles. Reformers argued that grounds for divorce should be expanded to include physical and mental cruelty, willful desertion, intemperance, and temperamental incompatibility. Such arguments paved the way for no-fault divorce, which established "irretrievable breakdown of the marriage" as sufficient cause for marital breakup. Taking hold in the 1970s, no-fault divorce has become widespread.

Continuity of Concerns About Family Problems

Just as the early history of constructed solutions to family problems points to the continuity of such constructions over time, articles appearing in professional journals in the early 20th century reflected many of the same concerns about family life and family disruptions that find expression in professional journals today. In 1905, several articles appeared in *Charities,* a publication devoted to the promotion of local and general philanthropy dealing with the problems of family desertion and nonsupport (Baldwin, 1905; Wade, 1905). Just as today, nonsupport at that time was held to be a criminal offense in all states except Iowa, Minnesota, Nevada, Oregon, Tennessee, and Texas. One article dealt with the twin topics of mothers' poor health and broken families (Brandt, 1905).

A later article titled "The Influence of Mothers' Aid on Family Life" that appeared in a 1915 issue of *Survey* magazine, a leading social work journal of that time, similarly expressed concerns of today. Shades of all the years to follow, the author wrote that while the Massachusetts Legislature in 1914 granted $175,000 for relief under the Mothers' Aid law, it reduced the appropriation necessary for hiring visitors (staff) to carry out the law (Sheffield, 1915). Improvements in family life, she declared, called for relief that was not merely enough to save families from starvation but sufficient to maintain their health and decency and enable mothers "to give their children training," just as many advocate today.

The Role of the Federal Government

Except for the creation of the U.S. Children's Bureau, which pioneered in federal maternal and child health programs and the establishment of rehabilitation services for war veterans early in the 20th century, the federal government was not involved in advancing the health and well-being of American families on a massive scale until 1935, when Social Security was enacted. With its enactment, the federal government assumed a broad base of social obligation and responsibility for meeting the needs of large segments of the population (Morris, 1987). It did so in 1935 in response to the economic hardships that individuals and families were experiencing as a result of the Great Depression when, according to President Franklin D. Roosevelt, one third of the nation was ill clothed, ill fed, and ill housed.

Although subsequent amendments to the Social Security Act were important to the further development of programs under the Act, it was not until the 1960s that Congress again enacted social and health legislation as sweeping as Social Security or that directly affected as many individuals and families—the food stamp program, Medicare and Medicaid, the Aid to Families with Dependent Children's Unemployed Parent program (AFDC-UP), housing subsidies, job training programs, economic opportunity programs, and so on. Again, none of these policies and programs were conceptualized at the time in terms of family policy.

■ Factors Contributing to the Growing Awareness of and Interest in Family Policy

The 1960s: The Swedish Experience

What accounted for the change in conceptions of the policies that governments enacted vis-à-vis families? Although such change can in part be attributed to the expansion of government's role in matters pertaining to families from the mid-1960s to the mid-1970s, it was Alva Myrdal, a Swedish sociologist, who first introduced the idea of family policy. Her book *Nation and the Family* (1941, 1968) was based on Sweden's experience in the development of a democratic welfare state. Replacing a strong centralized monarchy, Sweden's democracy was based on a highly developed bureaucratic model of centralized administration and control made possible by the homogeneity and size of its population and circumscribed geography (Dempsey, 1981). In a series of systematic efforts to better understand and address the demographic and social implications of its dramatically falling birthrates, Sweden intuitively made the connection between population policy and family policy. From the beginning, it set goals and initiated ways of attaining them with respect to families. In the 1968 edition of her book, Myrdal argued that any country without a conscious family policy leaves to "chance and mischance" an area of social reality of great importance, exposing it to the untrammeled and frequently undesirable consequences of policies in other areas, maintaining that family policy was nothing less than social policy.

The prime reaction to Myrdal's book in the United States was largely skepticism. The prevailing attitude was that because the two countries differed in fundamental ways, the Swedish "experiment" had little to offer the United States. In contrast to Sweden, it was said, the United States was a large country in terms of both geography and population size, and also highly diverse (Dempsey, 1981). Moreover, its tradition of decentralized government and state and local, not federal, control meant that a national family policy was likely to be much more difficult to achieve there than in Sweden.

Nevertheless, many social scientists and family professionals in the United States followed the Swedish experience with interest. That experience planted the idea of something called *family policy,* which appealed to a society that almost uniformly valued family. But with divorce rates rising and family size declining in the 1960s, the United States was beginning to worry about whether the family, as an institution, was just changing or dying. The notion of family policy brought to consciousness the fact that from unwritten common law to contemporary federal and state legislation, the family as a subject and object of law and legislation was, by and large, not a conscious part of the American tradition.

The Moynihan Factor

Indeed, because family professionals and academicians themselves had not neglected the family, many were surprised to realize that the United States had no explicit comprehensive national family policy. The absence of such a policy suddenly seemed reckless and irresponsible. While European innovations in child care, maternity leave, children's allowances, and so on continued, evidence began to surface in the United States that some of the changes in the family that worried people resulted from the failure to consider the family implications of policies that had been enacted. The Aid to Families with Dependent Children (AFDC) program, which supported families *after* they broke up (excluding families with an unemployed man in the home for the first 25 years of the program), was a prime example. In one of the first articles on family policy in this country, Daniel Patrick Moynihan (1965) cited a precedent-setting speech by President Lyndon Johnson on the policy neglect of families in the United States. To Moynihan, the expanding economy of the 1960s, coupled with an increasingly favorable political climate, was the opportune time for the country to initiate some family policy initiatives.

Moynihan at the time conceptualized family policy as a general statement of intent rather than a series of specific solutions to specific family problems. A national family policy, he held, needed only to declare that it was the policy of the American government to promote the stability and well-being of the American family, that federal social programs would be formulated and administered with this objective in mind, and that the president, or his or her designee, would report to Congress on the condition of the great range of American families, regionally, ethnically, and economically.

The Sciences and Professions

As government's role in matters pertaining to families increased, interest in the study of public policy related to families increased accordingly, especially among those sciences and professions oriented toward social change. Such scientists and professionals became increasingly interested in assessing the effectiveness of government programs and policies for families. They also wanted to be better able to understand and influence these programs. Hence, the policy literature that resulted was not a political science literature for understanding the political system but an action literature intended to increase the participation of scientists and professionals in policy formation and evaluation (Dempsey, 1981).

Nonetheless, articles on family policy that appeared with increased frequency in the 1960s tended to be more philosophical than empirical. In 1967, the *Journal of Marriage and the Family* devoted an entire issue to the topic of public policy and the family. Paradoxically, the article that Nathan Cohen and Maurice Connery (1967) wrote for that issue was about families as the foundation of society, not about family problems that government policies could address. Alvin Schorr (1968), in his book *Explorations in Social Policy,* questioned the likelihood of family policy in the United States, asserting that even if family goals were not subordinated to the individualistic traditions of the country, dedication to private enterprise and small government would make such goals difficult to achieve in this country in any case.

Although articles had been written about the family effects of various federal programs prior to the 1960s (as, for example, some of the articles cited earlier in the chapter), few found their way into the bibliographies of scholars who wrote about family policy in the 1960s and later, probably because such articles were not identified as being about family policy. Family policy was seen as something new, something different, requiring a whole new literature (Dempsey, 1981). That family policy was viewed as a thing apart and extraordinarily new was evident in the failure of many students of family policy to recognize the relevance of the 1935 Social Security Act for families, which up until then was the most significant piece of family legislation that Congress had ever enacted. It remains so into the new millennium.

The 1970s:
The Continuing Expansion of Government Programs

The years after the 1960s saw the continuing expansion of the federal government's role in relation to families. In 1973, such legislation included:

■ Title XX social services

■ A block grant for 23 different social services

■ Supplemental Security Income (SSI), which collapsed Aid to the Blind (AB), Aid to the Disabled (AD), and Old Age Assistance (OAA), which were part of the Social Security Act, into a single federal program for income eligible persons

■ The Earned Income Tax Credit (EITC) for poor working families

The Mondale Hearings on the State of the Family

Giving viability to the idea of family policy in the 1970s were the hearings Senator Walter Mondale from Minnesota held for 3 days in 1973 before the subcommittee on Children and Youth of the Senate Committee on Labor and Public Welfare. Senator Mondale later became vice president in the Carter administration and was a presidential candidate in 1988. The purpose of the hearings was to learn about the problems that American families were experiencing and the ways in which public and private programs helped or hurt them (Dempsey, 1981). The hearings were held following reports of children who had been placed in foster care and languished there, some for as long as 8 years, without being returned to their parents.

Predicated on the belief that nothing was more important to a child than a healthy family, the hearings not only gave visibility to the idea of family policy but helped to legitimize it (Zimmerman, 1988a). Despite their divergent views, the 14 experts who testified at the hearings were in agreement as to the enormity of the problems families were facing at the time: unemployment and underemployment that threatened the financial stability of families; the declining quality of parenting as measured by time spent with children; the erosion of family life ideals; the weakening of natural support systems, such as neighborhoods and communities made up of extended families; the failure of government support systems to explicitly address the problems of families, like welfare policies that hurt recipient families, tax structures that tempted middle-class parents of college students to cope with college costs by divorcing; and finally, the absence of family-sensitive government policies that protected and respected the autonomy and self-determination of families.

The hearings also prompted presidential candidate Jimmy Carter to propose, in the 1976 presidential campaign, holding a White House Conference on Families. His 1976 campaign speech on the family in New Hampshire sparked so much interest in the topic that Joseph Califano, who became secretary of the U.S. Department of Health, Education and Welfare in the Carter administration, was directed to compile a report on the status of the American family. In his report, Califano (1976), like the panel of experts at the Mondale hearings 3 years earlier, identified rising unemployment as the principal problem plaguing American families. Indeed, unemployment was the central family issue in the 1980 presidential election 4 years later.

The Literature on Family Policy in the 1970s

Interest in family policy evidenced itself not only in the political arena during this period but also in academic journals and programs. In the 1970s, many articles began to appear on family policy-related issues (Chilman, 1973; Dumon & Aldous, 1979; Giele, 1976; Kamerman, 1976; Kamerman & Kahn, 1978; Leik & Hill, 1979; McDonald, 1979; Moroney, 1976; Rice, 1977; Schorr, 1972; Tallman, 1979; Zimmerman, 1976, 1979). In 1979, the *Journal on Marriage and the Family* devoted another entire issue to family policy, as did *Daedalus*

(Journal of American Academy of Arts and Sciences) and *Social Work*. The articles in these three journals reflected a general maturation and collectively demonstrated the enormous scope of topics that were coming to be viewed as part of family policy. Although many of these articles dealt with traditional social policy issues—poverty, income support, inadequate housing, juvenile justice—reflecting what Alva Myrdal (1968) had said earlier—that family policy was nothing less than social policy—others focused on conceptualizing the relationship between families and public policy, largely in systems terms (Zimmerman, 1976, 1979).

Unlike most of the work that had been published in the 1960s, which, according to Robert Leik (1979), leaned toward advocacy, many of the articles dealing with family policy issues in the 1970s were empirical. Among such work was Robert Moroney's (1976) study, which examined the question of whether families in England had relinquished their caregiving functions for disabled children and elderly parents to the state. Based on the interviews he conducted with parents of disabled children and adult children of frail elderly, Moroney reported that no evidence could be found to support such a view, that inter- and intragenerational contact and support were prevalent among the families in the study, that the social care families provided for members far exceeded the social care the state provided, that no monetary value could be assigned to such care, nor could the costs to the state be calculated if families indeed decided to relinquish their caregiving function.

Bringing an international perspective to the topic, in 1978, Sheila Kamerman and Alfred Kahn, Codirectors of Cross National Studies at Columbia University, compiled 14 articles on the state of family policy in 14 countries, including the United States. Collectively, the papers offered an unusual multidisciplinary assessment of family policy, reflecting the perspectives of economics, sociology, psychology, medicine, social work, political science, and public administration. Certain themes emerged: changing family roles and structures, gender and racial equality, demographic shifts, changes in the economy, and the implications of increasing numbers of mothers employed outside the home for society. The interplay between these several trends, the editors maintained, contributed to the focus on family policy as a possible framework for responding to the variety of problems confronting families in these different countries. Of interest here was the editors' view that no country had yet developed an ideal model of family policy that other countries could adopt—not even Sweden. Based on their analysis, Kamerman and Kahn (1978) concluded that family policy in 1978 was in the middle of many societal contradictions and that the family, if seen as a central institution, would be viewed as a critical agent both for those who seek change and those who strive to avoid it, a conclusion supported by later developments.

To chart the growth of scholarly interest in families and family policy, in 1979-80, Reuben Hill (1980), founder and director of the Family Study Center at the University of Minnesota, undertook an inventory of all the scholarly work that had been published between 1900 and 1980 on those twin topics (Dempsey,

1981). Worldwide, he found that about 25,000 scholarly books and journals had been published during the study period. Two thirds of the literature was in English, most of it published since the end of World War II, when the number of publications on the family exceeded 2,000 annually. One cannot even hazard a guess as to what that number might be today. In 1980, the number of journals that published articles on family research, as distinguished from family policy research, approached 800.

With respect to scholarly work published on family policy per se, although some appeared in the family field before the 1960s, the first continuous thread of scholarly interest in family policy did not appear until the 1965-72 period. Prior to that time, according to the Hill inventory, almost all the published writing on family policy was entirely European, but during the 1965-72 period, half of it was American. Hill did not find any journals that specialized on the topic, however, nor have any done so since.

Three of the many conclusions Hill drew from his inventory that are of relevance here were the following:

1. The volume of interest in the family within the professional scientific community was immense and growing.
2. Interest in family public policy, though of relatively recent vintage, was increasing.
3. Although growth in substantive knowledge about the family was impressive, there was no scientific consensus about many important extensively examined topics, such as the totality of the impact of a changing, industrializing society on the family as an institution.

At this writing, the impact of a changing postmodern, postindustrial, global society on the family might be an additional contested topic.

Family Impact Analysis

In addition to the expansion of government programs in the 1960s and 1970s and growing awareness of the family dimensions of the policies governments enacted, the emergence of family impact analysis (FIA) as an analytic research tool was integral to the development of family policy as an area of study during the late 1970s and early 1980s. FIA emerged in the 1970s as a potential research tool for predicting the likely consequences of government policies on families (Dempsey, 1981). The model for such analysis was environmental impact analysis, which aimed to predict the consequences of public and private actions on the natural environment. Also contributing to its conceptualization was Wolf's (1976) model of social impact analysis (SIA) for anticipating "the unanticipated consequences of purposive social action." Applying such systematic analysis to public actions related to families, Kamerman (1976) asserted, would make possible the development of family impact statements that made their family consequences explicit. Such a statement was seen as necessary for assessing all relevant federal legislation and for identifying alternative values and the degree to which each would be realized by a given course of action. It also was seen as necessary for identifying the potential consequences of alternative courses of action for different sets of values: family well-being, individual rights, equality, social integration, and so on. Where value conflicts occurred, the final decision would be made in the political arena. Although the ultimate goal of family impact statements was to improve conditions for families, their more immediate goal was to raise national consciousness about policies that affected the lives of families and their members.

Because FIA was such a new analytic tool, the literature on it was as limited as its use. By late 1976, a few family impact papers began to appear (Leik, 1979). Paul Mattessich (1976a) developed a guide for writing state-level family impact statements and prepared an annotated bibliography of useful materials. Except for Kamerman's paper, however, none contained the title of FIA. Although the literature on FIA was scanty, Mattessich (1976b) found an extensive literature on policy analysis and evaluation from which he said FIA could draw. Evaluation research, viewed as policy assessment (Rossi & Wright, 1977), included procedures for determining policy outcomes and identifying preferred choices (i.e., cost-benefit analysis) and for projecting trends via time series analyses or simulation modeling. To provide a broader context for the existing literature, Leik (1979) suggested that FIA be treated as a special type of family policy analysis.

■ Family Impact Analysis Training Programs, 1970s: University of Minnesota

In keeping with developments in family policy and the growing interest in the effects of individual policies on families, the Family Study Center at the University of Minnesota secured funding in 1976 from the National Institute for Mental Health (NIMH) to train selected pre- and postdoctoral students to assume the role of FIA specialists in government, industry, and public and private social agencies (Leik, 1979). Program requirements included a continuous internship in family-related nonacademic settings, a staff-trainee seminar focused around the internships, and the preparation of a series of family impact analyses related to the internship experience that also incorporated research training. For information about the curriculum in the FIA program at the University of Minnesota and the backgrounds of students in the program, please see the Notes at the end of this chapter.[1]

Funding for the FIA Training Program at the University of Minnesota ended in the early 1980s; the Minnesota Family Study Center closed its doors soon after. Since then, the term *family impact analysis* has taken on the more modest cast of *family policy research*.

■ Family Impact Analysis Training Program: Duke University

The FIA Training Program at the University of Minnesota was situated within the Minnesota Family Study Center, but the training program in National Policy and the Family at Duke University at that same time was positioned in the multidisciplinary Institute of Policy Sciences and Public Affairs (NIMH Post Doctoral Training Program, 1976). Its purposes were similar but different from Minnesota's program. It was designed to train social scientists to identify and analyze a broad range of laws, policies, or regulations affecting all families or certain categories of families and to produce "family impact statements." Not as theoretically or statistically oriented as the FIA training program at Minnesota, Duke's program was more policy oriented, consisting of coursework on family policy, policy decision making, community-based internships, direct supervision by sponsoring faculty, and the development of practical policy recommendations as working papers.

■ The Washington-Based Family Impact Seminar

In addition to the FIA training programs at the University of Minnesota and Duke University, an independent Family Impact Seminar was established in 1976 at George Washington University in Washington, D.C., under the leadership of Sidney Johnson, a former staff director of the Senate Subcommittee on Children and Youth under Senator Mondale. The Seminar was comprised of 22 leading scholars and policy makers with expertise in family research and public policies affecting families. This program, like the programs at Minnesota and Duke, also aimed to systematically examine the impacts of government policies on families (Dempsey, 1981).

One of the Seminar's projects was an inventory of federal programs that appeared to have an impact on families. Of the 1,044 federal programs, only 2 related to families: family medicine and family planning. Of these 1,044 federal programs, 268 provided financial assistance in the form of in-kind subsidies and services to individuals and families. The programs were housed in 17 federal departments and agencies, most in the Department of Health, Education and Welfare. Categorized in terms of their family functions—membership, material support, nurturance, and health—63 of the 268 programs were judged to be explicit family policies to varying degrees. Based on its analysis, the Seminar concluded that the United States had many family-relevant programs with varying degrees of family explicitness.

Another project the Seminar undertook was the testing of the feasibility of family impact statements. To do this, it developed model statements on two policies—government as employer and foster care—at state and local levels. It surveyed federal employees about standard and flextime schedules to determine how work schedules affected their family roles, and it also looked at policies and practices that encouraged or inhibited the reunification of children in foster care with their biological families.

After 2½ years of study, the Seminar issued an interim report that cautioned against hasty action in the largely unexplored area of FIA (Schaar, 1978). In particular, it recommended against predicting the family effects of *proposed* policies in the manner of FIA, recommending instead examining the family effects of existing policies—in short, family policy research that in effect joins family and policy questions.

The Seminar's interim report also expressed reservations about the idea of a comprehensive national family policy. Instead, it proposed new legislative initiatives to make public policies more sensitive and responsive to the needs of diverse families. Warning against the development of governmentwide processes for FIA, it urged that the concept first be carefully tested at state and local levels through model impact statements on selected public policies such as foster care and teen pregnancy.

Underscoring the limitations of any analogy between FIA and environmental impact analysis, the report also advised against the creation of a federal bureaucracy comparable to the Council on Environmental Quality with the authority to require family impact statements to be included in all policies and programs affecting families. As Sidney Johnson noted, although FIA was easily defined, it was less precisely researchable and more complex, value ladened, personal, private, and sensitive than environmental impact analysis (Dempsey, 1981).

Just as the Seminar was hesitant to advocate the insertion of FIA into the then current federal policies affecting families, it was especially wary about doing so for proposed policies, in part because of the problems in identifying all the variables that might need to be included in such analysis *prior* to the enactment of a given policy and then finding all the data needed to carry out the analysis. Then, contrary to the Seminar's conclusions and indicative of the confusions and contradictions that abound in the area of family policy—and in all areas of policy—the report advised against FIA because social problems and the policies designed to address them were generally defined in terms of individuals, not families. One reason for this state of affairs, it said, was the widespread belief that families were private and largely untouched by public policies. It also emphasized the need for examining the effects of policy on mediating structures such as neighborhood, church, and voluntary associations vis-à-vis families, or structures that link state and federal agencies to families and their members—in effect, policies that affect families indirectly.

Scheduled to be released early in 1979 prior to the White House Conference on Families (WHCF), the Seminar delayed release of its recommendations until the Conference convened in June 1980. Conflicts over the leadership of the Conference and the potentially explosive issues the Conference itself were expected to evoke—abortion and homosexual rights—contributed to its delay, suggestive of just how sensitive and political the family as a topic had become.

The 1980s:
The 1980 White House Conference on Families

Just as the Mondale hearings gave viability to the idea of family policy, the WHCF in 1980 did too, sparking the interest not only of academics and politicians but also of community groups and the general public. Key to understanding the Carter administration's approach to family policy and the ostensible purpose of the WHCF was a paper prepared by Joseph Califano for President Carter, urging that public and private policy "restore the Family to its rightful place as the cornerstone of American well-being" (White House Conference, 1977-78, p. 4). Califano wrote that the Conference would seek to improve understanding of the trends and forces that influenced families and the problems and opportunities resulting from such trends. Most important, Califano said, the Conference would be designed to transmit and translate knowledge about policies that "strengthen families rather than weaken them."

The WHCF was sponsored by a coalition of 28 widely diverse national family-oriented voluntary organizations. Controversy surrounded preparations for the Conference and was also embedded in the proceedings. Held in three different cities in the United States—Los Angeles, Minneapolis, and Baltimore—the WHCF in effect was constituted of three conferences. Attempts by pro-life groups to shape the outcomes of the conferences met the resistance of pro-choice groups. In Baltimore, pro-life groups staged walkouts in opposition to delegate recommendations supporting the Equal Rights Amendment (ERA) and choice with regard to abortion, charging that the Conference had been "rigged" to support more government involvement in family life instead of less ("Family Delegates," 1980).

In Minneapolis, the conservative coalition staged a similar walkout to highlight differences in the views of elected and appointed delegates. A dissenter within the conservative caucus charged the caucus with racism, saying that because government often intervened in the lives of black families, less government in family life meant that delegates wanted less government in the lives of black families as well (Byrne, Benidt, & Hudgins, 1980). In Los Angeles, similar conflicts occurred. The National Pro-Family Coalition charged conference planners with rigging the conference to reflect the views of social service professionals and federal bureaucrats who had a vested interest in government spending, and an evangelical group met separately in an alternative conference to write its own recommendations.

In the end, delegates to the conferences were able to agree on 60 recommendations in the following topics: (a) family and economic well-being, (b) the challenges and responsibilities of families, (c) families and human needs, and (d) families and major institutions. Five of the defeated recommendations were supported by the pro-family coalition made up of pro-life groups (Zack & Klauda, 1980). The defeated measures included anti-ERA and antiabortion recommendations. Another controversial issue, the definition of family, was resolved by the adoption of "two or more persons related by blood, heterosexual marriage and adoption" as the definition, thereby excluding proposals for the inclusion of homosexual and heterosexual unions not formed through legal marriage and also, it should be noted, three- and four-generation families as well. Delegates also recommended tax credits for homemakers, changes in Medicare and Medicaid regulations to include home care provisions for older and disabled family members, and the repeal of the marriage penalty, issues still with us more than 20 years later. In keeping with the times, other recommendations called for greater sensitivity to families on the part of government and a systematic analysis of the impact of laws and regulations on families (Klauda, 1980).

Despite the controversies that plagued it, the Conference was useful in highlighting just how important the issues embedded in family policy were to people. Following the WHCF and Ronald Reagan's pledge in the 1980 presidential campaign to "get government off the backs of families," the country experienced a retreat on the part of the federal government on policy matters pertaining to families. Perhaps inspired by the controversies that attended the WHCF, Gilbert Steiner (1981), in his book *The Futility of Family Policy*, concluded that the search for a comprehensive national family policy, though high sounding, was a futile endeavor and that the problems that family policy would be required to address were simply too complex to fit into a coherent package with universal appeal.

Beyond the 1980s: Academic Programs and an Expanding Family Policy Literature

Despite the retreat of the federal government from the problems of families during the 1980s, the role of the federal government was reactivated in this regard in the 1990s, beginning with the enactment of the Family and Medical Leave Act (FMLA) in 1993, which provided (a) working parents with 12 weeks of unpaid leave to care for a child or sick family member, (b) domestic abuse laws, (c) the Children's Health Insurance Program (CHIP), and others, about which much more will be said in subsequent chapters.

In the meantime, interest in family policy in academia during both the 1980s and the 1990s continued unabated. In a survey of family studies departments in the United States, Elaine Anderson and Denise Skinner found that much of the literature on family policy that appeared in journals in the 1970s and 1980s had been incorporated into ongoing courses on family policy at many universities (Anderson & Skinner, 1995). Such courses constituted what Anderson and Skinner called family policy education. The broad objective of such courses was to empower students with a better understanding of families and their problems, policies that address their problems, and the political process (Quoss, 1992).

Another survey conducted in 1995 by the Irving B. Harris Graduate School of Public Policy Studies at the University of Chicago documented the vibrancy of child and family policy studies in schools of social work, public affairs, and child development as well (Gordon & Chase-Lansdale, 1995). Universities that at the end of the 1990s were known to have organized undergraduate and graduate programs in family policy studies included Iowa State, Cornell, and Chicago, with others in the process of being developed. Despite an extensive Internet search, however, Leslie Koepke (1999) found such programs hard to identify, highlighting, she maintained, the need for ongoing discussion about viable family policy studies programs and the importance of promoting family policy studies to students.

Since the 1980s, the literature on family policy has grown tremendously, as any reference list will show. That literature in the 1980s and 1990s includes entire issues of such publications as the *Journal of Family and Economic Issues,* the *Journal of Family Issues, Policy Studies Review, Policy Studies Journal,* the *Journal of Social Issues, Family Relations,* the *Journal of Marriage and the Family,* to say nothing of individual articles that have appeared in these and other professional and academic journals. It also includes the publication of several textbooks on family policy during this period (Zimmerman, 1988a, 1992a, 1995a).

■ Summary and Conclusions

Thus, despite Schorr's doubts of the applicability of family policy to the United States and Steiner's admonition of its futility in light of the complexity of family problems, family policy as a concept and field of legislative activity, programs, and practice is alive and well in the United States today. Within a relatively short period of time, it has moved from being for all practical purposes nonexistent to forming the basis for full-fledged academic programs. Today, Web sites with the term also exist.[2] Its application as a term has made clear that although many policies may not be explicit as to their family objectives, they nonetheless affect families directly or indirectly, intentionally or not, helping to uncover their latent family dimensions and objectives as well.

Factors contributing to the development of family policy as it is most commonly understood in the United States today include the following:

- Alva Myrdal's work in the 1960s
- The influence of Daniel Moynihan
- The expansion of government programs for families from the 1960s on
- The interest of family scientists and professionals in the formation and evaluation of policies related to families and the ideas they communicated in the literature
- Events such as the Mondale hearings on the state of American families in the 1970s and the 1980 WHCF
- The emergence of university-based programs of study in family policy and FIA as an analytic tool

Although not discussed here, mention should be made of all the advocacy groups for families that also contributed to the development of family policy in this country.

As a domain of policy study and activity, family policy is constituted of many hotly contested issues, as highlighted in the discussion of the 1980 WHCF. Unlike the 1960s, when problems such as poverty were not likely to be couched in family terms, by the late 1990s, they often were. Although discourse on family problems in the 1960s was premised on the assumption that government had a responsibility for helping individuals and families meet their needs, such discourse in the late 1990s and into the new millennium was premised on the assumption that individuals and families were responsible for meeting their own needs—which we now recognize as also constituting a family policy of sorts. What has not changed in this regard are the contradictions and ambiguities embedded in family policy activities and discourse—and indeed, in all policy discourse—and the ambivalence such discourse evokes.

In a very real sense, government itself, by its earlier funding of academic training programs in family impact analysis, the WHCF, the research undertakings of family policy scholars, and its role in funding an ever-increasing number of family and family-related programs, has contributed to the development of family policy as an increasingly differentiated field of study and activity that spans the life cycle, from birth to death, in the areas of health, education, social services, housing, employment and manpower, income maintenance, family law, and taxation—which explains why we are talking about family policy here—keeping in mind the roots of family policy in the United States: the English Poor Law.

As Chapter 2 will show, knowledge-producing activity in family policy can be as contentious and political as the issues that underlie family policy itself. It would be wise to heed the advice of Sanford Schram (1995), who counseled that just as the term *family* can be used irresponsibly to justify almost all that is done in its name, it also can be used to limit consideration of policies and practices that deserve to be affirmed in their own right, even if they cannot be justified on the basis of serving the good of the family. Taking a leaf from Alva Myrdal, though, examples of such policies are hard to come by—both practically and empirically.

Before turning to the next chapter, think about the following questions.

■ Some Questions for Your Reflection and Discussion

1. What is family policy?
2. What value traditions have governed our approach to family policy in the United States?
3. Why is it said that the country's value traditions run counter to the idea of family policy?
4. What terms (language) are associated with family policy?

5. What is meant by *explicit* family policy?

6. How does *explicit* family policy differ from *implicit* family policy? Give an example of each.

7. What is meant by "constructed" solutions to family problems?

8. What accounts for the delay in awareness of the family dimensions of governmental policies in this country?

9. What is the significance of the English Poor Law for family policy in the United States?

10. In what ways is the PRWORA like English Poor Law?

11. What contributed to an increased interest in family policy in the United States?

12. What are some of the ways in which such interest has been and is manifested?

13. What is FIA?

14. Does this book take a broad or narrow approach to the topic of family policy? Elaborate.

15. What was Alva Myrdal's advice with regard to family policy?

Now that you have answered these questions, it is time to turn to the next chapter.

■ Notes

1. The curriculum in FIA at the University of Minnesota Family Study Center included coursework in social policy and social theory, policy analysis, and economic theory and methods in addition to coursework on families. The program included training in research methods and in different approaches to data analysis. In the fall of 1976, the Center's program combined training in family theory, policy formation, research, and FIA, targeting three levels of potential family impacts: the family as an institution, families as functioning groups, and individual family members whose primary sources of socialization, personal maintenance, and mental health were their families.

The program was interdisciplinary in nature and attracted students from social work, sociology, and family social science. Trainees' employment experiences and substantive interests included sociology, public health, social work, and counseling psychology in academic and nonacademic settings such as public and private agencies and the military. Several of the trainees were later employed at major universities teaching courses in family policy and engaging in family and family policy research. Among them are Elaine Anderson, Phyllis Moen, and Shirley Zimmerman.

2. The two Web sites are the Family Policy Studies Centre in London, 222.fpsc.org.uk, and the Institute for Child and Family Policy at Columbia University, www.childpolicyintl.org.

CHAPTER 2

Family Policy Discourse

The Construction of Family Problems and Their Solutions

■ Discourse in Family Policy

With the introduction of terms such as *family policy* and *family impact analysis (FIA)* into policy discourse, there has been an increase in awareness of the family dimensions of the policies that are enacted. We can see this in the frequency with which public officials and advocacy groups evoke the term *family* when they argue on behalf of various policies. *Family policy discourse* refers to the written and verbal communication of thoughts and ideas about the problems that families experience in relation to society and policy solutions to them—whether by political candidates, elected officials, advocates, or ordinary people in public and private settings. In general, discourse analysis attempts to connect beliefs and attitudes to broader social and political practices and meanings and various forms of power relationships (Doherty, 1997). We can see these same attempts in family policy discourse analysis. Discourse analysis itself involves the description of recurrently used words, phrases, and linguistic devices that categorize and reproduce the social world (Parker, 1992). In focusing on discourse in the area of family policy, I draw on the work of Murray Edelman (1968, 1975, 1985) and others who approach the analysis of public policy from a postmodern perspective, as the discussion below will show.

Postmodernity and Modernity

Postmodernism refers to the historical period that began in the 1970s (Doherty, 1997) and was born partly out of the social revolutions of the 1960s and the growing dominance of new technologies that transformed modes of communication. This period is characterized by cultural fragmentation; changes in the experience of time and space; new modes of experience, subjectivity, and culture; fluid and ambiguous social organization; and postindustrial and global economies.

In contrast, the social organization of modernism is characterized as fixed and clear, its economies industrial and regional, not global. A 17th-century phenomenon out of which postmodernism arose, modernity is continuous in the sense that it did not occur all at once in any one particular country or segment of society. The ideas associated with modernism—rationalism, scientism, humanism, democracy, individualism, romanticism—took root and flourished in different places at different times (Elkind, 1994). Although some places even today are more feudal than modern, modernity arose in revolt against the autocracy of the premodern world, eventually overturning medieval forms of government, religion, science, art, and education.

The conceptual foundations of modern developments in the 19th and 20th centuries included, first, a belief in *progress* and the constant improvement of society and humankind. Coupled with the growth and accumulation of knowledge about human problems, this belief was based on a belief in science, the same conditions that gave rise to developments in family policy in the 1970s. Second, it included a belief in *universality,* in which nature everywhere operates according to universal principles—natural laws—that human beings can discover and understand through the exercise of rational and creative thought. The belief in universality led to a third foundation of modernity, notions of *regularity and predictability* based on the belief that the physical and social worlds are governed by universal natural laws in regular and predictable ways. Underlying the growth of modern science, these ideas were incorporated in all modern social institutions, including the nuclear family.

When language rather than reason is ascendant, however, a different set of themes moves into prominence (Elkind, 1994). Postmodernism arose not so much as a revolt against the beliefs of modernity but as a set of attitudes designed to correct and modify modern ideas that proved to be overly broad or narrow. Belief in the unmitigated benefits of science and technology is an example. Postmodernism questions the certainties associated with modernism, holding that the latter's beliefs are often overly idealized and blind to the dark side of human behavior and technological development such as urban sprawl, alienation and isolation, the proliferation of weapons of human destruction, and the degradation of the environment. A postmodern perspective is first and foremost a critical attitude toward the values and beliefs of modernity, including notions of rationality, individual freedom, and progress, and suggests that just as language changes without necessarily progressing, the same holds true for the world around us.

Emphasizing the embeddedness of all human knowledge in a social, historical, and linguistic context, postmodernism offers elaboration, eclecticism, and inclusiveness instead of the purity, order, clarity, and analytical abstraction of modernism. Postmodernism's emphasis on diversity joins themes of difference, particularity, and irregularity in recognition of differences but not superiority. In postmodern terms, such emphasis and themes offer evidence of each person's embeddedness in his or her own experience and interpretation of it. Post-modernism's openness to diversity is seen in such social movements as the civil rights movement, the women's movement, the gay rights movement, and provisions for people with disabilities. The ongoing elaboration of family policy that finds expression in contemporary family policy discourse also can be viewed in postmodern terms. Examples include an emphasis on highly particularistic and targeted solutions to a range of diverse problems that families of diverse ethnic, racial, and socioeconomic backgrounds experience, and a preference for state and local as opposed to federal solutions, and market (i.e., goods and services bought and sold privately) as opposed to public solutions, reminiscent of the country's earliest days. As Esping-Anderson (1996) suggests, the much greater occupational and life cycle differentiation that characterizes postindustrialized postmodern societies, to say nothing about the cultural and racial differentiation that characterizes them, implies that the needs and expectations of individuals and families also are more diverse and heterogeneous as are the risks they face. When Esping-Anderson talks about increased occupational and life cycle differentiation, she is talking about the increased specialization of jobs and more finely graded life cycle stages—that is, newborns, toddlers, kindergartners, young-old, old, old-old—that have grown with increased knowledge about human development and the lengthening of the life span. Increased cultural and racial differentiation refers to the multiplicty of cultural and racial groups in the society with which individuals identify, socially and psychologically.

Such differentiation and elaboration also may be seen in the many divisions within the domain of family policy. Although many of these divisions are discipline based—economics, sociology, psychology, political science, social work, and so on, each discipline having its own knowledge base, language, and sources of power—others are based on ideology and specialized family interests. Ideological differences pertain to beliefs that people hold about family/government/market relations, and the latter pertains to life cycle foci: aging; child and youth development; parenting; different family problems that provide the focus for family services and practices such as domestic abuse and school failure; and different approaches to family problems, such as family life education, family counseling, family resource management, and advocacy on behalf of particular family policies.

The postmodern perspective, in contrast to the modernist perspective, which sees power and knowledge as separate from one another, sees the two from an embedded perspective, never separate from each other. Thus, it is not surprising that the divisions within the domain of family policy often lead to competition and conflict in the construction of family problems and their solutions. A news report on a complaint registered by the Council on Contemporary Families against the Institute on American Values, an influential New York think tank that promotes the return of the two-parent family, is a case in point. The Council called the Institute's construction of the solution to the one-parent family as consisting of oversimplified, politicized "sound bites," identifying themselves as *serious* researchers who had neither the time nor the money to organize and inform the debate on family values (Smith, 1997).

Postmodern Policy Analysis

Postmodern policy analysis that reflects the importance that postmodernism attaches to language emphasizes the role that language and discourse play in subjectively shaping social institutions and politics. Postmodernism views language as a system of signs or words whose meanings derive from relations of difference and contrast (Seidman, 1994). It views words that connote opposites such as man/woman, body/mind, reason/intuition, worthy/unworthy poor, dependence/independence, old/young, pro-family/anti-family as binary oppositions that structure language and the broader cultural and institutional organization of society. Binary oppositions are instrumental in producing linguistic and social hierarchies; they define a thing by what it is not. Hence, the two-parent family may be defined in terms of the one-parent family and vice versa. Moreover, the two terms that constitute binary opposites are not regarded as equal: two-parent families are viewed by groups such as the Institute on American Values as superior to one-parent families. Hierarchical oppositions structure linguistic and discursive meanings and shape social practices as they become part of institutions and the popular culture. Because these linguistically organized subjective and social orders are never fixed or stable, meanings, according to Seidman (1994), are always unstable, shifting, and multivocal sites of contestation, as, for example, the changing meanings of family.

Political Discourse and Family Policy

A brief review of the political history of family policy reveals the unstable, shifting, and multivocal sites of contestation that have attended its development. *Multivocal sites of contestation* refers to the multiplicity of contesting voices that can be heard on almost any family policy issue, much as were heard in the White House Conference on Families (WHCF). Although the term *family* is a symbol of two divergent views of the role and responsibilities of government, in the 1980s it was was invoked by politicians from both political parties to advance their different political agendas (Mintz & Kellogg, 1988). Conservatives, largely Republicans, used the term as a synonym for *traditional social values* and as a way of expressing their opposition to the expanded role of government and what they said were liberal welfare policies. Liberals, largely Democrats, used the term as a synonym for government programs designed to help individuals and families suffering from poverty, abuse, and other afflictions.

Ronald Reagan emphasized the themes of family, work, and neighborhood in his rhetorical agenda and tried to capture the term *family* as an issue for Republicans in the 1980 presidential campaign. He argued in campaign speeches that federal programs that were supposed to provide family services had instead promoted indolence, promiscuity, easy abortion, casual attitudes toward marriage and divorce, and maternal indifference to child-rearing responsibilities—in effect linking government programs to an increase in family problems. Many former Democrats and religious activists, concerned about abortion, school prayer, pornography, and the increased number of out-of-wedlock births and single-parent families, resonated to his call for a return to traditional family values. The solution that Republicans constructed to the family problems they identified—which also were politically constructed—was a counterrevolutionary move against the New Deal of the 1930s and the Great Society of the 1960s and 1970s in the form of cuts in federal spending for social programs.

Following Reagan's election in 1980, Democrats also began to emphasize the family theme, demonstrating that they too were in touch with mainstream middle-class Americans and aware of the increasing number of baby boomers who were marrying and having children. Based on such recognition, they called for flexible work hours, maternity and paternity leaves, federal financial support for child care and uniform child care standards, increased spending on nutrition and health care for poor children, and federal enforcement of court-ordered child support to strengthen families and assist custodial parents in caring for their children.

The solutions that Democrats constructed to family problems differed from those constructed by Republicans in part because they constructed the problems of families differently. Democrats in the 1984 presidential election, in contrast to the Republicans, linked the term *family* to issues such as poverty, the federal budget deficit, and child care, and they connected the $2 trillion federal debt to the threat that it presented for the well-being of future generations of families. Daniel Moynihan associated the term with a new generation of poor children and adolescents growing up in single-parent households mired in a cycle of poverty.

Based on the belief that government had a responsibility to help meet the needs of the nation's families, the solutions that Democrats constructed to family problems during these years emphasized social integration, inclusivity, and caring. Jesse Jackson, a prominent black civil rights leader, for example, in emphasizing the term *family*, linked it to the need for building a sense of community to replace the inward-facing individualism of the Reagan years. Governor Mario Cuomo of New York said at the 1984 Democratic National Convention that Democrats believed in a government that was strong enough to use words like *love* and *compassion*, and that by recognizing that we were all bound to one another, we collectively were the family of America ("Transcript of Keynote Address," 1984). Bill Clinton invoked the term *family* in both the 1992 and 1996 presidential elections, saying in 1992 that he wanted an America that included all families, traditional families, extended families, two-income families, single-parent families, and foster families (Clinton, 1992).

Al Gore, in announcing his candidacy for the Democratic nomination for president in the year 2000, also invoked the term *family* when he asked for help to strengthen family life in America, pledging that if he were entrusted with the presidency, he would marshal its authority, resources, and moral leadership to fight for America's families (Gore, 1999). George W. Bush, when announcing his plans to run for the Republican presidential nomination, referred to the conservative principles "ingrained in his heart," which, in addition to local control and private property as the backbone of capitalism, included the importance of family and the need for personal responsibility (Bush, 1999).

Family also is freely invoked by politicians at state and local levels. Steve Kelley, a Democratic state senator from Minnesota, in announcing his candidacy for the U.S. Senate on the Democratic ticket in the year 2000, said that he was running for the Senate because Minnesota families, and all American families, were on the threshold of a new era of achievement, and that if our nation was a family, "we would make the same sound decisions a Minnesota family makes every day and develop public policies that work for the families of our state and the nation" (Reilly, 1999).

Such discourse is embedded not only in the politics of family policy, and in the knowledge-producing activities that constitute and accompany it, but also in the everyday practices of most institutions—families, community organizations, the workplace, legislative bodies, government and corporate bureaucracies—and in the experiences and activities of individuals and families as beneficiaries of different services. It also is embedded in the activities and practices of individual service providers: doctors, nurses, teachers, social workers, other agency staff, and politicians and policy makers themselves. It is embedded in such knowledge-producing activities as research, conferences, and news stories that focus on family problems and policies. In essence, discourse about families, family problems, and family policies is a political arena in which sets of activities, discursive and material (i.e., talk and practical assistance), affect one another in mutually reinforcing ways (Leonard, 1997), as the previous chapter in fact illustrated.

From Discourse to Practice

Constituted of a set of practices, discourse about families, their problems, and policies that affect them varies with agency setting and professional role. Such practices may consist of giving information, referring individuals and families to sources of help, certifying the eligibility of individuals and families for cash or other kinds of assistance, counseling them about their problems, advocating on their behalf, planning services and programs for them, or legislating on their behalf. These practices as historical products are subject to change over time, as is the discourse that gives rise to them. An example of a historical practice is the Temporary Assistance to Needy Families (TANF) program, which requires county social service workers to inform TANF mothers, immediately upon their receipt of assistance, that they must either go to work or prepare themselves for work, and furthermore, that such assistance is limited to 2 years at a time and 5 years over a lifetime. Not required prior to TANF, such a practice that could change because of the enactment of new legislation is the historical product of presidential and congressional discourse in the early 1990s "to end welfare as we know it." The term *historical* calls attention to the time period in which the practice is located.

Another example of a practice that is a historical product of implicit relevance to families is state-sponsored gambling, which, according to George Will (1999), a conservative journalist whose column appears in newspapers throughout the country, was ubiquitous in the 1990s. Will cited the 37 states that ran lotteries to raise funds for dedicated purposes like education in 1998, and reported that over two thirds of all Americans said they had gambled at least once that year. He mused that the practice of state-sponsored gambling was transforming a rare and highly stigmatized activity considered a social disease just a generation ago into social policy by the end of the 1990s. Such a change is an example of implicit family policy with the potential of undesirable family consequences. It also is illustrative of what is meant by the shifting meanings of historical practices.

Still another example of a historical product of family policy discourse, and perhaps of more explicit relevance to families, was the legislation that Congress enacted in 1996 requiring insurance companies to allow mothers of newborns to remain in the hospital for 48 hours rather than the 24 hours that had been their practice. Not too many years ago, before the days of managed health care, hospital stays of 5 days were the norm for these mothers.

The Construction of Family and Other Social Problems

As I noted in Chapter 1, the problems of families in relation to society is a paramount theme in family policy discourse. Family problems are persistent troubling or undesirable conditions (Edelman, 1968). However, because governments shape public beliefs and attitudes, the attitudes that people hold about families and their problems do not necessarily reflect how individuals and families with these problems see them. Problems come into discourse in family policy not just because they exist and have consequences for families and their well-being, but because they reinforce ideologies about their causes and the respective roles of government and families in addressing them. For example, discourse about the child support responsibilities of noncustodial parents depicts the failure of noncustodial parents to provide such support as a cause of child poverty and welfare dependency, but it also reinforces prevailing beliefs about parental responsibility and the causes and treatment of child poverty and welfare dependency as family problems. By naming the problem, such discourse also signifies which parents act responsibly and which do not. Discourse about chronic sex offenders that emphasizes helping young people stay out of trouble in the first place similarly acts to reinforce prevailing beliefs about the cause and treatment of sex crimes.

Diversity of Meanings of Problems

If diversity is a hallmark of postmodernism, the diversity of meanings assigned to every constructed family or social problem is inherent in them (Edelman, 1985). Meanings that do not necessarily flow from language itself are a function not only of the context in which language is used but also of the diverse needs and concerns of interested publics and persons situated in different positions in the sociopolitical-economic structure—and also in the structure and organization of family policy activities themselves. Such diversity stems in part from the range of their different concerns. Debate over the federal tax cut bill in 1999 in the context of a projected budget surplus is an example of such differences. Although the two political parties agreed about the tax cut, they differed about (a) the size of the cut; (b) the specific taxes that were to be cut: the capital gains tax, the inheritance tax, the marriage tax, and so on; and (c) the individuals and families who should benefit most from the tax cut—middle- or upper-income families (Stevenson, 1999a).

The tax cut also had different meanings for individual lawmakers, even those belonging to the same party. To moderate Republicans, the $792 billion tax cut over 10 years that the House passed was too big and left none of the budget surplus available for debt reduction and needed spending (Stevenson, 1999b). To other Republicans, returning excess revenues to taxpayers meant that Republicans would be able to advance their goals of reducing the power of the federal government and increasing prosperity, which they thought would help them recapture the conservative fervor of Ronald Reagan's first term as president. To Democrats, the Republican tax cut plan meant risking the return of the budget deficits and higher interest rates that plagued the country following the Reagan years and the chance to shore up Social Security and Medicare and invest in education, health care, the environment, and the military. To President Clinton, it meant, in addition, not being able to "take care of our kids," whereas to Alan Greenspan, head of the Federal Reserve Board, big tax cuts meant risking inflation and an overheated economy.

Nondecisions and Problems

If problems are constructed from undesirable conditions that hurt families, it is not thereby evident that such conditions are then constructed as problems. For a condition to be constructed as a problem, a sizable portion of the population must accept its depiction and explanations for it. Poverty, an undesirable condition that hurts families, was not constructed as a problem in the 1990s, even though the Census Bureau reported that almost one fifth of all children in the United States were poor in 1996 (Uchitelle, 1999). Indeed, if the income threshold for living above poverty were raised, as the Census Bureau proposed, from $16,600 to $19,500 for a family of four, the national poverty rate would be 17%, not the 12.7% reported in September 1999. Despite the proclivities of some congressional lawmakers such as Senators Ted Kennedy from

Massachusetts and Paul Wellstone from Minnesota, the lack of affordable housing is another undesirable condition that Congress has not constructed as a
problem requiring a decision to address it.

Nondecisions about troubling conditions are attributed in part to prevailing
ideologies and beliefs that connect conditions such as child poverty, for example,
not to inadequate government solutions but to the failure of individual parents.
Based on social cues rather than rigorous analysis, beliefs tend to be impervious
to developments and empirical evidence (Edelman, 1975) that might challenge
them. Holding alternative and often conflicting sets of cognitive structures, people tend to interpret developments to match their beliefs. To give an example:
TANF's family cap is a preestablished dollar limit on TANF benefits that ignores
family size. Governor Christine Whitman of New Jersey, despite evidence to the
contrary, said that New Jersey's family cap on TANF benefits should be continued, because she believed the cap was a factor in the decline in out-of-wedlock
births in New Jersey. Similarly, in a congressional debate about the social or
genetic basis of homosexuality, Trent Lott, Senate Majority Leader in the 106th
Congress, based on his beliefs, maintained that homosexuality was socially
based and therefore subject to the control of individuals.

Nondecisions about undesirable conditions also can occur because powerful
political groups can block decisions and practices that disadvantage them. An
example are the nondecisions on gun control legislation to address the problem
of school violence after 2 students fatally shot 12 fellow students and a teacher at
Columbine High School in Littleton, Colorado, in the spring of 1999. Because of
the opposition of one politically powerful group, the National Rifle Association
(NRA), which claimed that restrictions on the sale and purchase of guns
infringed on the constitutional right of individuals to own and bear arms, decisions on gun control measures were effectively blocked, resulting in a nondecision with respect to such measures.

Often not recognized as ideological, nondecisions also occur because troubling conditions many times are more or less accepted as the way the world is
constituted. Consensus on long-standing practices such as gun ownership, for
example, means that only a small subset of related practices are likely to be constructed as problems. In the case of guns, NRA members say that it's too bad that
some people are accidentally killed by guns, but as they see it, the problem is not
guns but people who do not know how to use guns, thereby making nondecisions about the situation tolerable for the NRA. Similarly, consensus about
regulations restricting the placement of children to two-parent heterosexual
families makes nondecisions about the shortage of good foster care families tolerable for foster care workers.

The Construction of Undesirable Conditions as Problems

For a condition to be constructed as a family or social problem that requires a
policy solution, depictions of and explanations for it must not only be accepted
by a sizable portion of the population, but the solutions proposed to remedy it

must similarly be accepted by a sizable portion of the population (Edelman, 1968). Such acceptance requires, first of all, gaining the public's attention, a matter of no small moment. Sequentially aroused, reassured, engaged, and bored, the public's attention is simultaneously absent and present in the construction of problems and their solutions. Yet, unless a condition and accompanying explanations for the condition are accepted together with remedies for it, public officials and interest groups cannot use it to their advantage in constructing solutions to family problems.

Construction of Groups

How can the public gain acceptance of troubling conditions as problems? Useful for this purpose is the construction of groups as agents of one or another course of action (Edelman, 1968). Examples of such groups in the area of family policy include the following:

- Action Alliance for Children
- American Association of Retired Persons
- The ARC [formerly Association for Retarded Citizens]
- Children Now
- Children's Defense Fund
- Christian Coalition
- Coalition That Supported the 1980 WHCF
- Coalition to Stop Gun Violence
- Eagle Forum
- Families USA
- Family Health International
- Family Research Council
- Feminist Majority Foundation
- Focus on the Family
- Gray Panthers
- Initiatives for Children
- Mothers Against Drunk Driving
- National Association for the Education of Young Children
- National Committee to Preserve Social Security/Medicare
- National Fatherhood Initiative
- National Immigration Forum
- National Organization for Women
- National Partnership for Women & Families
- National Right to Life Committee
- Parents, Families and Friends of Lesbians and Gays
- Parents Television Council
- Planned Parenthood

Some of these groups might be labeled conservative, some liberal, because of their beliefs and attitudes about families and the role of government in promoting their well-being. Not equally powerful, their influence in the family policy arena shifts over time.

Explanations for Problems

Just as the public may accept some groups and not others, it may accept some explanations of troubling conditions as problems but not others. Edelman

(1985) says accepted explanations are notable not for their rigor, verifiability, or explanatory power but for the diversity of causes and ideologies they represent. Thus, with respect to managed health care, the loss of professional autonomy may be the explanation for the undesirable condition that doctors depict as the problem of the declining quality of health care—and also their patients vis-à-vis the treatment of breast cancer, for example. But for insurance companies, employers, and managed health care corporations, the condition they say is the problem is the rising cost of health care. Power considerations also play a role in the acceptance of explanations for troubling conditions as problems, since some explanations serve to advance the authority of some individuals and groups while threatening that of others, such as doctors and insurance companies in the area of health care. History and social structure also account for the acceptance of some explanations and the nonacceptance of others as ways of knowing and acting strategically. Thus, with regard to health care, the enactment of legislation in 1996 to ensure the portability of health insurance coverage when workers changed jobs was a strategic move that signified acceptance of the reason so many families were without health insurance (i.e., they lost it when parents changed jobs).

Signifiers of Family Policy Problems

A signifier of a family policy problem can be identified by focusing on a name for an undesirable condition (e.g., high unemployment or the loss of health care insurance) and by an accompanying rationalization of activities, governmental and nongovernmental, to remedy the condition. Comprised of ambiguous language claims, the names of problems are important political symbols (Edelman, 1985), although the activities that accompany their names may or may not ameliorate the problems with which they are associated (Edelman, 1968). As noted earlier, the *declining quality of health care* is a name for an undesirable condition that threatens family well-being, but it was *the rising cost of health care* that in 1999 was the name assigned to the undesirable condition.

Problems and Crises

Whether a condition is depicted as a problem or a crisis, both terms aim to entice the public to accept the deprivations associated with it. Such deprivations could include higher taxes or higher patient costs (in the case of health care) or health care rationing, depending on the troubling condition that is accepted as the problem. Because problems often connote conditions that stem from entrenched institutional features that resist easy solution (like the structure and financing of Medicare and Social Security), those affected negatively or positively by these programs learn that such conditions are likely to continue. By contrast, a crisis such as the farm crisis or the drought of 1999 signifies instability. Instability usually means that people must endure new forms of deprivation for a period of time, such as higher food prices in the case of family consumers or the foreclosure of family farms in the case of farmers. In the conventional view, problems are seen as chronic, whereas crises are seen as acute, although because problems often instigate crises, such a distinction may not always hold. George W. Bush, in campaigning for the presidency in 2000, said he was proposing a $5 billion program to address what he called a national literacy "crisis" among children (Levy, 2000).

From Problems to Solutions

According to Leonard (1997), solutions to problems can be constructed so that "the truth" suggests a set of political arguments that includes their solutions, the assumption being, according to Gergen (1999), that "truth" can be depicted by language. One of these truths in 1999 was that despite the general prosperity of the country, some pockets of the country were largely untouched by it. In 1999, unemployment and poverty in eastern Kentucky were two to three times higher than the national average (Applebome, 1999). As one solution to the area's impoverishment, President Clinton presented a package of proposed solutions that included federal tax credits and loan guarantees to entice private companies to build plants and stores in Appalachia. The political argument he used was that during this period of economic prosperity, not only was it the right time to bring more jobs and hope to families in areas of the country that had not fully participated in the country's economic recovery, but the country had an obligation to do so (Broder, 1999).

Typically, solutions to problems come before their definitions, both chronologically and psychologically, according to Edelman (1968). Because it is effective in legitimizing government's role and in quieting dissatisfied groups, the most common course is to enact a law that promises to solve or ameliorate a problem, even though its chances of doing so may be slim (covenant marriage laws to discourage divorce or child support enforcement laws to solve family poverty could be examples). Solutions, like problems, are labels for categories of differences, such as (a) school vouchers to increase school choice and thereby improve the educational experience of children; (b) higher property taxes to more adequately fund public education and thereby improve the educational experience of children; or (c) differences over taxes that some said were too high and others did not in relation to the budget surplus in 1999-2000. Among Americans nationwide, however, tax cuts ranked last among potential solutions to the budget surplus problem. The House, as its solution to the budget surplus problem, passed a far-reaching $792 billion tax cut, which included a 10% reduction in individual income tax rates, a repeal of the inheritance tax, and a reduction in the capital gains tax (Dao, 1999a). Threatening the return of the three-martini lunch, it also included an increase in the tax deduction for business meals (Mitchell, 1999b).

Embedded in solutions to problems are the ambiguities and contradictions that emanate from the ambivalences and vacillations of advocates. Congressional debate over the marriage tax in 1999 is an example of such ambivalence.

Though not really a tax, marriage tax relief was a concept embraced by those who thought federal tax policy should be biased in favor of, not against, marriages—good ones, bad ones, rich ones, or poor ones (Reno, 1999). The deep divisions that emerged in the Republican party between Wall Street Republicans, the Christian Coalition, and moderate Republicans over the marriage tax measure caused some to wonder whether the Republican party stood for Wall Street wealth or the family values of the Christian Coalition—motherhood and righteousness—or both.

The Functions of Political Language

Language is important in shaping appraisals of conditions constructed as problems at local, state, and national levels of governments. It is also important in catalyzing and shaping perceptions and behaviors in the construction of solutions to remedy such conditions (Edelman, 1985). Typically surrounded by uncertainty and controversy, the language used to construct problems and their solutions in family policy discourse can both arouse and intensify fear and anxiety in large numbers of people. Consider, for example, some of the problems addressed in the Patients' Bill of Rights debated in Congress in 1999. One problem was the premature discharge of patients from the hospital following a mastectomy and the right of women to remain in the hospital for as long as their doctor deemed medically necessary. The language that Senator Barbara Mikulski, Democrat from Maryland, used to construct both the problem and its solution during Senate debates served to arouse anew anxieties and fears about the declining quality of health care in this country. "Make no mistake," she said, "a mastectomy is an amputation and it has all the horrible, horrific consequences of an amputation," adding that even so, women in some cases were told to call a cab and go home (Mitchell, 1999a).

Language, cognition, and social conditions, which are all important in the construction of problems and their solutions, shape each other in ways that make the contradictions and dilemmas embedded in their constructions and the chronic inability to resolve them tolerable, as, for example, the contradictions embedded in the 1999 tax cut debates with respect to Wall Street and family values. Language also is important in appeals for support by public officials, aspirants to public office, and interest groups. Such appeals can be understood as affirmations waiting to be ignored, qualified, or accepted. The same is true of preambles to public proceedings, statutes, court rulings, and popular discussions of public issues. To illustrate the latter point, Paul Weyrich, a founder of social conservatism, in reflecting on the achievements of the Christian Right in American politics, recounted Bob Dole's response when he was told of the amount of time that Gary Bauer and Phyllis Schalfly, leaders of the Christian Right, spent working on the Republican platform in the 1996 presidential campaign. In one brief sentence, Bob Dole, Republican presidential candidate that year, in effect dismissed their efforts, saying that he had never read the platform and did not feel bound by anything in it (Dreble, 1999).

Because people are eager to believe that government can and will protect them from evil and threats to their well-being, people are susceptible to political language. The backdrop of anxiety and ambiguity embedded in the dilemmas for which government solutions are sought means that people are vulnerable to social cues, that is, language emanating from sources they want to believe are authoritative and competent enough to cope with evil and threats. Senator Bill Frist from Tennessee, who, before becoming a senator, was a physician and therefore in a position to speak authoritatively during the Senate debates on the issue of patient rights, said reassuringly that Congress would come up with a good patient rights bill that would guarantee access to specialists. In effect, by assuring the American people of substantive rights to health care, he attempted to ease their fears about threats to their health care.

Language and language claims also link family problems to material benefits by way of the allocation of values in the political process. For example, the current quality of health care was linked to Medicare and Medicaid spending cuts through the language claims of doctors, patients, and insurance companies in the 1999 congressional budget process. Language claims also serve to assign blame to the origins of problems, such as the attribution of poverty to teen childbearing, unemployment, or divorce—in other words, to individual behaviors, the state of the economy, or liberal divorce laws.

Linguistic Cues: Metonyms and Metaphors

Linguistic cues and references evoke entire cognitive structures. A cognitive structure defines ambiguous situations by focusing on only one part and comparing it to a situation with which people are familiar. Sets of beliefs about social issues, the meanings of family and social problems, feelings about problems, role definitions, and self-definitions, as integral parts of a single cognitive structure, define and reinforce the others (Edelman, 1975; Levi-Strauss, 1966; Mead, 1934). *Helping, welfare, family,* and *family values* are examples of commonly employed linguistic cues. Presidents, presidential candidates, legislators, advocates, interest group spokespersons, and others commonly employ such cues.

Linguistic cues and references are comprised of metaphors, metonyms, and syntax. *Metonymy* refers to the use of the name of one thing for another thing with which it is associated. For instance, in Louisiana, the use of words such as *ma'am* and *sir* in addressing teachers (which is now required by law) is associated with respect ("Use of 'Ma'am,' " 1999). *Metaphor* refers to a figure of speech in which one thing is likened to another—such as "squeaky clean" in reference to the untarnished reputation of Vice President Al Gore, the Democratic presidential candidate in 2000—is probably the most common of the linguistic cues. Remember Ronald Reagan's reference to "welfare queens," which he used to arouse hostility toward and cast suspicion on mothers receiving Aid to Families with Dependent Children (AFDC)? Steve Kelley, Democratic candidate from Minnesota for the U.S. Senate in 2000, used the metaphor of nation-as-family when he said that families worked hard to invest in their futures—putting money into education for their children, making sure they had decent health insurance, paying off their bank loans, and making sure they had enough saved for retirement—which he said was just plain common sense that could be applied to develop policies that would work for the families of Minnesota and the nation (Reilly, 1999).

Syntax refers to the way words are used to evoke feelings about an issue, as, for example, when Senator Barbara Mikulski, as mentioned earlier, said, "Make no mistake, a mastectomy is an amputation and it has all the horrible, horrific consequences of an amputation," and then added, "Even so, in some cases, a woman is told to call a cab and go home." (Mitchell, 1999a). Senator Barbara Boxer's charge in those same debates over the Patients' Bill of Rights that all but three Republicans turned their backs on the women of America was designed to have the same effect.

Linguistic References in Naming and Classifying Problems

Linguistic references name and classify family and social problems such as poverty, crime, mental illness, drug abuse, failing schools, unwed parenthood, and suicide. They also evoke cognitive structures and beliefs that include solutions to the problems (Edelman, 1975). Though symbolic cues are not all-powerful, they help to define the physical features and representations of such features that constitute our political world. Generated subtly by the terms used to signify them, the beliefs and perceptions evoked by their classification typically are accepted uncritically. By implying that problems are distinct and separate from each other, their classification also implies that the causes and symptoms of problems are different—poverty, out-of-wedlock births, and homelessness being examples.

Given that the naming of problems involves alternative scenarios, each with its own set of facts, value judgments, and emotions, and that self-conceptions are embedded in cognitive structures in the naming of problems, the passion with which developments are interpreted, together with efforts to make them consistent with existing cognitive structures, can be better appreciated. One example of this phenomenon is the argument raging among family professionals in different disciplines about whether heterosexual marriages are essential for child well-being; different advocates adamantly hold different positions and interpret research findings in ways to make such findings consistent with *their* cognitive structures. The same applies to suicide and whether it should be seen as a medical problem, a psychological problem, a problem of moral or social or family failure, or an assertion of individual freedom and autonomy (Smith, D. 1999). The naming of problems also has consequences for the ways in which governments as organizational entities are structured. It has resulted, for example, in separate governmental departments staffed with people trained to focus on a particular set of symptoms and to believe in a distinct set of causes to supposedly distinct problems. Thus, the naming of problems in family policy discourse is a matter of some consequence not only for family policy but for families themselves. An example is the naming of welfare dependency as a problem associated with child care rather than the naming of child care as a problem associated with child development.

■ Summary and Conclusions

Family policy discourse, like language itself, is always in flux. A subcategory of social policy, family policy is a product of modernity that rests on three conceptual foundations: progress, universality, and regularity/predictability. Postmodernism, in contrast, emphasizes difference, particularity, and irregularity and diversity. These characteristics are embedded in contemporary family policy discourse and increasingly in family policy itself, as evidenced by its increasingly differentiated organization, structure, and practice. Never fixed or stable, its meanings are contested by many groups in many locations, just as the term *family* is.

Postmodernism entails some risks for family policy. With so many sources of information and avenues of communication, its emphasis on diversity jeopardizes a shared view of the common good and of family well-being as the goal of family policy not only among social scientists, family professionals, and policy makers but also among the general public—which indeed many think already has occurred; a shared view is perceived as necessary for reconstructing undesirable conditions that hurt families into policy solutions that help families. Moreover, its focus on language, discourse, meaning, and constructionism could deflect attention from objective social and economic realities that create harm for families such as sex and racial discrimination, economic hardship, growing income inequalities, increased market competition and growing economic insecurities, growing isolation, and police brutality.

Just as Elkind (1994) argues that the postmodern attitude does not deny longstanding moral principles in insisting that universal principles must arise out of consensus rather than rational argument or sacred text such as the Bible, it also could be argued that postmodernism's emphasis on diversity and differentiation could help to ensure the well-being of *all* families, regardless of family structure and ethnic or racial or economic background, achieving perhaps in its emphasis on diversity the universality that has eluded family policy for so long in this country. Indeed, if it is true that family policy is nothing less than social policy except for its focus on the family dimensions of social policy, then the differentiation of family policy from social policy, like many of the programs and practices that constitute family policy, is itself a postmodern turn.

If Arac (1989) is correct in saying that the personal has become political because of public agitation for public remedies in areas long considered private, the same may be said with respect to family: The family has become political because of public agitation for public remedies in the private family area. Because the meanings of terms like *family* and *public* or *government* or *policy solutions* are always in flux, it seems reasonable to ask, in light of the present discussion, what *family* means in the postmodern era. Has its meaning changed over time? If so, how? These are the questions that the next chapter addresses.

But before turning to the next chapter on changing families and changing meanings of family, reflect on the following questions.

■ Some Questions for Your Reflection and Discussion

1. What are the characteristics of postmodernism?
2. What are the conceptual foundations of modernism?
3. What is the postmodern critique of modernism?
4. How is the domain of family policy reflective of the differentiation and elaboration associated with postmodernism?
5. How does postmodernism view language?
6. What are binary opposites? What are their function?
7. How has the political discourse of Republicans and Democrats differed in family policy developments? Give some examples.
8. What is meant by *historical* practice?
9. What are some of the factors that contribute to the acceptance of undesirable family conditions as family problems that government should address?
10. Why are some undesirable conditions accepted as problems and not others?
11. Of what consequence is the naming of problems for family policy—and families?
12. What is the difference between a *problem* and a *crisis?*
13. What are the functions of language in the construction of problems and solutions?
14. What are linguistic cues? What is a metaphor and a metonym? Give examples.
15. What are some of the risks of postmodernism for family policy?

CHAPTER 3

The Many and Changing Meanings of Family

◻ The construct *family policy* is new in policy discourse, but the term *family* is not, although its meanings have changed over time due to changes in the social, economic, political, and cultural context in which it is embedded. Because family is both the subject and object of family policy, this chapter reviews some of the historical changes in family life, some explanations for such changes, different constructions of such changes (sociological, cultural, feminist, psychological, and so on), and the implications of such changes and their constructed meanings for the construction of policy solutions to family problems.

■ Families Defined: Definitional Diversity

In the popular vernacular, the term *family* is used broadly and loosely (Mintz & Kellogg, 1988). Never fixed or stable, it can refer to any group of persons of a common ancestry, to any group of individuals residing under the same roof, and to a unit comprised of one or more adults living together and participating in the care and rearing of their own or adopted children. Social scientists, in attempting to disentangle its diverse definitions, make the distinction between family and household, defining family as a legal kinship unit based on marital, adoptive, or biological relatedness and linkages, and household as a residential unit composed of a group of kin and/or nonkin. The U.S. Census Bureau makes the distinction between *family* and *family group*. It defines family as two or more people living together who are related by blood, marriage, or adoption, one of whom is the householder, and the housing unit is owned or rented in that person's name. A family group includes all family living arrangements: families, related subfamilies, and unrelated subfamilies (Bryson & Casper, 1998).

Some students of families focus on their organizational structures (Mintz & Kellogg, 1988). The nuclear or conjugal family is a unit composed of a husband, wife, and dependent children living in an independent household, separate from other family or nonfamily members. Other types of family structures include the consanguinal family (a unit comprised of a single parent and children) and various kinds of complex families based on blood and generational ties. Examples of the latter include three-generation families and families that include two married siblings, their spouses, and children.

Recent scholarship emphasizes the developmental cycle of families, relating changes in family structure to key life events that individual family members experience—marriage, the establishment of independent households, births, and deaths—highlighting the fact that over time, life events will change family size, composition, membership, and organizational structure. Although the timing of such events pertain to age of marriage, age of entry in the labor force, age of childbearing, and the spacing of children may represent the decisions of individual family members, such decisions are made within a particular historical and cultural context. Together, historical and cultural context combine to order the developmental sequence of family households and the timing of life cycle events.

By kinship, social scientists refer to genealogical relationships among groups of families. The term *extended family* refers to a large group of relatives who live separately from each other. In small-scale societies, where kinship is the fundamental organizing principle, kinship groups have important cultural and social functions, such as housing, social control, welfare, socialization, and economic activity. They also have certain political powers.

Kinship groups can be structured in a variety of ways. In small-scale societies, social organization is based on descent group structures, that is, on paternal or maternal ties (patrilineal or matrilineal) or both (cognatic). Descent group organization structures not only the family and religious life of the society but also its politics and economy. In large-scale societies such as modern industrial societies like the United States and other Western countries, public institutions and the marketplace have assumed many of the functions formerly assigned to kinship groups. Nonetheless, extended family ties remain important even in urban and industrial societies. Relatives help their kin carry out a variety of tasks, such as the care of young children, and are sources of mutual aid and assistance in times of emergency.

Until recently, most Americans shared a common set of beliefs about family life that were so widespread they were largely taken as fact (Mintz & Kellogg, 1988). These beliefs that:

- A family is comprised of a married couple and their minor children living together in a common residence.
- The father, as household head, is the sole earner of the family's income and decides where the family lives, and his surname is his wife's and children's.
- The mother, as full-time homemaker, is devoted to child rearing and homemaking, and is her husband's faithful companion and helpmate and the facilitator of her children's development and education.
- Marriage is a lifelong commitment with sexual relationships confined to the marital partner.

- Before kindergarten, parents are solely responsible for their children's care.
- Parents are free to discipline and care for their children as they see fit, without outside interference.
- Families whose behaviors do not conform with one or more of these assumptions can be thought of as troubled.

Today, the term *family* no longer is exclusively attached to conjugal or nuclear families comprised of a husband, wife, and dependent children. It is applied to almost any grouping of two or more people living together. These family groupings include single-parent households, blended families made up of stepparents and stepchildren, adoptive parents and their children, grandparent families, and couples cohabiting outside wedlock, including gay couples.[1]

■ Families Historically

Such changes in the application of the term *family*, although constituting a fundamental reorientation in American family patterns, have their precedents. Over the past 300 years, American families have undergone a series of far-reaching "domestic revolutions" that have profoundly altered family life, repeatedly transforming their demographic characteristics, organizational structure, functions, conceptions, and internal dynamics (Mintz & Kellogg, 1988). Although the family is seen as a social institution resistant to change, it is as deeply embedded in historical processes as are other institutions. A conservative institution in terms of the transmission of moral and cultural values from one generation to the next, the family clearly is not a static institution.

Families in Colonial Times:
"Little Commonwealths"

Three centuries ago, when the country was founded, the American family was the fundamental economic, educational, political, and religious unit of society (Mintz & Kellogg, 1988). The family, not the individual, was the unit on which church and state were based. The household as a unit of production was the institution responsible for the education of children, the transfer of craft skills, and the care of elderly and infirm members. During the early colonial era, when the family performed many functions that have since been relegated to nonfamilial institutions, it was an integral part of the larger society. As a "little commonwealth," a microcosm of the larger society, it was governed by the same principles of hierarchy and deference that governed other institutions. All aspects of life—economics, religion, law, politics—were part of a single, unitary, mutually reinforcing set of relationships. Hence, distinctions between kin and nonkin were more blurred in preindustrial Europe and colonial America than they are today, and the language of family was more open and fluid (Gillis, 1996). Children were taught by their parents not to rely on blood ties alone, and

New England Puritans constantly reminded themselves not to love their spouses and children too much, because doing so might detract from their love of God. People gathered to work or pursue communally organized leisure, not for family occasions.

Families in the 19th Century: Separate Spheres

By the time Alexis de Tocqueville came to the United States in 1831, family patterns were very different from those of the settlers who left England in the 17th century. Instead of a little commonwealth, the family had been replaced by a new image—a "haven in a heartless world," a mainstay of morality and tender feelings and a refuge from the aggressive and selfish world of commerce (Mintz & Kellogg, 1988). The origins of the new image and emphasis on sentiment and self-fulfillment lay in the upper-class and merchant families of western Europe of the 1600s and 1700s, and did not spread to the masses until the late 1800s and early 1900s.

The increased emphasis on feelings and self-fulfillment transformed the family in the 19th century into a private place, a shelter for higher redeeming values and from the temptations and corruptions of the outside world. Relations within the new "democratic" family were less formal and hierarchical than had been the case in the 17th- and 18th-century household. Marriages increasingly were based on romantic love, relations between husbands and wives were increasingly affectionate and egalitarian, children remained at home for an increasingly longer time, and parents devoted more time and attention to the care and nurture of their children. In this family, relations were organized around the principle of "separate spheres," whereby each family member had a special role, or sphere, appropriate to his or her age and gender.

Families in the Early 20th Century: Companionate Families

The 19th-century family gave way to the construction of the companionate family: a new family ideal in the early decades of the 20th century. Responding to the rise in divorce rates, falling birthrates, the changing position of women, and the revolution in morals and manners, educators, legal scholars, social workers, and social scientists extolled the new ideal of family life as one in which spouses would be friends and lovers and parents and children would be friends (Mintz & Kellogg, 1988). According to this new ideal, relations within the family would be based not on patriarchal authority but on affection and mutual interest. The traditional conception of marriage as a sacred duty or obligation gave way to a new ideal of sexual satisfaction, companionship, and emotional support. To achieve this ideal, influential groups recommended liberalized divorce laws, programs of marriage counseling, domestic science, sex education, and child-rearing practices that emphasized freedom and self-expression over impulse control.

Families in the 1950s: Family Togetherness

Although the intellectual roots of the companionate family lay in the 1920s, the Great Depression and World War II delayed the impact of this new ideal until after the war. By the mid-1950s, the ideal of the companionate family seemed well on the way to fulfillment. Family "togetherness" became the cultural norm (Mintz & Kellogg, 1988). Couples married earlier than their parents had, and women bore more children, had them at younger ages, and spaced them closer together. They divorced at a slower rate than in preceding years. Rising incomes permitted a growing majority of families to buy their own homes, even as outside institutions continued to assume many of the functions that families had previously performed. As the proportion of the population over the age of 65 increased, public and private pensions increasingly helped families shoulder the economic burdens of elderly parents. Separate age-segregated institutions, like nursery schools, assumed more responsibility for the education of children.

Families Since the Late 1950s: Personal Freedom and Autonomy

Since the late 1950s, the family increasingly has come to be seen as an impediment to individual self-fulfillment. During these years, the relationship between family values and values of individualism and personal autonomy has become more and more problematic. One source of strain is the continuing escalation of expectations of marriage that have proven difficult to meet. An increased desire for personal fulfillment, coupled with the belief that such fulfillment can be achieved only through a successful, independent career, conflicts with the more traditional view of marriage as an institution in which the wife, not the husband, is expected to sacrifice for the good of the family (Mintz & Kellogg, 1988). As notions of individual autonomy and freedom became the framework for constitutional and family law, the importance of family in mediating individual and community interests and in creating democratic citizens eroded accordingly (Hafen, 1990). The desire for greater personal freedom and fulfillment can be seen in the sharp rise in the number of couples cohabiting outside of marriage and the number of persons living alone. In 1997, persons living alone constituted 83%, or almost all of the nonfamily households (Casper & Bryson, 1998a).

Families Since the 1960s: Diversity

Given the desire for greater personal freedom and self-fulfillment, it should not be surprising that since the 1960s, the distinguishing characteristic of

American family life has been the increasing diversity in family living arrangements. Survey findings reported in the 1999 General Social Survey (GSS) revealed a continuing rapid decline of traditional family living arrangements and an even starker picture of marriage in the 1990s than the Census Bureau's findings ("Poll Reveals Another Sign," 1999):

■ In 1996, only 56% of the adult population in the United States was married, down from 75% in 1972, when the survey first was taken ("Poll Reveals Another Sign," 1999).

■ In 1998, almost 10% of the population was divorced (Lugaila, 1998), up from just over 6% in 1980 and 3.2% in 1970 (U.S. Bureau of the Census, 1994).

■ In 1998, just over half of all children lived in a two-parent households, compared with 73% in 1972 ("Poll Reveals Another Sign," 1999).

■ The percentage of households consisting of unmarried persons with no children in 1998, 33%, was more than twice the rate in 1972 ("Poll Reveals Another Sign," 1999).

■ The percentage of children living with single parents in 1996, 18.2%, was 4½ times greater than in 1972 ("Poll Reveals Another Sign," 1999).

■ The average number of children under 18 per family in 1998 was 1.84, down from 3.58 in 1970 (U.S. Bureau of the Census, 1986, 1998).

Part of the decline in married couple households can be attributed to the growing number of young adults who are deferring marriage (U.S. Bureau of the Census, 1998). Since 1970, census data show an increase in age of first marriages for both men and women, many cohabiting before marriage. Although the percentage of women who had ever cohabited and were cohabiting in 1998 was relatively small (just 7%), almost a quarter of those who had ever cohabited reported they had cohabited before marriage. In addition to the postponement of marriage by young adults, part of the decline in married couple households also can be attributed to a decline in marriage rates for both first marriages and remarriages (as the latter pertain to divorced and widowed persons). Since 1990, the decline in married couple households with children has slowed (Casper & Bryson, 1998a). Divorce rates also have slowed from their high of 5.3 per 1,000 population in 1979 and 1981 (U.S. Bureau of the Census, 1986) to 4.1 in 1998 (U.S. Bureau of the Census, 1998).

Despite the slowing rate of decline in married couple households and the slowing of divorce rates, more and more people now live alone—in all age categories—but women more than men, especially among those 75 years and older, reflecting in part life span differences between the sexes (U.S. Bureau of the Census, 1998). A quarter of all American households consisted of just one person who lived alone in 1998, up from 18% in 1970. In San Francisco, more people also were dying alone with no one to arrange their funerals, settle their estates, or mourn their passing (Nieves, 2000). In the first 6 months of 2000, 275 people died this way, according to city officials, compared with about 300 per year for the last decade.

Increased divorce rates have led to an increased number of stepfamilies; indeed, the number of stepfamilies is projected to outnumber nuclear families by 2007 (Herbert, 1999). A more inclusive estimate of people involved in step relationships of any kind—stepparent, stepdaughter or son, stepsibling, stepgrandparent and stepgrandchildren, stepparents and uncles, stepnieces and nephews, and so on—is about 60% of the population. Higher divorce rates have led not only to an increased number of stepfamilies, but coupled with a sharp increase in the number of children born to single women, they also have led to a marked upturn in the number of female-headed families (U.S. Bureau of the Census, 1998). In 1997, almost a quarter of all family households with children under 18 were headed by mothers only. Mother-only families accounted for over 20% of all white families, almost 60% of all black families, and over 30% of all Hispanic families. Just 5% of all family households with children under 18 in 1998 were headed by fathers only, 2½ times more than in 1970. Just as the number of families headed by single parents has increased, so has the number of families maintained by grandparents (U.S. Bureau of the Census, 1998).

As is commonly known, women with children are much more likely to work outside the home today than in the past. Over 75% of all married mothers with school-age children worked outside the home in 1997 as did almost two thirds of all mothers with preschool children. For single mothers, labor force participation rates were almost 75% for those with school-age children and 65% for those with preschool children (U.S. Bureau of the Census, 1998). Nationwide, a large percentage (76%) of preschool children with employed mothers were regularly cared for by someone other than their parents in 1997.

Child care arrangements are as diverse as family living arrangements. For more than half of preschool children with employed mothers, the primary child care provider was not related to the child (Capizzano, Adams, & Sonenstein, 2000). About 32% of children were in center-based child care arrangements, and about half as many, 16%, were in family child care. A relatively small percentage of children (6%) were regularly cared for by a baby-sitter or nanny in the child's home. Almost half of all preschoolers whose mothers worked were cared for by relatives (Casper, 1996). In poor families, relatives provided care for almost two thirds of the preschoolers whose mothers worked (Casper 1997a). The percentage of married fathers who cared for their preschoolers while mothers worked increased from 23% in 1988 to 30% in 1991, attributable in part to the economic recession of that period, when job layoffs made fathers more available for child care and parents looked for a way to cut child care costs. As the economy began to recover and fathers found jobs, the percentage caring for their preschoolers while mothers worked declined to 25% in 1993 (Casper, 1997b).

Because these data are for the population as a whole and not broken down by race, ethnicity, or geographic region, they do not fully depict the extent of the diversity that exists between families and their living arrangements in the United States. The data also do not include other types of family relationships—such as same-sex partnerships, multiracial families, families with disabled children and adults—that also speak to such diversity.

■ What Has Made Families Evolve and Change?

What accounts for the extraordinary evolution and transformation of the American family over the past 3 centuries? As Mintz and Kellogg (1988) and others point out (Zimmerman 1992b), the critical transformations in family life are aspects of broader demographic, economic, social, and cultural changes that have reshaped all facets of American life. Of these, changes in the demographic makeup of the country, in the economy, and in the role of women are all paramount.

Changes in the Economy

Changes in the economy have been a principal force for change in all facets of American life. Three centuries ago, most American families were largely self-sufficient agricultural units. Few families sought to maximize their income by producing goods destined for distant markets. Their goal was to build up family farms or enterprises to maintain family independence, to protect family property and status, and to produce dowries or an inheritance for their children. Although shoes, saddles, hats, iron implements, and men's clothing were made by specialized craftspersons, most families used the goods they themselves produced: food, furniture, cloth, soap, candles, and leather. Parental authority was reinforced through the control of property (i.e., land) or through the generational transmission of craft skills. The family was not merely the site of emotional attachments but was also an economy made up of interdependent family members who participated in and contributed to it. It was, in short, a "family economy."

By the late 19th century, economic relationships among family members had loosened dramatically, a transition marked by the diminishing control of parents over children's choice of marriage partners. As a growing number of farm households began to specialize in the production of cash crops and use the proceeds to purchase household goods produced outside the home, the self-sufficiency of family households diminished accordingly. Domestic industries that formerly employed large numbers of women and older children gradually disappeared. For the middle class, older children, no longer employed in household industries or fostered out as servants or apprentices, lost their value and status as economic assets. Instead, they became economic dependents requiring significant investments in their human capital in the form of education. As a result of these changes, the family was transformed from a more public institution serving as workplace, school, and social welfare agency into a more private and specialized institution serving the emotional needs of family members.

The 1990s and the years beyond are to be noted for the globalization of the economy, whose full family effects are as yet unknown. Globalization, which is associated with postmodernism, involves the integration of free markets, nation-states, and information technologies that enable individuals, corporations, and nations to reach farther, faster, deeper, and cheaper around the world than has been known in the past (Friedman, 1999). The symbol of globalization is the World Wide Web, which not only connects people around the world but also increases their power to influence markets and nation-states. Questions about the sustainability of the new system come at a time when the world has been and will continue to be destabilized by economic crises that can rapidly spread from one continent to another. Noting the effects of globalization and rapid technology on every aspect of national policy—health care, welfare, education, job training, the environment, market regulation, Social Security, free trade, and military strategy—Friedman warns that global financial crises could be the norm in the coming era, with booms, busts, and recoveries all coming faster.

In 1999, a meeting of the World Trade Organization (WTO) in Seattle brought protesters to the streets, charging that globalization was a threat to human rights, the environment, and the wages of working families. The WTO is an international organization of 135 countries that strive to ensure the freest possible flow of trade in the world. Known as the ultimate capitalist club, its headquarters are in Geneva, Switzerland ("Just What Is the WTO?", 1999), and to join, countries agree to follow broad principles of openness in their economies and to move away from government subsidies. No country is required to join, but with the growing importance of the world economy to the economic prosperity of nations—and to the economic well-being of families, it might be added—nations generally are eager to become members.

Advocates have long argued that free trade is key to curing the social ills of the world. As wages rise, they say, and countries around the world prosper, the market's invisible hand, unfettered by parochial regulation, will somehow pressure governments to clean up the environment, outlaw child labor, and enact workers' rights laws (Lighthizer, 1999). Speaking to the WTO, President Bill Clinton, an advocate of free trade, voiced the concerns and complaints of environmental and labor groups about free trade. Without suggesting specific solutions, he more or less acknowledged that a global free market would not by itself raise family living standards throughout the world, nor would corporations and countries that got richer necessarily do the right thing for the environment, child labor, and workers' rights.

Changes in Demography

Demography, along with the economy, also has been a potent force for change in American family life. Such population characteristics as age distribution and sex ratio exert strong influences on the size and composition of families, the marriage rate, the death rate, the birthrate, and other aspects of family life (Mintz & Kellogg, 1988). The gradual reduction of the size of the family has had especially far-reaching consequences for family life. Beginning in the last quarter of the 18th century, American women began bearing fewer children, spacing them closer together, and ceasing childbearing at younger ages. Smaller families meant that parents could invest more emotional and financial resources in each child, and closer spacing of children meant that mothers could expect to devote fewer years to bearing and rearing children.

A second fundamental demographic change affecting family life has been the aging of the population. Some 150 years ago, the average age in the United States was 17. In 1997, the median age was 35 (U.S. Bureau of the Census, 1998), giving the country one of the oldest populations in the world. For whites, average life expectancy at birth in 1995 was 73.4 years for men and 79.8 years for women; for blacks, it was 65.2 years for men and 73.9 years for women (U.S. Bureau of the Census, 1998). This demographic shift means that a growing proportion of the population now experiences aspects of family life that were less well known in the past—grandparenthood, prolonged widowhood, and concomitantly, the care of elderly parents—some of which are more pleasurable than others.

Changes in the Role of Women

A third factor that has changed family life are the profound transformations in women's roles. During the early 19th century, when economic production (e.g., canning, sewing, working on the farm) increasingly was transferred out of the home, married women lost many of their economically "productive" roles (Mintz & Kellogg, 1988). As a result, many middle-class women instead concentrated on motherhood and household management. A new conception of sex roles in the home and the economy was taking place. The task of women, according to this new model, was to shape the character of children, make the home a haven of peace and order, and exert a moral and uplifting influence on men. The task of men, as breadwinners, was to provide for their families. With the dramatic increase in the participation of married women in the labor force during World War II—spurred in part by the shortage of workers as men left to join the war effort—the process of privatizing women's roles was reversed, making wives less financially dependent on their husbands. The entry of so many women into the labor force called into question traditional assumptions about the sexual division of housekeeping and childrearing roles, which constituted the domestic sphere of family life. After the war, however, when the men returned, women's domestic roles were glorified, and women were pulled back into the home. Since the 1960s, traditional assumptions about the sexual division of labor in families gradually changed as women again joined the workforce in ever-increasing numbers.

■ Practical Consequences of Changing Families in Changing Contexts

For over 3 centuries, Americans have worried about the future of the family. Within decades of the Puritans' arrival in Massachusetts Bay Colony, Puritan jeremiads decried trends they saw at the time: the increasing fragility of marriage, the growing selfishness and irresponsibility of parents, the increasing unruliness of children (Mintz & Kellogg, 1988). Despite all these centuries of worrying that the family was disintegrating, the family as an institution, although changed in important ways, has done more than just survive.

To illustrate: Families today are much less likely than those in the past to lose children, as evidenced by declining rates of infant mortality, and children are much less likely to be orphaned. Unlike parents in the past, parents today can expect to see all their children reach adulthood. Since mothers no longer bear children every 2 years after marriage until menopause or death, they also can expect to spend a smaller proportion of their adult lives rearing young children and can more easily combine family life with a career. Longer life expectancies and spacing children closer mean that married couples can have time together after their children have ceased to be responsibilities to enjoy each other as friends and lovers and nurture their relationship.

At the same time, because families today are perceived to be more isolated from the worlds of kinship and community life than their predecessors, many regard the contemporary family as more fragile as an institution (Mintz & Kellogg, 1988). Shorn of traditional educational and productive functions, the stability of today's families rests on the tenuous foundations of affection, compatibility, and mutual interest. Family members no longer are bound together by their mutual participation in a collective family economy. Closer spacing of children and fewer children mean that parents can devote more time to the quality of their interpersonal relations. Parental authority, no longer reinforced by control of property, the transfer of craft skills, or the supervision of the surrounding community, also is no longer supported by the common values and beliefs of large groups of people. Given the erosion of earlier kinds of supports and longer life spans, it is not surprising that families today are more likely to be disrupted by divorce than premature death. At the end of the 20th century, the proportion of marriages likely to be disrupted by divorce was about the same as those disrupted by death in earlier centuries (Stone, 1977).

The historic transformation of the family in the United States in recent decades—which is as dramatic and far reaching as the transformation that took place at the beginning of the 19th century with the advent of the Industrial Revolution—has generated a profound sense of uncertainty and ambivalence about its future. In particular, such change has given rise to concern about the role such transformation might play in increased child neglect, teen pregnancy, delinquency, suicide, school failure, and drug and alcohol abuse (Dawson, 1991). These concerns appear to be based on data showing a relationship between these problems and (a) a decline in the percentage of children being raised in two-parent families, from 85% in 1970 to 68% in 1997; (b) an increase in the percentage being raised in mother-only families, from 11% in 1970 to 24% in 1997; and (c) an increase in the percentage being raised in father-only families, which, like mother-only families, more than doubled in this same period, from 4% in 1970 to 8% in 1997 (Ladd, 1999).

Although the percentage of children living in two-parent families declined for both blacks and whites over this period, racial disparities are dramatic. In 1970, for example, 90% of all white children were being raised in two-parent families but only 59% of all black children were. By 1997, 75% of all white children were being raised in two-parent families, and only 35% of all black children were (Ladd, 1999). The percentage of black children living in mother-only families increased, from 30% in 1970 to 52% in 1997; the percentage living in father-only families remained almost constant—12% in 1970 and 13% in 1997. Survey responses to questions about the family experiences of respondents when they were growing up reflected these trends: Over three fourths of the respondents in 1973 said they lived with both their mother and father when they were 16, and by 1997, that percentage had declined to 69% ("Material Status," 1999). For those who were not living with both parents when they were growing up, those who attributed their family situation to the death of a parent declined from 61% in 1973 to 28% in 1998, whereas those who attributed it to parental divorce increased from 32% to 52%.

■ Different Constructions of Changes in Family Life

Families as Worlds of Our Own Making

What is to be made of the transformations, especially since the 1960s, in the family as an institution and in family life in general in the United States? What meanings have been attributed to those changes? According to John Gillis (1996), who agrees that modern family life has changed and is changing, the idea that the family is not what it used to be never seems to change. He maintains that families past are presented not only as more authentic and real than families present but also as more stable. Moreover, because families past belong to the past, they are regarded as traditional. Thus, when people talk about the traditional family, they describe changes in family life in terms of the disintegration of the family and the loss of what they call the traditional family. The fact is, Gillis says, the notion of the traditional family is a myth, and that despite popular beliefs and images, the desire for closeness for the sake of closeness was notably absent among families past.

Nonetheless, people want to believe that families past were less fragmented, discontinuous, and divided than families present, Gillis (1996) says, despite the absence of historical evidence to support such beliefs. The ideal of family life, he says, sustains our economy, dominates our politics, and holds us hostage to the culture wars being waged in the name of the family. *Culture wars* describes the sharp divisions in American society with regard to certain values and ideals, such divisions fostering antagonism, avoidance, distrust, and even hatred toward groups holding opposing views (Gergen, 1999). As Peter Leonard (1997), a Canadian social work professor, notes, the power of the traditional family in many Western countries has not been fatally weakened, despite the growth of single-parent families, "blended" families, partners without children, and same-sex partners with or without children. Indeed, the strength of the traditional family was abundantly in evidence in debates about welfare reform and whether state-provided services weakened family values. What has changed, according to Gillis, are the cultural resources that different periods offered for coping with the perpetual challenge of creating a sense of continuity and permanence. Earlier references to globalization and the increasing rate of change that characterizes postmodern, postindustrial societies are pertinent here.

Gillis concludes by asserting that if history has a lesson for people today, it is that no one family form has ever been able to satisfy the human need for love, comfort, and security, that families are worlds of our own making and that our images, rituals, and myths must continually be open to revision and never be allowed to be dominated by any orthodoxy or serve the interests of any one class, gender, or generation.

Public Families, Private Families: Institutional Meanings

Cherlin's (1996) construction of the family change is both the same as and different from Gillis. He holds that although the family as a social institution has experienced much change, it has handled some aspects of change well and other aspects less well. Thus, he maintains that in debates about the state of the American family between those who argue that the family is in deep decline and those who say otherwise, neither assertion is true. He says that although history has shown the family to be a resilient institution, able to alter its form to fit changing conditions, there are limits to its adaptability.

Making the distinction between *public* and *private* families, Cherlin distinguishes the public family by its contribution to the public welfare in the form of the services that family members provide by taking care of one another. Public families are comprised of one or two adults related by marriage, partnership, or shared parenthood who take care of dependents and are identifiable by the presence of dependents, both young and old. Because society has a stake in how well families manage the care of dependents, the law allows for some regulation of public families, despite strong sentiment against intervening in private family matters.

The term *private family* connotes intimacy, emotional support, and love. Indeed, most people today think of the family and experience it in terms of the private family. The private family refers to two or more individuals who maintain an intimate relationship that they expect to last indefinitely—or in the case of a parent and child, until the child reaches adulthood—who live in the same household and pool their income and household labor. Whereas questions about the public family pertain to how families care for dependents, questions about the private family center on the intimacy and emotional support that people provide to each other. Although neither the public nor private family that Cherlin depicts requires opposite sexes, they both require long-term commitment and a partnership that involves the sharing of daily problems and pleasures. Currently, because most Americans seem to view the family primarily as the private family, they pay less attention to the commitments and obligations of the public family, according to Cherlin.

Commenting on the implications of the changing emphasis on private as opposed to public families, Cherlin notes that although the family was designed for scarcity, the family is now required to perform in an era of affluence that, although not uniform, is far greater than in the past. Historically, he explains, subsisting from day to day and season to season was the primary preoccupation of the family, not intimacy and personal fulfillment. Marriage and family provided an efficient labor pooling of women and men, which was necessary for growing food or making enough money to buy it, making or buying clothes and other goods, and raising children as future sources of labor. Today, these basic tasks are taken for granted, and families now are responsible for providing not merely material sustenance for family members but emotional sustenance as well. Moreover, the family that in most places and times was dominated by men now is required to function in and adapt to a society in which women have substantial independence.

What has helped to ensure the continuance of the family and family life, Cherlin says, is that most adults continue to desire the experience of lasting bonds of intimacy and affection and to have children—in other words, they value the private family, the family responsible for the emotional nurturance of members. Some sociologists think these desires are solely the result of the powerful socialization children receive early in life. But other theories suggest a psychoanalytic component derived from early experiences with parents or an evolutionary component derived from the need to reproduce. The law and social norms also provide strong support and guidance for the roles of spouse and parent for couples in first marriages. Whichever may be the case, Cherlin says that as an institution, the family has demonstrated a remarkable ability to assume a great diversity of forms in different cultures and different eras and thus to outlast its critics and pessimists. For this reason, Cherlin concluded that although he did not think the family was disappearing, he was unsure about where it may be heading.

Families and the Market: A Postmodern Perspective

When Gillis (1996) advised that the family not be allowed to be dominated by any one orthodoxy or to serve the interests of any one class, nation, or generation, he was speaking to some of the same concerns that preoccupied Peter Leonard (1997) in his postmodern discussion of the family in terms of the state's retreat in the face of market advances. Leonard argues that to understand such changes in state and market involvement at the end of the 20th century, it is necessary to appreciate the profound changes underway in the culture, in the social organization of society, and in conceptions of the person—changes that emerged during a period of what he called "late capitalism," the capitalism of mass consumption within global markets.

Under such conditions, Leonard argues, the family household provides a site for the continuing though weakening and contested promotion of the ideology of familism, which he says celebrates the virtues of the nuclear family, the nurturing roles of women, the subordination of children, and other aspects of the social order. The family household is also where the exchange of ideas about work, consumption, and sexuality plays a significant part in how the different views of family members interact and in messages they convey in what they talk about. Leonard uses the word *subject* to refer to the focal person in the discourse, or as presented here, the family member as speaker or actor. Leonard sees discursive support for familial hierarchies. Family hierarchies relate to the superiority of husbands in relation to wives, parents in relation to children, and the opportunities such hierarchies provide for the abuse of women and children. He sees support for such hierarchies as taking place in a wider context in which family members, especially adults and older children, make work and consumption the foci of their discourses—what they talk about. These discourses, he says, aim to construct and reinforce the commitment of people to productive or domestic labor and child care according to gender within the context of the different circumstances and norms of specific cultures and class positions.

Such discourses also serve to manufacture desire and encourage market dependency, Leonard goes on to say. The market enters directly into family discourses and practices through television programs and advertising that open up an ever widening range of commodities. As bearers of the idea of consumption, older family members present each other and younger members with the possibilities of fulfilling the desire for commodities generated through cultural production. Older family members also provide models of the good consumer, just as they might do for the hard worker, the caring mother, or the dutiful daughter. In short, just as Gillis maintains that the traditional family is a myth in the service of the market economy, Leonard in postmodern language does too.

Noting that the dominant discourses in the larger society stigmatize and condemn welfare dependency, which involves dependency on the state, they approve of dependency on the market because the market is necessary to the dynamic of the capitalist system. Market dependency goes by another name, however, Leonard points out; it is called *independence*. Independence is fostered by dominant discourses in part because market conditions of late capitalism require people to depend on the market as a necessary condition of life and also because such discourse must counter the reality that individuals are more convincingly seen as "interdependent."

Leonard holds that people's needs must be met if they are to be moral agents and advises that only the state can provide the structure, resources, and protections necessary to ensure that their needs *are* met—health care, education, social care, and income maintenance being primary elements. The problem, he says, is that the state is locked into the contradictory legacy of modernity and implicated in the political economy of late capitalism. For this reason, he advises that collective resistance to the power of dominant cultural discourses, such as the market, needs to be strengthened. The aim of such resistance, he says, is for people to resist the cultural messages that (a) exploit them, (b) homogenize their differences, and (c) encourage a profound dependency on the market. Seeing the family as a site for discourse and practices involving the market could make it a prime area for mobilizing such resistance.

Family Roles and Relations: A Postmodern Perspective

David Elkind (1994), a psychiatrist, focuses his discussion of the postmodern family not on its relation to the market, as Leonard does, but on parent-child relations and elaborates on the insights provided by Gillis. The advent of the postmodern era, with its emphasis on difference, particularity, and irregularity, notably from the 1970s on, has produced a change in all assumptions about kinship, according to Elkind. He notes that during the modern period, social scientists did not hesitate to apply the notion of social progress to the evolution of the family. They argued that the family, like other social institutions, had evolved to its current ideal state—monogamy—after passing through the more primitive stages of sexual promiscuity, group marriage, and polygamy (Goode, 1963).

The idea of the nuclear family evolved into the popular belief that the nuclear family represented everything good and warm in human relationships, a center of love, solidarity, and harmony in which each person fulfills personal needs and contributes to the well-being of other family members (Elkind, 1994). Even though this belief recognized the existence of dysfunctional families, the assumption was that these families were exceptions and attributable to the personal failings of family members, not to structural problems of the family itself (Skolnick & Skolnick, 1977). The belief in universals was mirrored in the specialized functions that members of nuclear families were expected to perform and in the increasing role differentiation among members, paralleling earlier discussions of the separate gendered spheres that characterized family life in the late 19th and early 20th centuries. Although parents may have found the roles of breadwinner and homemaker restrictive, the role of children as pupils ensured that their needs for protection and guidance would be met by parents and the larger society.

Parent-child interactions were governed by a set of underlying contracts in the modern nuclear family—unverbalized rules, understandings, and expectations that ensured orderly and predictable attitudes and habits (i.e., regularity) (Elkind, 1994). Contracts were based on the unquestioned unilateral authority of parents to set rules, limits, and standards for their offspring. Three basic contracts predominated:

1. Parents would provide freedom when their children demonstrated appropriate responsibility, such as an infant's feeding herself or himself or an older child's crossing the street by himself or herself.

2. Parents would provide support in return for their children's achievements (i.e., to show pleasure when children say their first word or toilet train themselves).

3. Parents would demonstrate commitment to children in return for their demonstration of loyalty.

These implicit contracts ensured that the child would be properly socialized and able to function productively in the larger society. The regularity that parent-child contracts provided was weighted in favor of the needs of children over those of their parents.

Postmodern emphases on role dedifferentiation and kinship diversity have changed the nature of parent-child relationships, Elkind contends. Parent-child contracts were based on the assumption that regularity was desirable and healthy. Irregularity forced on many parents by the pressures of family and work has led to an erosion of contractual relationships. Unable to fulfill their end of the bargain to support their children's achievements by attending plays, ball games, recitals, and so on, many tired parents use schedules and lists in place of contracts. Schedules and lists, unlike contracts, are variable and irregular and have no underlying agreement that teaches children the skills of organization and discipline, both of which are basic to survival in the postmodern world, Elkind maintains.

Moreover, the change from contracts to schedules and lists has shifted the balance of authority in postmodern families, Elkind adds. When parents have contracts, they operate under unilateral authority in which they hold the power to give or withdraw support, freedom, and commitment. Unilateral authority is the kind of authority that all citizens are obliged to obey. Examples include stopping and going at traffic light signals, paying taxes, keeping sidewalks shoveled in winter, and generally conforming to local, state, and federal laws. With schedules and lists, however, a different form of authority comes into play, Elkind says—mutual authority—which means that equals mutually create, accept, and enforce the rules of their relationship. In contrast to mutual authority, which minimizes differences between adults and children, unilateral authority is based on such differences. The shift from unilateral to mutual authority within the family has been coupled with a similar change in the larger society, which Elkind argues is a major contributor to a new imbalance in family and other institutional relationships.

The modern belief in universals contributed to the belief in progressive role differentiation, just as the postmodern belief in human diversity and particularity is leading to the opposite, namely role dedifferentiation at home and work: for example, male airline stewards, female truck drivers, and househusbands. This radical difference in family roles not only extends to children and adolescents who participate in cooking and housecleaning and to their parents, but it also has contributed to the blurring of the boundaries between home and workplace. Millions of people now have space set aside in their homes where they do some or all of their paid work. Many firms now either support child care services or have child care facilities on the premises. In short, just as the home is moving into the workplace, the workplace is moving into the home.

The blurring of home and workplace also extends to the blurring of boundaries between public and private families, benefiting parents and adults more than children, Elkind says in expanding on Cherlin's terminology. The destruction of the ideal of the happy nuclear family has led to the public airing of what is wrong with modern private family life. Divorce, he goes on to point out, is a publicly visible yet private hurt. Children are transported outside the home to talk to strangers (i.e., therapists) about what goes on within it. Elkind maintains that children need boundaries and protected spaces, and that in general, loss of privacy harms children more than adults. He adds that permeable family kinship forms often contribute to children's feelings of insecurity.

Although the postmodern recognition of particularity and the multifaceted nature of individual interests, abilities, and talents should in theory lead to the dedifferentiation of rigid gender and parental roles, Elkind, along with many others, states that it also imposes a heavy burden on mothers who work outside the home. The permeable family frees postmodern mothers to work and pursue careers, but it has not liberated them from the modern role of child-caregiver and homemaker. In addition, just as Gillis and Leonard noted with regard to social supports in general, Elkind points out that many options now available to parents have not been accompanied by a comparable expansion of programs that provide quality accessible and affordable child care.

The Postmodern Family: A Feminist Perspective

Judith Stacey (1996), like Elkind, uses the term *postmodern family* to indicate the contested, ambivalent, and undecided character of contemporary family cultures. Looking at the problem from a feminist perspective, she holds that the postmodern family condition signaled that moment in history when belief in the logical progression of stages has broken down, and the postmodern family incorporates both experimental and nostalgic dimensions as it lurches forward and backward into an uncertain future.

Although it was once predicted that modernity would produce a singular family system, Stacey notes that we instead are converging toward the postmodern family condition of diversity, flux, and instability, and that under conditions of postmodernism, the social character of practices of gender, sexuality, parenting, and family life become visible and politically charged. If we recognize the contradictions inherent in the ideology, principles, and practices of the modern family system, the most glaring of which is the tension between volition and coercion, some perspective on contemporary family turmoil can be gained, she says.

The acceptability of the contradiction between egalitarian principles of free love and companionship and inegalitarian forms of material and cultural coercion depended on the availability and accessibility of a male breadwinner's wages, Stacey maintains. Despite the patriarchal-capitalist bargain negotiated between male factory owners and laborers, it was not until the 1950s and 1960s, she says, that most industrial workers earned enough to support a full-time housewife; soon after they did earn enough, deindustrialization and post-industrialization conspired to eliminate their jobs and erode their earnings. As that strand of the bargain began to unravel during the 1970s and 1980s, the fragility of the entire gender and family order came into full view, provoking widespread consternation over a "family crisis" throughout industrial societies.

Patriarchal crises, Stacey argues, are always moments of danger and opportunity. As women become less dependent on male earnings, they are freer to leave or avoid abusive or hostile relationships. At the same time, men seem less obliged to commit themselves to familial or parental responsibilities. As women struggle to survive diverse patriarchal crises, they too could become nostalgic for the relative security provided by prior, more stable, patriarchal families. The feminization of poverty around the globe, Stacey maintains, is a direct product of the feminization of family life that has taken place ever since the collapse of the modern industrial order, upon which the modern family rests.

Historically, all stable systems of marriage and family life have rested on measures of coercion and inequality, according to Stacey. Family systems appear to have been most stable when women and men have been economically interdependent, when households served as units of production with sufficient resources to reproduce themselves, and when individuals lacked alternative means of economic, sexual, and social life. Family units of this sort have always been embedded in and supported and sanctioned by wider sets of kinship, community, and religious ties. Disturbingly, Stacey adds, all such family systems have been patriarchal. She takes issue with claims that family breakdown is the principal source of what's wrong with our society. She maintains that most of the problems people experience are traceable to the incomplete transition into newer structures after the breakdown of existing economic and social structures.

Family as Natural Selection: An Evolutionary Biological Perspective

Evolutionary biologists construct the changes that have occurred in family life differently from Stacey, Gillis, Cherlin, Elkind, and Leonard. According to Steven Pinker (1997), an evolutionary biologist, the application of basic principles of Darwinian science to family behaviors can illuminate family dynamics in ways the social sciences (which generally emphasize the cultural, psychological, and economic roots of behavior rather than biological ones) cannot. Families are not unique to human beings, Pinker says, so consideration of the conditions that foster family formation among other species could give new insights into the origins of the human family as well as into the motivations and impulses lying just beyond the forebrain's grasp.

Illustrative of the motivations and impulses that could foster family formation in humans under conditions of late capitalism from the evolutionary biological perspective is the case of a photographer who offered fashion models as egg
donors to the highest bidders, auctioning their ova on the Internet to would-be
parents willing to pay up to $150,000 in hopes of having a beautiful child
(Goldberg, 1999b). On the Web site, the photographer quoted a study that
looked at personal ads to determine the "market value" of mate choice and
found that men wanted youth, beauty, and social skills, and women who had
those qualities wanted rich, good-looking, and young men. According to the
photographer, this was Darwin's natural selection of the very best. "The highest
bidder gets youth and beauty." Such a Darwinian view could not only provide
insights into the origins and motivations of the human family, Pinker says, but it
could also cast much needed light on the conditions that tend to strengthen kinship ties and those under which families are likely to bicker, wobble, and finally
collapse.

Some evolutionary biologists, hypothesizing that families are inherently unstable and are kept together out of necessity rather than choice, assert that many
homebound people would just as soon pack up tomorrow if they had anywhere
better to go. This casts a different light on the instability of family life that characterizes the postmodern era. At the same time, Pinker warns that in this era of
serial marriages, the most unstable and strife-prone families are stepfamilies in
which one parent is not the biological relative of resident offspring. One corrective solution to this problem could be extending legal rights to stepparents, similar to England's Children Act of 1989, that would legitimate their role in both
the family and society and enhance their status as stepparents (Herbert, 1999).
Noting that although rich families have been portrayed as tinderboxes of
intrigue, conflict, and debauchery, Pinker says that evolutionary biologists can
offer examples from the nonhuman world of how comparative wealth generally
binds relatives together, encouraging them to remain on the family estate and
expand family boundaries over time. Although this is not meant to be a recipe
for rescuing what he calls the much beleaguered American family, Pinker says
that evolutionary biologists believe that the forces of natural selection have
shaped much of the underlying drama of the family life we are witnessing today.
Whether the ways in which evolutionary biologists have constructed the problem of family instability can offer insights into the changes that have occurred in
the human family over time remains a question.

■ Summary and Conclusions

What is notable from the present discussion is the diversity of ideas available
for depicting families and the perspectives that underlie such constructions—
historical, organizational, sociological, cultural, feminist, economic, psychological, biological, and postmodern. It is clear from this discussion that the family
has evolved as we know it over time from what has been characterized as a "little

commonwealth" to "separate spheres" to companionate to isolated "together-ness" to an expression of personal freedom and autonomy, and finally to diver-sity, that as an institution, the family is dynamic and ever changing in relation to the social, economic, cultural, and political contexts in which it is embedded.

Explanations for such evolution lie in the changing economy, demography, and role of women. Although many people today worry about the family's future, such worries have persisted since the country was founded. Regardless of which of the above constructions the reader accepts, they all connect family instability to postmodern conditions of instability, fluidity, and impermanence and also to the belief that because of the high value most people place on fami-lies, the family as an institution will survive into the future just as it has in the past, although in different forms.

Today, the United States is a society without a clear unitary set of family ideals and values. Many Americans, groping for a new model of American family life, are confused, ambivalent, and fearful of the meanings of the changes that have taken place in families in recent decades, and hence, of the solutions that should be constructed to address their problems. Such confusion and ambivalence can be seen in some of the policy solutions that were constructed to family problems in the 1990s, the topic of later chapters.

Given the changing meanings of family, the changing context of family life, and the profound meaning families have for most people, it is not surprising that the term *family values* has entered into policy discourse related to families. What *are* family values? What are values? Of what consequence are they for families and family policy? These are the questions that frame the discussion of the next chapter.

Before turning to the next chapter though, I have provided some questions below for you to think about in relation to what was said in this chapter.

■ Some Questions for Your Reflection and Discussion

1. What are some of the ways in which families have been defined?
2. What do social scientists mean by *kinship?*
3. What are some of the beliefs about families that until recently were shared by most Americans?
4. What characterized families in colonial times? Elaborate.
5. What characterized families in the 19th century? Elaborate.
6. What characterized families in earlier decades of the 20th century? Elaborate.
7. What characterized families in the 1950s? Elaborate.
8. What has characterized family life since the late 1950s and the 1960s? Elaborate.
9. What are some of the factors that account for the ways families have changed? Explain.
10. What are some of the consequences of the family changes that have occurred? Explain.

11. How do Gillis and Leonard construct the changes we are witnessing in family life?

12. What is the difference between *private* and *public* families in Cherlin's formulation? What are the implications of an increased emphasis on private as opposed to public families?

13. How does the market enter into family discourses, according to Leonard, and what are the implications of this phenomenon for families and the larger society?

14. How does Elkind construct the changes that have occurred in family roles and relations?

15. How does Stacey construct the changes that have occurred in family life?

16. How does Pinker construct the changes the have occurred in family life?

17. Which of these representations of the meanings of changing families fits best for you? Why?

18. What do you conclude from this chapter about the family's survival in the future? Why? Draw from the authors cited in the chapter.

19. What do Beutler and his colleagues mean by the terms *family realm* and *family transcendence?* Explain in terms of the changes in family life cited in the chapter. Also see Note 1.

And now to the next chapter and the question of *family values.*

■ Note

1. Beutler, Burr, Bahr, and Herrin (1989) offered terms such as *family realm* and Bahr and Bahr (1996) *family transcendence* in constructing their definitions of family. These scholars see family life as an experience in connectedness, combination, and commitment, much of it long term or open ended. To say a relationship is like family, Bahr and Bahr advise, is to say it resembles kinship, the family realm being just another name for kinship networks.

Family transcendence refers to the expression of distinctive elements that contribute to the uniqueness of families. A unifying theme, the core of the disparate elements that constitute family transcendence, is a combination of the fundamental elements of birth and generational ties and other attributes. Family transcendence is the essential familial connection to life and the cosmos and to what has been and what could be, Bahr and Bahr (1996) hold. To transcend is to go beyond the limits of or to overstep or exceed. Family transcendence is the idea that familial ties go beyond other ties in some way. Family connections, these authors say, stretch beyond the present or the present situation and group, linking family members to social and genetic heritage, to meaning systems, ascribed statuses, present identity and future possibility, and to obligation, order, and opportunity.

Beutler and his colleagues identify three general categories of family transcendence: (1) generational transcendence, which pertains to connections among kin, extending both backward and forward in time; (2) the parent-child bond, involving deep emotion and intense commitment; and (3) ancestral linkages, with ties to posterity and immortality, impacting the meaning of life as well as death. Terms that transcend include fictive and symbolic relationships. Fictive kin are created by applying kinship terms to friends and neighbors and persons who may function as if they actually were kindred, assuming the appropriate obligations and roles (Stack, 1974). The application of family terminology and language transcends the culturally defined boundary between humans and other life forms and links them to the language of commitment and duty, extending the morality of kinship to a diversity of beings.

Postmodern in its emphasis on local reality and local authority, a family transcendence model affirms the right to have one's own subculture and personal or familial vision of things taken seriously, according to Beutler et al. (1989). It also coincides with many of the concepts and procedures of discourse analysis (Gubrium & Holstein, 1990). It includes an emphasis on subjectivity and everyday life; an overriding concern with meanings and their relation to language; awareness of multiple or indeterminate interpretations; sensitivity to various dimensions in the construction of reality; and attention to family embeddedness in an organizational, cultural, spatial, and temporal context.

CHAPTER 4

Family Values in the Context of Family Change

Although people have always worried about the family and its future, the changes that have occurred in the family have raised questions about the values that people today hold, whether such values have changed over time, and if so, how. Such values often are framed in terms of family values. Although the term *family values* has become part of the discourse on family and family policy, what people mean by those words is unclear. Also unclear are the connections people make between family values and family policy. The ambiguity of the term and its relevance for family policy is exacerbated by the problematic nature of values as subjects of study and research. Because values are so integral to policy, this chapter begins with a discussion of what values are, where they come from including family values, how such values have changed, factors contributing to such change, and what such change means for family policy and the construction of policy solutions to family problems.

■ Values

What Are Values? Where Do They Come From?

According to Peacock (1996), values are well-entrenched, culturally determined sentiments and beliefs produced by institutions such as the family, schools, and religion, and major historical events and developments. Examples of these sentiments and beliefs are the values underlying Protestant sectarianism: institutional individualism and instrumental activism (Peacock, 1996). Institutional individualism is the idea that society is a means or instrument for achieving individual ends, and instrumental activism emphasizes activism, as opposed to fatalism, for the achievement of those ends. Important to the earlier discussion of change—whether with reference to the family, the economy, the polity, or culture—is Peacock's contention that in Western societies, Protestant sectarianism has made change the constant by instilling discontent and dissatisfaction with the existing political and social order. By creating an incessant drive for change, Protestant sectarianism has, in effect, institutionalized anti-institutionalism, he says. Historical events shaping values in the United States include the Great Depression, World War II, and the Vietnam War (Lipset, 1996). Values that form the organizing principles of the United States are to be found in the Magna Carta, the Bill of Rights, and Protestant sectarianism.

Values, Attitudes, Norms: What's the Difference?

As conceptions of what is desirable, values are ideas that are also ideals (Peacock, 1996) that when applied to policy, represent policy goals. Just as individual well-being as a value is the goal of policy in general (Lasswell, 1968), family well-being as a value is the goal of family policy (Zimmerman, 1988a, 1992a, 1995a). Just as there are many ways to define families and family policy, there also are many ways to define family well-being. Because family well-being is the subject and focus of later chapters, I will not elaborate on it here except to say that well-being has been operationalized along economic, social, psychological, interpersonal, and family dimensions based on measures such as income, employment, satisfaction, self-esteem, and family functioning (Zimmerman, 1992a).

Values are a basis for guiding behaviors in terms of what people ought and ought not to do and involve morality and conscience (Peacock, 1996). Values incorporate ideas, symbols, and beliefs that help people make sense of their lives and the world in which they live. As such, they are subject to the challenges of diverse cultures and structural changes in the economy, families, and communities. Norms, in contrast to values, are the rules and laws that specify what people should and should not do to realize their values. Attitudes, which are more malleable than values and norms (Lipset, 1996), change in response to social and economic trends, such as economic downturns and eras of prosperity.

Variations in Values in Different Countries: What Accounts for Them?

The values that most specifically influence policy are those that vary among societies, cultures, and subcultures, according to Peacock (1996). Examples of these values are freedom, equality, and security: The degree to which governments in different countries are centralized or decentralized reflects values having to do with hierarchy and control. Peacock (1996) also says that the variations in values in different countries can be explained by the functional needs of different societies: economic, ecological, political, and psychological. Although all societies have the same functional needs—they all must feed their people, defend themselves when under attack, adapt to their environment, and manage people's tensions and fears—the ways they perform these tasks vary not only with their economy, demographics, and technological development but also with their values (Peacock, 1996). Indeed, how different societies accomplish their tasks and the values they seek to realize are mutually reinforcing. For example, while open elections reinforce democratic values of fairness and equality, such values require open elections, the two reinforcing each other.

The Study of Values

Scientific Biases

Social scientists have been slow to recognize the connection between values and public policy, tending to treat values, habits, tastes, preferences, and social norms as beyond the reach of public policy (Aaron, Mann, & Taylor, 1994). Yet, popular opinion focuses precisely on those values and norms many believe have contributed to the country's social and economic problems and think *must* be changed if such problems are to be solved.

What accounts for this gap between popular opinion and the social sciences in the formation of public policy, which here includes family policy? One reason is that economics, a discipline based on utilitarian philosophy, has dominated the policy arena. Utilitarianism views values as fundamental properties to be accepted as they are, not as subjects of scientific study and research or targets of change (Aaron, Mann, & Taylor, 1994). According to utilitarianism, the objective of a good society is the maximization of utility, or that which maximizes individual preferences and tastes.

A second reason is that values are hard to quantify apart from the behaviors they engender (Aaron, Mann, & Taylor, 1994). Because concepts like values are imprecise and nonquantifiable, they are difficult to incorporate into formal mathematical models, which typically are the mode of discourse in economics and other social sciences. For this same reason, hypotheses for testing values in relation to policy also have been difficult to formulate. Analytic statements about values often are simply critiques of behaviors that purportedly are treated objectively and reflective of values themselves.

A third reason is that the study of values and their relationship to policy has suffered from a lack of intellectual resources, in part because scholars in the disciplines generally concerned with policy—economics, political science, and sociology—have been otherwise engaged, namely in creating mathematical behavioral models based on utilitarian assumptions (Aaron, Mann, & Taylor, 1994). Indeed, the absence of scholarly attention to the role of values in the policy realm may help to account for the simplistic and judgmental nature of many of the appeals to family values in family policy discourse.

More recently, social scientists have begun to recognize the role values play in public policy and that the two are *not* independent of each other. Such recognition, in conjunction with the recognition that responses to public policies also are value based, has led to thinking how policy might change values, directly or indirectly, and thereby change responses to public policies themselves.

Perspectives on the Study of Values in Public Policy

The study of values in public policy has been approached from different perspectives. One perspective emphasizes the problem of the conflicts involving justifiable and worthwhile but irreconcilable values, a common travail of those trying to work their way toward a common view (Aaron, Mann, & Taylor, 1994). Conflicts between grandparents' rights and parents' rights or children's rights and parents' rights are cases in point. Here, the story of Elian Gonzalez is pertinent. Elian is the 6-year-old boy who was rescued at sea after surviving a crossing from Cuba in which his mother and 10 other people drowned in November 1999. The boy was caught in a custody dispute involving his father in Cuba, who came to the United States to bring the boy back to Cuba, and the relatives with whom Elian had been living in Florida, who wanted him to remain in this country, insisting that life in Cuba was not in his best interest. After exhausting all legal remedies to prevent him from being returned to Cuba, the relatives were forced by law to acknowledge the father's right to bring his son back with him to Cuba, and in June 2000, the two flew back home together.

A second perspective focuses on the values of a deviant minority, such as computer hackers who invade people's privacy and people who traffic in drugs and prey on others' addictions. From this point of view, the problem does not represent a conflict between worthwhile values but is rather the failure of mainstream society to transmit positive values to particular subgroups.

A third perspective for approaching the study of values in public policy reflects a fear that broad consensus on values is eroding in the United States, if it has not already done so—a fear that extends to values pertaining to families. The problem here is seen not as a conflict between worthwhile values but as the subtle contagion of values by the media and other cultural venues that infect and undermine the culture. Many people hold this view about the effects of X-rated movies and TV programs in which sex and violence are featured and sold as products to the consuming public.

Language in the Construction of Values

A society's values and general perceptions are revealed and guided by language (Edelman, 1985). Thus, a society's language and the adequacy and character of its vocabulary are seen as central to the construction of values. When President Bill Clinton, for example, in his State of the Union address to Congress in 2000 ("Text of President Clinton's State of the Union Address," 2000), said the country needed a 21st-century revolution to reward work and strengthen families by giving parents the tools to succeed at work and at the most important work of all—raising their children—he in effect was using language to reveal and guide the country's values of work, families, children, and success, all underscored in his speech.

Embedded in such language—the language that discloses and guides a society's system of values—are past beliefs and values that continue to draw attention and evoke responses from people (Edelman, 1985). Thus, when President Clinton emphasized success, work, children, and families in his State of the Union address, he was calling up not only past beliefs and values central to America's historical tradition but also beliefs and values that have strong emotional appeal for people today. Language also can be used to deflect criticism of government's role in solving family problems and in describing and evaluating government actions with regard to such values. Who in the name of family well-being, for example, would criticize government's role in mandating counseling and parent education for parents lacking the knowledge and skills to protect their children from harm, except when its role is not performed effectively?

Since the 1970s, political candidates have incorporated the language of family values into their political rhetoric. Such language conveys a sense of decency and morality, evokes images of the family as a safe haven and refuge in a heartless world, and has proven to be infinitely malleable as a symbolic resource in corporate-sponsored media politics (Kolbert, 1995). Because it can be used for multiple purposes—to sell air time, to intimidate political opponents, to garner support for political candidates and causes—the language of family values is attractive to both entertainers and politicians. Resonant, it has functioned less as verbal communication that informs and enlightens than as an image to arouse emotions, as evidenced by Vice President Dan Quayle's invocation of Murphy Brown and her out-of-wedlock pregnancy (Stacey, 1996) to depict an antifamily values' stance. The terms *family* and *family values,* politically important in the 1992 presidential campaign for capturing public attention and gaining support for particular constructions of family problems, proved to be as important in the 1996 presidential campaign and held the promise in the 2000 presidential campaign as well.

Critics are skeptical of the incantation of family values and the presentation of the candidate as a family member in political campaigns, calling them obvious attempts to manipulate public opinion. They say that the depiction of government as every family's best friend implicitly justifies government's intrusion into many more aspects of family life than most people are likely to accept (Greenfield, 1996). These critics further charge that applying the family values' standard to public policies and programs encourages politicians to avoid acknowledging the contradictions in their public positions and pronouncements. They cite as an example some politicians' position on welfare reforms that could jeopardize the well-being of children from poor families by forcing their mothers to work without ensuring adequate, affordable child care. Moreover, critics have said, the evocation of family and family values has enabled political candidates to overlook their own shortcomings, citing the behaviors of many politicians preaching the sanctity of a good marriage, good parenthood, and fidelity that have been found wanting in this regard (Greenfield, 1996). Newt Gingrich, Speaker of the House in the 105th Congress, is an example—as is Bill Clinton. Recalling the White House Conference on Families of the Carter administration, the language of family values also can be politically treacherous, critics point out.

■ Family Values

Defining Family Values

According to the economist Herbert Stein (1995), family values are really the human values that are desired in relationships outside and inside the family. Alvin Schorr (1972) says family values broadly encompass the objectives a nation professes for families, such as financial independence or parent responsibility, as well as patterns of family structure and activity to which people by their practices show attachment, such as having dinner together as a family on a regular basis, delaying childbearing until marriage, or negotiating differences in cases of marital conflict so that both parties win. Despite value traditions of individualism, private property, and minimal government and liberal political theory—which celebrate the individual but say nothing about the family (Wilson, 1993)—the family spirit people brought from Europe when the country was founded, coupled with the isolation of the frontier, sustained the feeling that the family was primary, according to Schorr (1972). Based on Schorr's account, family values pertain to the feeling that family is primary and are reflected in the objectives we as a nation profess for people and patterns of family structure and activity to which people themselves show attachment. According to Seymour Lipset (1996), family is an important value anchor.

For people with a more ideological bent, the term *family values* has other meanings, depending on where these people fall on the liberal-conservative continuum. To many liberals, the term connotes the perpetuation of male control and authority, the denial of the hard-earned rights of women, and a license for abusive or neglectful parents to mistreat their children free of prompt and decisive social or government intervention (Wilson, 1993). To other liberals, the term suggests that human nature is to some degree fixed and immutable. To conservatives, it connotes mainline resistance against homosexual marriages, bureaucratic child care, compulsory sex education in the schools, and a planned society. Most mothers and fathers, Wilson (1993) argues, hold views that are less dogmatic, agreeing with both conservatives and liberals.

Survey Respondents' View of Family Values

How do respondents to surveys, as distinguished from scholars and ideologues, view family values? To answer this question, Daniel Yankelovich (1994, 1998) founder and chair of the Daniel Yankelovich Group (DYG) and analyst of social trends and public attitudes, analyzed responses to survey questions measuring values and value changes since the 1950s. When asked to define *family values* in the 1990s, respondents endorsed the following 11 meanings, 6 of which Yankelovich said were traditional and 5 a blend of newer and traditional values. The 6 traditional meanings included the following:

- Respecting one's parents
- Being responsible for one's actions
- Having faith in God
- Respecting authority
- Being married to the same person for life
- Leaving the world in better shape

The other 5 were a blend of traditional and newer values that Yankelovich called expressive. These included the following:

- Giving emotional support to family members
- Respecting people for themselves
- Becoming more skilled at communicating feelings
- Respecting one's children
- Living up to one's potential as an individual

Notable among the family values of the 1950s not endorsed by survey respondents in the 1990s were being married, having children, earning a good living, and being financially secure. Although pessimistic about marriage and family in general, most people in the 1990s felt they were better off than their parents at a comparable stage in life and expected a more satisfying life than their parents. Although people in the 1990s realized they were better off than their parents in many ways, they also were aware of the threat many newer values posed for individual families and the family as an institution—which Yankelovich said was more important to them now that it could no longer be taken for granted. In a poll conducted by the *Washington Post* in collaboration with Harvard University and the Henry Kaiser Family Foundation in 1998, 9 out of 10 Americans agreed that the country would have fewer problems if traditional family values were emphasized more (Marin & Broder, 1998).

Survey Respondents:
Their Views of Cultural Values in General

To provide context for survey respondents' answers to questions about family values and to determine those values that have changed and those that have remained more or less the same over time, many of which pertained directly to families, Yankelovich (1994, 1998) analyzed their answers to questions about broader cultural values.

Cultural values that have remained more or less the same over time include the following:

- Freedom: Political freedom, free speech, freedom of religion, freedom of movement, and the freedom to pursue personal happiness
- Equality before the law: The same rules of justice apply to all, rich and poor, black and white
- Equality of opportunity: The expression of freedom and individualism in the economy, helping to alleviate some of the tensions between equality and freedom
- Fairness: An emphasis on people getting what they deserve as a result of their own individual actions and efforts
- Achievement: Emphasis on the efficacy of individual effort and the belief that hard work pays
- Patriotism: Emphasis on loyalty to the United States and to the way of life it represents
- Democracy: A belief that the judgment of the majority should form the basis of governance
- American exceptionalism: A belief in the special moral status and mission of the United States
- Caring beyond the self: An emphasis on concern for others such as family or ethnic group, neighborliness, and community
- Religion: Looking beyond the secular and practical
- Luck: A belief that good fortune is temporary and that good and bad fortune can happen to anyone at any time

The cultural values that have changed over time, which Yankelovich expressed in relative rather than absolute terms, include the following:

- Less emphasis on duty or what one owes to others as a matter of moral obligation
- Less emphasis on social conformity (i.e., keeping up with the Joneses)
- Less emphasis on respectability and symbols of correct behavior for people of a particular social class
- Greater acceptance of differences in ethnicity and lifestyles
- Less emphasis on sacrifice as a moral good but more emphasis on when and where it is necessary
- More emphasis on choice and individuality that express one's unique nature
- More emphasis on the natural environment and its preservation
- More emphasis on technological solutions to problems and challenges
- A loosening of some but not all norms of sexual morality but less emphasis on "correct" sexual behavior
- Greater emphasis on pleasure and fun as positive (i.e., good)
- Greater emphasis on family life, extending the concept of family beyond the traditional nuclear form
- A shift from role-based obligations to shared husband-wife responsibilities
- Greater emphasis on personal responsibility for maintaining and enhancing health

- Less emphasis on the intrinsic moral value of work and more emphasis on work as a source of personal satisfaction
- Greater emphasis on women's achievement of self-fulfillment through their own choices
- A shift from sharply differentiated roles for men and women to a blurring of roles and a different conception of marriage

What Accounts for Value Transformations?

What accounts for the changes that have occurred in both cultural and family values over time? According to Yankelovich (1994), such value transformations were attributable to factors such as (a) rapid technological advances; (b) the troubled and ambiguous outcomes of various national experiments involving government in the solution of social problems; (c) the episodic but relentless process unleashed by the Enlightenment and the emancipation of the individual from all forms of tutelage (the state, revealed religion, and ancient custom); and (d) the end of the struggle between Soviet-style command economies and democratic capitalism—to which the new global economy might now also be added.

Perhaps the most pronounced factor, according to Yankelovich, for the transformation of values in industrial democracies—the United States, Western European countries, and Japan—was the affluence effect, that is, people's reactions to the experience of affluence since the end of World War II (Yankelovich, 1994) or the *meanings* people assign to their affluence or lack of it. As Mintz and Kellogg (1988) note, between 1950 and 1970, median family income tripled, increasing opportunities for education, travel, and leisure, which in turn heightened expectations for self-fulfillment. Affluence increasingly enabled many people, though certainly not all, to provide for themselves many of the services they may have received from community organizations and agencies that bound people together in the past. Higher incomes meant greater freedom from community pressure—and in the process, the loss of social support and nurturance from the community as well. Although economic change by itself has not transformed values, Yankelovich says, people's perceptions of such change have. The effect of affluence on value change, he said, was indirect; it was mediated by people's perceptions and interpretation of the objective reality of their economic situation—or their constructions of their affluence.

The human potential and counterculture movements of the 1960s and the drive toward self-fulfillment and liberation that characterized the 1960s and 1970s (Mintz & Kellogg, 1988) also contributed to the transformation of values, including family values. Like the human potential movement, the New Left also was concerned with the psychological repression of individuals' instinctual needs, its goal being the liberation of eros (i.e., total sexual gratification, including bisexuality). The women's liberation movement, which attacked the family's exploitation of women, challenged family values that subordinated women to men and children to parents. During the 1960s and 1970s, broad segments of society were influenced by and participated in these value shifts. Following the assassinations of Martin Luther King Jr. and Robert Kennedy, the ordering of the bombing of Cambodia by President Richard Nixon, the shooting and killing of student protesters by police at Jackson State University in Mississippi and Kent State University in Ohio, and Watergate, many also lost faith in their government.

The Affluence Effect and Family Life and Values

Of all these influences, however, the affluence effect was the most significant for the transformation of family values, according to Yankelovich. Because of it, individuals and families could experiment with forms of self-expression and individuality unthinkable or impractical in earlier times, sweeping aside traditional values rooted in generations of want and scarcity. As Cherlin (1996) observed, the family was designed for scarcity and was now being asked to perform in an era of greater, although not uniform, prosperity, with many families still experiencing severe economic hardship. People throughout most of history, Cherlin says, were preoccupied not with personal fulfillment but with simply subsisting from day to day and season to season. Marriage and family offered an efficient way for men and women to pool their labor and grow enough food or make enough money to buy it, to make or buy clothes and other goods, and to raise sources of future labor—that is, children. Today, most people take these basic family tasks for granted, asking that families provide not merely material sustenance but emotional sustenance for members as well.

Psychological Stages of the Affluence Effect

Based on his analyses of the surveys his firm has conducted since World War II, Yankelovich (1994) says that the affluence effect evolves in three stages, which, given the economic prosperity of the late 1990s, could be subject to revision when applied to that historical period. Stage 1 of the affluence effect occurs when affluence is new and people do not believe their economic good fortune is real. In Stage 2, they swing from undue skepticism about their economic prospects to undue optimism—the feeling, for example, that the stock market boom of the late 20th century will continue indefinitely. In Stage 3, which Yankelovich periodicized as the early to mid-1990s, people fear the loss of affluence.

In Stage 1, Yankelovich continues, values remain conservative and traditional. The focus is on social bonds, sacrifice, hard work, and saving for the future. Personal choice is limited. It was not until the late 1960s that Americans who had lived through the Great Depression were able to put aside their depression psychology and the fear and insecurity it engendered. Between Stage 1 and Stage 2, a sharp psychological break occurs, according to Yankelovich. Almost overnight, the feeling changes from "it won't last" to "it will go on forever" and "now we can afford to do what we want."

The hallmark of Stage 2, psychologically, is the delight people experience as a result of expanded choices. People relish their newfound freedom to choose careers and lifestyles according to their individual predilections and not the expectations of others. The search for self-expression and self-fulfillment becomes less inhibited. When people feel financially well off, they assume they can live for today, and tomorrow will take care of itself. In Stage 3, people grow apprehensive that opportunities for jobs, income growth, home ownership, higher education for children, and retirement are at risk.

The Affluence Effect in Historical Context

Putting the influence of the affluence effect on cultural values into historical context, Rolf Dahrendorf holds that all historic shifts in Western culture have involved efforts to balance freedom and relationships, or choice and bonds (Yankelovich, 1994). Choice enhances individualism and personal freedom; bonds foster social cohesion and stability. The tension between bonds and choice has characterized the evolution of American cultural values in the post-World War II period, according to Yankelovich. Driven by the affluence effect, people's striving for greater individual choice has conflicted with the obligations and social norms that held families and communities together in the past, he explains. As a nation, we came to experience the bonds of marriage, family, children, job, community, and country as unnecessary constraints.

Commitments Loosened Accordingly

Gradually, as the affluence effect has evolved, Americans have begun to shape a synthesis between expanded choice and the need for enduring commitments, which parenthetically could be an extension of the affluence stages Yankelovich (1994) depicted. People have modified their values as they have learned from experience. According to Yankelovich, they have learned that:

- Expanded choice created time pressures and mounting financial debt.
- Work could be less satisfying and secure than they had assumed and that giving too much to work and career could undermine family and the quality of life.
- The quest for greater self-expression could take a heavy toll on personal relationships, as evidenced by growing numbers of families at risk, more complicated and unstable male/female relationships, and frustrated needs for affiliation.
- Some forms of pleasure seeking, like substance abuse, were deeply unsatisfying.

Such lessons, according to Yankelovich, did not necessarily mean a return to traditional marriages and families, to older definitions of status and success, to social conformity and family togetherness, but rather that people were creating distinctive blends of bonds and choices, shaping novel patterns of culture—very much in keeping with postmodernism.

The Affluence Effect on Family Policy

Just as the affluence effect has played a role in transforming personal and family values, it also has played a role in family policy and the transformation of government's role in constructing solutions to family problems. From the late 1960s to the mid-1970s (which, in Yankelovich's formulation, represents Stage 2 of the affluence effect), people were willing to help others and, if necessary, pay extra taxes to do so. In the period of transition of rising expectations in Stage 2 to the diminishing expectations of Stage 3 (which here, according to the Yankelovich formulation, refers to the 2 years before the 1992 presidential election), people began to reconsider the role that government should play in their lives, giving priority to its role in addressing long-term problems plaguing the economy such as slow economic growth, lagging competitiveness, a ballooning federal budget deficit, and high unemployment. Not foreseeing the prosperity of and the budget surplus at the turn of the new century, Yankelovich's formulation of affluence effect stages does not extend to the late 1990s.

The affluence effect in its latest stage, Stage 4, exerted its influence on family policy in the 1990s in several ways. It especially changed the conceptions of fairness as a value to be achieved in family and public policy more generally, and it raised, as a consequence, fundamental questions about the moral basis of public and family policy. One definition of fairness is that people are entitled to receive help because they worked for it and therefore deserved it, and the other is that people are entitled to receive help because they need it. In the mid-1990s, a new value consensus was reached about fairness that shifted the moral foundations of entitlements from a one-way transaction—namely that if individuals and families need help, they are entitled to receive it—to a social contract arrangement incorporating the concept of reciprocity—that is, if a person is helped by society, he or she should in some way return the help and not expect it as a matter of right. Thus, in return for the subsidized housing they receive, people are now expected to provide some form of community service. In New York, for example, a plan was in place to make homeless families work for their shelter that threatened them with expulsion if, on the one hand, they failed to comply with shelter work rules and charges of child neglect, and on the other, if they did not comply with welfare rules regarding the care of their children.

The affluence effect also has shown its influence on the idea of fairness in the area of taxes: Polls compiled from Associated Press wire reports show that most people favor elimination of the estate tax, which affects only about 2% of the population in any given year (Von Sternberg, 2000). After attracting little or no interest for 84 years, when it was incorporated into the nation's progressive tax system to help pay for World War I (Wolfe, 2000), the estate tax suddenly was a potent issue in 2000, tapping into feelings about family and inheritance rights based on family relationships. Attributable to this development were a number of factors:

- Baby boomers' anticipation of the largest transfer of assets in the nation's history upon the death of their parents
- The booming stock market, which, by creating an astonishing number of millionaires, made the tax tangible for more people than ever before
- Republicans' charge that the tax was unfair
- "Simple greed," as Paul Light, a Brookings Institution scholar who has studied the boomer generation, speculated (Von Sternberg, 2000)

Repeal of the tax would take an estimated $105 billion out of the federal budget through 2010 and $750 billion in the decade after that, which, in the name of fairness and families, could be spent on affordable housing for low- and middle-income families, affordable day care for their children, prescription drugs for the elderly, and so on.

The Dialectic Nature of Values Change

What is important for the present discussion is that values and cultural changes do affect families and public and family policy. As Yankelovich points out, however, values change is not linear but dialectic, swinging to opposite extremes at first, followed by a series of multidirectional movements as people adapt the values they have newly acquired to more traditional ones and to changing circumstances. Attempts to synthesize old and new values lead to new patterns that sometimes appear to be a return to the past. The case of welfare reform is an example, as is store-bought prepared meals for family gatherings to accommodate the time and energy limitations of working mothers. When values conflict, people vacillate between old and new values, trying to hold on to both until they can no longer manage the conflict and are forced to choose between one or the other or arrive at some sort of compromise—or synthesis. Family values are at the center of such conflict. Based on the values people profess to be most important to them, however, family ranks at the top of most people's values list.

The Role of Government and Family Values

As to government's role with respect to values in general and family values in particular, answers are not so clear, because values emerge from lessons taught by family, friends, and community and are acquired under the influence of parents, schools, neighbors, and the media throughout infancy, childhood, and adolescence and continue to evolve gradually during a lifetime of adult experiences (Aaron, Mann, & Taylor, 1994). Adding to the complexity of government's role in influencing family values is the fact that because people live in a social context, they also are subject to the influence of community norms, which may or may not support family values. Here, the efforts of a group of suburban parents in Minnesota in urging other parents to insist that coaches, dance instructors, and choir leaders scale back their youngsters' activity schedules to make more time for family are pertinent (Cummins, 2000).

Respondents to a 1999 CBS poll were about equally divided when asked whether government could or should promote family values or remain neutral on the matter. Roughly half in 1999 said government should do more to promote traditional family values and the other half said it should remain neutral and not favor one set of values over another ("Polity Watch," 1999). Here, Peacock (1996) advises that because values are pervasive, enduring, and derived from religious or similar sources, sensitivity is required to the potentially unstated religiosities that may be an integral part of seemingly value-neutral policies. Peacock in fact advises that policy makers—whether by supporting policy initiatives to transform values or by engaging in dialogue and participatory processes about values—must be prepared to deal with powerful, explosive forces that could set off transformative movements that could destroy a heritage of millennia while instituting values that could endure for centuries.

To avoid such a possibility, Peacock suggests the economists' use of incentives for changing or supporting particular values. Examples of such incentives pertaining to families might be family policies that do the following:

- Increase the minimum wage to encourage low-income parents to work
- Lower interest rates on home mortgages so that families can own their own homes
- Provide child care subsidies to enable parents with preschool children to work or subsidies to enable parents to care for their children at home
- Compensate family members who care for ill or disabled family members at home
- Increase the earned income tax credit for low-income families to better support their work and family efforts
- As proposed in Minnesota, increase filing fees for divorce to discourage married couples from divorcing while reducing marriage license fees to encourage couples to marry

But governments have employed other strategies that have proven effective in this regard. Informational campaigns about the hazards of unprotected sex have effected changes in teen sex behaviors that presumably reflect changes in the values underlying their behaviors. The same is true of abstinence education and informational campaigns about alternative contraceptive technologies. Prohibitions of certain forms of racial discrimination—although not directly aimed at families but affecting them nonetheless—have forced changes in public behaviors and thus presumably in values with respect to different ethnic and racial groups. Among some groups, antismoking ordinances have led to a decline in smoking and the enhancement of family health values. Similarly, time limits on the receipt of public assistance have effected changes in the labor force participation of poor parents and, in the process, has effected a change in the values of some with respect to work and financial independence.

Another way that governments can influence values is to replace misperceptions with accurate information. Informing teen girls about the demands and meaning of parenthood to correct misperceptions about parenting, especially parenting alone, is an example. In the same way, if people were not as misinformed about the estate tax as they reportedly are, they would be less sanguine about the fairness of its repeal. Much of the support for the tax's repeal in the summer of 2000 was based on misinformation or no information about the tax: Fully 17% of Americans said they would benefit from its repeal and 40% said they had no idea if they would benefit from it (Von Sternberg, 2000). The fact is, as noted earlier, only 2% of the population—the richest 2%—would benefit. Another approach to altering family values goes beyond merely presenting information: It enlists the help of public figures such as Jane Fonda, who is working to persuade adolescent girls to remain in school, delay sex, and get additional training.

Judith Stacey (1996) suggests that a better way for policy to influence family values is to redefine such values democratically by extending full rights, obligations, resources, and legitimacy to a diversity of intimate bonds. Another way she suggests is to elevate the cultural status and responsibility of fatherhood, given that fatherless families seem to be disproportionately harmful to women, children, and civil society.

When survey respondents were asked how family values could be strengthened, they identified more time for parents to spend with their children as central (Yankelovich, 1994). Yet, when asked what government could do to strengthen family values, they were hard-pressed for an answer. They thought churches, synagogues, and schools could do more in this regard and that television could offer better role models, but they did not see measures such as day care for children of working parents, flexible work schedules for parents, or work-from-home arrangements for parents as solutions to the weakening of family values. Such responses did not necessarily mean that these solutions were unimportant to the survey respondents, but rather that they did not connect such remedies to having more time to spend with their children—or in their terms, to family values. Thus, one way to enhance family values might be to educate the public about the myriad connections—both direct and indirect—between public and family policies and everyday family life. Indeed, Generation-Xers already appear to have made such connections after watching their parents' generation sacrifice time for their careers, saying that flexible hours were more important to them "for a life in balance" than financial incentives and rewards (Lang, 2000).

■ Summary and Conclusions

Despite being subject to political abuse and misuse, the term *family values* has meanings for people that go beyond family to encompass relationships, feelings, and ideas people associate with family but are not confined to family. The feeling that family is primary as one definition of family values was operationalized by survey respondents in traditional ways: as respect for one's parents, responsibility for one's actions, faith in God, respect for authority, being married to the same person for life, and leaving the world in better shape. In the spirit of postmodernism, these definitions blended with newer expressive family values involving giving emotional support to family members, respecting one's children, becoming more skilled at communicating feelings, respecting people for themselves, and living up to one's potential as an individual. Interestingly, even though respondents were almost evenly divided about whether or not government should promote traditional values, most agreed that the country would have fewer problems if traditional family values were emphasized more. Embedded in the term *family values* are well-entrenched culturally determined sentiments and deeply held beliefs about family. These beliefs are produced and reinforced by family, schools, religion, and major historical and economic events.

The transformation of values in relation to the family and family policy has been brought about not only by technological developments, the social movements of the 1960s and 1970s, and major historical developments but also by the affluence effect, which led to expanded choice and personal freedom. The affluence effect refers to people's definitions and interpretation of their material situation. Because personal freedom and choice proved to be at odds with people's need for enduring commitments, they tried to effect a synthesis of newer expressive and more traditional family values in the last decade of the 20th century. Values that have changed in families include the following:

- An extension of the concept of family beyond the traditional nuclear form with a continued emphasis on family life
- A shift from role-based obligations in husband-wife relationships to shared responsibilities
- A shift from sharply differentiated roles for men and women to a blurring of roles and a different conception of marriage
- A greater emphasis on women's achievement of self-fulfillment through their own choices

Thus, although individual emancipation and choice represent cultural challenges to family values, family values are still an important area of social reality to which people continue to show attachment, with newer and older family values accommodating each other. With respect to family policy, the affluence effect has shown its influence on changing conceptions of fairness as a value or goal, as in the case of both welfare reform and taxes, with obvious implications for the construction of policy solutions to family problems.

Because of the public functions that families perform, Stein (1995) advises that we as a nation should try to strengthen families in any way we can—by both private example and public policy—adding that even families that function well need the support of other institutions. These institutions include governments whose wide-ranging functions, from education to child abuse prevention, are generally accepted, policy playing a role in shaping values both directly and indirectly. Examples include information and educational campaigns and financial incentives to encourage desired behaviors on the part of families and their members, and financial subsidies to community organizations and institutions that help to establish community norms that support families.

Although few families today represent the mythical traditional form, the term *family values* seems to express ideas and feelings that most people share about families. It connotes the idea that family is primary. As Stein (1995) said, the family is still the most likely of society's institutions to be governed by values like love, responsibility, and voluntary commitment to the care and welfare of others, including those least able to fend for themselves. Despite being subject to political use, abuse, misuse, traditions that promote other values— individualism, private property, and minimal government—and liberal political theory that ignores family, and despite the ideological meanings it connotes for some, to most the term simply means family comes first.

Although values are important for guiding behaviors, attitudes are more specific expressions of values. To better understand the values and attitudes underlying the construction of policy solutions to family problems, the next chapter focuses on the attitudes that people hold toward government, families, the economy, and their relationship to each other—and other matters pertinent for family policy and its construction. But before addressing that topic, consider the following questions about this chapter.

■ Some Questions for Your Reflection and Discussion

1. What are values? How do they differ from attitudes and norms?
2. What is the role of language in the construction of values?
3. How have family values been defined?
4. What does the term *family values* mean to people responding to surveys on the question?
5. Which family values have stayed the same? Which have changed?
6. What are some of the political uses of the term *family values?*
7. Which cultural values, as distinguished from family values, have remained the same? Which have changed?
8. What accounts for some of the changes that have occurred in family and other cultural values?
9. What is the *affluence effect?*
10. What role has the affluence effect played in government's role in constructing solutions to family problems?
11. How has the affluence effect manifested itself in family policy?

12. How do people manage their value conflicts?
13. What are some of the strategies that have been identified for changing values?
14. What is the importance of values for family policy?
15. What has impeded the study of values in public policy?

And now to Chapter 5 for a look at attitudes underlying the construction of policy solutions to family problems.

Attitudes Toward Government, Families, and the Economy

If values are well-entrenched, culturally determined sentiments produced by institutions such as family, schools, religion, or major historical events, which result in deeply held beliefs that are the organizing principles of different societies, what are attitudes and what role do they play in family policy and family policy discourse? Attitudes have been defined as specific expressions of values or beliefs applied to concrete objects or situations involving positive or negative evaluations and a readiness to respond to related objects or situations in a characteristic and predictable manner (Theodorson & Theodorson, 1969). As noted in Chapter 4, attitudes are sensitive to social and economic conditions and developments such as economic downturns, crime waves, and stock market gains and losses. Attitudes change in response to these conditions and thus are more malleable than values (Lipset, 1996). Attitudes are important not only because they affect a person's exposure to information and perceptions about and actions toward given objects (Zaltman, Duncan, & Holbeck, 1973; Zimmerman, Mattessich, & Leik, 1979) such as government and families but also because the strength and intensity of the feelings associated with them—their affective component—provide the impetus for behaviors. For this reason, the attitudes that people hold toward government, families, and the economy are important for family policy, constraining or facilitating the construction of some solutions to family problems and not others.

What are some of the attitudes and beliefs that people hold about families, government, the economy, and their own position within the political-economic-social structure in particular? Although people may want to believe that government can protect them from misfortune, as Edelman says, the survey data cited in Chapter 4 indicate that many do not necessarily connect government policies and programs to the problems families are experiencing, such as lack of time as a major factor in the weakening of family values. Even Bill Bradley, Democratic presidential hopeful in the 2000 election, asserted in one campaign speech that Americans outside Washington, D.C., did not see it as a place that had much to do with their lives (Clymer & Seelye, 2000). He is not alone in making this charge.

This chapter addresses this important question. It is based on attitudinal surveys pertaining to families, government, and the economy conducted by various survey organizations that report their findings in *Public Perspective,* a publication of The Roper Center for Public Opinion Research. In conjunction with these survey findings, *Public Perspective* also publishes relevant census data from time to time. The discussion is placed in the context of the changes in values identified in Chapter 4 that Yankelovich said presented the country in the 1960s and 1970s with one of the sharpest discontinuities in its cultural history.

■ Changing Values, Changing Attitudes

The 1960s and 1970s have been variously depicted as "the me-generation," "post-materialist" (Inglehart, 1990), and "expressive individualism" (Yankelovich, 1994, 1998). The value changes associated with these terms, as Yankelovich noted in the last chapter, involve the twin issues of expressiveness and individualism as influences in people's lives that reflect the belief that everyone, not just artists and writers, should be able to develop their inner potential for self-expression. Although the belief in individualism is as old as the nation itself, prior to the 1960s, it manifested itself primarily in the political domain—in the freedom of people to speak their minds, to follow their religious beliefs, and to live where they chose. A nation of political individualists, America was also a nation of social conformists. The 1960s saw a radical change in this regard as individualism in the political domain was extended to personal lifestyles. By the 1980s, the ethos of expressive individualism had grown into a national preoccupation.

To track the era of expressive individualism in its initial stages of development, the Yankelovich survey firm identified a group of "forerunner" college students in the 1960s who had begun to question some of their parents' core values. The students concluded that working hard and keeping their nose to the grindstone, as their fathers had done, and sacrificing themselves for the family, as their mothers had done, did not make sense in an era of growing affluence. Although they viewed sacrifice for family as fine if it was financially necessary, they questioned its logic if it was not. Between the mid-1960s and the late 1970s, such student attitudes spread beyond the nation's universities—from just 3% of the population in the mid-1960s to 80% of the adult population by the late 1970s. The important value shifts of this period were outlined in Chapter 4.

Yankelovich (1998) described the processes by which such change occurred in terms of "lurch and learn," explaining that societies learn and react differently to events and developments than individuals do: Social learning is far more abrupt and extreme than individual learning, which is more incremental. To account for the discontinuities in such societal-level processes, he theorized that a typical pattern of social change begins with a sharp shift or lurch in an opposite direction, which is followed by a series of complex modifications based on trial-and-error learning.

Such lurches seem to be precipitated by changed circumstances and the failure of institutions to respond to such change, according to Yankelovich. Individuals who can exert some control over their lives tend to overreact to changes in circumstances in the form of a lurch as a result of the frustration they experience in dealing with society and its institutions, over which they have little or no control, he says. The process often leads to serious mistakes before corrective learning takes hold. In the lurch phase, people are prone to error, but because of the intensity of their feelings, they are oblivious to the positive aspects of that which they are reacting against. Some changes that occurred in the 1960s and 1970s relevant to this discussion include lurches from the following:

- An automatic sacrifice for the family to the view that sacrifice is unnecessary
- A conviction of the importance of observing society's rules to the view that if something is not illegal, it is not wrong
- Puritanism to casual sex experimentation
- Acceptance of government's role in society to the view that government has no role to play in society

Then in the late 1990s, after more than 3 decades of experimentation, a new conception of individualism seemed to be evolving. People in the 1990s, upon learning they liked many of the aspects of expressive individualism, wanted to hold on to them. These included:

- The emphasis on health and fitness that emerged in the 1970s.
- Sexuality as an inherent good to be openly but prudently expressed.
- Self-expressiveness as a major life goal and changing conceptions of the individual as a self, important because the ability of cultures and civilizations to adapt to change is closely tied to how people see themselves.

These aspects of expressive individualism were accompanied in the 1990s by:

- A shift away from the doctrine of need-based rights and toward the concept of reciprocity and the idea that people should not expect to get something for nothing and should give back that which they have received.
- A greater emphasis on self-reliance and the notion that in life, there are both winners and losers, ideas captured by the term *Social Darwinism,* which limits society's moral and legal obligations but does not preclude compassion, according to Yankelovich.

The 1990s saw other attitudinal changes as well. One was that if people wanted their children to become caring, responsible, and effective adults, they would have to sacrifice more of themselves than many may have assumed neces-sary. Such change, Yankelovich maintains, was accompanied by an emerging conception of the self as an individual that was less preoccupied with rights and more preoccupied with community and society. In this view, individuals saw themselves not so much as independent power centers engaged in a struggle to maximize satisfactions, often at the expense of others, as in the 1960s. Rather, he says, people in the 1990s were beginning to see themselves as part of a larger whole, cooperating with each other in a variety of ways to make their communi-ties better. Such cooperation did not necessarily extend to government, however, nor did it manifest itself in voter participation rates in the United States, the low-est among the world's industrialized democracies (Putnam, 2000)—voting being one of the cooperative acts of citizenship.

■ Attitudes Toward the Economy

Economic Progress

How did the transformation in cultural values and attitudes toward govern-ment and families manifests itself in the attitudes that people held toward the economy and their own economic status in 1999? Or did it? Everett Ladd, editor of *Public Perspective,* says that on virtually every count, pollsters found that people viewed the United States as a better society at the end than at the begin-ning of the 20th century (Ladd, 1999). Yankelovich's survey respondents said that people in the 1990s had better nutrition, housing, and health care, longer spans of productive life, more leisure time and recreational opportunities, and greater opportunities to continue their education (Ladd, 1999). Despite a sharp rise in income for most, however (personal income having doubled between 1965 and 1999), they also thought poverty was all too prevalent in everyday life, especially in female-headed families.

A remarkable commentary on the 20th-century experience that both speaks to and reflects the relationship between economic developments and attitudes to which reference was made earlier was that so many people in the late 1990s said they were satisfied with their economic circumstances and confident of their futures (Ladd, 1999). Although most people in the late 1970s and early 1980s doubted their children would do as well or better financially than they had, most in 1999 expected their children to do as well or better than they had, just as they themselves had done better than their parents at the same age.

Even more important, according to Ladd, was the widespread sense that the economic system was broadly fair—that it extended real opportunity and rewarded people for their efforts ("Legitimacy," 1999). Compared to 1980, when over 30% of those surveyed said they did not think America was a land of opportunity where everyone who worked hard could get ahead, only 15% held this view in a 1997 survey by Opinion Research Corporation. Most survey respondents thought the country's economic system in the 1990s was basically fair and provided plenty of opportunity for people to get ahead, and a sizable proportion, over two fifths, thought it provided more opportunity than in the past.

These attitudes were reflected in respondents' definition of the "good life," which 1999 surveys undertaken by the Roper Center found to be considerably more materialistic than in past decades (Crispell, 1999). The proportion who said that "a lot of money" was part of the good life (38% in 1975) rose to 63% in 1999. The proportion who said a job that paid much more than average was part of the good life similarly increased during this period, from 45% in 1975 to 62% in 1999. By the same token, those saying that having an interesting job was part of the good life declined from 69% in 1975 to 51% in 1999.

The Class Factor

Despite analysis that showed the shrinking of the middle class, the percentage of persons who viewed themselves as middle class was almost the same in 1939 (63%) as in 1998 (61%), some 60 years later, in surveys by Gallup in both data years (Ludwig, 1999). In his study of middle-class attitudes, Alan Wolfe (1998) defined *middle class* not only in terms of income but more broadly to incorporate attitudes, beliefs, practices, and lifestyles that he says define what it means to live in a way not so poor to be considered dependent on others and not so rich that one lost touch with common sense. He used the term *middle-class morality* to characterize the values of people who strived to earn enough to feel in control of their lives and emphasized individual responsibility, family, and obligation to others as principles to live by. As in the case of persons identifying themselves as middle class, about the same percentage of respondents viewed themselves as lower class or poor in 1998 (6%) as in 1939 (5%). Disparities occurred in the percentage of persons who classified themselves as lower class and lower income—12% in 1939, when the country was just emerging from the Great Depression, and 21% in 1998, a period of growing affluence—and in the percentage who identified themselves as upper class or rich: 6% in 1939 but only 1% in 1998.

Disparities in the percentage of persons identifying themselves as working class and middle class similarly appeared in surveys by the National Opinion Research Center General Social Survey (NORC GSS) in 1949 and 1998, 61% and 45%, respectively, in the case of the working class, and 32% and 46% in the case of the middle class. In terms of respondents' identification with lower class and upper class, the percentages remained pretty much the same in both data years: for lower class, 3% in 1949 and 5% in 1998, and for upper class, 2% in 1949 and 4% in 1998. These are clearly increased percentages, but they are still representative of a relatively small number of respondents. Thus, when 60% of the respondents in Gallup surveys in 1988 and 1998 said they did not view the United States as a country of haves and have nots, it was consistent with their view of their own position on the social class continuum and also with their placement of themselves in the haves or have nots categories: 59% in 1988 and 67% in 1998 in the case of the haves. Paradoxically, again, in the case of the have nots, a larger though relatively small percentage placed themselves in the have nots category in 1998 than 10 years earlier: 24% and 17%, respectively.

Interestingly, when immigrants were asked in a 1995 Gallup survey to place themselves on the social class continuum, those from Great Britain and central and Eastern Europe placed themselves in higher percentages in the upper middle class than immigrants from other countries ("The American Ethnic Experience," 1998). Three fifths of the immigrants from Great Britain and Europe identified themselves as upper middle class, but less than a third of immigrants from Africa did. Like most Americans, the majority of immigrants from most countries identified themselves as middle class.

The Gender Factor

What about the gender factor? Did it play a role in survey respondents' attitudes about the economy and their own economic circumstances? The generally positive attitudes respondents expressed toward the economy and with regard to their own economic circumstances also were reflected in the responses of women to questions about their financial status and security compared with their mothers' and about sex discrimination in the workplace (Fox-Genovese, 1999). According to a Gallup survey in 1999, most women in 1999 considered their financial status as better than their mothers'. Although two thirds thought society still treated men better than women, especially in pay, two thirds thought their current pay was about the same as it would have been if they were men. Suggestive not only of perceptions of declining sex discrimination but also of respondents' general satisfaction with their gender status were their responses to a question in both 1946 and 1995 asking whether they would rather have been born female or male. In 1946, more than 25% of the female respondents said they would rather have been born male, as contrasted with just 8% in 1995. However, when the Roper Center asked both men and women whether they thought more advantages accrued to being a woman or to being a man in 1979, 1985, 1989, and 1994, a higher percentage of both men and women said there were more advantages to being a man in all data years, although by 1994, the percentage holding this view declined for both men and women.

The Race Factor

Responses from blacks and whites alike to questions about race relations over the last half century, as in other areas related to economic progress, conveyed a sense that progress had been made in this area, although blacks were more inclined than whites to emphasize continuing racial discrimination (Ladd, 1999). Despite sharp differences in economic circumstances, most black respondents (67%) in surveys conducted by the Roper Center, Gallup, and NORC GSS in 1993, 1994, and 1995 believed that if people worked hard, they could get ahead, and over half of all black respondents (51% in 1995) said that people living in poverty have a realistic chance of getting out of it ("Belief in America's Promise," 1996). In both instances, however, the percentage of white respondents answering similarly was higher, suggesting that although more than half of all black respondents were optimistic about their economic prospects, white respondents were optimistic in larger numbers.

As to a middle-class lifestyle, a larger percentage of blacks (70%) than whites (30%) surveyed by the *Washington Post* in 1995 said they had less opportunity to live a middle-class style ("Ethnicity," 1998). Yet, in a 1994 survey by NORC GSS, a larger percentage of black (70%) than white (60%) respondents agreed that blacks had a good chance of improving their standard of living. Over half the respondents in both groups thought people living in poverty had a realistic chance of escaping from it. Although more white (66%) than black (54%) Americans agreed that anyone who worked hard enough in the United States could make it economically, the substantial agreement between the two groups on this question was noteworthy.

When asked if they thought conditions for black people in the United States had improved, the two groups were in substantial *disagreement*, however. In a 1995 survey by the Yankelovich firm, blacks, in higher percentages than whites, said blacks suffered from discrimination in the workplace with respect to wages and access to middle-level management and high-level executive positions. In the 1994 NORC GSS survey, fewer black (about one third) than white (about three fifths) respondents thought conditions had improved for blacks ("Ethnicity," 1998). For both groups in a Louis Harris & Associates survey, though, more respondents thought that conditions for black people had improved or were the same than thought they had worsened.

The Ethnic Factor

Most immigrants, like Americans in general, were high on the U.S. economy. In a 1995 Gallup survey, 75% thought that opportunities for their children in the United States were better than they themselves had experienced ("The American Ethnic Experience," 1998). Almost all expected their family's economic situation to improve in the next year, saying that opportunities for good jobs were better in the United States than in their homelands. Immigrants from all countries were more satisfied than dissatisfied with their financial situation. The percentage of immigrant respondents who agreed that people who worked hard to better themselves could get ahead in the United States was even higher than the 85% for adults in general in the United States, regardless of the length of time the immigrant respondents had lived here—whether for 10 years or longer or for less than 10 years.

■ Attitudes About Helping People Experiencing Economic Hardship

Government's Role

Attitudes about government helping people who are experiencing financial hardship, which are central to the construction of policy solutions to family problems, were reflected in the hardening of views on this issue in the 1990s (Mann, 1998). For example, in 1991 surveys by *ABC News/Washington Post* and the *Los Angeles Times* that asked in a period of economic downturn whether government should be responsible for finding a job for everyone, over two fifths of survey respondents said government definitely should be responsible. But in 1996, when times were better, less than two fifths thought government should be responsible, and three fifths said it definitely should not, as contrasted with just over one half in 1991, pointing again to the influence of economic and other developments on attitudes (Mann, 1998). Although more people in 1990, 1991, 1992, 1993, 1994, and 1996 agreed that the federal government was responsible for improving living standards *and* also that people were responsible for taking care of themselves, a larger proportion of survey respondents in 1996 (25%) than in 1991 (20%) said that people should take care of themselves.

Similarly, when people were asked whether poor people had it easy or hard *prior* to the enactment of the Personal Responsibility and Work Opportunity Reconciliation Act (PRWORA), 42% in 1992 said they thought poor people had it easy contrasted with 53% in 1994 and 1995. When asked in 1994 how upset they would be if new limits on welfare cut off benefits to poor families even when work was not available, only 40% said they would be somewhat or very upset; almost 25% said they would not be upset at all. Even after PRWORA was enacted, the percentage of those surveyed in 1997 who thought poor people had it easy was higher than in 1992. In a similar fashion, over three fifths of those surveyed by the Hart & Teeter Research Companies for *NBC News* and the *Wall Street Journal* in 1995 said people were poor because they did not do enough to help themselves. The percentage that attributed their condition to both lack of sufficient effort and to circumstances beyond their control shrank to just 7%, down from roughly 20% in 1990. *After* PRWORA was enacted, almost half (49%) in 1997 surveys by *ABC News/Washington Post* and the *Los Angeles Times* said they thought poor people led hard lives, and more than two thirds of those surveyed in 1996 said the federal government did not do enough to help poor people, again suggestive of the contextual basis for attitudes.

Middle-Class Attitudes

In Wolfe's (1998) study of the attitudes of middle-class persons living in the suburbs in different urban centers of the country, a larger percentage of respondents (48%) *opposed* reductions in welfare benefits for people living in poverty than favored them (31%). Almost two thirds also said they would be willing to have their taxes increased to provide job training to help people get off welfare. In general, persons in Wolfe's survey supported the idea of welfare, despite its negative associations with teenage pregnancy, drug use, poverty, and dependency. They recognized that people sometimes needed help, and they were not prepared to see welfare cut off without a safety net. Some of their attitudes were based on personal experience; in other cases, religious belief formed the foundation for a strong sense of altruism and obligation.

As in other surveys, however, the attitudes of middle-class persons toward welfare in Wolfe's study were characterized mostly by ambivalence. Their support for welfare was undermined by the idea that people have a right to welfare; their view was that welfare in America was based on the obligation to provide, not the right to receive. Their sense of obligation came from many sources: God, the idea of doing the right thing, the idea of charity and alms, and the view that the poor should not have to depend on the largesse of the rich. The right to welfare, unlike the right to free speech, according to the middle-class respondents in Wolfe's study, required not protection from government but action from government. In general, their view was that government should be a provider of last resort and that government assistance should be temporary, limited, but always reliable when times got hard. Similar to previously cited surveys, Wolfe found that participants in his study strongly believed that welfare should emphasize personal responsibility and go only to those who deserved it.

The Attitudes of Whites and Blacks

On the question of government's role in helping people who are experiencing severe hardship, the attitudes of blacks and whites diverged sharply. In a 1995 survey by the *Washington Post,* 70% of black respondents thought the federal government could do something to help black Americans with severe problems, but 60% of white respondents disagreed. Likewise, 65% of black Americans in 1996 said that the country was spending too little to help blacks, and only 17% of white Americans agreed. Similarly, in contrast to the 58% of black Americans who in 1995 did not think government programs went far enough to help blacks, only 20% of white Americans shared their view in a 1995 Yankelovich survey.

Income Disparities and the Role of Government

As to rising income disparities between the rich and the poor in the United States, and whether government should be responsible for reducing them, attitudes remained stable between 1991 and 1996: A little less than half of those surveyed said it should, and just over half said it should not, according to survey findings from the NORC GSS. Survey data from the Roper Center in 1939 and Gallup in 1998, however, show that a higher percentage of people in 1998 (45%) than in 1939 (35%) thought government *should* redistribute wealth, although the percentage that thought it should not do so by imposing heavy taxes on the rich remained roughly the same in 1998 (51%) as in 1939 (54%). Even so, data from the Yankelovich firm show that since 1974, the percentage who thought income in this country should be more evenly distributed declined dramatically, from 84% in 1974 to 63% in 1998. Most, 52%, thought the distribution of wealth and money in the United States was basically fair, even those whose annual household income fell below $15,000. Respondents from both races in a 1994 Roper Center survey were in substantial agreement on whether there should be a top limit on incomes that people earn: 68% of black Americans and 78% of whites said there should be no top limit. Nevertheless, despite general satisfaction with the fairness of the income distribution in the United States, there were distinct undertones of dissatisfaction that, although related to socio-economic status, were not restricted to just those at the lower end of the income distribution.

Indeed, more people in 1998 (25%) thought there were too many rich people in the country than did in 1990 (21%), but a higher percentage thought there were too few. Most (54%), in fact, did not think the gap between rich and poor was a problem that needed fixing. Similarly, most (60%) did not think of American society as divided between the haves and have nots or that such a division, if it existed, was bad for the country or mattered very much in any case.

The attitudes of immigrants on the issue of income disparities in the United States were consistent with those of most other respondents ("The American Ethnic Experience," 1998). In a 1995 Gallup survey, half or over half of all immigrant respondents from France, the Scandinavian countries, England, and Ireland did not think government had a responsibility to reduce income differentials between high- and low-income groups; the percentage of Canadians who held this view was highest. African immigrants in higher proportions than immigrants from other countries thought government did have such a responsibility.

■ Attitudes Toward Government

What about government itself? If attitudes toward helping people who are experiencing economic hardship had become more resistant during the 1990s, what attitudes did people hold with respect to government itself, and how might their attitudes have changed? These questions are central to the construction of policy solutions to family problems. In general, the attitudes that people held toward government were less than positive. According to survey data from the 1996 International Social Survey Project (ISSP) cited by Thomas Mann (1998), over three fifths of those surveyed in 1995 said they thought the federal government had too much power, and more than four fifths in a 1996 Gallup survey said government policies had served to weaken moral values over the last 25 years. Over half thought the new cutbacks and limits on federal and state welfare benefits ended a system that kept poor people in poverty; they did not think the cutbacks represented the relinquishments of government's proper role in helping people who were poor. However, in a 1999 survey by CBS that asked whether it was government's responsibility to take care of people who could not take care of themselves, a large 69% responded in the affirmative ("Role of Government," 1999), which again speaks to the contradictory views held in this area. As to which had the greatest responsibility for helping the poor—churches, private charities, government, families and relatives, or the poor themselves—more people (40%) in that same 1999 survey said families of the poor and the poor themselves than did in 1990 (30%), the percentage naming government, churches, and private agencies all declining over this period (Ludwig, 1999).

According to Mann (1998), director of Governmental Studies at the Brookings Institution, the renewed emphasis on self-reliance and "doing it yourself" occurred in conjunction with the loss of confidence in the capacity of government to solve problems that worried people the most. Mann attributed the loss of confidence in government to solve people's problems to the series of traumatic events that the country had experienced since the 1960s: assassinations; a failed war; White House scandals; a long period of slow economic growth accompanied by stagnant wages; high federal budget deficits; alarming increases in violent crime, drug use, and out-of-wedlock births; and the apparent rejection of conventional values of personal responsibility and self-sufficiency by a subset of the population. Buffeted by cultural wars, Americans had been subjected to an increasingly shrill and polarized debate among politicians who routinely denigrated the government in which they served and deployed with relish their new weapon of choice—the moral annihilation of opponents. Americans' attitudes toward politics and government were further shaped by a mass media that thrived on scandals and reports of program abuse and failure.

Between the 1960s and 1990s, the proportion of Americans who thought government in Washington could be trusted to do what was right declined precipitously, from three fourths in the 1960s to less than one fourth in the 1990s, in surveys by the *Los Angeles Times* and the Princeton Survey Research Associates for *Newsweek*. All through the 1990s, just over a half to over three fourths of those surveyed by *ABC News* said they trusted government to do what was right only some of the time. Few trusted government to *always* do what was right and just; in fact, more respondents said they did not trust government to *ever* do what was right than said they trusted it to always do what was right.

In addition to losing trust in government, most respondents in the early 1990s expressed a lack of confidence in government's problem-solving abilities. Indeed, the percentage of those who said they had some confidence that Washington could solve problems declined during the 1990s, from 46% in 1992 to 35% in 1996, in polls conducted by *ABC News* in 1992 and the Center for Survey Research at the University of Virginia in 1996. More disconcerting was that almost one fourth in both 1991 and again in 1995 said they had no confidence that when government in Washington decided to solve a problem, the problem would be solved, which, it should be noted, declined to one fifth in 1996. Just 4% of those surveyed during this period expressed a lot of confidence in government in Washington as a problem solver. Asked in 1991, 1992, 1993, and again in 1994 whether their lack of confidence in the federal government was attributable to the difficult nature of the problems to be solved or governmental incompetence, three fifths or more attributed it to the latter.

These attitudes, paradoxically, coincided with a major expansion of the public agenda since the 1960s, when government, especially the federal government, had come to be seen as a critical instrument for correcting unacceptable wrongs, for grappling with deep-seated social problems, and for reducing the risks of physical harm and financial destitution. Issues long the responsibility of local and state governments—education and public safety—had gravitated to Washington as entrepreneurial politicians sought to respond to those areas of greatest public concern (Mann, 1998). Within this context, questions about the credibility of government should not be surprising. Doing more, looking worse, and producing disappointing economic and social results, government in the 1970s and early 1980s came to be seen by many as the problem more than the solution, which conservative politicians, namely Ronald Reagan, seized upon and used to win substantial victories at the polls. Successful Democratic politicians, like Bill Clinton, acknowledged rather than contested that reality and sought to work around it.

Because Americans are more pragmatic than ideological, their attitudes toward government, though shaped by socialization and partisanship, also are rooted in experience, not philosophy (Mann, 1998). Despite value traditions of individualism and minimal government and a loss of confidence in government, over the years they have come to take for granted a substantial governmental role in virtually every aspect of the economy and society, sometimes so much so that they fail to acknowledge that essential programs like Social Security and Medicare are public, not private, programs. Thus, Americans expect their government to stabilize the economy; provide for national defense; insure citizens against the risk of disability, unemployment, and poverty and illness in old age; improve the life prospects of young children; finance and improve public education; facilitate job training and placement; promote public safety; explore space; fund scientific and medical research; help citizens acquire health insurance; ensure quality medical care; protect the environment; ensure food and product safety; regulate financial institutions; control air traffic; administer parks; promote the arts; protect against police discrimination; curb unfair and harmful business practices; build highways; promote exports; ease home buying; provide for veterans—in short to respond to almost every economic and social need imaginable, despite the disparaging views they hold toward government.

About the only federal programs the public targeted for reductions in the 1990s were welfare and foreign aid, whose outlays people thought were a lot more than they actually were, according to Mann (1998). Resistant to what they viewed as the squandering of public resources on undeserving recipients—individuals, corporations, or countries—the public at the same time expressed a willingness to help those who help themselves, to lend a helping hand but not to subsidize a permanent lifeline. There was little evidence among ordinary citizens of a libertarian resistance to government in principle. The public attitude, Mann said, was more nuanced, opposing public programs that violated its core values, appeared wasteful of substantial resources, achieved meager results, and benefited narrow interests with special access to policy makers.

Of all the indicators that something might be wrong with American public life, among the middle-class persons in Wolfe's study (1998), none was as persistent over the last quarter century as their dislike of government and politics. Yet, they too understood that in the contemporary world, government had obligations to people they did not know and, in that sense, recognized the necessity of morality writ large. A few of those with whom Wolfe spoke expressed themselves in a postmodern voice, finding traditional conceptions of morality not to be universal and timeless but rather nakedly partisan efforts by more powerful individuals and groups that wanted to impose their conception of the good life on others. Common were declarations of loyalty to moral principles combined with determined revisions to account for contemporary circumstances. People said that old virtues considered to be sacred should be maintained, but there should be flexibility. Rules, they said, were not meant to be broken, but they *were* made to be bent.

Given the above, it should come as no surprise that Bill Clinton and the Democrats were able to defend against Republican efforts to scale back the role and size of government in the 1990s, especially given Republicans' strategy of coupling Medicare reductions with tax cuts and allowing the federal government to be shut down (Mann, 1998). Lacking confidence in a major expansion of government such as the Clinton health reform plan envisioned, was not the same as embracing a radical reduction in public programs, or even a modest one, Mann reminds us. Indeed, public hostility toward government showed signs of easing a bit in the 1990s, particularly in light of a booming economy, increases in real wages, a vanishing budget deficit, falling crime rates and teen birthrates, and government leaders articulating values that most Americans cherished.

Attitudes Toward Government in the United States and in Other Countries

A comparison of attitudes that people in the United States hold toward government with the attitudes of people in other countries is illuminating: Despite the demands people place on government, over two thirds of the respondents from the United States in a 1996 ISSP survey thought government had too much power. Americans were much less inclined than people from other countries to think government was responsible for reducing the income gap between people with high and low incomes: under one third in the United States compared with almost three fourths in France and Spain. Only in Canada did a smaller percentage (35%) than in the United States (39%) think government was responsible for providing jobs for everyone. Americans also were much less inclined to agree that government is responsible for providing a decent standard of living for those who were unemployed than people in other countries—only 48% in the

United States compared to 90% in Ireland and Spain, 91% in Sweden, and 93% in Norway.

The Ethnic Factor

A 1995 Gallup survey showed that the attitudes of more recent immigrants toward the United States were less positive than those who had lived in this country longer. Small by historic standards, the proportion of foreign-born Americans in 1996 (a little over 9%) was larger than in the years 1960-1980, compared with almost 15% in 1890 and a little over 13% in 1920 ("The American Ethnic Experience," 1998). According to a 1996 Current Population Survey of the U.S. Census Bureau, the top 10 countries from which today's foreign-born Americans come were Mexico, the Philippines, China, Cuba, India, Vietnam, El Salvador, Canada, Korea, Germany, the Dominican Republic, and Jamaica. Of these countries, most immigrants were from Mexico.

The relative reluctance in the United States to use the state to provide social benefits can be explained by a number of factors, many of which have already been identified:

- Institutional biases toward inaction
- The absence of a feudal experience
- A strong antifederalist tradition rooted in entrepreneurialism and evangelicalism
- The widespread practice of private provision of health and pension benefits, that is, benefits attached to the workplace (Mann, 1998)

Under these circumstances, what is most striking about government's size in the United States over the last four decades was its stability relative to the economy, not its precipitous growth. Most of the growth in government during this period occurred at state and local levels, not federal. The United States retains a substantial localism in public affairs, with much initiative and innovation originating far from the nation's capital. And despite costly litigation prompted by regulatory policies, most students of such policies concede that the American workplace remains comparatively unfettered and its enterprises sufficiently flexible to respond effectively to a rapidly changing environment.

■ Attitudes Regarding Family Matters

What about family matters? What are some of the attitudes that people expressed about families? For 25 years, NORC GSS has regularly asked married people whether they are very happy, pretty happy, or not too happy with their marriages (Bowman, 1999). The results have been positive and stable. In no year have even 5% of married people described their unions as not too happy. Male-female differences in perceptions of wedded bliss were generally small. These findings are corroborated by other surveys such as those by ABC in conjunction with the *Washington Post* and *CBS News* and *ABC News* separately. Almost two thirds upon questioning in 1995 and again a year later said that knowing what they now knew, they were certain they would marry the same person if they had to do it all over again; only 9% said they might not ("The Family," 1998). Similarly, in Gallup polls taken almost 50 years apart, majorities said they would marry the same person again (Bowman, 1999). Only about 10% were willing to say they might not. In questions that asked for a straight yes or no response, roughly 85% said they would do it all over again. Seventy-six percent even described their marriages as perfect or nearly perfect, only an inconsequential 3% admitted to having serious marital problems, and just 1% said their marriage was in serious trouble ("The Family," 1998).

According to data comparing married people with those currently divorced or never married in the 1970s, 1980s, and the 1990s, married men and women were happier than those who were divorced or never married (Bowman, 1999). Furthermore, the relationship between marriage and happiness was consistent across nations. Using data from a 1991 World Values Survey, Steven Stack and Ross Eshleman (1998) found that in 16 out of 17 industrialized nations, marital status was positively and significantly related to happiness, the exception being Northern Ireland. Married people were not only happier than their nonmarried counterparts, but they also appeared to have fewer emotional and health problems. A review of 130 empirical studies undertaken by Richard Coombs (1991) on alcoholism, suicide, mortality and morbidity, schizophrenia, and other psychiatric problems provides additional empirical evidence of the therapeutic benefits marriage confers on people.

In a 1995 CBS survey asking respondents to compare their marriages with those of their parents, over half the respondents said their marriages were better than their parents'; only 3% said they were worse. There were gender differences, however. Women (63%) were much more inclined than men (49%) to say their marriages were better than their parents, and men (43%) were more likely than women (29%) to say their marriages were about the same as their parents, but not necessarily worse.

Views of marital happiness existed side by side with the long-standing belief that the institution of marriage was weaker today than in the past. Although almost no one in 1981 or 1990 thought that marriage was an outdated institution, and almost everyone in 1991 and again in 1994 said they held old-fashioned values about marriage and family, almost 70% of those surveyed in 1995 agreed that compared to 10 years ago, the institution of marriage in the United States was weaker ("The Family," 1998). Hardly anyone thought it was stronger (Bowman, 1999).

A Roper Center worldwide poll also revealed growing pessimism about the institutions of marriage and family: 19% in 1974 as contrasted with 31% in 1997 were pessimistic. Expectations for lasting marriages were low. Fifty-five percent said most people who married expected that they would divorce sooner or later, and only 36% expected their marriage last forever. Indeed, the proportion that agreed that people who get married expected to have their marriages to last forever had shrunk from one half in 1991 to a little over one third in 1995, just as the proportion that thought most people who got married expected to divorce sooner or later increased from 42% in 1991 to 55% in 1995.

Middle-Class Attitudes

Based on his analysis of the attitudes expressed by the middle-class participants in his study, Wolfe (1998) developed a typology of their attitudes on issues related to family: traditionalists, postmodernists, realists, and ambivalents. *Traditionalists* were wary of the changes that had taken place in family life and were convinced of the goodness of the nuclear family that they associated with simpler times and thought people should return to. *Postmodernists* held diametrically opposite views, maintaining that the benefits of postmodern family relationships have been positive for women, gays, and children. Such attitudes, which represented an extreme minority taste, were more popular on the coasts than in the heartland of the country, according to Wolfe. The rejection of an "anything goes" approach to family life that Wolfe discovered was actually in accord with national survey data cited in this chapter.

Realists were those who thought that women ought to work and that access to divorce should be available when a marriage becomes unbearable, since both developments promoted greater equality between the sexes. The realist's temperament, Wolfe said, was practical rather than ideological, an acknowledgment of the changes that had occurred in family life and the adjustments that were required. *Ambivalents* were those who were divided between traditional and postmodern conceptions of family, positions impossible to reconcile, such as the desire to see taxes cut and favorite government programs expanded at the same time.

For all their uncertainty about the family, the middle-class people that Wolfe surveyed were nonetheless fairly certain that families should be organized to fit the needs of the individuals who comprise them rather than organized to fit the needs of individuals to some preconceived family structure. Given the many kinds of people and many kinds of families, respondents thought the best way to fit the one to the other was to allow people to make those decisions that fit best for them, an idea that nourished critics' concerns that Americans have become too focused on themselves to appreciate the degree of commitment and loyalty that stable families require.

Ambivalence about family matters signified to Wolfe that people were reluctant to choose on matters pertaining to family and did not want to have to make choices, for example, between work and family. What was most noticeable about the way middle-class Americans discussed family matters, he said, was that guilt was rarely an issue. Most people were reluctant to pass judgment on the choices of others; questions about how things should be were second to how they actually were. A disappointment to those who invested significant meaning in the family, Wolfe found that the language of family life among middle-class Americans was more profane than sacred.

Attitudes About Divorce

Attitudes about lasting marriages were reflected in attitudes about divorce and also in divorce behaviors. Although the divorce rate in the United States was leveling off, one out of every two marriages taking place in a given year still resulted in breakup (Bowman, 1999), which in 1996 represented 4.3 divorces per 1,000 population and 8.8 marriages per 1,000 population (U.S. Bureau of the Census, 1998). The United States, which liberalized divorce laws before many other Western nations, has the highest divorce rate in the Western world (Bowman, 1998).

Over the past quarter century, attitudes about the easy availability of divorce have hardened, just as they have about welfare. Survey data from NORC GSS show that in six different data years—1990, 1991, 1993, 1994, 1996, and 1998—over half of those surveyed thought divorce should be more difficult to obtain, compared to 42% of those surveyed in 1974. Gender differences were slight, a larger percentage of women (53%) than men (50%) saying divorce should be made more difficult.

Among immigrant respondents in a 1995 Gallup survey ("The American Ethnic Experience," 1998), at least half, regardless of their country of origin—Asia, Eastern and central Europe, France, Germany, Great Britain, Ireland, Italy, Norway, Sweden, Denmark, the Netherlands, American Indians, Canada, and Mexico—said divorce in the United States should be made more difficult; indeed, three fifths of the survey respondents from the Netherlands thought so.

Respondents attributed increased divorce primarily to the failure of couples to take marriage seriously (45%), in a survey by the Yankelovich firm in 1997. Other reasons included its acceptance by the larger society (15%), more liberal divorce laws (10%), the selfishness of partners (9%), and changes in earning capacity (7%). In a different poll taken by the Yankelovich firm the same year, a larger percentage of respondents attributed increased divorce to changing attitudes on the part of women (38%) more than men (18%), although almost one third attributed it to the attitudes of both men and women ("The Family," 1998).

Since the early days of polling when pollsters first explored the topic, infidelity has been thought to be a primary reason for marital dissolution (Bowman, 1999), sexual fidelity ranking at the top or pretty close to the top in polls that asked people what they thought made a good marriage. The importance of sexual fidelity can be seen in the strong views people held about extramarital relationships, suggesting that, if anything, an already conservative public had become even more so. In 1973, when people were asked about sexual relations with someone other than their marriage partner, almost 70% said they were always wrong, which increased to 80% by 1998, undoubtedly due to the Clinton factor. Of survey respondents in 1998, 86% said infidelity among married men was morally wrong, up from 76% in the late 1970s. The percentage also increased for those who said infidelity among married women was morally wrong. By contrast, the proportion that said cohabitation among unmarried couples was morally wrong was about the same as in 1977: not quite 45%. Most, 75%, disagreed that infidelity was unavoidable in married life, married men and women responding similarly. As to whether respondents thought more people were committing adultery today than in the past, most said people were just more willing to talk about it.

Most of those surveyed by the Yankelovich firm in 1992, 70%, regarded parental divorce a big problem for children ("The Family," 1998). The percentage that said it was always best for children to be raised in a home where a married man and woman were living together as father and mother increased from 69% in 1993 to 78% in 1995, in surveys conducted by the *Los Angeles Times* in each of those years. Nonetheless, 61% of those surveyed by the Yankelovich firm in 1992 said they no longer believed that couples with children should remain together if they were unhappy, men being more inclined (54%) than women (48%) to favor divorce as a solution to marriages that were not working out, in a 1995 CBS survey.

Attitudes Toward Working Mothers

Almost all those surveyed in 1994 said mothers should work outside the home full or part time *before* they had children and again after the children left home, 87% and 84%, respectively, according to an NORC GSS survey ("The Family," 1998). When children were under school age, however, almost 50% said mothers should stay home, as contrasted with just 8% who said mothers should stay home even after their youngest child started school. Almost 70% in 1997 said it was better if the mother rather than the father stayed home; almost three fifths agreed it was generally better for society if the man rather than the woman achieved outside the home and the woman stayed home to take care of the children and family. Two fifths of those surveyed thought mothers working outside the home was not good for society.

Attitudes About Children

Just as attitudes about divorce and working mothers are central to the concerns of family policy, so are attitudes about children. In a 1996 survey by the Public Agenda Foundation, over four fifths of the respondents said they thought growing up as a child in the United States was harder today than in the past ("The Family," 1998). Over three fourths of those participating in a 1995 Gallup survey agreed that most parents do not discipline their children often enough, and over half (56%) in an NORC GSS survey said that compared with 10 years ago, American children were much worse off in terms of the supervision and discipline they received from parents. Nonetheless, fewer respondents approved of the spanking of children in 1997 (67%) than in 1946 (76%) in surveys by Gallup in each of those years. When parents of children aged 18 or younger were asked to compare their disciplinary styles with those of their parents, almost two fifths said they were more strict, a little over one third said they were less strict, and one fourth said they were about as strict as their parents were, in surveys by Gallup in 1995 ("Bumps in the Road," 1999). In another survey by Princeton Survey Research Associates for *Newsweek* in 1995 asking the same question of parents of children 17 years old and younger, almost one half, 48%, said they punished their children much less severely than their parents, 38% about the same as their parents, and only 9% reported more severely. Common forms of discipline included taking away children's privileges, timeouts, and reasoning with them; spanking or slapping them, yelling at them, and not talking to them were far less common forms of discipline.

In surveys by the *Washington Post* in 1997, 79% of the respondents said that having children was important to them, and in a 1994 NORC GSS survey, an even larger percentage (81%) agreed that watching children grow up was one of life's greatest joys ("Americans on Parenting," 1999). Although 75% strongly disagreed that having children interfered too much with the freedom of parents, 52% also strongly disagreed that people who have never had children lead empty lives. Fifty percent in 1997 said they thought two or fewer children was the ideal family size, compared with 17% in 1962. In 1996, 33% said the ideal family size was four, as contrasted with only 9% in 1997 ("The Family," 1998), according to Gallup survey data. In surveys by Princeton Survey Research Associates for *Newsweek* in 1995 comparing the respondents' parenting to their parents, roughly the same percentage said they thought their parenting was better or about the same as their parents', 45% and 49%, respectively; 60% said they spent more time with their children than their parents had spent with them; 62% said they understood their children better than their parents had understood them; and 51% said that being a parent was more important to them than it had been to their parents ("Measuring Up," 1999).

However, when exploring the ways in which parents frequently spent time with their children—eating together, watching TV together, going shopping together, sitting and talking with one another, taking a vacation together, and attending religious services together—the only shared activity that showed an increase in frequency in 1997 over 1976 was shopping together, in a survey by Roper Starch Worldwide. For all the other activities, frequencies declined.

Most respondents (63%) in a Princeton Survey Research Associates survey in 1996 thought parents needed help in raising their children ("Helping Hands," 1999). When asked who outside their immediate family was involved in their children's lives, most parents of children aged 6 to 17 named their children's grandparents (78%), other relatives (72%), and friends (75%). Parents worried more about their children's success in school than about the threat of drugs and crime or their economic security ("The Heart Stands Still," 1999), which may say more about the seemingly increasing competitive nature of education today than about the school achievement of children. Some worried a lot that their children might get hurt or into trouble during after-school hours, but over a third did not worry at all. Most worried a lot about their children's safety on the street (57%), at shopping malls (56%), and only a little about their safety at school (44%) and at friends' homes (48%). In general, the views of parents with regard to their parenting would seem to be at odds with the views of respondents who said children were worse off than in the past in terms of parental attention, supervision, and care.

■ Summary and Conclusions

What is striking about the attitudes reported here is the optimism they conveyed about almost all facets of respondents' lives involving family, government, and the economy, especially in the late 1990s, a change from earlier decades. For most respondents, the 20th century was viewed as one of great progress on most counts: housing, nutrition, health care, longevity, economic security, leisure time and recreation, educational opportunities, and so on. At the end of the 1990s, survey respondents were not only satisfied with their economic circumstances but were confident of their futures. For women too the 1990s were seen as a decade of progress. Though continuing to lag behind men in pay, women felt better about their status in the 1990s than in years past. Immigrants also were satisfied with the U.S. economy and with their economic circumstances and expected it to improve.

Like other respondents, black Americans also were optimistic about their economic situation and progress. Indeed, they thought they had greater opportunity to live a middle-class lifestyle than white Americans thought they did. Although white and black Americans were in substantial agreement that anyone who worked hard could make it financially in this country, they were in substantial *disagreement* about whether conditions for black people had improved: fewer black than white respondents said conditions for blacks had improved. Fewer respondents in either group, however, thought conditions for blacks had worsened.

In the context of greater prosperity, most respondents in the 1990s defined "the good life" in terms of making money, not in terms of a satisfying job, as they had in the past; as a result, they were more materialistic. The economic system, they thought, was fair, providing plenty of opportunity for people to get ahead and "make it." Despite a general sense of optimism and progress among black respondents, however, the world clearly looked different to white and black Americans with respect to economic opportunity and racial discrimination.

Paradoxically, given the shifts in the economy over time, a higher percentage of people thought of themselves as lower class/income in 1998, when times were prosperous, than in 1939, when the country was just emerging from the Great Depression, and a smaller percentage identified themselves as rich. In the context of greater prosperity, the smaller percentage of people identifying themselves as rich in 1998 than in 1939 may be attributable to comparisons that persons who are rich make with those who are even richer, which then makes them feel not so rich, even though by all objective measures they are. Or the smaller percentage of people identifying themselves as rich could be attributable to the higher income standards resulting from such prosperity. In both 1939 and

1998, most people in fact identified themselves as middle income/class, just as roughly the same percentage identified themselves as poor both data years. Immigrants, like Americans in general, identified themselves as middle class.

Although respondents were aware that poverty was prevalent in the United States in 1998, an increasing number thought people were poor because they did not do enough to help themselves, not because of circumstances beyond their control. At the same time, most survey respondents thought that government was not doing enough to address the needs of the poor. Despite the emphasis they placed on self-reliance, most respondents thought government had a responsibility to take care of those who could not take care of themselves. Based on personal experience and also a sense of obligation and altruism, middle-class respondents living in the suburbs recognized that people sometimes need help and thus supported the idea of welfare, despite its association with teenage pregnancy, drug use, and dependency. Like respondents in other surveys, however, they emphasized self-reliance and personal responsibility and held that welfare should go only to those who deserve it.

Although they may have thought government had a responsibility to take care of those who could not take care of themselves, most survey respondents were not disturbed about the growing income disparities in the United States and did not think government should redistribute wealth and income by imposing heavy taxes on the rich. These attitudes had not changed from earlier in the 1990s or, for that matter, from 1939, and pertained regardless of income, race, and ethnic group. In fact, most in 1998 did not think the income gap was a problem in need of fixing.

In this regard, the attitudes of Americans differed from those of people from other countries in that the latter were more predisposed than Americans to think that government did have a responsibility to close the income gap and was responsible for providing a decent standard of living for those who were unemployed. Reluctance to use government for constructive purposes on the part of Americans was attributable to the country's historical and cultural traditions and institutional framework, to which references were made earlier and about which more will be said in later chapters.

Renewed emphasis on self-reliance coincided with a loss of confidence in government's capacity to solve problems that worried people the most. Loss of faith in government was attributed to a series of traumatic events the country had experienced since the 1960s, as well as to polarizing attacks by politicians who regularly denigrate government and to a mass media that thrives on scandal and government wrongdoing and incompetence. Negative attitudes toward government were prevalent even as the public's agenda for the federal government was expanding in the 1990s.

As to family matters, almost no one in the 1980s and 1990s thought the institution of marriage was outdated; almost everyone claimed to hold old-fashioned values about marriage and family themselves. Just as they had for over 25 years, most described their own marriages as very happy, declaring that if they had to do it all over again, they would marry the same person. Almost no one admitted to having any serious marital problems. Gender differences were small. Married men and women reported being happier than those who were divorced or never married and having fewer emotional and health problems, marriage seeming to act as a prophylactic in protecting people against these kinds of difficulties.

Yet, almost everyone thought the institution of marriage had grown weaker over time, saying that expectations for lasting marriages were low, attitudes supported by the reality of increased divorce rates. Attributing increased divorce primarily to the failure of couples to take marriage seriously, it is not surprising that the percentage of people who thought divorce should be more difficult to obtain increased in 1998 over the 1970s, when no-fault divorce laws were first enacted. Immigrants also thought divorce should be more difficult to obtain. Although most thought parental divorce created a problem for children, an increasing percentage of survey respondents in the 1990s did not think couples with children should remain married if they were unhappy. Women, less than men, favored divorce as a solution to unhappy marriages.

Most viewed life for children as harder than in the past. Although most thought parents did not discipline their children enough, a declining percentage approved of spanking for disciplining children. Forms of discipline included withdrawing privileges, giving timeouts, spanking, yelling, and not talking. Large percentages said they punished their children much less severely than their parents had punished them.

Survey responses to questions about the importance of children in the lives of respondents present a challenge to critics who charge parents with self-centeredness and parenting failure. Almost all respondents in 1997 said having children was important to them and that watching children grow up was one of life's greatest pleasures. Indeed, most said that being a parent was more important to them than it was to their parents when they as children were growing up. They also rejected the notion that children interfered unduly with parental freedom. In general, respondents thought they were better parents than their own parents were when they were children, understand their children better, and spend more time with them.

Most, however, thought that parents needed help in raising their children. Contrary to prevailing assumptions about the isolation of contemporary families, most said that grandparents, other relatives, and friends were very involved in their children's lives. Parents worried more about their children's success in school than about the threat of drugs and crime or their economic insecurity. Some worried a lot about their safety on the street and at shopping malls, which clearly says something about the times and communities in which we live.

Whatever kinds of families people lived in themselves, America's debate over the family involved public rather than private questions, according to Wolfe. The politicalization of family issues runs against the grain of middle-class sensibilities. Unhappy with the impact of contemporary life on their children, middle-class Americans, Wolfe speculated, could be susceptible to dubious claims about the sources of the problems facing children today. Conservatives in particular sensed middle-class anger about such problems—bad schools, loss of parental control over children, the decline of discipline, sex education, gay rights, and the seeming contempt for "middle-class morality" on the part of teachers and social workers—that have formed the basis of campaigns to assert "parental rights" and used to justify home schooling and vouchers for religious education. Parents' rights legislation, however, has failed in states such as Colorado, Kansas, North Dakota, and Virginia.

Just as Americans in general were ambivalent about the role of government and the changes that had taken place in families, middle-class Americans living in America's suburbs also were ambivalent. Persistent over the last 25 years was their dislike of government and politics. Reluctant to choose on matters pertaining to family or to make choices between family and work, guilt was not the issue for them. Probably to the disappointment of those who invest considerable religious meaning in family, Wolfe found that the language of family life used by middle-class Americans was more profane than sacred.

Clearly not accepted as a problem in need of a solution, should anyone wonder why a solution has not been constructed to effect a more equal distribution of income and wealth in this country, one need only consider the attitudes that most people hold about the matter. What is surprising, however, is that these attitudes pertained regardless of income, gender, ethnicity, and race. Most people simply thought the economic system was fair and that income and wealth as presently distributed was not a problem.

The optimism expressed in the different surveys cited in this chapter could be attributable to the affluence effect to which Yankelovich attached such importance with regard to the values transformation that has occurred in this and other industrialized countries. Such attitudes could easily shift with less favorable developments than the country experienced at the beginning of the 21st century, particularly in the economic realm, as earlier surveys in fact reveal, again underscoring the relationship between attitudes and developments and the malleability of attitudes. The positive attitudes people held about their marriages and children and the involvement of extended family and friends in their and their children's lives were at odds with prevailing views of marriage and family as crumbling institutions. Similarly, the negative attitudes people expressed toward government were at odds with their expectations of government and the demands they place upon it. In short, with respect to both government and family, attitudes were both contradictory and ambivalent, the very ingredients that could make people susceptible to the influence of those with extreme agendas.

Given that attitudes are relatively specific expressions of values or beliefs that provide impetus for action, knowledge about the attitudes that people hold about matters related to government, the economy, and family is important for the construction of solutions to problems that families may be experiencing and to the strategies used to construct them. The question is, What have the survey findings on attitudes reported in this chapter meant for family policies constructed at state and federal levels? This is the question that frames the discussion of the next three chapters, but before turning to them, consider the questions I have listed below for you to think about—and answer.

■ Some Questions for Your Reflection and Discussion

p84

1. What are the terms that Yankelovich uses to depict the processes by which the value transformations he identifies have occurred? Explain.

p84

2. What attitudes are associated with "expressive individualism"?

3. What attitudes are more characteristic of the 1990s than the 1960s and 1970s?

4. What were the views of most about the economic system and their own economic circumstances?

5. In terms of the 1990s, what characterizes the "good life"?

still behind, but better.

6. How do most persons classify themselves in terms of class? What changes have occurred in how people classify their class position? How does Wolfe define "middle class"?

7. How do women view their economic status relative to men's?

8. In what ways are the views of black Americans similar to and different from white Americans' with regard to economic opportunity, fairness of the economic system, and government's role in helping people?

9. How did survey respondents in the chapter regard growing income disparities?

10. What are some of the expectations that people hold for government?

11. What are some of the attitudes people expressed toward government in the 1990s? What accounts for these attitudes?

12. How do the attitudes that people in the United States hold toward government compare with the attitudes of people in countries like Sweden and Norway?

13. What attitudes did people express toward marriage in general and their own marriages in particular?

14. What attitudes did people express toward divorce? To what did people attribute increased divorce?

15. What attitudes did people express about working and mothers with young children?

16. What attitudes did people express about children growing up in the United States today?

17. What attitudes did people express about parenting?

18. Of what relevance to family policy are the attitudes that people expressed?

And now, what have the attitudes reported in this chapter meant for the construction of solutions to family problems at the federal level? For the answer to this question, please turn to the next chapter.

From Attitudes to Constructed Solutions to Family Problems

☐ The three chapters that constitute Part II are based on the content analysis of three different sets of data: (1) congressional roll call votes on explicit family legislation at the federal level for selected years in the 1980s and 1990s, (2) the *Congressional Record*, containing verbatim the congressional debates of the Defense of Marriage Act of 1996 (DOMA), and (3) the legislative summaries of the explicit family policies enacted by six states with different political cultures in the 1990s and for three of the states in the 1980s. Based on the assumption that attitudes provide impetus for action, the congressional roll call votes were seen as actions emanating from congressional members' attitudes on a wide range of explicit family issues, just as the explicit family legislation the states enacted over the study period also were seen. Readers should note that findings from the analysis of congressional roll call votes do not connote the actual passage of legislation but rather the number of votes taken over the study period in both the House and Senate that made explicit mention of families or that contained manifest family content and the categories of problems in which such votes were taken. The analysis of the congressional debates over DOMA documented the attitudes that were in fact expressed during the debates and that led to its passage.

Readers may find some of the procedures used in these analyses useful for examining the explicit family legislation enacted by their own state as a way of learning about the policy solutions their own state constructs to family problems—and the kinds of solutions it constructs. Such analyses offer a way of monitoring constructed solutions to family problems, as an aspect of fancy policy practice.

CHAPTER 6

Family Policies Constructed at the Federal Level for Selected Years in the 1980s and 1990s

Because attitudes as specific expressions of values and beliefs (Theodorson & Theodorson, 1969) provide the impetus for action in concrete situations (here in the form of congressional votes on legislative provisions related to families), what attitudes can be inferred from House and Senate roll call votes related to families in the 1980s and 1990s? Did they reflect some of the attitudes people expressed in the surveys cited in Chapter 5? What might such votes depict about the kinds of policy solutions that were constructed in addressing the problems that families were experiencing in the last decades of the 20th century and about the role of government in relation to families? How did policy solutions to family problems in the 1990s, the Clinton years, compare with those constructed in the 1980s, the Reagan/Bush years?

To answer these and other questions, a content analysis was undertaken of the descriptive summaries of all the measures on which House and Senate members voted for selected years in the 1980s and 1990s—1983, 1985, 1991, 1993, 1995, 1996, and 1997—that made explicit mention of the term *family* or any of the terms associated with it: *spouse, children, parent, grandparent, relatives,* and so on. These terms served as a measure of semantic validity, which refers to those words or coding units that possess similar connotations about which persons familiar with the language agree (Weber, 1985). Although the analysis focused primarily on roll call votes with *explicit* family content, it also included roll call votes with *implicit* family content that affect families directly. Examples are votes on the minimum wage, education, and some health provisions whose summaries may not have included family language but conceptually and empirically pertain to families, having implications for family functioning and the role performance of family members. In this regard, I heeded the advice of Alva Myrdal (1968) and Sanford Schram (1995), who counseled against limiting consideration of policies and practices that may not be justified in the name of the family but affect families nonetheless.

The data source for the analysis was the Congressional Roll Call, a compendium of House and Senate roll call votes published by the *Congressional Quarterly* at the end of each congressional session. For details about how the study was conducted, see Note 1.[1] Notice that recorded votes do not necessarily imply the passage of given measures; rather they signify the range of policy solutions that lawmakers constructed to a range of family problems over the observational period, or as Edelman (1975) put it, the range of alternative scenarios they constructed in addressing such problems.

The selection of the years for the analysis was based on some of the attitudinal and ideological differences they represented as expressed by Ronald Reagan, Republican president from 1980 to 1988; George Bush, Republican president from 1988 to 1992; and Bill Clinton, Democratic president from 1992 to 2000. It was President Reagan's view that government was the problem and not the solution to family problems. Charging that government social programs undermined family life and encouraged family breakup, teen pregnancy, and poverty, he advocated for less government and lower taxes (Zimmerman, 1992a). He opposed affirmative action, abortion, and school busing as strategies for effecting gender and racial equality and reducing some of the social and economic disparities between black and white and one-parent and two-parent families. An advocate for increased military spending, he nonetheless adamantly opposed increased taxes. His guiding assumption was that as resources for social programs shrank, spending for them would shrink as well—and so would the role of government. The legacy he left to George Bush, who succeeded him, was a dramatic increase in the federal debt and budget deficit that seriously constrained solutions to family problems.

George Bush was elected to office to ensure that the country's dominant value traditions—individualism, minimal government, and private property—continued to be reflected in its policy approach to families. Connecting the problems of the late 1980s to the collapse of the family, he said such problems called for the construction of new solutions to deal with what he said was a "crisis" (Bush, 1989). Although holding more positive attitudes toward government than President Reagan, President Bush viewed government's ability to act on such problems as limited (Wines, 1992), parenthetically adding that funds were low in any case. He constructed voluntarism as the solution to family problems, likening it metaphorically to a "thousand points of light" and urging that people become personally engaged in the lives of others in the spirit of goodness and courage. President Bush's veto of the Family Leave Bill in 1990 and opposition to an increase in the minimum wage were acts that expressed his attitudes about the role of government in addressing family problems. His comments alleging that government social programs "have tried to assume roles once reserved for families and schools and churches" (Pear, 1991) were similar expressions of his attitudes about government's role.

With the recession in the early 1990s, people were resensitized to the need for government to play a larger role in mediating the problems confronting families such as unemployment and slow economic growth. Bill Clinton ran for president in 1992 on the Democratic platform that called for a *third* way, one aimed, it said, at strengthening the family and putting government back on the side of citizens who played by the rules. The platform set forth two principles: (1) no one who is able to work could stay on welfare forever and (2) no one who worked should have to live in poverty. It called for investments in education, job training, child care, and health care to help families make a transition from welfare to work. Bill Clinton, in running on that platform, called for a new approach to government, envisioning a government, he said, that offered "more empowerment and less entitlement, a government that was leaner but not meaner." He said that if parents failed to meet their child support responsibilities, government would force them to do it, adding that government did not raise children, parents did, all suggestive of the attitudes underlying his construction of policy solutions to family problems—and reflective of some of the attitudes revealed in the surveys cited in Chapter 5.

Based on the attitudinal differences underlying President Reagan's, President Bush's, and President Clinton's construction of solutions to family problems, I hypothesized that more solutions to family problems would be constructed in the Clinton years than in the Reagan and Bush years and also that the nature of such solutions would differ in terms of their categorical or substantive labels as well. The methods used in the research appear in Note 1. What did the data show? What policy solutions did lawmakers construct in the early to mid-1980s and throughout most of the 1990s vis-à-vis families?

■ The Senate: Substantive Votes

As Table 6.1 shows, the substantive categories of measures on which roll call votes related to families taken in the 7 data years were:

- Child care
- Defense/military families
- Domestic abuse
- Education
- Employment
- Family farms
- Health
- Immigration
- Income security
- Marriage
- Taxes

TABLE 6.1   Senate Roll Call Votes on Legislative Provisions With Explicit Family Content[a]

	1983	1985	1991	1993	1995	1996	1997	Total
Child care	1	1	—	1	—	1	3	7
Defense/military families	2	1	2	—	1	—	—	6
Domestic abuse	—	—	1	1	2	1	1	6
Education	—	2	—	1	4	—	5	12
Employment	—	—	1	8	1	1	1	12
Family farms	—	—	—	3	—	—	—	3
Health								
Abortion	4	4	5	3	7	4	4	31
Health insurance revisions	—	—	—	—	1	6	1	8
Medicare/Medicaid	—	2	—	1	10	3	12	28
Services/standards								
Breast cancer screening	—	—	—	—	—	—	1	1
Child immunization	—	—	—	1	—	1	—	2
Children, elderly, pregnant women	—	—	—	—	1	—	1	2
Obstetric services	—	—	—	—	1	—	—	1
AIDS patients, spousal notification	—	—	—	—	1	—	—	1
Minimum hospital stays after birth	—	—	—	—	—	1	—	1
Seniors' health programs	—	—	—	—	—	—	1	1
WIC	1	1	—	1	—	—	—	3
Sex survey for school children	—	—	1	—	—	—	—	1
Total for category								80
Immigration	1	—	—	—	—	1	1	3
Income security								
AFDC	—	1	—	2	1	—	—	4
Welfare reform (PRWORA)	—	—	—	—	22	9	1	32
Social Security	1	—	—	4	3	—	—	8
Supplemental Security Income	—	—	—	—	—	—	1	1
Unemployment insurance	—	—	1	4	—	—	—	5
Total								50
Marriage (DOMA)	—	—	—	—	—	1	—	1
Taxes	—	1	—	2	11	—	7	21
Total by year and for all years	10	13	11	32	66	29	40	201

a. Connotes references to families in Senate's roll call votes on various provisions; includes procedural votes, votes of rejection, and votes of passage.

Child Care

As Table 6.1 shows, most of the Senate votes in the area of child care over the observational period occurred in 1997. In 1983, they pertained to day care centers for children of Senate employees; in both 1985 and 1993, they pertained to Head Start; and in 1996, to child care centers. In 1997, in addition to Head Start and day care centers, votes pertained to home child care providers and tax credits for employers who provide quality child care for their employees' children.

Defense/Military Families

Defense, not a category usually associated with family, nonetheless included roll call votes on measures related to families in four of the data years: 1983, 1985, 1991, and 1995. In 1983, the two votes pertained to measures related to families of military personnel missing in action in Southeast Asia. In 1985, the vote pertained to armed forces and their families in Nicaragua. In 1991, one vote pertained to veterans' compensation and another to parents in combat. In 1995, the one vote pertained to benefit cuts for veterans accompanied by a provision calling for a child impact statement. No votes occurred on measures related to families in this category in 1993, 1996, or 1997.

Domestic Abuse

With regard to domestic abuse, roll call votes occurred each year of the analysis in the 1990s but not in 1983 or 1985. In 1991, the vote pertained to child abuse and domestic violence prevention; in 1993, to a violence against women measure; in 1995, to measures on domestic violence and unfunded mandates related to child abuse; in 1996, to a measure on a domestic violence gun ban; and in 1997, to temporary work requirement waivers under the Temporary Assistance for Needy Families (TANF) program for victims of domestic violence.

Education

Although no Senate votes were taken in the area of education in 1983, 1991, or 1996, two votes were taken on such measures in 1985, one in 1993, four in 1995, and five in 1997. In 1985, one of the votes pertained to school prayer and the other to student aid and loans. In 1993, the sole education vote also pertained to student loans and aid. Student loans and aid were again the subject of roll call votes in 1995 and 1997. Other Senate votes in the area of education in 1995 pertained to student loans, to protecting student college aid from budget cuts, holding the line on education accounts, and direct as opposed to indirect college loans to students. In 1997, in addition to student aid, votes pertained to vocational training for needy families, school choice for crime victims, school breakfast programs, and child literacy initiatives, most of which represented investments in the role performance of family members and the future functioning of families.

Employment

In the area of employment, no Senate roll call votes were taken in 1983 and 1985. The predominant Senate vote in this category, especially in 1993, pertained to the Family and Medical Leave Act (FMLA). Here, votes were taken on measures related to tax credits for employers of employees responsible for the care of children or elderly parents, compensatory time, part-time workers, optional benefits, written notice requesting leave, and 12 weeks of unpaid leave to care for family members except for national service participants. The vote taken in 1995 pertained to displaced homemakers; in 1996, to an increase in the minimum wage; and in 1997, to the form of private sector compensatory overtime (i.e., compensatory time off or compensatory pay).

Family Farms

By virtue of their naming, measures pertaining to family farms are examples of explicit family policy. The only three votes taken on such measures in this category over the observational period occurred in 1993. The three votes pertained to taxes, tax increases, and family farm ombudsman.

Health

Family language was particularly prominent in the summaries of Senate roll call votes in the health area. In 1983, four votes were taken in this area, all in relation to abortion and its prohibition: a constitutional amendment to overturn *Roe v. Wade;* the prohibition of the use of federal funds for abortion except in cases of rape, incest, and mother endangerment; a permanent ban on federal funding for abortion; and the denial of federal health insurance coverage for abortions for federal employees. The Senate also voted on supplemental appropriations for the Women's, Infants', and Children's (WIC) program in 1983. In 1985, the Senate voted on four additional measures related to abortion: population planning; human rights violations; the prohibition of the use of federal funds for abortions for prison inmates and its constitutionality; and the prohibition of the use of federal funds for abortions in the District of Columbia. Two votes were taken on the funding of Medicare and Medicaid and one vote on full funding for WIC. Of the six votes in 1991, five were in the context of abortion: pregnancy counseling; parental consent; the gag rule; the prohibition of abortion advocacy; and a general appropriations bill. The sixth vote pertained to a parental consent for sex surveys involving school children.

Three roll call votes were taken on abortion measures in 1993: the prohibition of abortion in federal health insurance plans; reduced penalties for violent objectors at abortion clinics; and the continuation of restrictions on federal funding for abortions. A vote also was taken in 1993 on child immunization requirements, funding for Medicare, and full funding for WIC. In 1995, seven votes were taken on measures having to do with abortion: incentives to states for reducing out-of-wedlock births without increasing abortions; the banning of late-term abortions; penalties on physicians performing abortions; adverse health exceptions to abortion; prescription drugs related to abortion; and the prohibition of abortion in federal health insurance plans and in international family planning programs. Votes also were taken on assorted Medicare and Medicaid measures in 1995: cost cutting; the restoration of Medicare cuts; Medicare reform; Medicare fraud and abuse; Medicaid mandates; Medicare premium protections; nursing home standards; Medicaid eligibility; Medicaid entitlement; and child Medicaid health care insurance. Other votes in 1995 in the area of health included spousal notification of AIDS-infected patients; higher standards for obstetric services; and the exemption of child and elderly health care regulations from federal mandates.

Votes to ban abortions continued in the Senate over the observational period. In addition to the four votes on abortion in 1996, votes also were taken that year on several health insurance measures: medical savings accounts; mental illness coverage; the portability of health insurance; the coverage of preexisting conditions; increased tax deductions for health insurance premiums (from 30% to 80%); and minimum hospital stays of 48 hours for mothers of newborns. Votes on Medicare and Medicaid per se pertained to nursing home standards, Medicaid eligibility, and managed care options.

Many roll call votes in 1997 were a repetition of votes to ban abortion: in overseas military hospitals, on doctors performing abortions, on late-term abortions, and in federal health insurance plans. Votes also occurred on the prohibition of federal funds for assisted suicide and on health regulation exemptions pertaining to children, the elderly, and pregnant women from federal mandates; children's health and a balanced budget measure that also included banning the use of federal funds for abortions; the prohibition of the use of fetal tissue in research on Parkinson's disease; and federal funds for breast cancer research. With regard to Medicare and Medicaid, votes in 1997 pertained to Medicare home health copayments; an increase in Medicare age eligibility; cost cutting; Medicare means testing; home health benefits; Medicare premium protections; nursing home standards; Medicaid spousal impoverishment; child Medicaid health care insurance; Medicaid eligibility of disabled children; medical savings accounts; a 100% deduction for health insurance premiums of the self-employed by 2007; and senior citizens' health programs under the Older Americans' Act. One vote was taken in health insurance revisions: a 100% deduction for health insurance premiums of the self-employed by 2007.

Immigration

Senate votes in the area of immigration were confined to 1983, 1996, and 1997. In 1983, the vote pertained to visa allotments being contingent on employing others outside their families. In 1996, such votes pertained to restrictions on illegal immigration and the creation of legal family categories, and in 1997, to family remittances to Cuba. Such remittances related to limitations on travel to Cuba and a limit of $200 on funds sent to family members living in Cuba.

Income Security

Most Senate votes in the category of income security pertained to welfare reform, Social Security, and unemployment benefits. In 1983, 1985, and 1991, only one vote was taken in each of these data years. In 1983, the Senate voted on a measure to amend the income threshold for Social Security and reduce the Social Security marriage penalty; in 1985, on the termination of the Work Incentive (WIN) program in relation to the Aid to Families with Dependent Children's (AFDC) program (and jobs and training); and in 1991, on unemployment benefits.

Although other votes were taken on measures related to AFDC in 1995 having to do with entitlement caps and work requirements, votes in the area of income security centered primarily on welfare reform. Included were votes on welfare recipients who were felons; delinquent child support payments; child care; food stamp work requirements; wages and transitional aid; vouchers; work assistance; the elimination of family caps; Indian family assistance grants; out-of-wedlock births; foster care and adoption programs; the denial of federal funds for teen mothers of illegitimate children living with parents; incentives to states for the reduction of out-of-wedlock births; the denial of assistance for illegal aliens; noncustodial fathers; naturalized citizens; legal alien eligibility; drug and alcohol addiction programs; food assistance grant exemption; extended child aid; and preserving the entitlement status of AFDC.

With regard to Social Security, most Senate roll call votes occurred in 1993 and 1995. In 1993, such votes pertained to measures aimed at reducing the marriage penalty in the calculation of Social Security benefits, Social Security taxes, cost of living (COLA) increases, and the earnings test. In 1995, they pertained to the earnings test, the earnings limit, and a balanced budget without cuts in Social Security. The earnings test and earnings limit pertains to the amount of money people can earn *up to* age 70 before their benefits are reduced.

Senate votes on unemployment benefits were largely confined to 1991 and 1993. In 1991, such votes pertained to unemployment benefits generically. In 1993, they more specifically related to the extension of unemployment benefits from 7 to 13 weeks, depending on state unemployment rates; funding for extended benefits for workers who exhausted their 28 weeks of unemployment insurance; retroactive taxes on extended unemployment benefits; and a general vote on unemployment insurance.

In 1996, Senate votes in the area of income security pertained to the adoption tax credit, school breakfast programs, child subsistence vouchers, legal immigrant benefits, work requirement penalties, family caps, abstinence education, and the family assistance formula. Except for votes on legal immigrants' benefits and Supplemental Security Income (SSI), no other Senate votes were taken in 1997 in this area.

Marriage

An obviously explicit family policy, the only measure on which Senate votes were taken in this category pertained to the Defense of Marriage Act (DOMA) in 1996. It is the sole subject of the next chapter. DOMA defines marriage as a union between one man and one woman, which in effect rejects the practice of same-sex marriage.

Taxes

Most Senate votes in the area of taxation occurred in 1995 and 1997. In 1985, the only Senate vote in this area pertained to a family cap on income tax cuts. No Senate votes related to families were taken in this category in either 1983 or 1991. In 1993, the votes pertained to tax increases and high-income exclusions. In 1995, they pertained to the Earned Income Tax Credit (EITC), middle-class tax cuts, family tax relief, refundable child tax credits, college tuition deductions, tax break limits taking family income into account, estate taxes, and home office deductions. In 1997, such votes pertained to a $500 per child tax credit, estate tax exemptions for family-owned businesses and farms, an adoption tax credit that was part of welfare reform, the expansion of tax-deferred IRAs, a reduction in the capital gains tax, and a nonrefundable tax credit of up to $1,500 per student for the first 2 years of college. As in 1995, Senate votes pertaining to the EITC and estate tax breaks and restrictions also occurred in 1997.

In all, 201 roll call votes related to families were taken in the Senate over the observational period, broken down as follows:

- 7 in child care
- 6 in defense measures
- 6 in domestic violence
- 12 in education measures
- 12 in employment measures
- 3 in family farms
- 80 in health-related measures
- 50 in income security
- 3 in immigration
- 1 in marriage
- 21 in taxes

■ The House: Substantive Votes

What about the House? How did House roll call votes compare with those of the Senate? The House of Representatives, being over four times larger than the Senate, took many more roll call votes on family-related provisions over the observational period, but it also took many more nonfamily-related roll call votes. Table 6.2 shows the categories of measures on which House roll call votes were taken in which explicit family language or terms associated with family were used or that had manifest family content. These included:

- child and family welfare
- child support
- crime
- defense/military families
- education
- employment
- health
- housing
- immigration/refugees
- income security
- institutional (i.e., the creation of congressional committees, offices, and procedural rules)
- marriage
- taxes
- veterans affairs

Thus, the scope of the measures in the House was somewhat broader than in the Senate, and the naming of categories and subcategories was slightly different. Furthermore, both the categories and subcategories of House votes were constituted of many more specific family-related measures, as the discussion below will show.

Child and Family Welfare

House votes in the category of child and family welfare occurred mostly in 1995, 1996, and 1997. In 1983, only one vote was taken on a measure, namely the Child Protection Act, and no votes occurred in 1985, 1991, or 1993. In 1995, such votes pertained to several provisions with regard to the protection of family privacy rights, such as written parental consent for minors to participate in surveys, prohibition of the use of federal money to conduct surveys of minors without parental consent, and a parental consent requirement before minors can participate in surveys distributed under federal programs. House votes in 1996 pertained to parental control technology and to many measures pertaining to adoption. The latter included appropriations for adoptions, Indian child adoptions, tax credits for adoption expenses, and nondiscrimination in matching

TABLE 6.2 House Roll Call Votes on Legislative Provisions With Explicit Family Content[a]

	1983	1985	1991	1993	1995	1996	1997	Total
Child and family welfare								
Adoption	—	—	—	—	—	3	2	5
Au pair program	—	—	—	—	—	—	1	1
Child Protection Act	1	—	—	—	—	—	—	1
Family Privacy Protection	—	—	—	—	4	—	—	4
Foster care	—	—	—	—	—	1	—	1
National Center, Missing/ Exploited Children	—	—	—	—	—	—	1	1
Parental Control Technology	—	—	—	—	1	1	—	2
Total								15
Child support	1	—	—	—	3	—	1	5
Crime								
Child sex crimes	—	—	—	—	2	—	1	3
Domestic violence/violence against women	—	—	—	1	—	—	—	1
Rape and assault	—	—	—	—	—	1	1	2
Violent crimes, children, elderly, etc.	—	—	—	—	—	1	—	1
Sex offenders' release disclosure	—	—	—	—	—	1	1	2
Crime victims, families, trials	—	—	—	—	—	—	1	1
Total								10
Defense/military families								
Abortions	—	—	—	—	3	1	—	4
Housing	—	—	—	—	1	—	1	2
Quality of family life	—	—	—	—	1	—	—	1
Child care food programs	—	—	—	—	1	—	—	1
Total								8
Education								
School lunch/nutrition	—	3	—	1	1	—	—	5
Handicapped children	—	1	—	—	—	—	—	1
Student loans	—	2	1	—	2	—	—	5
Head Start	—	—	1	—	—	1	—	2
National Service	—	—	—	7	—	1	—	8
National education goals	—	—	—	1	—	1	1	3
Vocational/adult education	—	—	1	—	—	—	1	2
Youth Fair Chance	—	—	—	1	—	—	—	1
Women's Educational Equity Act	—	—	—	—	1	—	—	1
Voc-tech education/displaced homemakers	—	—	—	—	—	—	1	1
Scholarships/low-income DC students	—	—	—	—	—	—	1	1
Education savings accounts	—	—	—	—	—	—	1	1
Charter schools	—	—	—	—	—	—	1	1
Total								32

(continued)

TABLE 6.2 (Continued)

	1983	1985	1991	1993	1995	1996	1997	Total
Employment								
Compensatory time off/wages	—	—	—	—	—	1	1	2
Jobs/training, food stamp recipients	—	1	—	—	—	—	—	1
Plant closing notification	—	5	—	—	—	—	—	5
Job Corps increases	—	—	1	—	—	—	—	1
Employment aid/elderly poor	—	—	1	—	—	—	—	1
Family/Medical Leave	—	—	1	6	1	—	—	8
Minimum wage	—	—	—	—	—	1	—	1
Striker replacement	—	—	—	3	1	—	—	4
Job training	—	—	—	—	—	1	1	2
Total								25
Health								
Abortion	1	4	7	13	11	8	8	52
AIDS program reauthorization	—	—	—	—	1	—	1	2
Assisted suicide, funding ban	—	—	—	—	—	—	1	1
Breast cancer research	—	—	—	2	—	—	1	3
Child safety protections	—	—	—	2	—	—	—	2
Health insurance, domestic partners	—	—	—	1	1	—	—	2
Family planning	—	1	—	4	1	1	1	8
Health insurance	—	—	—	—	—	8	1	9
Research	—	—	2	—	—	3	—	5
Medicaid	—	—	—	—	1	1	3	5
Medicare	—	1	1	1	2	1	3	9
WIC	1	—	—	—	—	1	1	3
Misc.: Reproductive disorder pollutant	—	—	—	—	1	—	—	1
Population activities (UN)	—	1	—	—	—	—	—	1
Total								103
Housing								
Loan programs	2	—	—	—	—	—	—	2
Multifamily housing	3	—	—	—	—	—	1	4
Home investment partnerships (HOPE)	—	—	1	1	—	—	—	2
Affordable housing program	—	—	—	1	—	—	—	1
Exempt from federal mandates, protections against adult/ child homelessness/hunger	—	—	—	—	2	—	—	2
Senior housing/can't exclude children	—	—	—	—	1	—	—	1
Seniors/housing safety, home equity protections, housing assistance	—	—	—	—	1	—	1	2
Assisted housing	—	—	—	—	1	—	—	1
Rents, rental assistance	—	—	—	—	1	2	2	5
Public housing overhaul	—	—	—	—	—	3	5	8
Pets	—	—	—	—	—	1	—	1

TABLE 6.2 (Continued)

	1983	1985	1991	1993	1995	1996	1997	Total
Assistance, elderly, disabled, AIDS victims, homeless	—	—	—	—	—	4	—	4
Total								33
Immigration/refugees								
Targeted assistance/social services	—	2	—	—	—	—	—	2
Immigration restrictions	—	—	—	—	—	1	—	1
Illegal aliens	—	—	—	—	—	3	1	4
Welfare overhaul, deny assistance to	—	—	—	—	—	1	—	1
Temporary agricultural worker program	—	—	—	—	—	1	—	1
Grants/help refugees adjust	—	—	—	—	—	—	1	1
Total								10
Income Security								
AFDC	—	1	—	—	—	1	—	2
Death benefits, survivors of police and firefighters killed in line of duty	1	—	—	—	—	—	—	1
Food stamps	—	—	—	—	—	1	1	2
Social Security, debt limit, SS card, COLA, taxes/cuts earnings test	—	1	1	—	1	3	—	6
Supplemental Security Income, legal immigrants, 5-year wait	—	—	—	—	1	—	—	1
Delay ending SSI/legal immigrants	—	—	—	—	—	—	1	1
Unemployment benefits	—	—	1	4	—	—	—	5
Unfunded mandates, low-income entitlement programs	—	—	—	—	2	—	—	2
Welfare overhaul	—	—	—	—	12	9	—	21
Total								41
Institutional								
Select Committee on Children, Youth, Families, hold hearings	1	—	—	—	—	—	—	1
Separate office, FMLA compliance	—	—	—	—	1	—	—	1
Gift ban rule, exception family	—	—	—	—	—	1	—	1
Taxpayer Advocate Office, in IRS	—	—	—	—	—	1	—	1
Total								4
Marriage (DOMA)	—	—	—	—	—	1	—	1

(continued)

TABLE 6.2   (Continued)

	1983	1985	1991	1993	1995	1996	1997	Total
Taxes								
EITC	—	—	—	1	3	—	—	4
Family tax relief	—	—	—	—	—	—	1	1
$720 family limit, 10% tax cut	1	—	—	—	—	—	—	1
Minimum federal income tax	—	1	—	—	—	—	——	1
Tax overhaul	—	2	—	—	—	—	—	2
Social Security, tax benefits	—	—	—	1	—	—	—	1
Tax/spending cuts								
Child tax credit	—	—	—	—	2	—	2	4
Marriage penalty ease	—	—	—	—	1	—	—	1
Tax incentives, education	—	—	—	—	—	—	1	1
Miscellaneous	—	—	—	—	5	1	1	7
Total								23
Veterans Affairs								
Veterans' compensation	—	1	1	1	—	—	—	3
Health insurance/health care	—	—	1	1	—	2	—	4
Reproductive health services, no abortion	—	—	1	—	—	—	—	1
Housing	—	—	1	—	—	1	—	2
Education	—	—	1	—	—	—	—	1
Total								11
Total by year and overall	12	27	24	53	74	75	56	321

a. Connotes reference to families in House roll call votes on various provisions; includes procedural votes, votes of rejection and votes of passage.

children with adoptive parents. They also pertained to appropriations for foster care and to a prohibition against children under 17 controlling an airplane, a solution House members constructed in response to a child who piloted an airplane with the permission of his father.

In 1997, House votes were related to the au pair program that gave English-speaking Western Europeans 18 to 25 years of age an opportunity to live with an American family for 1 year while assisting with child care; missing and exploited children; and two adoption measures, one pertaining to incentives to increase adoptions of children in foster care for 18 months or more and the other to exemptions of foreign children adopted by U.S. parents from immigration vaccination requirements.

Child Support

Most of the votes on child support measures in the House occurred in 1995. The two exceptions were a vote on one measure in 1983 requiring states to institute mandatory procedures for withholding payments from the wages of parents in arrears in child support payments and one measure in 1997 pertaining to United Nations' personnel who fail to comply with child support orders that were linked to delinquent U.S. dues payments to the United Nations. The three measures in 1995 pertained to state exemptions from unfunded federal mandates for child support payment collections; child support liens against the property of persons owing overdue child support in the states in which they own property; and the suspension or withholding of driver, professional, or recreational licenses of persons delinquent in child support payments.

Crime

No votes were taken in the House on crime issues in 1983, 1985, or 1991. In 1993, the only measure on which House votes were taken pertained to domestic violence grants to states. In 1995, they pertained to child sex crime prevention, increased penalties for child pornography, and state exemptions from federal mandates requiring states to maintain national data for tracking child molesters, all designed to aid parents in protecting their children. In 1996, they pertained to several measures dealing with rape and sexual assault, such as life sentences without parole for rapists who cross state lines upon a second conviction; increased penalties for violent crimes against children, the elderly, and other vulnerable persons; and in both 1996 and 1997, the mandatory disclosure of the release of sex offenders from prison. Other votes in 1997 pertained to the review of federal sentencing guidelines for rape and sexual assault, state registries of sex crimes against children, and allowing crime victims and their families to attend the trials of those accused of the crime and to testify in the sentencing phase of the trial.

Defense/Military Families

Most of the votes in the House in the category of defense/military families were taken in 1995. None occurred in 1983, 1985, 1991, or 1993. Votes in 1995 pertained to a measure stating that the quality of life for military families was not to be affected as an offset to unbudgeted military operations, the equal treatment of children on military bases in child care food programs, and to funds for family housing for military personnel. The remaining three votes pertained to abortion (e.g., allowing abortions for military personnel and their dependents at overseas military bases as long as women paid for the procedure themselves); prohibiting abortions at overseas military facilities unless the life of the woman is in danger or the costs associated with abortion are reimbursed with private money (rejected); and prohibiting abortions at overseas military facilities unless the life of the woman is endangered. The only family measure on which a vote was taken in 1996 also pertained to abortion, namely a measure to repeal current law with regard to abortions in overseas military hospitals. In 1997, the only vote pertained to family housing for military personnel.

Education

In the area of education, no votes were taken in the House in 1983. In 1985, three votes pertained to school lunch and child nutrition programs, one vote pertained to handicapped children's education, and two votes pertained to two measures having to do with student loan payments and repayments. In 1991, such votes pertained to student loans, funding for Head Start, and vocational and adult education. In 1993, they pertained to 2-year education awards for persons volunteering for national service; student aid programs; reduced education awards; federal match for local programs with regard to stipends, health, and child care costs; national education goals, standards, and texts; stipends for youth participating in education/training programs while participating in paid work experience (e.g., Youth Fair Chance); and school lunch programs with an emphasis on whole milk.

In 1995, votes pertained to funding for direct student loan programs, a federal cap on direct student loan programs, and school lunch and breakfast programs. In 1996, such measures included funding for Head Start as in 1991, the elimination of the National Service Program, the elimination of Goals 2000, school reform programs, and the Women's Educational Equity Act. In 1997, Goals 2000 are identified in the table as national education goals, which includes a provision for parent involvement in the education of children. Other measures on which votes were taken in 1997 included votes on vocational and adult education for high-risk youth as in 1991; voc-tech education for displaced homemakers; scholarships for low-income students in the District of Columbia to attend private or public schools; education savings accounts; and federal grants for public charter schools.

Employment

In the area of employment, no votes occurred in the House in 1983. Votes in 1985 pertained to a 3-year employment and training program requirement for food stamp recipients and to plant closing notification regulations having to do with company size and time requirements for prior notice. The three votes in 1991 pertained to job corps increases; employment aid for elderly poor; and FMLA, which was subsequently vetoed. However, after the 1992 presidential election, the measure was introduced again in 1993. In 1993, six votes were taken in relation to the FMLA. These included votes on a cafeteria benefits plan; reduced leave for employees without employers' consent when medically necessary; employers' discretion in granting medical and family leave to employees; and unpaid leave of up to 12 weeks for medical and family reasons required of employers of 50 or more employees.

In 1995, the only votes had to do with FMLA and striker replacement. In 1996, the three measures on which votes were taken pertained to an increase in the minimum wage, job training, and overtime pay or compensatory time off for overtime. In 1997, such votes were confined to a job training program block grant, largely for summer youth employment, and, as in 1996, to compensatory time off/wages for overtime.

Health

Over the observational period, votes escalated in the health area with regard to abortion. In 1983, only one vote was taken on the issue, namely to prohibit the use of federal funds to pay for abortions. In 1985, four votes were taken on the issue: one to demand that China cease its practices of forced abortions and sterilization in the implementation of its one child per couple policy; another to deny funds to countries based on the types of family planning programs they promoted; another to bar the Legal Services Corporation from using federal funds for abortion-related litigation; and one to bar the District of Columbia from using federal funds to pay for abortions.

In 1991, such votes pertained again to a prohibition on the use of federal funds to pay for abortions and China's forced abortion and sterilization policies in addition to votes prohibiting the use of federal funds to provide information about abortion in family planning programs (otherwise known as the gag rule); the prohibition of the use of local taxes to pay for abortions in the District of Columbia; the denial of federal funds to foreign nongovernmental organizations that provide abortions or abortion counseling; the prohibition of federal funds to support family planning programs in countries such as China via the U.N. Population Fund; and fetal tissue research, namely to lift the ban on induced abortions to facilitate fetal tissue research and protections for women having abortions for that purpose. The three nonabortion votes in 1991 pertained to human sexual surveys to reduce the incidence of sexually transmitted diseases and cuts in Medicare spending to reduce the budget deficit.

China's abortion and sterilization policies, which were the subjects and objects of House votes in 1985 and 1991, continued to be the subjects and objects of House votes in 1993, 1995, 1996, and 1997. House votes on abortion measures in 1993 pertained to federal criminal and civil penalties for the use or threat of the use of force to block access to abortion clinics; prohibitions on the use of federal funds for abortion except in cases of rape, incest, or mother endangerment; role expectations of antiabortion counselors; 48-hour parental notice in abortion cases involving a minor; and lifting the ban on induced abortions for fetal tissue research. Just as votes taken in the House in 1993 pertained to the preservation of the U.N. Population Fund, with prohibitions on funding to support family planning programs in many countries, such votes also occurred in 1995 and 1997.

Other measures on which votes were taken in addition to abortion in 1983 pertained to the WIC program, namely to protect the program from budget cuts to prevent an increase in domestic hunger. In 1985, they pertained to Medicare spending cuts (as in 1991 also), and they earmarked assistance for population activities from the U.N. Population Fund. The third vote was on the extension of assistance to states for family planning. In 1993, such votes pertained to breast cancer research; breast and cervical cancer prevention; child safety protections; child safety restraints in airports; the eligibility of domestic partners in the District of Columbia for group health insurance; lifting the gag rule; the extension of federal aid for family planning assistance; clinic programs; standards for patient advisers; state control of Title X funds; the distribution of condoms; and an increase in the payroll tax for Medicare.

In addition to votes on China's abortion and sterilization policies in 1995, House votes on abortion also pertained to federal employees and the deletion of a provision prohibiting them from obtaining abortion services through federal health insurance policies except in cases of rape, incest, or endangerment of the mother's life; the denial of funding for foreign nongovernmental organizations that provide abortions or abortion counseling; restrictions on funds for overseas abortions; revocation of a requirement that foreign organizations receiving U.S. aid certify that they do not violate or lobby to change U.S. abortion laws; the use of block grant monies for the protection of abortion clinics; a prohibition on Medicaid funding for abortions except when the life of a woman is in danger; a prohibition on the withholding of funds and accreditation from medical training programs that do not offer training in abortion procedures; a ban on partial birth abortions; and a prohibition on federal funding for abortions, directed pregnancy counseling, lobbying, or political activity advocating abortion.

Nonabortion measures in 1995 pertained to the AIDS Program Reauthorization Act; revocation of a law allowing city workers in the District of Columbia to buy health insurance for domestic partners; block grants terminating the Title X family planning program; maternal and child health and Community and Migrant Health Center programs; Medicare spending cuts; a freeze on Medicare reimbursement rates; and the exemption of reproductive disorder pollutants from federal mandates related to reproductive disorders in humans; and federal funding caps on the WIC program based on the number of WIC participants.

In 1996, House votes on abortion measures pertained to prohibitions on federal employees from obtaining abortion services through federal health insurance policies; barring the use of federal funds to pay for abortions in the District of Columbia; prohibiting Medicaid funds from being used to pay for abortions except when the life of the woman is in danger (as in 1995); a ban on partial birth abortions (also as in 1995); and a shift in the burden of proof from the defendant to the prosecution to show that an abortion procedure was not necessary to save the woman's life.

Nonabortion votes in 1996 pertained to the encouragement of parent involvement in family planning programs; a ban on the use of federal funds for embryo research; the portability of health insurance; prohibitions on the cancellation of insurance by insurers based on employees' health; increased deductibility of health insurance premiums for self-employed persons; medical savings accounts; mental health insurance coverage without an increase in premiums; a requirement that health insurance plans covering mental illnesses establish limits on coverage at the same level as physical illnesses; a 48-hour hospital stay requirement for mothers of newborns and 96 hours for mothers having

Caesarean sections; a prohibition on funding for human embryo research; and Medicaid and Medicare spending cuts.

Abortion continued to be a focus of House votes in 1997. Roll call votes pertained to the denial of U.S. visas to Chinese officials involved in population activities resulting in forced abortions or sterilizations; restrictions on the use of funds for overseas abortions; the elimination of provisions requiring foreign organizations receiving U.S. aid to certify that they do not violate or lobby to change U.S. abortion laws; the U.N. Population Fund; penalties on persons performing partial birth abortions; parent notification in abortion cases involving a minor; a ban on the use of funds for international family planning activities by family planning organizations that use private funds for abortions; and the rights of doctors facing penalties for performing abortions to have a hearing before a state medical board to determine whether the procedure was medically necessary.

Nonabortion measures in 1997 pertained to breast cancer research; early release of funds for international family planning activities; medical savings accounts (as in 1996); uninsured children; Medicaid spending cuts (again); a child health assistance block grant as well as Medicaid eligibility for disabled children who lose their SSI benefits; a freeze on Medicare reimbursement rates; and a ban on funding for assisted suicide.

Housing

In 1983, five roll call votes related to families were taken in the area of housing: one to allow postponement of the repayment of loans to the Farmers' Home Administration; another to a temporary loan program to help unemployed homeowners with their mortgage payments; another to prevent federal funds from going to communities that place rent control requirements on housing projects; another to a home ownership program for low- and moderate-income families and a rental assistance program; and still another to the establishment of a multifamily rental housing production program.

No House votes were taken in the area of housing in 1985. The only votes taken in 1991 pertained to home investment partnerships, otherwise known as HOPE (Home Ownership and Opportunities for People Everywhere), and shelter care programs, on which House votes were taken in 1993 also. Another family-related housing measure in 1993 pertained to the expansion of the Resolution Trust Corporation (RTC) and affordable housing to avoid the displacement of tenants that resulted from single-family property requirements.

In 1995, housing measures pertained to unfunded federal mandates that exempt programs protecting adults and children, separately, from hunger and homelessness; federal housing benefits for families that participate in welfare-to-work job training programs as part of welfare reform; housing for older persons that prevents the exclusion of families with children; assisted housing that included an increase in the percentage of family income used to calculate rental assistance; a rental assistance exemption that waived rules on a 70-unit family housing apartment in Madison, Wisconsin, to allow for rentals on a mixed-income basis; and to a Senior Citizens Housing Safety provision that, in addition to protections for disabled seniors from seniors whose disability involved drug or alcohol abuse, pertained to a reverse mortgage program to protect the home equity of seniors.

In 1996, family-related housing votes included the consolidation of federal funding for public housing and low-income rental assistance through a block grant; federal caps on families' rent contributions; a minimum limit of $25 per month on public housing rent contributions, or rental waivers in cases of financial hardship; and homeless assistance appropriations.

In 1997, such measures pertained to multifamily rural rental housing for low- and moderate-income families; reverse mortgages (as in 1995); further consolidation of federal funding for public housing; low-income rental assistance (as in 1996); an 8-hour-per-month community service requirement for public housing with restrictions on evictions; exemptions of single parents of young children and primary caregivers of seniors and disabled persons from the 8-hour service obligation; a requirement that pay for community service be no lower than the minimum wage; tenant rents based on 30% of adjusted family income; and family income requirements for rental vouchers.

Immigration/Refugees

Almost all the House votes taken in the area of immigration occurred in 1996 and 1997, most in 1996. In 1985, two roll call votes were taken in this area: one deleted funding authorization for targeted assistance to communities with large refugee populations, and the other froze authorization for refugee social services and medical screening programs at the 1985 level. In 1996, one of the measures pertained to restrictions on family reunification and employment-related visas and the denial of SSI, food stamps, and Medicaid to illegal aliens as part of the overhaul of welfare. Another measure relaxed the provisions that prevented undocumented aliens from applying for food stamps and Medicaid for their children and allowed parents to challenge a state's decision to deny public education to their children by proving their U.S. citizenship and lawful presence in the country. In 1997, such votes pertained to relocation assistance for displaced illegal aliens and grants to private organizations helping refugee families adjust to life in the United States.

Income Security

Just as most of the roll call votes taken on measures in the area of immigration occurred in 1996 and 1997, the same was true of votes on income security. In 1983, a vote was taken in this area pertaining to death benefits for survivors of law enforcement officers and firefighters killed in the line of duty; in 1985, only two votes taken in this area related to families, one pertaining to AFDC and the other to the elimination of the cost-of-living adjustment (COLA) for Social Security in combination with tax increases and spending cuts. In 1991, votes were taken on the earnings test for Social Security; another pertained to the extension of the emergency spending for unemployment insurance benefits in response to the high unemployment rates at that time. Votes on the latter were taken again in 1993 along with another vote to eliminate extension of COLA; a vote to extend unemployment benefits for long-term unemployed persons; and a vote to disallow extension of federal unemployment insurance benefits in states having unemployment rates below 5%.

In 1995, votes on measures included increases in the earnings limit for Social Security; exemptions from unfunded federal mandates that would threaten the health and safety of children and unemployed parents on welfare; and the application of federal mandates to any changes in low-income entitlement programs such as Medicaid, AFDC, SSI, and WIC. Votes also were taken on several welfare overhaul measures that incorporated such disparate measures as reductions in welfare eligibility; limits on federal welfare spending; state flexibility in the provision of social services; reductions in illegitimate births; work participation requirements; shielding states' child protection laws from the federal government; the timely adoption of children; vouchers instead of cash benefits for teen mothers; state discretion with regard to the denial of cash benefits to teen unwed mothers; vouchers for newborn babies and assistance to families; a food stamp block grant and food stamp work requirements; federal control of the entitlement status of welfare benefits; the preservation of the entitlement status of welfare and related benefits; and welfare overhaul involving five block grants to states (for cash welfare, child welfare, school meals, nutrition programs, and child care), state flexibility, a 2-year time limit for securing employment after benefits are first received, and a 5-year limit on benefits over a lifetime.

In 1996, most votes pertained to welfare reform. These included cuts in aid to legal immigrants; cuts in food stamps; the end of the federal guarantee of welfare benefits; block grants; work requirements coupled with a 2-year time limit for securing employment and a 5-year lifetime limit; avoidance of cost shifting from state to local governments; avoidance of an increase in the number of children in poverty; maximization of the availability of food stamps and vouchers for children; guaranteed Medicaid coverage; and the application of realized savings to the reduction of the budget deficit. Such measures also specifically pertained to Wisconsin's welfare program, namely to waivers and Wisconsin's replacement of AFDC with work and a 5-year limit on benefits over a lifetime.

Other votes in 1996 pertained to AFDC; food stamp reauthorization; Social Security benefits and the debt limit; Social Security identification cards; the Social Security earnings test; and tightened welfare eligibility for disabled children and legal immigrants. In 1997, the only measures on which roll call votes were taken pertained to postponement of the termination of SSI benefits to legal immigrants and disregarding prisoners as household members in the determination of family eligibility for food stamps.

Institutional

Votes on measures that explicitly mentioned families and pertained to structures and rules for carrying out the wishes of Congress on matters relating to families are categorized here as institutional. In 1983, a roll call vote was taken on a measure to establish a Select Committee on Children, Youth, and Families for the purpose of holding hearings on family-related matters. A roll call vote in the institutional category in 1995 pertained to the creation of a separate office to oversee compliance with FMLA and other labor laws. In 1996, a vote pertained to a gift ban rule prohibiting House members and staff from accepting gifts, meals, and trips except from personal friends and family, and another vote created a Taxpayer Advocate Office in the Internal Revenue Service, taxpayers representing family tax concerns.

Marriage

The only House roll call vote in the category of marriage pertained to DOMA in 1996. As in the case of the Senate, this measure will be discussed in greater detail in the next chapter to show how language is used to convey attitudes and evoke corresponding emotions in the construction of problems and their solutions in congressional debates on controversial measures.

Taxes

In 1983, a roll call vote was taken in the House on a $720 per family cap on a 10% individual income tax cut. In 1985, votes were taken on three measures: (1) a minimum federal income tax; (2) a tax overhaul involving the restructuring of income tax laws, reductions in tax rates, increases in personal exemptions and standard deductions, and the elimination of an investment tax credit; and (3) the creation of an alternative minimum tax. In 1993, votes pertained to an expansion of the EITC for low-income families and tax increases in the benefits of better-off Social Security beneficiaries.

Many more votes were taken in 1995 than in 1993. Among these were votes on the expansion of the EITC (as in 1993); cuts in the EITC; tax relief for working poor families with children; a child tax credit of $500 per child for families with incomes less than $200,000 per year; the elimination of the alternative minimum tax; a reduction in the capital gains tax rate from 28% to 20%; tax cuts for families earning less than $85,000 per year; tax deductions for student loans; individual retirement accounts (IRAs); child tax credits for families with incomes up to $100,0000 per year; expansion of eligibility for IRAs; the elimination of the marriage tax penalty; and repeal of the tax increase on Social Security benefits.

In 1996, in addition to a roll call vote to create a Taxpayer Advocate Office in the IRS that was classified under institutional because of its structural nature, a vote was taken with regard to a constitutional amendment requiring a two-thirds majority in the House to raise taxes. In 1997, votes taken in the area of taxation pertained to permanent tax relief for families; a reduction in the capital gains tax rate from 28 to 20% (as in 1995); a refundable child tax credit and the EITC; tax cuts over 5 years; and tax incentives for education including a non-refundable credit for the first 2 years of college.

Veterans Affairs

No votes were taken in the area of veterans affairs in 1983, and only one was taken in 1985: a vote on COLAs for veterans receiving disability compensation and dependents and survivors receiving indemnity compensation. Measures in 1991 pertained to service-connected disabilities for veterans of the Gulf War; veterans education, employment, and training programs under the Veterans War Act; and veterans housing programs. In 1993, the only measures on which votes were taken pertained to COLA in veterans benefits and the increased cost of drugs. Votes in 1996 pertained to uniform eligibility standards for health care for veterans and their families and to a measure directed at children suffering from spina bifida who had a parent who had been exposed to Agent Orange while serving in Vietnam.

In all, 321 roll call votes related to families were taken in the House over the observational period: 15 votes were in the child and family welfare category, 5 in the category of child support, 10 in the area of crime that pertained to families, 8 in defense/military families, 32 in education, 25 in employment, 103 in health, 33 in housing, 10 in immigration, 41 in income security, 4 in the institutional category, 1 in marriage, 23 in taxes, and 11 in veterans affairs.

■ What Proportion of the Family-Related Votes Did the Different Categories Represent?

Table 6.3 shows the proportion of roll call votes related to families in the different categories for both the Senate and House over the observational period.

Based on a total of 201 roll call votes on family-related measures in the Senate over the observational period, Table 6.3 shows that the largest share of votes occurred in the health category—40%—almost 40% of which pertained to abortion and 35% to Medicare and Medicaid. Senate votes in the area of income security represented the next largest share—25%—almost two thirds pertaining to welfare reform. This was followed by votes in the tax category, which represented the next largest share of Senate votes—10%. As Table 6.3 shows, the remaining categories of roll call votes represented a very small share of Senate solutions to family problems over the observational period.

Based on a total of 321 roll call votes related to families in the House over the observational period, Table 6.3 shows that, as in the Senate, the largest share of House votes occurred in the health category (32%), half of which pertained to abortion and 14% to Medicare and Medicaid. House votes in the area of income

TABLE 6.3 Senate and House Roll Call Votes on Legislative Provisions With Explicit or Manifest Family Content, Percentages by Category Over the Observational Period

	Senate (N = 201) %	House (N = 321) %
Child and family welfare	—	5
Child care	4	—
Child support	—	2
Crime (domestic abuse)	—	3
Defense/military families	3	3
Domestic abuse	3	—
Education	6	10
Employment	6	8
Family farms	2	—
Health	40	32
Abortion[a]	39	51
Medicare/Medicaid[a]	35	14
Housing	—	10
Immigration	2	3
Income Security	25	13
Welfare reform[a]	64	51
Institutional	—	1
DOMA	.5	.3
Taxes	10	7
Veterans Affairs	—	3

a. Percentages are based on the number of roll votes in the subcategory relative to the number of roll call votes in their category, not relative to the total number of roll call votes.

security represented the next largest share (13%), over half of which pertained to welfare reform. This is followed by votes in the education and housing categories (10% each) and then taxes (7%). Thus, in both the House and Senate, solutions in the areas of health (primarily with respect to abortion) and income security predominated. The House, however, voted on a larger share of measures in the areas of housing and education than the Senate and a smaller share of measures in the area of taxes. Just as in the Senate, House votes in the other categories represented a very small share of House solutions to family problems over the observational period.

■ How Did the Share of Family-Related Votes Vary by Year?

Table 6.4 shows the frequency and proportion of roll call votes related to families for both the House and Senate, irrespective of legislative category, for each data year over the observational period. As Table 6.4 shows, the largest share of such votes occurred in the Senate in 1995 (33%), followed by 1997 (20%) and 1996 (14%). In 1983, 1985, and 1991, such votes represented less than 10% of all the family-related Senate votes over the observational period.

TABLE 6.4 Senate and House Roll Call Votes on Legislative Provisions With Explicit or Manifest Family Content, Frequencies and Percentages Relative to Total Votes on Such Provisions Over Observational Period, by Year

	Senate (N = 201)		House (N = 321)	
	N	%	N	%
1983	10	5	12	4
1985	13	7	27	8
1991	11	6	24	8
1993	32	16	53	17
1995	66	33	74	23
1996	29	14	75	23
1997	40	20	56	17

In the House, the largest share of family-related roll call votes occurred in 1996 and 1995, 23% each year, followed by 17% both in 1997 and 1993. In 1983, 1985, and 1991, such votes represented less than 10% of all the family-related votes in both the House and Senate over the observational period.

■ What Was the Share of Family-Related Role Call Votes Relative to Total Roll Call Votes?

What proportion of all Senate and House roll call votes did those that were family related represent in the 7 data years? Table 6.5 shows that of the 371 roll call votes in the Senate in 1983, less than 3% (N = 10) related to families, and that of the 381 roll call votes in 1985, just over 3% were family related (N = 13). In 1991, almost 4% of the votes were family related, based on a total of 289 Senate roll call votes, only 11 of which pertained to families. Beginning with 1993, the relative share of family-related votes in the Senate increased. Family-related votes constituted 8% (N = 32) of the 395 Senate votes in 1993, 9% (N = 29) of the 306 votes in 1996, 11% (N = 66) of the 613 votes in 1995, and 13% (N = 40) of the 1997 298 Senate votes.

In the House, the big year for family-related roll call votes was 1996, when such votes (N = 75) represented almost 17% of the 454 House votes that year. This was followed by 1993, when such votes represented almost 9% (N = 53) of the 597 House votes; then 1997, when family-related votes also represented almost 9% (N = 56) of 633 House votes; then 1995, when the 74 votes represented over 8% of the total 867 votes; then followed by 1985, when 27 family-related votes represented just over 6% of the total 439 votes that year; then 1991, when 24 family-related votes represented over 5% of the total 444 votes; and finally by 1983, when the 12 family-related votes represented only a little over 2% of the total 498 total in the House that year.

TABLE 6.5 Senate and House Roll Call Votes on Legislative Provisions With Explicit or Manifest Family Content, Frequencies and Percentages Relative to Total Roll Call Votes, House and Senate, by Year

	Senate		House	
	N	%	N	%
1983				
Total roll call votes	371		498	
Votes/explicit family content	10	3	12	2
1985				
Total roll call votes	381		439	
Votes/explicit family content	13	3	27	6
1991				
Total roll call votes	289		444	
Votes/explicit family content	11	4	24	5
1993				
Total roll call votes	395		597	
Votes/explicit family content	32	8	53	9
1995				
Total roll call votes	613		867	
Votes/explicit family content	66	11	74	9
1996				
Total roll call votes	306		454	
Votes/explicit family content	29	10	75	17
1997				
Total roll call votes	298		633	
Votes/explicit family content	40	13	56	9

Thus it can be seen that beginning with 1993, the proportion of family-related roll call votes increased in both the House and Senate relative to the total number of roll call votes in the two bodies over the earlier years of the observational period, suggesting that more family-related solutions were constructed to address family problems—or that more family conditions were constructed as needing such solutions in the 1990s than in the 1980s, as hypothesized. Readers also should note how the two bodies differed, both in terms of the number of roll call votes taken each year and in the relative share of their votes that were family related.

■ Summary and Conclusions

What can be said about House and Senate roll call votes as constructed solutions to family problems? For one, many more family conditions were constructed as problems in need of solutions in the 1990s than in the earlier period, as hypothesized. Comparing 1993-95 with 1983-85, votes were taken on over three times as many family-related measures in the House in 1993-95 ($N = 127$) than in 1983-85 ($N = 39$), and in the Senate, on over four times as many measures, 98 in 1993-95, than in 1983-85 ($N = 23$).

Not only were more votes taken on more measures related to families in 1993-95 than in 1983-85, but the nature of the family problems such measures addressed differed markedly, also as hypothesized. For example, in the Senate, votes on school prayer were taken in 1983 but not in 1993 or in any subsequent data year, whereas several votes were taken on measures related to FMLA in 1993 but not in 1983 or 1985. (In 1990, President Bush vetoed such a measure.) Nor were problems such as Medicare/Medicaid funding and health insurance as prominent in the 1980s as they were in the 1990s. The same is true of most of the income security measures: welfare reform, social security, and unemployment insurance.

Similarly, in the House, solutions to problems in the area of child and family welfare, except for the Child Protection Act in 1983, were not constructed until 1995, when protection from government agencies was constructed as a solution to problems involving family privacy. Child support enforcement was constructed as a solution to a family problem in 1983 but not in 1985, whereas in 1995, it was the object of votes on three separate measures. Domestic abuse, child sexual assault, and sex offenses in general, which also were not constructed as problems that required governmental solutions in 1983-85, were so constructed in 1993 and each data year thereafter. Abortion, though prominently constructed as a problem in the 1980s, did not permeate areas such as defense and foreign affairs as it did in the 1990s. In this respect, the 1990s were more extreme and restrictive than the 1980s with regard to abortion.

Breast cancer, cervical cancer, assisted suicide, partial birth abortions, and domestic partnerships all constituted problems for which federal solutions were sought in the 1990s but not in the 1980s. The same pertains in the housing area, although in 1983, the House did vote on some housing measures to remedy problems encountered by families in this area. A similar statement may be made about votes in the areas of income security and taxes, the House voting on many more measures in these two categories in 1993-95 than in 1983-85.

With respect to the construction of policy solutions over the observational period as a whole, of all those related to families, none were more persistent than the restrictions placed on abortion as a reproductive choice for women with implications for the reproduction and membership functions of families. Such restrictions permeated policy measures in the areas of defense, foreign affairs, and income security vis-à-vis welfare reform (and even policy measures in its own category—health) involving Medicaid and insurance plans for federal employees. From this, it may be inferred that congressional members' understanding and knowledge of family problems in need of solutions centered in large part around the abortion issue, perhaps in part because of the mobilized efforts of groups organized for and against abortion that commanded congressional attention. However, although abortion remained the most persistent of all the problems for which congressional solutions were constructed over the observational period, those pertaining to welfare reform were perhaps as or even more pervasive in terms of their reach into areas not always associated with welfare: education, employment, child care, child and family welfare, housing, health, and so on.

Many family-related roll call votes represented alternative scenarios of family problems and their solutions, each with its own set of facts, value judgments, and emotions (Edelman, 1975). Examples include votes on the gag rule in 1991 prohibiting federal funds from being used to provide information about abortion, and votes in 1993 on a measure calling for the revocation of the gag rule; votes in 1993 calling for both the expansion of the EITC and cuts in the EITC; votes in 1985 to create an alternative minimum tax and in 1995, votes to eliminate the alternative minimum tax; votes in 1995 to establish federal control of the entitlement status of welfare benefits, and in that same session, votes to eliminate the entitlement status of welfare benefits through block grants to states and time limits on benefits. Also in 1995, there were votes allowing abortions for military personnel and their dependents at overseas military bases if women paid for the procedure themselves, votes to prohibit abortions at overseas military facilities unless the life of the woman is endangered, and votes on a child tax credit of $500 for families with incomes up to $200,000 and another calling for a child tax credit of $500 for families with incomes up to $100,000, and so on.

Many votes were reflective of some of the cultural changes and technological developments impinging on family life in recent years. Reflective of such cultural change, of course, was the vote on DOMA, which also was unique in terms of its subject matter at the federal level, because laws pertaining to marriage and divorce generally are the province of the states. Votes on breast cancer research, fetal tissue research, assisted suicide, family privacy protections, partial birth abortions, and so on, were reflective of technological developments. Many of these latter measures mirrored not only the growing influence of technology on the kinds of problems that families were seen as experiencing in the 1990s for which congressional solutions were being sought but also concerns about the moral implications of some of these measures, fetal tissue research being an example.

Other measures such as longer hospital stays for mothers of newborns, domestic violence prevention, home health care, breast cancer research, and related measures were undoubtedly attributable to the increased presence of women in Congress and in politics and society in general. Unpublished data from earlier analyses showed gender to be a factor on House votes pertaining to family and medical leave, abortion, budgetary measures, tax and spending bills, and welfare overhaul in 1985, 1990, 1993, and 1995 (Zimmerman, 1993a; Zimmerman & Gager, 1997). Their influence was not sufficient, however, to counteract the strong rejection of solutions involving fetal tissue research in addressing Parkinson's disease or restrictions on the reproductive choices of women, just as the increased activism of gays and lesbians in the political arena was not sufficient to defeat DOMA.

Overall, House and Senate roll call votes in the areas of health care such as minimum hospital stays for mothers of newborns, the portability of health insurance, a ban on insurance coverage exclusions based on preexisting health conditions, and some home health benefits, though positive and important, were relatively modest measures, especially when viewed against the health reform efforts of 1993 and 1994 that never came to fruition (Zimmerman, 1995a). Thus, solutions did not extend to the larger problems of health care financing and affordability in the later years of the 1990s, unless cuts in Medicare and Medicaid spending could be construed as solutions to the budget problems of the federal government, but certainly not of families.

As actions, congressional roll call votes reflected the attitudes that gave impetus to them, both the attitudes held by individual congressional members and those of their constituencies. Measures such as student aid and loans and welfare reform reflected attitudes embedded in Americans' cognitive structures with regard to independence, achievement, opportunity, and personal and family responsibility—and also the requirements of the new global economy. They also reflected a pullback from universality as a guiding principle for family policy, especially as it pertained to welfare reform, and the continuing devolution of responsibility for meeting the needs of families from federal to state governments—and to families themselves. They as well reflected an incremental, emergent approach to the construction of highly specific and particularistic solutions to family problems that in their entirety constituted the nation's family policy in the 1990s. To some extent, both the retreat from universality and the shift away from central to lower levels of government were in keeping with postmodern trends in society at large, as manifested in the blurring of policy solutions— adoption tax credits, for example—pertaining to both adoption and taxes. By the same token, measures designed to reinforce social and behavioral norms with regard to two-parent heterosexual families, personal and family responsibility, and abortion can be seen as efforts to counter such trends, although in the case of abortion, the blurring of policy solutions is abundant, as, for example, the joining of abortion with foreign and defense policy and other seemingly unrelated measures.

Whether the solutions that lawmakers constructed during the 1990s represented progress or regression vis-à-vis remedies to family problems depends on how such solutions are appraised—whether in the case of welfare reform, for example, the problem is constructed as welfare dependency or the persistence of child poverty in the United States. If appraised in terms of the former, votes on welfare reform in the House and Senate in 1995 and 1996 could be constructed as needed solutions. If appraised in terms of the latter, however, then votes on welfare reform together with votes on tax measures favoring higher-income over lower-income families would not be constructed as solutions but as problems in need of solutions. Although family-related votes clearly increased over time relative to all the roll call votes taken each data year, suggesting a shift from a more passive government role in terms of families to a more activist one (albeit conservative in both instances), the number and share of explicit or manifest family legislation remained small. If some of the more implicit family measures (e.g., minimum wage and some education and housing measures) had not been included in the analysis, the proportion of family-related roll call votes in both the House and Senate would have been even smaller. For those who worry that government is assuming too large a role in family life, this could be reassuring, but for those who worry that government is doing too little to support family life in more general ways, the findings from the analysis may be disheartening.

Some may fault the analysis on which these conclusions are based because it does not include each and every year of the 1980s and 1990s or because of the ambiguities in the classification of some measures or because some measures were more implicit than explicit with regard to their family content. Despite these limitations, however, the analysis sheds light on the kinds of solutions that lawmakers constructed to remedy problems in relation to families in selected years during the 1980s and 1990s. In addition, the analysis provides comparative data on which to base claims as to the expansion of family policy as a domain of policy, practice, and study in the future.

Although congressional roll call votes as actions related to families in the 1980s and 1990s may be suggestive of the attitudes that gave impetus to them, analysis of such votes could not reveal the attitudes that were expressed in the construction of family problems and solutions to them as represented by such votes. How do attitudes manifest themselves in the construction of policy solutions for families? To answer this question, the next chapter focuses on the 1996 congressional debates over DOMA. But first, I have provided some questions for you, the reader, to think about in relation to the federal solutions that were constructed to family problems as presented in *this* chapter.

■ Some Questions for Your Reflection and Discussion

1. What were Ronald Reagan's attitudes about the role of government in relation to families?
2. What were George Bush's attitudes about the role of government in relation to families?
3. What were Bill Clinton's attitudes about the role of government in relation to families?
4. What attitudes were embedded in congressional votes on welfare reform?
5. What attitudes were embedded in congressional votes on abortion?
6. What attitudes were embedded in congressional votes on education?
7. What attitudes were embedded in congressional votes on health care?
8. How did congressional votes in the 1990s differ from congressional votes in the 1980s and 1991?
9. Describe how congressional votes reflected the attitudes expressed in the surveys cited in Chapter 5.

And now to the congressional debates over DOMA.

▪ Note

1. To identify the measures on which House and Senate members voted each data year that related to families, the descriptive summaries of all measures that appeared in the Congressional Roll Call in 1983, 1985, 1991, 1993, 1995, 1996, and 1997 were scanned for their family content. The text of those that met the criteria established for inclusion in the analysis was typed onto 8½ × 11″ worksheets by data year. Each measure on which a vote was taken was then classified according to its substantive focus, such as child care, domestic abuse, and so on, by year, on separate worksheets. If a vote was taken on a child care measure, for example, it was classified accordingly and recorded with an X for that year and also for every other year in which votes on other measures in that category were taken. The analysis of House and Senate roll call votes on family-related measures in 1983 and 1985—which had been done earlier—provided a basis for comparing such votes with those taken in 1993 and 1995, 10 years later.

Because categories were comprised of several items, subcategories were developed that consisted of related measures within the larger categories. Both the subcategories and the measures that comprised them were then alphabetized to avoid duplicate entries and to facilitate a frequency analysis of the votes by category. Classification of measures followed their classification in the summaries. Thus, family housing measures that appeared in conjunction with defense and the armed forces, for example, were classified under defense rather than housing, in keeping with their presentation in the published summaries. With individual measures recorded down the left side and the years across at the top, the worksheets formed a grid. The grid allowed for the identification of those measures related to families on which roll call votes were taken in the House and Senate, separately within their respective categories and subcategories by year. These measures in effect provided a basis for inferring the attitudes that were embedded in congressional members' cognitive structures by way of family problems and shed light on the kinds of solutions that were constructed in addressing them in the early to mid-1980s and most of the 1990s.

Following these procedures, and to answer the study's questions, frequencies and percentages were obtained for the provisions that included family terminology or were manifest in the legislative summaries, by category and year, for both the Senate and House. Such procedures allowed for comparisons to be made among categories of roll call votes over time and thus for conclusions to be drawn about changes in constructions of family problems and solutions to them. Finally, to determine the relative importance of such constructions over the entire observational period, percentages were obtained for all the family-related measures on which roll call votes were taken in the House and Senate separately relative to *all* the other roll call votes in the two bodies for each year.

CHAPTER 7

The Defense of Marriage Act
The Construction of a Solution or a Problem?

Readers will recall from Chapter 6 that the Defense of Marriage Act (DOMA) was one of the family measures on which Congress voted in the 105th Congress. If you, the reader, might wonder how attitudes about families and government are embedded in constructions of family problems and legislative solutions to them, and how language is used in such constructions, you need look no further than the congressional debates over DOMA. This chapter is based on a content analysis of these House and Senate debates that took place in the House on July 11 and July 12 and in the Senate on September 10 and September 11, 1996[1] to uncover the themes that were emphasized in the debates. The attitudes embedded in congresspersons' constructions of same-sex marriage (Kohler & Zimmerman, 1999) are the subject of this chapter.

DOMA, enacted in 1996, defines marriage as a "legal union between one man and one woman as husband and wife" and grants states the authority to ignore same-sex marriages performed in other states. Before 1996, the sex of persons to be married was not specified. Enacted by wide margins in both houses of Congress, the passage of DOMA reflected the overwhelming acceptance of existing institutional arrangements with respect to heterosexual marriage on the part of the nation's lawmakers.

DOMA was important because it was a constructed response to challenges to institutional norms with regard to heterosexual marriage as the foundation of family life that growing numbers of people in the United States were willing to contest. It also was important because it created the circumstances for the first of its kind congressional debate. Indeed, it was the first time that marriage as a topic had been debated and voted on at the federal level by elected officials from every state and congressional district in the country. The *debates* over DOMA, as distinguished from DOMA itself, were important because they reflected the attitudes that congressional members held about marriage—same-sex and heterosexual—and the roles of state and federal governments in the regulation

The Social Change Model

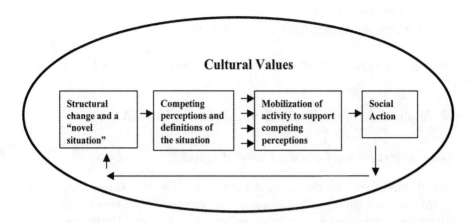

Figure 7.1. Social Change Model
SOURCE: Zimmerman, S. L. (1995). *Understanding family policy: Theories and applications.* (2nd Ed.). Thousand Oaks, CA: Sage.

of marriage. Thus, although the passage of DOMA represented congressional acceptance of same-sex marriage as the problem and DOMA as its solution, the debates over DOMA revealed the attitudes of congressional members that accounted for congressional acceptance of DOMA.

Discussion of the debates over DOMA is based on a social change model developed by Zimmerman (1982, 1988a, 1992a, 1995a, 1997a) and grounded in the work of Smelser and Halpern (1978). The model, as a representation of the processes involved in social change, offers a way of illustrating the attitudes that underlie the construction of policy solutions to family problems within the context of social change.

■ A Social Change Model

The social change model as depicted in Figure 7.1 is comprised of four process components that interact with each other in a repetitive fashion within the context of a society's cultural values. These four broad process components include:

1. A novel situation, that is, the emergence of something new and different in the society, like same-sex couple relationships

2. Different perceptions and definitions of the situation as articulated by different moral entrepreneurs who try to persuade others to accept their definition of the novel situation, like advocates for and against same-sex marriage

3. The organization and mobilization of groups that press for political action in support of their perceptions and definition of the situation, like gay rights groups and the Christian Coalition

4. The social action, which here pertains to DOMA

For a more complete presentation of the model, please see Notes 1, 2, and 3.[2]

■ Application of the Social Change Model to DOMA

The Context for the Debates: Cultural Values

Following the social change model outlined in Figure 7.1, the debates over DOMA occurred in the United States within the context of a larger debate over conflicting cultural values about the institution of marriage. The dominant cultural values structuring marriage in the United States are grounded in Judeo-Christian ideology. Historically, biblical and Talmudic teachings against homosexuality have been used to legitimate the prohibition of same-sex marriages in the United States (Tully, 1994). Although marriage laws in 47 state jurisdictions did not specify the sexes of the persons to be married until 1996, state courts have consistently concluded that marriage must be between members of opposite sexes, often referring to religious texts to support their decisions. As an example, in the 1971 *Baker v. Nelson* case, the Minnesota Supreme Court ruled that marriage as an institution, with the purposes of procreation and the rearing of children, was "as old as the book of Genesis." The Superior Court of the District of Columbia similarly cited passages from the Old and New Testaments in ruling against two men who petitioned for a marriage license (*Dean v. District of Columbia*) in 1990 (Eskridge, 1996).

Although the values and beliefs of many religious groups in the United States have led them to ban same-sex marriages, the heterosexual basis of marriage has been challenged as more mainstream Jewish and Christian faiths have debated, endorsed, or performed marriage services for same-sex couples. Religious practices have no direct effect on the legality of same-sex marriage in the United States, but the different cultural values endorsed by different religious communities are indicative of the cultural values and attitudes that surface in public debate and political discourse on matters related to same-sex marriage and marriage and family.

The Novel Situation

The novel situation in the context of the present discussion consisted of all the changes that have occurred in recent decades challenging existing social arrangements with respect to heterosexual marriage. Among such changes are domestic partnership laws enacted in the 1990s that provide rights to gay and lesbian couples that often parallel those provided to married couples. Many municipalities, universities, and private sector companies, for example, have granted certain legal protections to same sex or unmarried heterosexual couples who have lived together for a certain amount of time and signed documents of declaration (Tully, 1994), such measures enjoying greater acceptance at the local than at the state level, however. Only two states—Vermont and Hawaii—have extended domestic partnership legislation that covers all state employees. In April 2000, Vermont voted its approval of marriagelike civil unions for gay couples and offered marriage benefits to them, the first state in the country to do so.

The movement to legalize same-sex marriage that began in the 1970s preceded domestic partnership legislation. However, after the defeat of several lawsuits, same sex marriage became a low-priority issue for most gay rights organizations, due largely to the younger, more radical, leadership of many gay rights groups; organizational reluctance to infringe on a sexually free gay subculture; and organizational commitment to a number of other rights protection issues (Eskridge, 1996). It was not until the mid- to late 1980s that same-sex marriage returned as a major advocacy issue. Even today, some advocates within the gay rights movement, particularly feminist advocates, oppose legalizing same-sex marriage, arguing that because marriage is a patriarchal institution, it is inappropriate as a goal for gay rights groups.

The legal case that precipitated DOMA was the Hawaii lawsuit *Baehr v. Lewin* (1993) (subsequently *Baehr v. Mike*; currently *Baehr v. Anderson*). The *Baehr* lawsuit was filed in 1991, after the state of Hawaii refused to issue marriage licenses to one gay and two lesbian couples. Although the lawsuit was similar in content to several predecessors (e.g., *Adams v. Howerton*, 1980; *Baker v. Nelson*, 1971; *Jones v. Hallahan*, 1973; and *Singer v. Hara*, 1974), it fared differently in court. After a lower court initially ruled against the couples, the state Supreme Court in 1993 declared that the state's denial of marriage licenses to the petitioning couples was a violation of Hawaii's constitutional prohibition of sex discrimination and required Hawaii to prove a "compelling state interest" to justify its discriminatory practice (Dupuis, 1995). In 1996, a lower court ruled that the state had failed to prove such an interest and therefore had to permit same-sex couples to marry (Lambda Legal Defense and Education Fund, 1997-1998). The state subsequently appealed the decision.

Although DOMA could not directly affect the outcome of *Baehr v. Mike*, congressional opponents of same-sex marriage introduced it because they were fearful that if same-sex marriage were to be legalized in Hawaii, states throughout the country would be required to recognize it. Their fear was based on Article IV of the U.S. Constitution, the full faith and credit clause, which states that every state must recognize the "public acts, records, and judicial proceedings of every other state" (Art. IV, §3). Under the guise of protecting a person's vested liberty interest (here a person's freedom to marry), other legal experts argued that the Fourteenth Amendment's due process clause also could be used to require states to recognize legally performed same-sex marriages (Henson, 1993).

Mobilization of Activity

The introduction of DOMA was an outcome of both the Hawaii lawsuit and the mobilization of individuals and groups in favor of or in opposition to the legalization of same-sex marriages. Moral entrepreneurs—individuals and groups who defined and interpreted the novel situation with regard to same-sex marriage to their constituencies—organized new advocacy groups and mobilized existing groups to pressure congressional members to pass or defeat DOMA. Ralph Reed, who at the time headed the Christian Coalition, and Gary Bauer, the chair of the Family Research Council, issued statements in support of DOMA and used their political connections with certain congressional leaders to lobby for its passage. Other mobilized religious organizations that opposed same-sex marriage included, most notably, the Mormon and Roman Catholic Churches. The Mormon Church went so far as to file several unsuccessful requests to become a co-defendant with the state of Hawaii in the *Baehr* case (Dupuis, 1995; Partners Task Force for Gay and Lesbian Couples, 1998).

In opposition, mobilized gay rights, human rights, libertarian, and feminist groups pressed for DOMA's defeat, which was a particular priority for gay rights organizations whose efforts were spearheaded by the involvement of the Lambda Legal Defense and Education Fund in the *Baehr* case. In addition, new advocacy organizations were organized to fight on behalf of legalized same-sex marriage after Hawaii's 1993 Supreme Court ruling. Individuals associated with Lambda constructed the Marriage Project to "coordinate the legal and political groundwork" to attain legalized same-sex marriage (Lambda Legal Defense and Education Fund, 1997-1998). As of 1998, the Marriage Project was supported by nearly 50 civil rights and other professional organizations, including the American Civil Liberties Union (ACLU), the National Organization for Women (NOW), and the Human Rights Campaign. It also was supported by nearly 20 religious organizations that perform ceremonial same-sex marriages, including the Unitarian Universalist Association, the Society of Friends (Quakers), the Union of American Hebrew Congregations (Reform Jewish synagogues), and several other religious groups formed specifically for gay, lesbian, and bisexual congregations (Eskridge, 1996).

The Social Action: The Vote on DOMA

After extensive debate, a vote was taken on DOMA; the vote represented the social action component of the social change model. The vote was 342 votes for and 67 against DOMA in the House, and 85 for and 14 votes against it in the Senate, support for DOMA clearly crossing party lines. However, although Republicans almost unanimously supported the bill (224 to 1 in the House, 53 to 0 in the Senate), Democrats were more divided (118 to 65 in the House and 32 to 14 in the Senate). Thus, although opposition to the bill came almost exclusively from Democrats, a greater number of congressional Democrats supported the measure than opposed it. President Clinton signed the bill into law on September 21, 1996. Although the passage of DOMA represented congressional acceptance of the problem and its solution as proponents constructed them, the debates over DOMA reflected the attitudes underlying congressional acceptance of DOMA and also congressional attitudes about same-sex marriage. What were some of the attitudes expressed during these debates? How did such attitudes surface in the construction of the problems and solutions associated with DOMA? And given their different ideological orientations, did Republicans and Democrats differ in their constructions of the problem and its solution, and if so, how? Similarly, given differences in the composition and rules of the two bodies, did House and Senate members construct the problem of same-sex marriage differently, and if so, how?

To answer these questions, as mentioned earlier, a content analysis was undertaken of the debates as they appeared in the *Congressional Record;* a transcript of the debates was obtained from Thomas Legislative Information, the online congressional library. For a more complete explanation of how the analysis was conducted, please see Notes 2 and 3.[3] The 12 pattern codes that emerged from the analysis represented the four themes that were emphasized in the debates: (1) marriage and/or family; (2) the roles of state and federal governments in legislating marriage; (3) the rights of gay and lesbian individuals; and (4) attitudes toward gay and lesbian persons. A list and brief explanation of each of the 12 codes appears in Table 7.1. These pattern codes or themes became the basis of other analyses that followed and are described in Note 3.

What did the data show?

■ Findings

In all, 61 of the 435 members of the House (14%) and 30 of the 100 members of the Senate (30%) participated in the debates: 28 Republicans and 33 Democrats in the House and 14 Republicans and 16 Democrats in the Senate. Fourteen of the participants in the House were women (23%) as were five of the participants in the debates in the Senate (17%), which, in both instances, exceeded their proportion in the House and Senate in 1996 (11% and 8%, respectively).

Marriage and Family Life

The most commonly mentioned theme evoked during the debates by both Republicans and Democrats in both houses of Congress pertained to marriage and family life. Typically, when members evoked the theme of marriage and family, they connected it to marriage as an institution as commonly known in the United States. However, the attitudes that Democrats and Republicans in the House and Senate conveyed in evoking the theme were notably different. These differences were captured in five subthemes:

TABLE 7.1 Substantive Themes Emphasized in Debates Over DOMA, Pattern Codes, and Their Descriptions

Substantive Themes	Pattern Codes	Descriptions
Marriage/family life	Foundation of society	Marriage and/or family life are foundation of society
	Same-sex marriage threat to marriage itself and society	Gay/lesbian partnerships or same-sex marriage threatens society and/or institution of marriage
	Same-sex marriage not moral equivalent	Gay/lesbian partnerships are morally inferior to heterosexual relationships and/or marriage
	Same-sex relationships no threat to marriage	Gay/lesbian partnerships do not threaten marriage or society
	Marriage is private/personal	The decision whether or not to marry should be left to the parties involved; marriage is a personal decision
The roles of state and federal governments in legislating marriage	DOMA defends states' rights	DOMA defends states' rights to make own policies regarding gay/lesbian marriage
	DOMA usurps states' rights/authority	DOMA usurps right of states to make own policies regarding same-sex marriage; represents inappropriate federal intrusion into domain of law reserved for states
	DOMA redundant legislation, unnecessary federal intervention	Federal intervention unnecessary in this issue because states already have the right and authority to set their own policies regarding same-sex marriage; or because timing is premature—no state has legalized same-sex marriage
	DOMA offers states federal protections	DOMA provides uniform definition of marriage, thereby preventing the expenditure of federal funds on spousal benefits for same-sex marital partners
Gay/lesbian rights	Equal rights	DOMA discriminates against gays and lesbians; denies them their rights
Attitudes toward gays and lesbians	Negative attitudes	DOMA is based on and/or promotes negative attitudes toward gay and lesbian persons

TABLE 7.2   Themes Emphasized by Congressional Democrats and Republicans
Who Participated in Debates over DOMA (*N* = 91), Frequencies and
Percentages[a]

Themes	Democrats (N = 50)		Republicans (N = 41)	
	N	%	N	%
Marriage foundation of society (*N* = 24)	5	21	19	79
Same-sex marriage a threat to marriage and/or society (*N* = 20)	3	15	17	85
Same-sex marriage not moral equivalent of heterosexual marriage (*N* = 14)	2	14	12	86
Same-sex marriage does not represent a threat to heterosexual marriage (*N* = 23)	22	96	1	4
Marriage is private/personal (*N* = 7)	7	100	—	—
DOMA defends states' rights (*N* = 28)	3	11	25	89
DOMA usurps states' rights (*N* = 27)	27	100	—	—
DOMA redundant, unnecessary (*N* = 26)	26	100	—	—
DOMA offers states federal protections (*N* = 17)	2	12	15	88
Equal rights/gays and lesbians (*N* = 31)	30	97	1	3
DOMA based on and fosters negative attitudes toward gays/lesbians (*N* = 30)	29	97	1	3

a. Percentages are based on total number of Democrats and Republicans participating in the debates over DOMA who emphasized particular themes,, *not* the total number of Democrats and Republicans serving in the House and Senate in 1996.

1. Marriage is the foundation of society
2. Same-sex marriage is a threat to the institution of marriage
3. Same-sex marriage is not the moral equivalent of heterosexual marriage
4. Same-sex marriage is no threat to the institution of marriage
5. Marriage is personal

Here it is useful to point out that the subthemes dealing with threat and no threat to marriage represented binary opposites. Binary opposites, it will be recalled, refer to ideas and words that define a thing by that which it is not. Therefore, the subtheme "same-sex marriage is a threat to the institution of marriage" was defined by the opposite subtheme, "same-sex marriage is not a threat to the institution of marriage."

Marriage is the foundation of society. This subtheme was evoked primarily by DOMA proponents who emphasized the role of marriage and families in maintaining society as a whole during the debates. As Table 7.2 shows, almost all those who emphasized this subtheme were Republicans (80%).

Representative Steve Largent's (R-Oklahoma) statement is illustrative of this subtheme:

I would just like to say . . . the family is the cornerstone, in fact, the foundation of our society, and at the core of that foundation is the institution of marriage. . . . There is absolutely nothing that we do that is more important than protecting our families and protecting the institution of marriage.

Senator Phil Gramm (R-Texas) similarly claimed,

There is no moment in recorded history when the traditional family was not recognized and sanctioned by a civilized society—it is the oldest institution that exists. . . . So when some question what, 50 years from now, we are going to think about those [who] are defending the traditional family today, I would just remind them that the traditional family has stood as the seminal institution which has formed the foundation for civilized society for some 5,000 years. . . . We are here today because the traditional family is important to America.

The attitudes that Representative William Lipinski, a Democrat from Illinois, expressed were similar to those expressed by his Republican colleagues:

Marriage, no matter what your belief, is a sacred act. . . . Families are built on it and values are passed on through it. In our current age, where the sanctity of marriage is constantly being compromised, I feel that we must seize this rare opportunity to strengthen it.

Other Democrats, however, such as Senator Russ Feingold from Wisconsin, who also evoked this subtheme, countered the claims of his congressional colleagues when he said,

The institution of marriage is a vital foundation of any ordered society, including ours. However, . . . it is important amid all the talk about the need to defend marriage, that we look at the context in which this legislation is brought before this body [the lawsuit in the state of Hawaii]—having reviewed the arguments, I have reached the conclusion that this legislation is neither necessary nor appropriate for the federal government to enact at this time.

Same-sex relationships threaten marriage and are not its moral equivalent. Members often connected the subtheme "same-sex relationships pose a threat to the institution of marriage" to the subtheme "same-sex marriage is not the moral equivalent of heterosexual marriage," indicative of how some congressional members constructed the problem of same-sex marriage. When speaking of the threat that same-sex marriage and Hawaii's *Baehr v. Lewin* case posed for the institution of marriage, family life, and society itself, some also connected the threat subtheme to the belief that marriage and family were society's critical base, depicting homosexuality and same-sex marriage as morally inferior to heterosexual marriage.

As Table 7.2 shows, most of those who said same-sex relationships were a threat to heterosexual marital relationships were Republicans (85%), as were those who said that gay and lesbian relationships were morally inferior to marriage (86%). The following comments not only reveal the connections that were made between these two subthemes and hence of how the problem was constructed by those who emphasized them, but they also reveal the use of language and metaphors in the attempt to arouse the fears and emotions of congressional colleagues during the debates:

> [Same-sex marriage] is an issue that is being forced on us directly by assault by the homosexual extremists to attack the institution of marriage. . . . The very foundations of our society are in danger of being burned. The flames of hedonism, the flames of narcissism, the flames of self-centered morality are licking at the very foundations of society, the family unit. . . . What more does it take, my colleagues, to wake up and see that this is an issue being shouted at us by extremists intent, bent on forcing a tortured view of morality on the rest of the country. . . . Enough is enough. We must maintain a moral foundation, an ethical foundation for our families and ultimately for the United States of America. (Representative Robert Barr, R-Georgia)

Using terms such as *perversion* and *perversity* to construct what he saw as an undesirable condition or problem, Representative Tom Coburn (R-Oklahoma) also intended to evoke such emotion when he said,

> The real debate is about homosexuality and whether or not we sanction homosexuality in this country. . . . [My constituents believe that] homosexuality is immoral, that it is based on perversion, that it is based on lust. . . . It is time to say that homosexuality should not be sanctioned on an equal level with heterosexuality. . . . We hear about diversity but we do not hear about perversity, and I think that we should not be afraid to talk about the very issues that are at the core of this. . . . The fact is, no society has lived through the transition to homosexuality and the perversion with which it lives and what it brought forth.

Although the theme of marriage and family life was emphasized by Republicans more than Democrats, the attitudes that Senator Robert Byrd, a conservative Democrat from West Virginia, conveyed in his statement emphasizing this theme were similar to those of his Republican colleagues. He argued,

> To insist that male-male or female-female relationships must have the same status as the marriage relationship is more than unwise, it is patently absurd. . . . Out of same-sex relationships no children can result. . . . Emotional bonding oftentimes does not take place, and many such relationships do not result in the establishment of families as society universally interprets that term. Indeed, as history teaches us, too often in the past when cultures waxed casual about the uniqueness and sanctity of the marriage commitment between men and women, those cultures have been shown to be in decline.

TABLE 7.3   Themes Emphasized by House and Senate Members in Debates Over
DOMA, Frequencies, and Percentages[a]

Themes	House & Senate (N = 91)		House (N = 61)		Senate (N = 30)	
	N	%	N	%	N	%
Marriage/foundation of society	24	27	13	21	11	37
DOMA threatens marriage/society	20	22	13	21	7	23
Same-sex marriage not moral equivalent of marriage	14	15	10	16	4	13
Same-sex marriage no threat to marriage/society	23	25	18	30	5	17
Marriage is personal/private	7	8	6	10	1	3
DOMA defends states' rights	28	31	12	20	16	53
DOMA usurps states' rights	27	29	19	31	8	27
DOMA redundant legislation, unnecessary	26	28	17	28	9	30
DOMA offers states federal protections	17	19	9	15	8	27
Equal rights, gays and lesbians	31	34	8	27	23	38
DOMA based on and fosters negative attitudes toward gays and lesbians	30	33	24	39	6	20

a. Percentages are based on number of House and Senate members who participated in the debates
over DOMA and emphasized different themes. The first column shows frequencies and percentages for both House and Senate members together. The second and third columns show frequencies and percentages for House and Senate members separately. Despite small Ns in many
instances, percentages were calculated to show relative importance of the different themes for
House and Senate members participating in the debates.

Same-sex relationships do not threaten marriage. Members who opposed
DOMA also referred to marriage and family life in their statements but challenged
the claim that same-sex marriage threatened the institution of marriage or society
as a whole. Of those who took this position, almost all were Democrats (96%) (as
shown in Table 7.2), House members evoking this theme more than senators, as
can be seen in Table 7.3.

Those who spoke to it often contrasted same-sex marriage with other family
problems and issues. Typically, they maintained that divorce, domestic violence,
substance abuse, unemployment, and extramarital sexual relationships posed a
greater threat to family life than same-sex marriage in arguing against DOMA:

> The truth that we know, which today's exercise ignores, is that marriages fall apart
> in the United States, not because men and women are under siege by a mass move-
> ment of men marrying men or women marrying women. Marriages fall apart
> because men and women don't stay married. The real threat comes from the at-
> titudes of many men and women married to each other and from the relation-

ships of people of the opposite sex, not the same sex. (Senator John Kerry, D-Massachusetts)

Representative Barney Frank, also a Democrat from Massachusetts, personalized the debate when he challenged House members to explain how his relationship with his same-sex partner constituted a threat to the institution of marriage and marital relationships:

> The most preposterous assertion of all [is] that marriage is under attack. . . . Mr. Speaker, whose marriage does it threaten? It does not threaten the gentleman's marriage. It does not threaten anybody's marriage. . . . The argument that it threatens the institution of marriage ought to be made by someone in an institution because it has no logical basis whatsoever.

Representative Steve Gunderson (R-Wisconsin), another openly gay congressional member in the 104th Congress, similarly argued,

> If marriage is at risk in this country, and it may be—there are more real factors at the heart of this problem. May I suggest that alcohol abuse, spousal abuse, and even Sunday football are far more likely to destroy marriage. Perhaps if people really meant it when they said their marital vows, marriage would be more stable. Perhaps if people were more willing to pursue marriage counseling, when necessary, the institution of marriage would be better off.

Marriage is personal. The final subtheme of the marriage and family life theme, "marriage is personal," was emphasized exclusively by Democrats and by Representatives more than senators (see Tables 7.2 and 7.3). Members who evoked this subtheme generally contended that marriage and family law was not the domain of the federal government:

> It is not right for this Congress to step in and intrude into the private relationships and the most personal decisions of our constituencies. Love and commitment can exist between a man and a woman and it can and does exist between men and between women. (Representative Patrick Kennedy, D-Massachusetts)

The Roles of State and Federal Governments

A second major thematic topic central to the debates over DOMA related to the roles that state and federal governments should assume in legislating marriage. Concerned about the impact of the potential legalization of same-sex marriage in Hawaii on other states and the federal government, members expressed concerns about the constitutionality of DOMA, particularly in relation to the Full Faith and Credit Clause. But again, although emphasizing the same theme, the attitudes members conveyed were different. The four subthemes that emerged within this larger thematic category were (1) defending states' rights; (2) usurping states' rights; (3) unnecessary federal intervention; and (4) federal protection against fiscal demands, with defending states' rights and usurping states' rights again representing binary opposites.

DOMA defends states' rights. Members who interpreted DOMA as a defense of states' rights typically referred to the potential impact of the Hawaii lawsuit on states' rights via the Full Faith and Credit Clause. These members constructed DOMA as a preventive strategy for ensuring the ability of states to enact laws banning same-sex marriage and relieving states from having to recognize marriages among same-sex couples returning to their home states after legally marrying in Hawaii. Republicans evoked this theme more than Democrats and senators more than representatives (see Tables 7.2 and 7.3). Illustrative were such statements as follows:

> The Defense of Marriage Act says that states should determine their own policy. This legislation is consistent with the need to return power and decision-making to the states where it rightfully belongs. (Representative John Ensign, R-Nevada)

> The bill is very clear in what it does. . . . It preserves the states' rights, so that one state, like the Supreme Court of the State of Hawaii, cannot mandate upon another state its interpretation of what marriage should be. (Representative Scott McInnis, R-Colorado)

> By defining the term [marriage], Congress is protecting the individual sovereignty of each state. No state will now be required to recognize a same-sex marriage—and no state will be prevented from recognizing a same-sex marriage. Passing the Defense of Marriage Act is the surest method of preserving the will and prerogative of each and every state. (Senator Frank Murkowski, R-Alaska)

DOMA usurps states' rights. Opposition to the proposition that DOMA defended states' rights came from congressional members who argued that DOMA represented an assault on states' rights and an improper extension of federal authority into the domain of marriage and family law that historically had been the purview of the states. This argument was advanced by Democrats exclusively (see Table 7.2), a somewhat surprising pattern, given that states' rights issues are more commonly associated with conservatives who are more likely to be Republicans than Democrats. Illustrative of the attitudes embedded in this subtheme were the following statements:

> H.R. 3396 [DOMA] is an unnecessary intrusion into the State domain of family law. It tears at the fabric of our Constitution. Historically, states have the primary authority to regulate marriage based on the 10th Amendment of the Constitution. The Supreme Court has supported this constitutional right. . . . Many on the other side of the aisle have been vocal and unceasing in their support for reversing the flow of power away from Washington and back to the states. Well, the laws governing marriage are traditionally and constitutionally under the authority of the states. If there is any area of law to which states can lay a claim to exclusive authority, it is the field of family relations. How can someone reconcile being for states'

[sic] rights while at the same time taking away a basic, constitutional right given to states by the Framers of our Constitution? (Representative Neil Abercrombie, D-Hawaii)

To my knowledge, never in the history of this nation—for over 200 years—has Congress usurped states' authority to define marriage or delineate the circumstances under which a marriage can be performed. If Congress can simply usurp states' authority to determine what the definition of marriage is, what is next? Will we tell states they are not required to recognize divorce judgments they disagree with? . . . Congress, in its 200 year history, has never once used the Full Faith and Credit Clause to nullify rather than implement the effect of a public act or judgment by a state. (Senator Dianne Feinstein, D-California)

We risk setting a dangerous precedent by crossing the threshold of preempting states by establishing a federal definition of marriage. Once we cross that threshold, what is to prevent the federal government from setting a national age of majority for marriage and preempting all states as in China, where the legal marriage age has been set as high as 28 years old, and changes almost annually? Furthermore, what is to prevent the federal government from setting new and rigorous standards for divorces preempting all state laws? (Representative Peter DeFazio, D-Oregon)

DOMA constitutes unnecessary federal involvement. Opponents of DOMA voiced a second concern about the involvement of the federal government in marriage and family law. In addition to perceiving the legislation as an inappropriate—even unconstitutional—invasion of the federal government into the affairs of the states, several members maintained that DOMA was unnecessary. Members expressing this view were exclusively Democrats (see Table 7.2). These members either perceived the Hawaii lawsuit to be a distant threat and believed that Congress was acting prematurely or that states already had the right that DOMA presumably provided—the right to ban same-sex marriages. They alluded to the public policy exception of the Full Faith and Credit Clause of the Constitution, which they reasoned already granted states the authority to set their own laws regarding marriage eligibility and to deny marriage benefits to couples who do not meet the criteria articulated in the policy, as, for example,

> The entire matter has very little to do with the federal government. It is a black letter law that the states are free to reject marriages approved by other states which violate public policy. It is pursuant to this authority that states have invalidated marriages consummated in other states which are incestuous, polygamous, based on common law, and involve underage minors. (John Conyers, D-Michigan)

> Under current law, states will continue to be free to decline to recognize same-sex marriages if they choose. To date, nearly 80 percent of the states, 37, have already addressed the issue of same-sex marriages in their legislatures. Eighteen states thus far have had legislation banning same-sex marriages. . . . These statistics hardly present a compelling mandate for the federal government to step in and rescue the states. (Representative William Coyne, D-Pennsylvania)

No state legislature is even suggesting that it recognize gay marriage, not one state in this Union. Not one person in the Senate or the House has introduced legislation to recognize gay marriage—not one. There is no bill pending before us to legalize gay marriage and provide benefits to these couples. Not one group has asked any of us, to my knowledge, to carry such legislation. We are told by constitutional scholars that even if one state does recognize gay marriage, other states have the option not to recognize it. . . . So why this legislation now? (Senator Barbara Boxer, D-California)

DOMA as federal protection against fiscal demands. The final subtheme within the larger theme of the roles of state and federal governments in marriage and family law, namely federal protection against fiscal demands, related to a provision in DOMA that pertained to the importance of defining marriage for federal purposes. Almost everyone who emphasized this subtheme were Republicans (88%; see Table 7.2), and senators emphasized it more than representatives (see Table 7.3). Their statements focused on the potential fiscal impact of the legalization of same-sex marriage on the federal government and the importance of uniformity in the federal code:

Federal policies could be dramatically affected by the Hawaii decision since the federal government generally recognizes state documents in granting benefits and privileges to married individuals. Veterans' benefits, labor policies, federal health and pension benefits, and Social Security benefits are just a few of the areas that would be subjected to substantive revision if Congress does not act soon. I think it would be wrong to take money out of the pockets of working families across America and use those tax dollars to give federal acceptance and financial support to same-sex marriages. (Representative David Weldon, R-Florida)

If, for example, Hawaii gives new meanings to the words "marriage" and "spouse," the reverberations may be felt throughout the Federal code unless this bill is enacted. For instance, a redefinition in Hawaii could create demands for veterans' benefits for same-sex spouses. . . . This bill anticipates future demands . . . and it . . . eliminate[s] legal uncertainty concerning federal benefits. (Senator Don Nickles, R-Oklahoma)

Gay and Lesbian Rights

A third major theme in the DOMA debates pertained to the impact of DOMA on the rights of gay and lesbian people. Those who evoked the theme of equal rights held that DOMA unfairly denied gay and lesbian individuals the rights accorded through marriage and therefore was discriminatory against gays and lesbians, often framing the issue as an affront to their civil rights. Almost everyone who emphasized this theme was a Democrat (97%; see Table 7.2), more representatives than senators emphasizing this theme also (see Table 7.3). Often when senators addressed the equal rights issue, they connected it to employment and the workplace—largely as a result of the merger of DOMA and the Employment Nondiscrimination Act (ENDA) in the debates. Coded statements included in the analysis pertained to both DOMA *and* ENDA but not to ENDA alone. Such statements not only reflected the view that gays and lesbians were denied equal access to many of the rights associated with marriage or marriage itself but also connected this theme to race- or ethnicity-based discrimination, comparing DOMA to prior antimiscegenation legislation, as, for example,

> In effect this bill would deny gay men and women hospital visitation rights, health coverage, and other forms of insurance, inheritance and taxation rights, government benefits for spouses, immigration rights for spouse, and other rights. . . . I swore to uphold the Constitution against enemies, foreign and domestic, to protect minorities and minority viewpoints from the tyranny of the majority, to protect African Americans from racism, Jews from anti-Semitism, Arabs from anti-Arabism, women from sexism, and gays and lesbians from homophobia and discrimination. With this vote, I am sending a message to all coalitions and those who have sworn to protect the Constitution that we will do just this that. We will protect their rights. (Representative Jesse Jackson, D-Illinois)

> This measure will federally codify discrimination against a group of Americans, striking a blow to justice and equal treatment for all people. Mr. Chairman, less than 30 years ago, many in this nation believed that allowing interracial couples to marry would seriously denigrate American society, and many State laws reflected that. . . . I recognize the general, pervasive discrimination gay men and lesbians face in society and in this House. . . . By advocating discrimination, we're breaking down the bonds which hold this Nation together when we should be strengthening them. (Representative Anna Eschoo, D-California)

> Mr. Speaker, I have served in this House for 24 years. . . . My partner, Dean, . . . is in a situation which no spouse of any Member of this House is in. . . . The spouse of every member of this House is entitled to that Member's health insurance, even after that member dies. . . . This is not true of my partner. . . . I have paid every single penny as much as every Member of this House for that pension, but my partner, should he survive me, is not entitled to one penny. . . . Do you think that is fair? I do not think most Americans think that is fair. (Representative Jerry Studds, D-Massachusetts)

> Gay and lesbian Americans . . . do not yet fully enjoy the equal protection of the laws promised to every American by the 14th amendment. And this legislation . . . is a step in the absolute opposite direction of extending the equal protection of the laws to Americans without regard to their sexual orientation, just as we moved so fitfully in this country to extend these protections of laws to Americans without regard to their race. . . . Strides have been made, Madam President, to provide gay and lesbian Americans the equal protection of the law, but DOMA is a retreat from that goal. (Senator Carol Mosely-Braun, D-Illinois)

Although Democrats emphasized this theme almost exclusively, a few Republicans did too, but the attitudes they conveyed were quite different, as, for example,

Let me say first of all that this is not about equal rights. We have equal rights. Homosexuals have the same rights as I do. They have the ability to marry right now, today. However, when they get married, they must marry a person of the opposite sex, the same as me. That is the same right that I have. Now, I would say that, just like a homosexual, I do not have the right to marry somebody of the same sex. It is the same for them as it is for me. (Representative Steve Largent, R-Oklahoma)

Negative Attitudes Toward Gays and Lesbians

A final theme emphasized in the debates over DOMA consisted of statements by members who argued that DOMA was rooted in and promoted negative attitudes toward gay and lesbian people. As a theme, it belonged almost exclusively to Democrats (see Table 7.2) and to members of the House more than the Senate (see Table 7.3). Members who emphasized this theme charged that DOMA was mean-spirited legislation that promoted bigotry and homophobia and capitalized on society's negative attitudes toward gays and lesbians to gain political advantage. Again the use of language to denigrate opponents' construction of the problem and to convince others to reject it as well is evident:

Mr. Chairman, the so-called Defense of Marriage Act should really be called the Republican Offense on People Who Are Different Act because it is nothing more than blatant homophobic gay-bashing. (Representative Cardiss Collins, D-Illinois)

Mr. Chairman, this is a mean bill. It is cruel. This bill seeks to divide our nation, turn Americans against Americans, sow . . . the seeds of fear, hatred and intolerance. . . . Mr. Chairman, I have known racism. I have known bigotry. This bill stinks of the same fear, hatred, and intolerance. It should not be called the Defense of Marriage Act. It should be called the defense of mean-spirited bigots act. . . . This bill appeals to our worst fears and emotions. It encourages hatred of our fellow Americans for political advantage. (Representative Robert Lewis, D-Georgia)

I regard this bill as a mean-spirited form of Republican legislative gay bashing cynically calculated to inflame the public eight weeks before the November 5th election. . . . The obvious explanation [for DOMA] is a crass desire for partisan gain at the expense of tolerance and mutual understanding. The bill is designed to divide Americans, to drive a wedge between one group of citizens and the rest of the country, solely for partisan advantage. It is a cynical election year gimmick, and it deserves to be rejected by all who deplore the intolerance and incivility that have come to dominate our national debate. (Senator Edward Kennedy, D-Massachusetts)

■ Summary and Conclusions

The social change framework provided the context for the analysis of the debates over DOMA, but the debates themselves revealed the attitudes underlying its passage, providing insight into the many meanings of the vote on DOMA. The debates also demonstrated how proponents and opponents of different constructions of DOMA and same-sex marriage used language to present and defend their position while casting the position of others in a negative and unfavorable light. In doing so, the debates also highlighted the attitudinal differences between individual congresspersons as Republicans and Democrats on the subject. For example, although Democrats tended to construct DOMA as the problem, Republicans tended to construct it as the solution. Democrats more than Republicans saw same-sex marriage as personal and no threat to society and DOMA as an impediment to the rights of gays and lesbians, as unnecessary federal intervention, as an usurpation of states' rights, and as an instrument for encouraging negative attitudes toward gays and lesbians. Republicans, on the other hand, were more likely to see same-sex marriage as morally inferior to heterosexual marriage and a threat to marriage and society and DOMA as an instrument for the preservation of marriage as the foundation of society, as federal protection against potential fiscal demands and as a defense of states' rights.

Although such differences may have been attributable to the values and attitudes embedded in the ways in which individual congresspersons had come to understand marriage and the roles of state and federal governments in relation to it—that is, their normative cognitive frameworks—they also reflected the ideological orientations of individual congressional members as Democrats and Republicans. Generally speaking, their constructions of same-sex marriage and DOMA were congruent with the ideological proclivities of their respective political parties. Such constructions were consistent with the more liberal orientation guiding the positions of Democrats and their emphasis on equality, rights, and social reform, and the more conservative ideology guiding the positions of Republicans and their emphasis on social stability and order (McClosky & Zaller, 1984; Zimmerman & Gager, 1997), individual congressional members holding such values to greater or lesser degrees.

Political party was inadequate for explaining some of the attitudes expressed during the debates, however, as, for example, Democrats' claim that DOMA represented improper federal usurpation of the rights of states to establish their own rules with respect to marriage. Here it is speculated that Democrats emphasized this theme to demonstrate the contradiction inherent in Republicans' penchant for restricting the role of the federal government and their support of DOMA, which expands government's role, not only in a matter regarded personal and private—marriage and family—but in a matter that traditionally lies in the states' domain.

Although attitudes did not differ as much on the basis of House and Senate membership as on the basis of party membership, some interesting differences were nonetheless evident. In particular, representatives more than senators constructed same-sex marriage as a nonthreat to marriage and society, arguing instead that marriage was a personal, private relationship, that DOMA was an infringement on gay and lesbian rights, and that it fostered negative attitudes toward gays and lesbians. The senators who participated in the debates, more

than the representatives who did, argued that DOMA offered federal
protections for states' rights and also the federal purse. Another notable difference was that representatives tended to use language that was much more
inflammatory and aimed at stirring emotions. Such distinctions could be attributable to differences in the rules governing the practices and procedures of the
House and Senate (Zimmerman, 1992a, 1995a), but they also could be attributable to differences in the rhetorical styles of members in the two bodies, for
example, Representative Robert Barr's use of metaphors to denigrate the position of others and evoke fear among those ambivalent about the matter, which,
although distinctive, was extreme.

Evidence of regional differences in the themes emphasized by individual congressional members during the debates could justify further investigation of the
attitudes embedded in their normative cognitive frameworks with regard to
same-sex marriage and DOMA. Two thirds of the House members who emphasized the theme of marriage as the foundation of society represented states in the
South, raising a question about the relationship between their states' political
cultures—that is, the values and attitudes that people in different states hold
toward government and other persons—and congressional members' construction of same-sex marriage and DOMA (Elazar, 1984, 1986; Zimmerman,
1992a, 1995a, 2000). Because the values and attitudes embedded in their ways
of understanding same-sex marriage could be a by-product of the political culture dominant in different states and geographic regions, it is not unreasonable
to hypothesize that the political culture of the state or region congressional
members represent could have been incorporated into the ways in which they
viewed and constructed same-sex marriage and DOMA.

Such speculation extends to other differences noted from the analysis as well.
One such difference is the overrepresentation of women who participated in
them—in both the House and Senate. Over 30% of the women in the House and
almost two thirds of the women in the Senate participated in the debates, rates
much higher than men's in either chamber. Although the small numbers of
women serving in Congress, particularly in the Senate, precluded analysis of
gender as an influence on constructions of same-sex marriage and DOMA, gender provides an important avenue for further investigation on the topic. Prior
studies that have examined the influence of gender on House votes (e.g.,
Zimmerman & Gager, 1997) found it to be significant on votes pertaining to
family and medical leave, tax and spending bills, abortion, welfare reform, and
others. Thus, it could have been an influence in the debates and vote on DOMA
as well.

Readers should be aware that analysis of the debates over DOMA was necessarily limited to only those members who participated in the debates, and that
despite party differences on how the problem and its solution were constructed,
DOMA was enacted with overwhelming bipartisan support. Although the vote
on DOMA was a vote *for* existing social arrangements with regard to heterosexual marriage, the social change model that framed the discussion in this chapter
suggests that groups will continue to mobilize and countermobilize around

those issues and values that are important to them and press for government action that supports their views and claims—here in relation to same-sex partnerships. Events leading up to the passage of civil unions in Vermont in 2000 are illustrative. With regard to the lawsuit in Hawaii that precipitated DOMA, the Hawaii Supreme Court ruled in December 1999 that the issue of same-sex marriage in Hawaii was resolved by the legislature's passage of a constitutional amendment banning gay marriages in 1998; the measure in fact passed by a ratio of 2 to 1 ("Hawaii Slams Door," 1999). These actions in Hawaii would seem to justify the claims of those who argued in the debates that DOMA was premature and unnecessary federal legislation. It also should be pointed out that many claims made during the debates with regard to marriage and family were at odds with historical research showing the evolving nature of the family as an institution and its changing meanings over time, as cited in Chapter 3.

The examination of policy solutions to family problems at the federal level in Chapters 6 and 7 leads to the questions of the next chapter: What solutions were constructed to the problems families were experiencing at the state level in the 1990s? Did states differ in their solutions to family problems, and if so, how?

In light of earlier discussion, these questions, not surprisingly, are framed within the context of political culture theory, but before turning to Chapter 8 for answers to them, you may want to answer the questions below with regard to the discussion in *this* chapter.

■ Some Questions for Your Reflection and Discussion

1. What was important about DOMA? What precipitated it?
2. What are the four process components of the social change model used to talk about DOMA?
3. What is the role of values in the model?
4. What are "moral entrepreneurs"? (See Notes and text.)
5. What does DOMA represent in the model?
6. What were some of the attitudes expressed in favor of DOMA?
7. What were some of the attitudes expressed in opposition to DOMA?
8. Cite an example of a metaphor used by Representative Bob Barr in the debates. What was his purpose in using it?
9. What precipitated DOMA?
10. How was the lawsuit in Hawaii finally resolved?

Now that you have answered these questions, please turn to Chapter 8.

■ Notes

1. This chapter is based on an analysis of DOMA undertaken by Julie Kohler, graduate student in Family Social Science, and a coauthored paper by Julie Kohler and Shirley Zimmerman, Professor

of Family Social Science, titled, "The Congressional Debate Over the Defense of Marriage Act (DOMA): An Examination of Competing Perceptions."

2. *The Social Change Model* (in brief). According to Smelser and Halpern (1978), in the historical development of any society, new ideologies and movements of public opinion emerge within the context of debates about institutionalized cultural values among committed individuals and groups. Out of such debate, certain value premises emerge as dominant, which in this chapter pertains to the superiority of heterosexual marriage over same-sex marriage. Such value premises become the basis for legitimizing the society's major institutional structures, its normative framework, and its systems of social control as exemplified in current marriage and divorce laws.

Structural change, which often produces new social arrangements that diverge from the ways in which people have come to understand the world in which they live—that is, their normative, cognitive frameworks—contributes to the conflict and contradictions inherent in novel situations as represented by structural change. Structural change refers to the introduction of some new or different phenomenon into the society, which here includes growing numbers of homosexual couples who seek legal recognition of same-sex marriage as an alternative institutional form to heterosexual marriage.

With the onset of such change—or novel situation—certain social processes typically begin to unfold (Smelser & Halpern, 1978). Initially, some individuals and groups begin to express alarm and concern and attempt to define, evaluate, and interpret the new situation to others—as they see it. The multiplicity of culturally provided value premises and perspectives available in the society for assigning meaning to new social phenomena means that a variety of definitions and perceptions of the situation are likely to emerge and compete with each other, as in the case of same-sex marriage. The ensuing struggle is over which definition or construction will prevail.

The struggle assumes a political dimension when certain individuals and groups attempt to spread their definition of the situation to politically significant or mobilized groups or begin to press for some kind of purposive social or political action that supports their definition of the situation or construction of the problem. The social action these "moral entrepreneurs" seek may be a moral crusade, legal regulation, or a new institution or organizational reform that accommodates the situation as they define or construct it. Here the social action being sought was the passage of DOMA.

The model, which is highly interactive and dynamic, is iterative. Thus, the resulting social action may constitute the condition for initiating another cycle of conflict and change similar to that which gave impetus to the action in the first place. In other words, the passage of DOMA as the resulting social action could become the novel situation in another cycle of change-producing processes similar to that which gave impetus to DOMA in the first place.

3. *Methods.* The Minnesota Contextual Content Analysis (MCCA) was used in the analysis. MCCA is a computer program that uses a preset dictionary to categorize text into categories of meaning and uncover patterns of emphasis in different texts within the context in which ideas are expressed (McTavish & Pirro, 1990). With a working dictionary of over 100 idea categories, the program quantitatively reveals patterns of emphasis within text by generating emphasis scores (E-scores) for each category of text. A category would receive a high E-score if certain words were used more frequently than others in the text.

By identifying the specific words that were emphasized during the debates, the E-scores provided the basis for a thematic analysis of the debates over DOMA. The E-scores not only provided the means for identifying the specific words that appeared the most frequently in the debates, but they also allowed for a comparative analysis of the themes that were emphasized.

With this in mind, a frequency analysis was undertaken of the specific words congressional members used during the debates. This analysis was followed by a thorough analysis of the transcripts of their entire statements, based on the words emphasized in the texts, such as *state* and *marriage,* as determined by MCCA, to which other recurring terms and phrases were added. To facilitate the analysis, notes were jotted in the margins that descriptively summarized the text (e.g., states' rights). These descriptive codes were further categorized to capture the range and diversity of attitudes and themes that DOMA evoked during the debates (e.g., defending states' rights, usurping states' rights). By analyzing members' statements in their totality, it was possible to ascertain the context in which particular words and phrases were spoken.

Inferential codes were then developed using the constant comparative method (Glaser & Straus, 1967; Straus and Corbin, 1990). This method involves labeling and comparing portions of texts. As a result, many of the original descriptive labels that were jotted in the margins were revised and collapsed into a smaller number of thematic categories. The pattern codes (Miles & Huberman, 1984) that ultimately resulted from this process facilitated the analysis of thematic and attitudinal differences between Republicans and Democrats and between senators and representatives with respect to the several issues that DOMA evoked.

Following these procedures, a frequency analysis was undertaken of the pattern codes or themes that were emphasized by individual congresspersons during the debates. Only the mention of a theme was coded, not the frequency with which it was mentioned. Themes mentioned by individual congressional members were coded as *1* for those members who participated in the debates. Thus, a *1* signified that a member mentioned a theme at least once in his or her remarks; a *0* signified no mention of the theme. These procedures allowed not only for a comparison of the different themes that surfaced during the debates but also for a comparison of the themes emphasized by Republicans and Democrats in both the House and Senate with respect to same-sex marriage as a problem and DOMA as its solution.

CHAPTER 8

States' Political Cultures and Their Constructed Solutions to Family Problems in the 1990s

◻ Given that states share with federal and local governments the responsibility for addressing the problems of families, it seemed reasonable to inquire about the solutions that states constructed to address such problems in the 1990s. Did their constructions of solutions to family problems differ from one another and from those of the federal government? And if so, how? To answer these questions, a content analysis was undertaken of the legislative summaries of six states—California, Florida, Minnesota, Nevada, New York, and South Carolina—for 3 data years: 1991, 1993, and 1995. The states were selected on the basis of Daniel Elazar's (1972, 1984) typology of states' political cultures—moralistic, individualistic, traditionalistic, and different mixes of the three described later in the chapter—to determine whether the family policies the states enacted varied with their political cultures on three dimensions: quantity, breadth, and focus. Readers will recall from the previous chapter the observation that some of the attitudes that congressional members expressed in the debates over DOMA seemed to vary with the geographic region of the state they represented. This observation provided the basis for speculating that such variations could have reflected the political cultures of the particular the state congressional members represented. This chapter speaks to states' political cultures and their relationship to the solutions that states constructed to family problems in the early to mid-1990s.

■ The Political Culture Perspective

What is political culture? What does it mean? Almond and Verba (1963, 1989) refer to political culture as a system of beliefs, values, and expressive symbols that structure the situation in which political action takes place. It also has been defined as the attitudes that people hold toward government and other people that, according to McClosky and Zaller (1984), can be determined empirically by the distribution of such attitudes in a population and also by the internal consistency of the attitudes that people hold toward different social policies (Devine, 1972). Just as attitudes provide the impetus for action, they also act as constraints on policy choices involving different but related public policies (Converse, 1964) and therefore on policy solutions. They help to explain why Norway, for example, with its commitment to social democracy, did not dismantle its social programs or privatize its public services (Ibrahim, 1996) in constructing its solutions to family problems in the 1990s although the United States, with its commitment to minimal government and the free market, did. Such attitudes also help to explain why the United States delayed for so long the enactment of legislation giving working parents 12 weeks of unpaid leave to care for newborn babies and sick family members and also why such leave is unpaid, not paid, as in Norway. According to Inglehart (1990), the political culture perspective constitutes one of the leading alternatives to rational choice theory as a general framework for explaining political behaviors and choices. Indeed, Barone and Ujifusa (1989) have asserted that cultural attitudes are far better predictors of policy choice than any other factor except party identification. Rational choice theory (which will be presented in its own chapter) refers to the selection of an alternative course of action that maximizes the values being sought in the action, here as it pertains to families and family policy.

Because the attitudes that people hold are acquired early in their socialization experiences and are incorporated into the ways they come to understand the world in which they live—their normative cognitive frameworks—Inglehart (1990) holds that attitudes are highly resistant to change. Almond and Verba (1989), who emphasize the importance of adult, not childhood, experiences in the political socialization process, also regard political culture as limited in terms of flexibility. Since culture is learned, variations in the attitudes people hold toward government and its role in society are seen to be attributable to variations in their acquisition of learned political-cultural values (Inglehart, 1990)

Daniel Elazar's typology of the political cultures of the 50 states represents the first systematic attempt to capture such attitudinal variations (Erikson, Wright, & McIver, 1993). Using the concept to connote differences in mass attitudes and general expectations and practices concerning the treatment of different needs and preferences in the political arena, Elazar (1984), in keeping with anthropologists' view of culture, sees political culture as an attribute of the political community more than a characteristic of individuals. As a result, his typology offers a way of making theoretical sense of differences among the states in the attitudes that people hold toward families and government and of tying together diverse behaviors and fundamental orientations toward elites, political participation, the role of government in society, and the centralization of government (Erikson, Wright, & McIver, 1993). In this respect, it differs from psychologists' approach to the study of attitudes, as represented in the survey data reported in Chapter 5.

Dividing the states and areas within states and using historical documents, Elazar (1984), as mentioned earlier, characterized the dominant political cultures of the United States as moralistic, individualistic, and traditionalistic, or some combination of the three. He characterized states as traditionalistic in part because their elites tend to ignore public opinion, individualistic because their politicians tend to be pragmatic, or moralistic because their politicians tend to impose their version of the public interest on their constituencies, cautioning that his typology represented ideal types not fully extant in the real world (Elazar, 1984).

States' Political Cultures

The Individualistic Political Culture

In abbreviated form, the individualistic political culture takes a utilitarian view of the role of government. It holds that government is instituted mainly for utilitarian reasons: to manage functions that people demand (Elazar, 1984). Emphasizing private over public concerns, it places a premium on limiting community intervention—governmental and nongovernmental—into private activities to the minimum necessary for keeping the market free and in proper working order. Government action in the individualistic political culture is generally restricted to the economic realm, its role being to encourage private initiatives and broad access to the marketplace. With few preconceptions about government goals, politics in this political culture is seen as a marketplace in which public officials broker constituent demands into public policy. Viewed as a business that the general public regards as necessary but unsavory and better left to those willing to engage in it, politics in the individualistic subculture tries to avoid ideology.

The Traditionalistic Political Culture

Rooted in an ambivalent attitude toward the marketplace and a paternalistic and elitist conception of the commonwealth, this largely Southern traditionalistic culture offers a different model for the role of government and democratic institutions. Accepting a substantially hierarchical society as part of the natural order in which those at the top of the social structure are authorized and expected to take a special and dominant role in government, social and family ties in this political culture are paramount (Elazar, 1984). Those without an assigned role in politics are not expected to be even minimally involved as citizens or even expected to vote, which explains why voter turnout in a traditionalistic state such as South Carolina was below the national average in six out of the last seven presidential elections (Barone & Ujifusa, 1997; U.S. Bureau of the Census, 1983, 1996).

Although government in the traditionalistic political culture is accepted as an actor with a positive role to play in the community, its role tends to be restricted to maintaining the existing social order. Wherever this type of political culture is dominant in the United States, political leaders such as Senator Strom Thurmond from South Carolina tend to play a conservative and custodial role rather than an initiatory and anticipatory one, unless pressured by external events to do so. The underlying features of the traditionalistic political culture include a general presumption against government action to solve people's problems and an overall assumption that the aim of politics is to serve the interests of traditional elites (Erikson, Wright, & McIver, 1993). In this regard, it is significant that a complaint filed with the Justice Department by a group of South Carolina voters in 2000 charged the Republican party in South Carolina with racial discrimination in the presidential primary elections in both 1992 and 1996. The charges involved the deliberate closing of polling places in black precincts, coupled with the failure to inform prospective voters that they were expected to travel to another precinct to vote; all polling places in white precincts were open (Firestone, 2000). South Carolina apparently is the only state in the country where political parties pay for and administer their primaries without supervision or oversight by a state elections board.

The Moralistic Political Culture

In contrast, the moralistic political culture emphasizes a concern for the public welfare (Elazar, 1984). It reflects the belief that government has a responsibility for promoting the general welfare and should take an active role in doing so. Committed to the use of communal power—governmental and nongovernmental—in promoting the public welfare, the moralistic political culture acts to constrain individualism. Guided by a sense of obligation for the community's welfare, political leaders in the moralistic political culture stand ready to undertake policy initiatives they think are in the public interest, even when the electorate does not demand them. Seeing politics as a means of dealing with the issues and concerns of civil society, the moralistic political culture regards politics as a matter of concern for everyone, not just those at the top of the states' socioeconomic-political structure or those pursuing political careers. Hence, it should not be surprising that in contrast to South Carolina, voter turnout in a moralistic state like Minnesota was higher than the national average in seven out of the last seven presidential elections (Barone & Ujifusa, 1997; U.S. Bureau of the Census, 1983, 1996). Similarly, national and Minnesota polls assessing voter interest in the 2000 presidential election found that Minnesotans expressed more interest in the upcoming presidential election in higher percentages than voters nationally. Whereas only 6% nationally said they had a great deal of interest in the 2000 presidential election, 27% of Minnesotans surveyed said they did; only 10% saying they had no interest in the election, compared with 52% nationally ("Who Cares?", 2000). Because issues are important in the moralistic political subculture, the culture is ideal for ideological activists, Paul Wellstone, the senator from Minnesota, being a prime example.

■ States' Political Cultures and Public Policy

The Elazar typology provides a way of making theoretical sense of not only atti-tudinal differences among the states but also of differences in the policies they enact as constructed solutions to family problems. Based on Elazar's typology (1972), which distinguishes not only the political cultures of different states but also the political cultures of different geographic regions within states, Johnson (1976) found that moralistic and individualistic states spent more per capita for social programs than traditionalistic states and that their policy activity was more innovative. Erikson, Wright, and McIver (1993) found that conservative policies or solutions were more characteristic of Southern traditionalistic states than other states. They also found a connection between the moralistic subcul-ture and liberal policies or solutions via the ideological preferences of states' political elites.

In another study that also was based on the Elazar typology, Zimmerman (1992a) found that states that were more individualistic spent less per capita for public welfare than states that were less individualistic, as measured by the mean percentage of state populations voting for Ronald Reagan for president in 1980 and 1984 and the frequency with which their per capita expenditures for educa-tion, health, hospitals, and public welfare were above and below the median that states spent in 1970, 1980, and 1985. Johnson (1976) also found that economic equality was greater in states with a moralistic political culture than other states, and Zimmerman (1992a, 1993b, 1995a) found a link between states' political cultures, their per capita spending for public welfare, and their suicide rates in 1985, and again in 1990. Fitzpatrick and Hero (1988) also found a relationship between states' political cultures and policy outcomes for people.

Elazar's typology also received support in an analysis that Zimmerman and Owens (1989) undertook of the explicit family policies enacted by three states in the early to mid-1980s: Minnesota, Nevada, and South Carolina. Minnesota, the singularly moralistic state, enacted more explicit family legislation than both South Carolina, the singularly traditionalistic state, and Nevada, the singularly individualistic state; South Carolina enacted the least. The term *singularly* refers to the fact that the political cultures of these three states represent only one rather than a mix of political cultures, as most states do. The core of the family legislation they enacted also differed in that Minnesota constructed relatively more family legislation that explicitly addressed the economic problems of fami-lies and Nevada enacted more family legislation related to the courts, child and family welfare, and child support and custody. What about the 1990s? Did such differences continue to pertain?

■ The Study's States

Expanding on the earlier study that Zimmerman and Owens (1989) undertook of the family policies enacted by Minnesota, Nevada, and South Carolina in the early to mid-1980s, the present research included—in addition to the three that were included in the 1980s' analyses—three states with mixed political cultures: California, Florida, and New York. The original three states were included not only because their political cultures were singular and seemed to distinguish their constructions of legislative solutions to family problems in the 1980s but also because their legislative solutions had not yet been analyzed for their explicit family content in the 1990s. The latter three states were selected because they represented different mixes of the political cultures identified by Elazar: California, a moralistic-individualistic political culture; Florida, a traditionalistic-individualistic political culture; and New York, an individualistic-moralistic political culture. According to Elazar's typology, the first of the paired cultures is the predominant one in a given state, with the second a strong strain. Thus, California would be characterized as being more moralistic than individualistic, New York as more individualistic than moralistic, and Florida as more traditionalistic than individualistic. The Elazar typology, which had not yet been applied to the explicit family policies enacted in the 1990s by the three states with singular political cultures, had *never* been applied to the policies enacted by states with mixed political cultures.

Given Elazar's characterization of their political cultures, and based on the research cited earlier showing that: (a) Policy solutions were more innovative in moralistic than in traditionalistic states (Johnson, 1976); (b) Economic equality was greater in moralistic than in other states (Johnson, 1976); (c) Predominantly moralistic states spent more for public welfare and had lower rates of suicide in both 1985 and 1990 than other states (Zimmerman, 1992a, 1995b); and (d) In moralistic states, people tend to view government as an instrument for promoting the public welfare and in constructing solutions to family problems.

It was expected that Minnesota as a moralistic state and California as a predominantly moralistic state would enact more legislation that explicitly addressed the problems of families than the other states. For similar reasons, it was expected that the family policies enacted by Minnesota and California would address a broader range of family problems and be more proactive in their constructed solutions to such problems. In the case of New York and Florida, it was expected that their constructed solutions to family problems in the form of the family policies they enacted would reflect the first of their paired political cultures more than the second in keeping with the Elazar typology—and California's would do the same.

■ Methodology

The data sources for the analyses were the legislative summaries produced by the six states. These were obtained from the legislative research offices of each of the states for each data year: 1991, 1993, and 1995. Legislative summaries are publications that list and summarize all the legislative measures that state legislatures consider and enact in any given legislative session. Not all states produce such summaries. Mississippi, for one, does not nor does Massachusetts. For states that do produce them, many do not retain copies from earlier years, thus restricting the pool of states whose legislation could be considered for the analyses to those that did, such as the six study states.

The amount of detail that legislative summaries provide varies. Minnesota's, for example, provides extensive information that details the history of and rationale for different legislative measures and the processes and procedures to be used in their implementation. It also combines separate but related measures into single legislative acts or chapters. In the summaries of other states, measures are identified by title and number and described in two or three brief sentences; some omit titles. All legislative summaries use some sort of classification scheme for the different measures states enact, such as aging, business, courts and corrections, education, economic development, families and children, health, taxes, and welfare. In some cases, subcategories are used also. Details about how the analyses were conducted can be found in Note 1.[1]

What did the data show? In what ways did the states differ in their constructed solutions to family problems as measured by the quantity, scope, and focus of the explicit family legislation they enacted over the observational period in the 1990s?

■ Findings

Quantity: Which State Enacted the Greatest Number of Explicit Family Policies?

As Table 8.1 shows, Minnesota, the singularly moralistic state, constructed relatively more legislative solutions that explicitly addressed the problems of families than any of the other states over the observational period, although in terms of absolute frequencies, California enacted much more. New York and Florida enacted relatively little explicit family legislation, and although similar in this regard, New York was legislatively more active than Florida, enacting much more family legislation and legislation overall. Important to note is that although the explicit mention of families was not a dominant feature of the legislation that any of the states enacted over the observational period, explicit mention of families increased over time in the legislation they enacted, especially in California's, the two exceptions being New York's and Florida's, which did not.

Focus or Content: Did the States Differ From One Another in the Kinds of Legislative Solutions They Constructed to Family Problems?

If the six states differed with respect to the frequency with which explicit family language was incorporated into their legislation and hence in the number of legislative solutions they constructed to family problems, did their constructions

TABLE 8.1 Explicit Family Policies Enacted by Six States in 1991, 1993, and 1995; Frequencies and Percentages of Total Legislation Enacted by Each

	Number of provisions enacted with explicit family content	Total number of provisions enacted	Percent of total number of provisions with explicit family content
California (moralistic/individualistic)			
1991	53	1,228	4
1993	63	1,307	5
1995	115	982	12
Total	231	3,517	7
Florida (traditionalistic/individualistic)			
1991	22	433	5
1993	19	417	5
1995	17	531	3
Total	58	1,381	4
Minnesota (moralistic)			
1991	50	356	14
1993	43	375	11
1995	55	265	21
Total	148	996	15
Nevada (individualistic)			
1991	37	729	5
1993	60	669	9
1995	59	730	8
Total	156	2,128	7
New York (individualistic/moralistic)			
1991	38	750	5
1993	25	731	3
1995	33	694	5
Total	96	2,175	4
South Carolina (traditionalistic)			
1991	9	248	4
1993	19	220	9
1995	24	279	9
Total	52	747	7

also differ in terms of substantive focus, core, or content and hence in the kinds of family problems they addressed? The categories in which family language appeared in the legislative summaries of the six states as a measure of the substantive focus of their family legislation appear in Table 8.2.

As can be seen, the categories of the family legislation the six states enacted for each data year were somewhat more differentiated than the legislative categories of congressional roll call votes in Chapter 6. Note that the only category in which all six states constructed family policy was in health care in 1991; in 1993, all six states enacted family legislation in both health care and child and family welfare; and in 1995, all six states enacted family legislation, in addition

TABLE 8.2   Substantive Categories of Explicit Family Policies Enacted by Six States in 1991, 1993, and 1995

Categories	CA	FL	MN	NV	NY	SC
1991						
Adoption	x		x	x	x	
Adult care	x					
AFDC/welfare reform	x		x	x	x	
Child abuse	x		x	x	x	
Child and family welfare	x	x		x	x	
Child care	x	x	x			
Child custody	x		x	x	x	
Child support	x			x		
Civil rights				x		
Courts, crime, juveniles	x			x	x	
Displaced homemakers				x		
Domestic violence	x	x	x	x		x
Education	x	x	x	x		x
Employment	x	x	x	x	x	
Family farms			x			
Family professionals	x			x		
Health care	x	x	x	x	x	x
Housing	x		x		x	
Marriage and divorce	x	x	x		x	
Mental health/developmental disabilities		x	x		x	
Survivors/death				x		x
Taxes			x			
Veterans/military affairs			x			
1993						
Adoption	x		x	x		
Adult care		x				
AFDC/welfare reform	x	x	x	x	x	
Child abuse/neglect	x	x	x		x	
Child and family welfare	x	x	x	x	x	x
Child care		x		x	x	x
Child custody	x	x		x	x	
Child support	x	x	x	x		
Civil rights			x			
Courts/crime/juveniles	x	x	x	x		
Displaced homemakers	x					
Domestic violence	x		x	x		
Education	x		x	x	x	x
Employment	x			x	x	
Family professionals	x					
Health care	x		x	x	x	x
Housing	x		x		x	
Human services			x			
Marriage and divorce	x	x	x	x		
Mental health/mental retardation			x	x	x	x
Survivors/death		x		x	x	
Taxes						
Veterans' affairs				x		

TABLE 8.2 (Continued)

Categories	CA	FL	MN	NV	NY	SC
1995						
Adult abuse		x				
Adoption	x		x	x	x	x
AFDC/welfare reform	x	x	x	x	x	x
Child abuse	x	x	x	x	x	x
Child and family welfare	x	x	x	x	x	x
Child care	x	x	x	x	x	x
Child custody	x	x	x	x	x	x
Child support	x	x	x	x	x	x
	(Minnesota and California enacted the most)					
Civil rights		x				
Courts/crime/juveniles	x	x		x	x	x
Displaced homemakers	x				x	
Domestic violence	x	x		x	x	x
Education	x	x	x	x	x	x
Employment				x	x	
Family professionals	x					
Health care	x	x	x	x	x	x
Housing	x	x	x	x	x	
Marriage and divorce	x		x	x	x	
Survivors/death	x		x			
Taxes					x	x
Veterans' affairs					x	x

to health care and child and family welfare, in AFDC/welfare reform, child abuse, child care, child custody, child support, and education. California was the only state to enact legislation pertaining to family professionals all 3 data years, joined by Nevada only in 1991. Florida was the only state to enact family legislation in the category of adult abuse; both Florida and California enacted family legislation in the area of adult care in 1991 and 1993. In the case of Florida, such legislative solutions undoubtedly were attributable to the large population of elderly living in that state. Human services appeared as a legislative category only in Minnesota and only in 1993. One other distinctive category in which family legislation was enacted was in the area of civil rights—by different states in each of the 3 data years: Nevada in 1991, Minnesota in 1993, and Florida in 1995.

Table 8.3 shows the relative frequency with which the term *family* was mentioned in the different substantive categories relative to all the other family legislation the states enacted in each of the data years—in percentage terms for categories in which families were mentioned at least four times in the legislative measures comprising the categories, allowing for comparisons to be made in the legislative focus of the six states. Thus, in 1991, for example, almost 10% of the family legislation California enacted was in the area of adoption, 11% in the area of child and family welfare, and so on, based on the total number of legislative measures California enacted that pertained to families in 1991 ($N = 53$). The

TABLE 8.3 Categories of Explicit Family Policies Enacted by Six States With Different Political Cultures, Percentages for Categories With Four or More Family Mentions by Year

Categories	CA %	FL %	MN %	NV %	NY %	SC %
1991	N=53	N=22	N=50	N=37	N=38	N=9
Adoption	9	—	—	—	13	—
Child abuse/neglect	—	—	8	—	24	—
Child and family welfare	11	—	—	11	—	—
Child custody	—	—	—	11	—	—
Child support	9	—	—	—	—	—
Courts, crime, juveniles	—	—	8	—	—	—
Domestic violence	9	18	—	—	—	—
Education	—	18	14	—	—	—
Health care	21	32	18	19	21	—
Marriage and divorce	—	—	8	—	—	—
Taxes	—	—	10	—	—	—
1993	N=63	N=19	N=43	N=60	N=25	N=19
Adoption	11	—	—	13	16	—
AFDC/welfare reform	13	—	—	—	—	—
Child and family welfare	9	—	—	—	20	—
Child custody	—	—	—	—	12	—
Child support	11	—	21	13	—	—
Courts, crime, juveniles	6	—	—	—	—	—
Domestic violence	14	—	—	7	—	—
Education	6	—	30	—	—	—
Employment	8	—	—	—	7	—
Health care	—	37	8	8	—	—
Housing	—	—	8	—	—	—
Marriage and divorce	6	—	8	—	—	—
Mental health/developmental disabilities	—	—	—	—	—	58
1995	N=115	N=17	N=55	N=59	N=33	N=24
AFDC/welfare reform	18	—	9	—	—	17
Child abuse/neglect	4	—	—	8	15	—
Child custody	—	—	7	8	15	—
Child and family welfare	10	—	—	14	21	—
Child support	4	—	18	—	—	—
Courts, crime, juveniles	10	—	—	14	—	—
Domestic violence	13	24	—	12	15	21
Education	10	—	11	10	—	—
Employment	—	—	—	7	—	—
Family professionals	4	—	—	—	—	—
Health care	12	—	18	10	—	—
Housing	3	—	—	—	—	—

same pertains for all the other categories for all the other states. If no percentages appear in the table (as signified by a dash), it is because family was not mentioned in a legislative category at least four times. As can be seen in Table 8.3, relative to all the other legislation the states enacted in 1991, they enacted more family legislation in the area of health care than in any of the other categories.

The two exceptions are New York and South Carolina; New York enacted more explicit family legislation in the area of child abuse.

In order of descending frequency, Florida enacted the most family legislation in the area of health care in 1991, followed by California, New York, Nevada, and Minnesota. Although Florida also enacted relatively more family legislation in the areas of education and domestic violence than the other states in 1991, it enacted fewer legislative solutions that explicitly attended to the problems of families than any of the other states except South Carolina, skewing categorical percentages. Because percentages were calculated only for categories with four or more family mentions, Table 8.3 shows that South Carolina did not enact enough family legislation in 1991 to warrant the calculation of percentages for any of the categories. Hence, it does not show that families were mentioned twice in the health care legislation that South Carolina enacted in 1991.

In 1993, Florida again enacted relatively more legislative solutions in health care than the other states but not a sufficient number of measures in other categories to calculate percentages for them. For California, the family problem that captured the most legislative attention was domestic violence, followed by AFDC/welfare reform, child support, and adoption; for Minnesota, it was education and child support; for Nevada, adoption and child support; for New York, child/family welfare and adoption; and for South Carolina, mental health/mental retardation.

In 1995, California enacted more legislative solutions primarily in AFDC/welfare reform, domestic violence, and health care; in Florida, domestic violence only; in Minnesota, child support and health care; in Nevada, child/family welfare, the courts, crimes, juveniles, and domestic violence; in New York, child/family welfare, domestic violence, child abuse/neglect, and child custody; and South Carolina, domestic violence and AFDC/welfare reform.

Breadth: Did the States Differ in the Breadth of their Legislative Solutions to Family Problems?

Table 8.4 shows pooled frequencies and pooled percentages for family measures enacted in each legislative category for each state for all 3 data years combined. Abuse/domestic violence is an example of the latter; the set of measures that comprise this category of constructed solutions includes child abuse, spousal abuse, and elder abuse legislation. By pooling the data for the 3 data years and grouping related sets of measures, readers can see that the scope of legislative solutions that Nevada enacted was the broadest of the six states, exceeding the number of categories of family legislation enacted by Minnesota by 1 ($N = 22$ and 21, respectively), followed by South Carolina, 19, California, 18, Florida, 17, and New York, 16.

Looking at the total percentages for each of the legislative categories, readers also can see that relative to all the family legislation it enacted, California enacted relatively more legislative solutions that addressed the economic problems of families than any of the other states, attributable largely to its very

TABLE 8.4   Explicit Family Legislation Enacted by 6 States; Legislative Measures, Pooled Frequencies, 1991, 1993, 1995; Categories of Measures, Pooled Percentages, 1991, 1993, 1995

Categories	CA N=231	FL N=58	MN N=148	NV N=156	NY N=96	SC N=52
Abuse/domestic violence						
Child	8	2	7	11	15	—
Spouse, significant other	29	8	3	12	5	6
Elderly				1		
Percent of total enacted family legislation for category	16	17	7	15	21	12
Child/family welfare						
Adoption	13	—	3	12	11	1
Foster care, family preservation	24	1	6	15	15	4
Percent of total enacted family legislation for category	16	2	6	17	27	10
Economic provisions						
AFDC/welfare reform	31	3	8	3	4	4
Employment-related benefits	8	3	3	10	4	2
Taxes, e.g., EITC			6	1		2
Child care	5	2	6	2	2	4
Domestic partnerships	2	—	—	—	—	—
Percent of total enacted family legislation for category	20	14	16	10	10	23
Courts, crime, juveniles	20	4	4	16	6	2
Percent of total enacted family legislation for category	9	7	3	10	6	4
Education	15	6	26	10	3	4
Percent of total enacted family legislation for category	6	10	18	6	3	8
Family roles & responsibilities						
Child custody	4	2	5	16	7	1
Child support	17	2	19	13	3	4
Displaced homemakers	1	—	—	2	—	—
Percent of total enacted family legislation for category	10	7	16	20	10	10
Health Care	28	16	23	18	10	5
Percent of total enacted family legislation for category	12	28	16	12	10	10
Housing	9	—	10	1	4	—
Percent of total enacted family legislation for category	4	0	7	1	4	0
Marriage and divorce	8	2	6	6	1	—
Percent of total enacted family legislation for category	3	3	4	4	1	0

TABLE 8.4   (Continued)

Categories	CA N=231	FL N=58	MN N=148	NV N=156	NY N=96	SC N=52
Miscellaneous						
Adult care	—	2	—	—	—	—
Civil rights, e.g., gays & lesbians/ marital status	1	1	1	—	—	—
Family farms	—	—	3	—	—	—
Family professionals/marriage & family therapists	8	1	—	1	—	—
Human services	1	—	3	—	—	—
Mental health/mental retardation	—	1	4	1	3	11
Surviving spouses/property rights, insurance	—	2	—	—	3	—
Families of murder/suicide victims, inheritance	—	—	—	2	—	1
Pension rights, one spouse cause of death of other	—	—	1	—	—	—
Veterans affairs	—	—	1	2	—	1
Percent of total enacted family legislation for category	4	12	9	4	6	25

substantial welfare reform efforts early on: child/family welfare, abuse/domestic violence, and health care. Florida enacted relatively more family legislation in health care and abuse/domestic violence; Minnesota, in education, economic provisions, family roles and responsibilities (namely child support and custody), and health care; Nevada, in family roles and responsibilities, child/family welfare, abuse/domestic violence, and health care; New York, more legislation also related to child/family welfare, followed by abuse/domestic violence, and family roles and responsibilities; and South Carolina, more legislation related to economic provisions, abuse/domestic violence, and mental health/mental retardation (under miscellaneous). Again, attention is called to the small frequencies on which percentages are based for both South Carolina and Florida.

Regardless of state and political culture, the legislative categories in which families were mentioned the least frequently were housing and marriage and divorce, in part because not many legislative solutions were enacted in these categories in any case. Of the six states, Minnesota enacted the most housing legislation that explicitly mentioned families, Florida and South Carolina, the least, that is, none. Unlike the other states, South Carolina also did not enact any legislation pertaining to marriage and divorce.

Other State Distinctions

Other differences also can be seen in the family policies the six states enacted during the study period. Florida was distinctive in that it was the only one of the six states to enact legislation related to adult abuse; Minnesota was the only state to enact legislation pertaining to family farms; and New York was the only state to enact legislation pertaining to the property rights of surviving spouses. Only California enacted legislation pertaining to domestic partnerships and, except for Nevada, was the only other state to enact legislation pertaining to displaced homemakers. In analyses not shown here, Nevada was the only state except for Florida to enact legislation pertaining to surrogate mothers, or more precisely, gestational surrogate contracts; and except for South Carolina, Nevada was the only state to enact legislation with regard to the inheritance rights and compensatory claims of families of murder/suicide victims.

South Carolina was distinguished not only by its legislative solutions to family problems in the areas of mental health and mental retardation but also by its legislative *inattention* to problems in the areas of child abuse and child/family welfare. In this regard, it mirrored the legislative pattern that it evidenced in the 1980s. Interestingly, South Carolina and Florida were the only two of the six states to enact family and medical leave legislation for state employees; New York was the only state to enact legislation creating an Alzheimer's Task Force charged with making recommendations to help families with a member suffering from the disease. Minnesota and California were both distinguished by their health insurance programs for low-income families, MinnesotaCare in the case of Minnesota and Medi-Cal in the case of California.

Although Minnesota clearly was the leader in emphasizing education as a solution to family problems, looking inside this category for examples of measures it included may help readers to better appreciate its substance—in the event they may think that education deals only with matters pertaining to academic curricula. As it pertains to families, it included measures as varied as AIDS prevention education for junior and senior high school students, prekindergarten early intervention programs, parenting workshops for parents of students with disciplinary problems, dropout prevention programs, parent involvement programs, dispute mediation in cases related to the educational placement of handicapped children, school lunch/breakfast programs, residency requirements, schooling for AFDC mothers, school tuition waivers, work curfews for high school students, parent notification, the creation of a Legislative Commission on Children, Youth, and Families and a children's cabinet in Minnesota to study various measures for increasing family participation in the schools, followed by the creation of a Department of Children, Families and Learning that incorporated the functions formerly assigned to the Department of Education and those of other state departments with programmatic responsibilities for children and their families.

The legislative solutions that explicitly addressed the problems of families in the area of health care were as varied as those in the area of education. Examples include abortion, breast cancer, health insurance coverage, public health programs for the prevention of child abuse and delinquency, breast feeding in public, prenatal care, adolescent pregnancy prevention, long-term care, Medicaid, HIV testing, child immunizations, the Women's, Infants' and Children's program (WIC), a legislative declarative with regard to assisted suicide in Nevada, drug and alcohol treatment for pregnant women, sperm donors, lead abatement, family planning services, surrogate mothers, hospital-based paternity incentive programs, living wills, organ transplant donors, and genetic testing in cases of contested paternity.

■ Summary and Conclusions

Based on these analyses, hypothesized differences in the quantity, breadth, and substantive focus of the legislative solutions that states with different political cultures constructed in the early to mid-1990s that explicitly mentioned families received mixed support. Minnesota as the moralistic state enacted relatively more legislation that explicitly addressed the problems of families than any of the other states, as hypothesized, and California, as a predominantly moralistic state, substantially more family legislation and legislation overall in terms of absolute frequencies. Readers will recall that according to the Elazar typology, moralistic states are oriented toward the use of government as an instrument for promoting the public good, here as it pertains to their construction of legislative solutions to address family problems. In relative terms, however, California enacted less than half as much family legislation as Minnesota—or about the same as Nevada and South Carolina, contrary to what had been expected.

Also contrary to what had been expected, the policy approach to family problems of Minnesota and California as moralistic states was not broader than that of the other states: Nevada's was broader, despite its cultural bias toward limited government, especially with regard to matters considered private. Nevada's legislation explicitly mentioned families in one more category than Minnesota's, in four more categories than California's, and in six more categories than New York's.

The findings show that the focus and content of the solutions the six states constructed differed and that the thrust of Minnesota's—education—was proactive, as hypothesized. However, the findings are more difficult to interpret in the case of California. Just as California, of the six states, enacted the greatest number of explicit family policies as legislative solutions to family problems, and indeed the most legislation overall in terms of absolute frequencies and the most legislation that focused on the economic problems of families, in relative terms, South Carolina constructed more of the latter. The same observation applies to health care. In terms of absolute frequencies, California enacted more legislative solutions to family problems in the area of health care than the other states, but in relative terms, Florida enacted more. Measures related to education, health care, and family economics are interpreted here as proactive in that they aim to address family problems *before* they occur. In contrast, the family policies enacted by Nevada and New York, the two individualistic states, could be characterized as reactive in that they aimed to address family problems *after* such problems occurred: abuse, family breakup, child support, and custody. Thus, depending on whether absolute frequencies or percentages are used to interpret the findings, the focus of California's constructed solutions to family problems was more—or less—proactive than that of the other states. Based on absolute frequencies, the focus of its legislative solutions to family problems would be as hypothesized.

Similarly with regard to the hypothesis that the family policies constructed by states with mixed political cultures would be more consistent with the first than the second of their paired cultures, again much depends on whether absolute frequencies or percentages are used to interpret the findings. Based on absolute frequencies, for example, the quantity and breadth of Florida's family legislative solutions are consistent with the state's traditionalistic culture and its presumption against the construction of government solutions to problems in general, consistent with the study's hypothesis. However, if based on percentages, the solutions that it did construct as measured by the focus of its family legislation—health care—would be viewed as proactive and thus contrary to the study's hypothesis. With respect to California, both the sheer quantity and focus of its family legislation—family economics—suggest that its family policies were more consistent with the moralistic than the individualistic side of its political culture, supporting the research hypothesis. Findings with regard to the family legislation that New York enacted also seemed to support the research hypothesis—and on all three dimensions: quantity, breadth, and core or focus—reflecting a preference for minimal government intervention into matters related to families, more in keeping with the state's individualistic than moralistic side.

Although Elazar's characterizations of the political cultures of the six states may not characterize the family policies they constructed on each and every dimension on which they were analyzed—quantity, breadth, and focus—his typology nonetheless offers a way of interpreting differences in states' constructed solutions to family problems as represented by the family policies they enacted. It also gives credence to speculations made in the previous chapter with regard to the attitudes embedded in congressional members' cognitive frameworks to which they gave voice in the debates over DOMA that might have reflected the political culture of the states they represented. Such a possibility pertains, despite the homogenizing effects of national influences and federal policies affecting what states do (Erikson, Wright, & McIver, 1993), as in the areas of child support, welfare reform, and domestic violence, or state demographics and fiscal capacities.

Although such differences cannot be attributed solely to their political cultures, the Elazar typology helps to interpret and make sense of the solutions that different states construct to family problems. For example, Nevada's divorce rate, which consistently ranks highest among the 50 states (National Center for Health Statistics, 1991; U.S. Bureau of the Census, 1998), could explain why its solutions to family problems were so strongly focused on child support and custody as problems, but such a focus also could reflect the pragmatism that characterizes the individualistic nature of the state's political culture, given the context of the solutions it constructed.

Similarly, although Minnesota's emphasis on education as a strategy for preventing family problems also cannot be attributed solely to its political culture, the two are highly consistent with Minnesota's per capita expenditures for education, which was the highest of the six states in 1995 (U.S. Bureau of the Census, 1997). Suggestive of the connection between its political culture, its spending to prevent family problems, and problems actually experienced by families was (a) the percentage of babies born to teen mothers in Minnesota in 1993, the lowest of the six states (U.S. Bureau of the Census, 1996); (b) the percentage of persons who were high school and college graduates in 1995, the highest of the six states (U.S. Bureau of the Census, 1996); and (c) the percentage of high school dropouts, the lowest of the six states (U.S. Bureau of the Census, 1993).

Vote data for the six states for the last seven presidential elections give further credence to differences in the states' political cultures as characterized by Elazar, voter participation rates being an indicator of attitudes toward government held by the populations of different states. As noted earlier, voter turnout in Minnesota was higher than the national average in seven out of the last seven presidential elections, whereas it was never higher than the national average in the other states, except in California in 1972 (Barone & Ujifusa, 1997; U.S. Bureau of the Census, 1990, 1993, 1996). Indeed, of the six states, voter turnout in Minnesota was the highest in all seven presidential elections, second highest in California in four of the seven presidential elections, second highest in New York in three of the last seven elections, and lowest in South Carolina and second lowest in Nevada in six out of the seven elections.

Another observation that should be made with regard to the study's findings has to do with the increased frequency with which families were explicitly mentioned in the legislation the states enacted over the study period for all but two of the states—New York and Florida—suggesting a heightened awareness on the part of states of the connections between the policies they enact and families and their well-being. For the three states included in the 1980s' analyses, the increase was dramatic: in the case of Nevada, it was three times greater than 10 years earlier and *over* three times greater in the case of Minnesota. It even increased in the case of South Carolina, by about 20%, although South Carolina's family legislation and legislative output overall remained the smallest of the three states. In this regard, the findings for these three states show patterns that were remarkably similar to the patterns they showed in the earlier analyses.

That families were increasingly mentioned in the legislation the states enacted should not be taken to mean that the solutions they constructed were necessarily supportive of families, however, or have had positive outcomes for families. Not only would such a conclusion require detailed analyses of the individual measures comprising the various categories, but carefully designed evaluation studies would have to be undertaken with experimental and control groups to determine the subsequent effects of the different measures on families. Some in fact may question whether the explicit mention of families in the legislation the states enacted is a valid measure of their family policies. Indeed, given that relatively few solutions were constructed to family problems by any of the states included in the analysis (as measured by the explicit family policies they enacted relative to all the other legislation they enacted) and that all policies affect families directly or indirectly (Kamerman & Kahn, 1976; Zimmerman, 1992a, 1995a), it would have to be said that most of the family policies the states enacted were implicit rather than explicit with regard to the families and their problems, just as at the federal level.

Thus, in addition to not providing information about the explicit family policies the six states enacted in 1990, 1992, and 1994, the even years of the early to mid-1990s, the findings do not provide information about their implicit family policies. Nor do they provide information about those family policies already incorporated into states' laws. Furthermore, because the states were not randomly selected, the findings cannot be generalized to the family policies enacted by the other 44 states in the country. All of these limitations convey something about the enormity of the task waiting for readers and researchers intent on overcoming them. In addition, unlike the analysis of the debates over DOMA that revealed the attitudes embedded in the solutions individual congressional members constructed to same-sex marriage, the analyses of the legislative solutions the six states constructed to family problems in the 1990s, like the analyses of the explicit family measures on which Congress voted during the 1980s and 1990s, did not. They ware inferred from the findings, based on the states' political cultures.

Nonetheless, the analyses do provide information about the explicit family policies constructed by six states with different political cultures for 3 data years, spanning a 4-year period from the early to mid-1990s. Moreover, the analyses, when viewed in conjunction with federal solutions to family problems, as in Chapter 6, allow comparisons to be made between the kinds of solutions that were constructed at the state level and the kinds of solutions that were constructed at the federal level. For one, abortion was not constructed as a problem as much at the state as at the federal level and thus did not permeate the family policies the states enacted. For another, state-level solutions, which in many instances complemented those at the federal level, were more programmatic, making manifest the policy, program, and practice connections. As readers may recall from earlier discussion, family policy may be seen as a political arena in which sets of activities, discursive and material, affect each other in mutually reinforcing ways.

Because political culture theory is not the only perspective that can help in understanding why some constructions of family problems and their solutions are accepted and others are not—at all governmental levels—the chapters in Part III provide additional perspectives for understanding such acceptance and nonacceptance. Further discussion of political culture theory is included to demonstrate its relevance to comparative analyses of policy solutions to family problems of other countries. But first, some questions are listed below for you to answer about the discussion in *this* chapter.

■ Some Questions for Your Reflection and Discussion

1. Define political culture.
2. What is the importance of political culture for family policy?
3. How does the anthropological approach to the study of attitudes differ from the psychological approach?
4. What three political cultures constitute Elazar's typology of states' political cultures?
5. What distinguishes each? Describe.
6. What are some variations of the three political cultures?
7. What political cultures do each of the states included in this chapter represent?
8. How did the six states differ in their construction of policy solutions to family problems?
9. For the six states as a whole, what conclusions were drawn about family policy at the state level in the 1990s?
10. In what ways do other data about the six states support the findings with regard to the policy solutions they constructed to family problems over the observational period, the six states being representative of different political cultures? Give examples from the chapter.

And now to Part III and the next chapter.

■ Note

1. The assistance of Lara Campbell, Meredith Fergus, Rachel Trovino, and Amy Weisenheimer in this project is gratefully acknowledged.

As in the analyses of congressional roll call votes, the criterion that was applied to the selection of items for the content analysis of the legislative summaries and used to measure the extent to which the six states explicitly addressed the problems of families in the legislative solutions they enacted was the incorporation of explicit family language in the titles or summaries of individual legislative measures. As in Chapter 6, such language as linguistic references included spouse, family, parent, father, mother, grandparent, relative, next of kin, and child within the context of the parent-child relationship. Just as in the analysis of the descriptive summaries of federal legislation reported in Chapter 6, these terms were measures of semantic validity. Readers will remember that semantic validity is defined as those words or coding units that possess similar connotations about which persons familiar with the language agree (Weber, 1985).

To identify the legislation that explicitly mentioned families, the entire legislative summary was scanned for each state and data year, page by page and line by line. Items that met the study's criterion for inclusion in the analysis were then typed onto sheets of 8½ × 11" worksheets, where the text of the items were recorded for each state for each year, retaining as much of the information that appeared in the text of the summaries as possible. The items were then classified into their respective categories (e.g., adoption, child abuse, domestic violence, health care, education), following their classification in the summaries, and recorded in abbreviated form onto other worksheets. Using keywords, individual items were then alphabetized within categories as a way of ordering them and avoiding double entries and duplicated counts, and recorded onto still other worksheets—for each state by year. This procedure allowed not only frequencies and percentages to be obtained for all the family policies that each state enacted for each data year and for all 3 years as a whole but also of the legislation each state enacted in the different categories. The total number of items that explicitly mentioned families relative to all the other legislation each of the six states enacted served as a measure of the extent to which their legislative solutions explicitly addressed the problems of families. The total number of items enacted in each category relative to all the items that explicitly mentioned families served as a measure of the core or focus of their explicit family policies. The number of categories in which families were explicitly mentioned in the legislation they enacted served as a measure of the breadth or scope of the family policies they constructed as solutions to family problems. It should be noted that these analyses differ from the analyses of congressional roll call votes presented in Chapter 6 in that they pertain only to the explicit family legislation states actually enacted, not to all the explicit family measures on which votes were taken.

To ensure reliability, each procedure was repeated at least twice to make sure (a) that all the legislation that explicitly mentioned families had been identified, (b) that such legislation had been accurately recorded and counted, and (c) that it had been classified the same way for all six states. In instances where legislation cut across categories reflecting the interrelated and interdependent nature of different family policies, items were classified according to their primary objective, such as health care in the case of HIV testing for victims of domestic abuse. These procedures were similar to those used by Zimmerman and Owens (1989) in their analyses of the family policies that Minnesota, Nevada, and South Carolina enacted in the 1980s.

Policy Frameworks:

What Accounts for the Policy Solutions That Are Constructed to Family Problems?

Although language is important in the construction of policy solutions to family problems (regardless of governmental level) and in revealing the attitudes embedded in such constructions, it also is important in understanding such constructions and what accounts for them. The diversity of meanings embedded in every constructed family problem and solution and the diversity of explanations for such constructions call for a diversity of conceptual frameworks—models, theoretical perspectives, or frameworks—to help in understanding such phenomena.

Part III consists of chapters that focus on policy frameworks that help shed light on the processes involved in the construction of policy solutions to family problems and the substance of such policies. As noted earlier, conceptual frameworks are clusters of interrelated concepts or ideas—in short, they are constructions that guide observations of different phenomena, here with respect to policies related to families and the selection of appropriate methods for making such observations (Hill & Hansen, 1960). Concepts are words or a set of words that express a general idea concerning the nature of particular phenomena or relations between phenomena (Theodorson & Theodorson, 1969).

I use the term *conceptual frameworks* the same way I use the terms *theoretical frameworks, theory,* or *theoretical perspective*. Like conceptual frameworks, theory consists of interrelated principles and definitions that conceptually organize selected aspects of the empirical or real world in a systematic way. Just as concepts are the basis of language, conceptual frameworks are the basis for generalizing and ordering phenomena in the real world. Focusing on certain aspects of phenomena while ignoring others, conceptual frameworks, as mental constructs, reflect a certain point of view, affecting perceptions of reality, which in turn have implications for the construction of policy solutions to family problems. The chapters that constitute Part III include conceptual frameworks or theories that help in understanding individual and collective behaviors in the policy and political arenas and also have implications for the construction of policy solutions to family programs. These include the following:

- The institutional framework, which views family policy as the outcome of institutional arrangements (Dye, 1975)

- Rational choice theory, which views family policy as the selection of the alternative with the highest net value ratio in the achievement of agreed-upon goals (Dye, 1975) (here with respect to family well-being)

- Incremental theory, which views existing policies and programs as variations of past constructions of policies and programs (Lindblom, 1959)

- Game theory, which sees family policy in terms of rational choice under competitive conditions of no authority (Dye, 1975)

- Political culture theory, which sees family policy as constrained by the attitudes that people hold toward government and each other (Inglehart, 1990; Zimmerman, 1992a)

- Interest group theory, which sees family policy as the equilibrium reached among contending interest groups (Dye, 1975)

- Elite theory, which sees family policy in terms of elite preferences (Dye, 1975), and

- Systems theory, which views family policy in terms of systems output (Easton, 1979)

As readers can see, there is no single, all-purpose framework that deals with all aspects of the policy situation. Because each focuses on somewhat different aspects of the policy situation, dealing with some aspects of the policy situation but not others, they each reflect a point of view. All the frameworks may appropriately apply to some issues, although only one or two may apply to others, depending on how contested the issues are. Social Security, health care reform, and welfare reform would be illustrative of the former and the reauthorization of funding for Head Start illustrative of the latter. The interests and preferences of the policy analyst also play a part in determining which of the frameworks is applied to the analysis of individual family policies, both as they are being constructed and after—upon their review and evaluation.

As to a framework for guiding the actions of those who would like to help shape the construction of solutions to family problems, much would depend on their role in that process—advocate, lobbyist, citizen, policy maker, agency staff, or researcher. As will be seen, the frameworks provide clues, not specifics, for carrying out such roles. For specifics, interested readers are advised to attend workshops that can help in this regard, although in the final chapter, I provide some suggestions that I hope will alert you to the requirements for different policy roles. Workshops on lobbying and advocacy also are offered by such organizations as the League of Women Voters and other public interest organizations in local communities, usually just prior to state legislative sessions. People certainly may and do engage in policy processes related to families *without* being familiar with the conceptual frameworks presented in these next few chapters, but the frameworks are useful guides for policy practice and for constructing a rationale for policy efforts.

The presentation of the policy frameworks in the discussion that follows includes their underlying assumptions and key concepts; these are accompanied by illustrative case examples. By their very nature, illustrative examples do not constitute a coherent story of the construction of a particular family policy. To tell such a story would require focusing on a particular issue, such as health care reform or welfare reform, and making it the central story. That is *not* what these next several chapters are intended to do. They are intended to present different conceptual frameworks that readers can use to answer one of the book's central questions: What accounts for the solutions that are constructed to family problems? The frameworks, each of which has its own conceptual configuration, are presented in the order in which they were listed earlier.

The length of the chapters in Part III vary with the complexity of the framework and the examples incorporated in the discussion.

CHAPTER 9

The Institutional Framework

*Family Policy as the Outcome of
Institutional Arrangements*

■ Definitions

This chapter focuses on the institutional framework as it applies to the construction of solutions to family problems via the policies that governments enact. An institution has been defined as an interrelated system of social roles and norms organized around satisfying some important social need or function (Theodorson & Theodorson, 1969) (here in relation to families). The legislation enacted by state governments in selected years of the 1990s and by the federal government in selected years of the 1980s and 1990s was intended to satisfy some family need, whether with respect to child care, employment, income security, or health care.

Such government policies have different policy functions: *regulatory, redistributive,* and *distributive.* The *regulatory* function acts to protect individuals and families and also the larger society by establishing rules for governing family behaviors and also the behaviors of governments and businesses. Illustrative of government's regulatory function in the family sphere are domestic abuse laws prohibiting parents from physically harming their children and spouses. Such laws at the same time also require governments through their relevant agencies to investigate suspected cases of child and spousal abuse and to act accordingly, depending on the outcome of their investigation.

The *redistributive* function pertains to the shifting or reallocation of resources from one program related to families to another. An example of such shifting or reallocation of resources was a county board of commissioners' plan to shift nearly one fourth of the money it needed to meet the increasing demand for programs for troubled children from social service programs for elderly, disabled, and low-income residents to child protection and mental health services for the county's most troubled children (Smith, M. 1999).

The *distribution* of resources, as differentiated from the *redistribution* of resources, refers to the allocation of *new* resources for programs such as child care as still another function of government policy vis-à-vis families. Such resources could come from budget surpluses or higher tax revenues, avoiding the need for shifting or reallocating resources from one program to another. Had the county board of commissioners, for example, been willing to ask taxpayers for more money, it might not have had to reallocate resources from social service programs for elderly, disabled, and low-income people to fund child protection and mental health services for troubled children. It could have simply *distributed* or *allocated* funds for such programs without cutting funds from other programs.

■ Government, the State, and Society

As an institution, government is associated with the modern state. The state refers to the nation as symbolized by government. Government is an instrument for carrying out the traditions and laws of a society by which a society is coordinated and administered (Theodorson & Theodorson, 1969). These definitions apply not only to the federal government but also, modified, to city, county, and state governments. Society itself is a comprehensive social system that includes all the basic social institutions required to meet basic human needs, such as the education of children, nutritional and housing needs for people, and so on. Society is independent in the sense that it includes all organizational forms necessary for its survival over a long period of time, recruiting members from within the group via biological reproduction and from outside the group via the recruitment of people from other countries and societies—or immigration.

■ Family Policy From the Institutional Perspective

The institutional framework highlights the importance of institutional structures, values, and roles for certain policy outcomes. Family policy, from this perspective, is defined as the outcome of the ways in which government as an institution is structured and the values and norms that underlie its structure (Dye, 1975). From the institutional perspective, all the legislative solutions to family problems enacted by the six states as reported in Chapter 8 and that Congress voted on as reported in Chapter 6 were outcomes of the ways in which government as an institution in the United States is structured and the values and norms that underlie its structures. Norms are rules that help control and predict human behavior and set the standards by which governments—national, state, and local—carry out their policy functions. Domestic abuse laws are illustrative of norms with regard to family behaviors that set standards by which governments carry out their regulatory and protective functions for families. These definitions are applicable to *all* institutions: social welfare, the family, education, financial, political, and so on. Each is an interrelated system of roles and norms organized around satisfying important needs.

The basic assumptions underlying the institutional framework as it applies to this discussion are as follows:

- As an institution, government in the United States is governed by the norms and values embedded in the Constitution and Declaration of Independence.
- The way in which government as an institution is structured reflects the norms and values of the society.
- The way in which government is structured and the norms and values underlying its structure favor some outcomes and not others, as for example, the vote over DOMA.
- Such outcomes (e.g., family policies) reflect the norms and values that underlie the structure from which such policies emanate.
- Characteristic of such outcomes are their legitimacy, authority, and universality.

Each of these assumptions, together with the concepts they incorporate, is discussed more fully in this chapter. The concepts—the language, the words, the terms—embedded in the institutional framework include:

- Values and norms
- Institutional roles
- Patterns of behaviors and activities
- Structures and structural arrangements
- Continuity over time
- The legitimacy, authority, and universality of policy outcomes

I begin the discussion with the U.S. Constitution as the country's institutional framework to both illustrate the framework and demonstrate how its conceptual language can be used to better understand family policy as the outcome of the ways government in the United States is structured and the values and norms that underlie its structure.

■ The Constitution: The Nation's Institutional Framework

The institutional framework of the United States is detailed in the Constitution. Embedded in it are the norms and standards that government and its leaders are expected to satisfy in performing their roles. The Constitution defines the role of the federal government in relation to the states and the people; the role of the president as chief executive and his or her relationship to Congress; the role of the Senate and House and their relationship to each other; the role of the judiciary; the role of citizens; and the relationship of each of these entities to the other, all playing a role in family policy—whether in its formulation, implementation, or evaluation. The Constitution also outlines the rights and duties of the three branches of government and the relationship of each of the three branches to each other. Although the Constitution provides the institutional context for family policy, it nonetheless is silent with respect to families.

Early History

The Constitution is pertinent to this discussion not only because it provides the institutional framework for our form of government but also because the process by which it came into being is illustrative of how a condition becomes accepted as a problem and a solution is constructed to address it (Edelman, 1968). Although the arguments and debates surrounding the adoption of the Constitution reflected the impossibility of marshalling evidence for or against its adoption that would be equally persuasive for everyone, the outcome of those debates helps answer the question What accounts for the policy solutions that governments construct to family problems?

The Constitution was constructed to address the problem of the Articles of Confederation, which, until 1789, when the Constitution was adopted, was the country's institutional framework (Bailyn, 1993). Although the Articles protected and jealously guarded colonial self-rule against Great Britain and the colonies against each other, they restricted Congress in performing the duties of a national government, such as the ability to levy taxes, to regulate foreign and interstate commerce, and to enter into treaties with foreign governments unless it had the approval of all 13 sovereign colonies or states. Accordingly, a Constitutional Convention was called in 1787 to revise the Articles. Instead of revising them, however, the Convention debated the merits of a new institutional framework for the country, as eventually embodied in the Constitution.

Reflected in the debates over the Constitution were the Founding Fathers' deepest fears of government domination and the loss of individual rights and freedoms. The Federalists, along with business interests, favored adoption of the Constitution and giving more power to the national government. Anti-Federalists, who wanted more power vested in the states, opposed its adoption (Draper, 1993). The debates were intense, both sides motivated by idealistic principles. The Federalists argued that the fate of the Constitution's adoption would determine whether the country would become a model of liberty and justice for the rest of the world to emulate—one, they said, that would transform the world, not just determine the form of government under which the American people as a nation would live. However, Patrick Henry, an Anti-Federalist, predicted that adoption of the Constitution would destroy individuals' and states' rights. Neither side had evidence to support its claims.

The Issue of States' Rights

When adoption of the Constitution was being debated, arguments for deferring to state or local control were based on the sanctity of regional differences in economics, customs, and values (Draper, 1993). The relative importance of

trade and agriculture, Anti-Federalists argued, was very different in Massachusetts and Virginia. Hence, the two states differed in their approaches to such
problems as bankruptcy and, later, the War of 1812. Today, arguments for
states' rights tend to be based on efficiency (the debates over DOMA being illustrative) and responsiveness to local concerns. Some political scientists argue that
decisions about programs like Social Security fall logically to the federal government, whereas other kinds of decisions, they argue, such as those pertaining to
economic development and many public services, fall naturally to states and
localities.

In 1999, a broad bipartisan coalition in the Senate and House of Representatives, hoping to shift political power back to the states, prepared legislation to
make it harder for Congress and the executive branch to adopt laws and rules
preempting the states on issues such as drugs, the environment, health, and
worker safety (Labation, 1999). The legislation would have given local authorities broad new powers to use the courts to challenge federal laws and regulations
that failed to explicitly identify state statutes and regulations being preempted.
Following three opinions handed down by the Supreme Court curbing the ability of Congress to make federal law binding on the states, the measure in the Senate was called the Federalism Accountability Act; in the House, it was called the
Federalism Act. Among other things, the legislation would have abolished the
legal doctrine of implied preemption.

Elected Officials and Their Constituents

Other issues surrounding adoption of the Constitution seemed on the surface
to be small matters of detail, such as how often elections should be held for members of the House and Senate. But underlying them were the Founding Fathers'
deep-seated fears of government oppression, which were based on their experiences of Europe under tyrannical monarchies. Elections under the Articles of
Confederation were held annually to prevent any one individual from accruing political power, but under the Constitution, Senate elections were scheduled
just once every 6 years. The infrequency of Senate elections worried the Anti-
Federalists. They argued that 6-year terms would create a permanent aristocracy
of lawmakers who associated only with each other, distancing them from the
experiences of ordinary people. For similar reasons, they objected to a 4-year
term for the presidency.

In this regard, it is interesting to speculate on how the Founding Fathers
would have reacted to the lack of voter participation in present-day elections
and whether they might have regarded the disengagement of voters from the
political process as the logical outcome of their worst fears—that government is
too far removed from the experiences of ordinary citizens, who, as a consequence, view politics as a waste of time and undeserving of even their minimal
attention (Teixeira, 1992).

Town hall meetings are a favorite forum for lawmakers to bring government
closer to people. Nearly all lawmakers hold them, bringing back to Congress

samples of public opinion to score particular political points (Ellperin, 1999). This time-honored tradition has its drawbacks, however. Such meetings tend to attract self-selected malcontents, whose quirky views often veer to the right or left of the average voter. Moreover, as more people have become disengaged from politics, fewer show up at meetings. The problem was exacerbated in the 1990s when redistricting tilted each lawmaker's district toward party activists in one party or the other.

The Bill of Rights: Individual Rights

Anti-Federalists worried about other issues in relation to the Constitution in addition to the length of terms for elected lawmakers and the seemingly limitless and unquestioned authority of the Supreme Court to decide all cases that came before it. What worried them the most was that the Constitution had no Bill of Rights. The Bill of Rights was not incorporated into the Constitution until the first Congress met under the new Constitution in September 1789, when the rights of individuals became one of the nation's few absolutes. Their experiences as subjects of tyrannical monarchs in Europe, where individuals had no rights, help to explain the solutions the Founding Fathers constructed to the potential threat of government-sponsored tyranny in America.

The basic assumptions underlying the Bill of Rights are outlined in the Declaration of Independence as follows:

- All people are created equal and have certain inalienable rights, among which are life, liberty, and the pursuit of happiness.
- To ensure these rights, individuals create governments that derive their power from the consent of the governed.
- Governments are responsible for carrying out the collective preferences of citizens whose fortunes and lives are bound to each other.
- Whenever any government becomes destructive of these ends, the people have the right to change or abolish it and to institute a new government based on principles that seem to have the greatest likelihood of ensuring the safety and happiness of all citizens.
- A system of checks and balances in the form of the separation of legislative, judicial, and executive powers is necessary to prevent the usurpation of individual rights.

Compromise and Nondecisions

Except for individual rights and their protection, the Constitution represents a series of compromises and second choices (Draper, 1993). Because the framers of the Constitution were willing to compromise, arguments over its adoption did not erupt into a civil war or prevent its ratification. The Federalists made one concession after another to achieve the goals they were seeking, which were a reasonably strong central government with the power to tax, maintain an army, and preserve the basic institutional structure they had outlined: a president, House of Representatives, Senate, and a Supreme Court. All powers not assigned to the federal government were to be reserved for the states. The Senate, with two seats for each state, large or small, was a concession to small states.

The issue of slavery was put on hold—as a nondecision—because it threatened ratification of the Constitution, postponing the civil war that was yet to come. In addition, once the vote was taken and the Constitution ratified, the Anti-Federalists conceded and did not revolt. Acceptance of the vote ratifying the Constitution, together with a willingness to compromise, reflected the norms that have since come to govern institutional practices in arriving at collective decisions and solutions to problems in this country, namely that the vote of the majority, however slim, gives such decisions their legitimacy and authority. Departing from these norms more recently was the unwillingness of congressional members to compromise on tax and spending bills, which caused the federal government to be shut down for a period of time in 1995.

▪ Distinguishing Features of Policy Choice From an Institutional Perspective

Despite noted departures from institutional norms, the three features that distinguish policy choices in the United States from an institutional perspective are their *legitimacy, authority,* and *universality.* Legitimacy refers to the lawfulness of policy and the processes that produce it; universality, to the applicability of such policy to all persons within the society to whom the policy applies; and authority, to the power of governments to enforce policy through the imposition of penalties on individuals and businesses that violate it. Tax policy is an example. Although tax policy may be contested, it becomes legitimized as law when a majority of elected representatives in both the House and Senate vote for it and the president signs it. It is universal in that it applies to everyone who pays taxes, and it carries with it the authority and power of the U.S. government to implement and enforce it—through the imposition of fines or, if necessary, imprisonment.

Even government officials—or maybe especially government officials—are expected to comply with the laws that are enacted. Whether elected or appointed, they are subject to arrest and lawsuits like everyone else. For example, President Clinton—rightly or wrongly—was sued in 1994 by a state employee in Arkansas who charged him with sexual harassment in 1991. Expectations of compliance with the laws that governments enact extend to those related to parent responsibility. Illustrative is a paternity suit a 17-year-old Michigan girl filed against the governor of Rhode Island, declaring he was her father ("Gov. Sundlun," 1993). Acceding to treating her as his child, the governor agreed to pay her college tuition, just as he did for his other children. In California, parents can be charged with a misdemeanor if they fail to provide "reasonable care" in supervising a child who commits a crime or delinquent act ("Parents," 1993). In

Minneapolis, parents of a 5-year-old boy who shot and killed himself with a gun the father had hidden in the boy's bedroom were charged, under a 1993 city statute, with the felony crime of child endangerment. All institutions have the power to impose sanctions to secure compliance with institutional norms, such as grounding children when they misbehave in the case of families, but government is the only institution that has the power to imprison and deprive people of their rights and freedoms (Dye, 1975).

■ Institutional Arrangements: The House and Senate Relationship

Just as the Bill of Rights reflected the Founding Fathers' fears of government domination, the structure of the government they created did as well. By creating two legislative bodies, the House and the Senate, they created not only a structure for ensuring a fragmented policy approach to families but also a structure for ensuring competition and conflict between the two bodies in lawmaking. As a result, the relationship between the House and Senate has always been characterized by tension and conflict (Merida, 1993).

Of the two, the House is less bound by tradition than the Senate; its members serve 2-year terms, not 6-year terms as senators do, and work in an environment four times larger than the Senate. For this reason, the two chambers differ in the ways they conduct their affairs and the rules that govern the way they conduct them. They also differ in their histories, their cultures, their style and temperament, and their personality. In the Senate, individual senators, including members of the minority party, enjoy considerable influence and status. Under Senate rules and precedents, a single senator can block legislation, force extended debate on an issue, and introduce amendments without warning. Congressional gridlock and failure to complete congressional tasks in a timely fashion is credited to the Senate's filibuster rule, which requires 60 votes to end debate instead of the 51 required for other votes. Senate rules also allow for a more leisurely and civil style of debate than House rules, which tightly control the time that members have on the floor, making polite debate a non sequitur. Pat Schroeder's observation characterizing the Senate as a peacock farm of strutting egos captures such differences. Schroeder, from Colorado, was a longtime House member who has since retired from that body.

■ Congressional Committees—and Families

Just as the relationship between the two chambers is structured for conflict, so also is the committee structure of the two bodies. Both the House and Senate conduct their business through a variety of committees and subcommittees, many of which compete with each other for jurisdiction over issues. Although the Founding Fathers may not have included families in their conception of the political order, many Senate committees and their several subcommittees deal with explicit family matters, as may be inferred from their titles. The function of congressional committees is to gather information by holding hearings on issues such as Medicare, the state of the economy, and the Patients' Bill of Rights that will aid congressional members in making policy choices. Family professionals with expertise in a particular family problem sometimes are invited to testify before such committees not only about the nature of the problem but also about solutions to address it.

In 1999, Senate committees explicitly related to families included the Committee on Aging, the Subcommittee on Social Security and Family Policy under the Senate Finance Committee, the Subcommittees on Aging and Children and Families under the Senate Committee on Health, Education, Labor and Pensions, and the Subcommittee on Youth Violence under the Senate Judiciary Committee. These committees are subject to change, and in 1999 there were fewer than in the past. The only House committee explicitly related to families included the Subcommittee on Early Childhood, Youth and Families under the House Committee on Education and the Workforce (Barone & Ujifusa, 1999). The different committees and subcommittees are created in response to the concerns of various interest groups and maintain and foster competition not only between themselves but also between the groups they represent. Committee specialization and overlap serve to intensify competition between committees and the fragmentation of policy effort.

In 1993, the Joint Committee on the Organization of Congress held a hearing on the topic of congressional committees. Former Vice President Walter Mondale testified that when he served in the Senate in the 1960s, he thought Congress needed more committees and larger staffs to study the problems that came to congressional attention. Some 30 years later, he recommended eliminating unnecessary committees and limiting the number of subcommittees, which by 1993 had grown to the hundreds. By 1999, the number of Senate committees had been reduced to 20 and subcommittees to 69; the number of House Committees was similarly reduced to just 20 and subcommittees to 89 (Barone & Ujifusa, 1999).

Regardless of their number, no congressional committee or subcommittee has jurisdiction over all the policy solutions that Congress enacts that affect families. None of the administrative agencies do either. Administrative agencies in the United States and elsewhere are organized around functions—health, education, income maintenance, housing, employment and manpower, commerce, agriculture, internal revenue, and defense—rather than around population groups such as the elderly, children, or families. Past experience in trying to structure activities around populations has not been particularly successful except for legislative oversight and the collection and dissemination of information. The experience of other countries in this regard has not been much different. The dilemma is that if family interests are defined too broadly, they exceed the boundaries and functions of a single agency. By the same token, if they are defined too narrowly, the sphere of agency activity is so tightly circumscribed that little of consequence can be accomplished (Kahn, Kamerman, & Dowling, 1979).

State Government Committees—and Families

State and local governments face problems similar to those at the federal level in terms of integrating broader family interests into their constructions of family policies as solutions to family problems. Efforts to incorporate family interests into government structures have been duplicated at state and local levels. Interagency committees on child and domestic abuse are common in many states and local communities (Zimmerman, 1988a). In 1985, two thirds of the states had some sort of committee within their governmental structures that focused attention on some family problem. Among the family issues or problems considered the most important at that time were child abuse, followed by teen pregnancy, drinking and driving, and foster care. Divorce, prayer in the schools, and euthanasia were considered the least important. Many committees were comprised of both legislators and interested citizens, including family professionals and practitioners, as another means of involving citizens in the construction of solutions to family problems and the affairs of government.

■ Rules for Governing Congressional Behaviors

The rules of state and congressional legislative bodies determine how committee specialization and competition play themselves out in the policy process. This evidenced itself in the jurisdictional dispute between the chairs of the Senate Finance Committee and the Senate Labor and Human Resources Committee when, in the 1993-94 debates over health care reform, each one argued for having the president's bill for health care reform under the jurisdiction of *his* committee. Senator Moynihan, chair of the Senate Finance Committee, argued that because his committee had the mandate to consider social security and tax-financed health care, his committee should deal with the bill in its entirety. Members of Moynihan's Finance Committee, many of whom were critical of the president's plan and sponsors of competing plans, also wanted the Finance Committee to have full responsibility for the bill.

However, large portions of the health care package were also within the purview of the Senate Labor and Human Resources Committee. Senator Kennedy, chair of that committee, proposed a division of responsibility between the two committees. He proposed that his committee handle the health and public welfare aspects of the package, including its insurance premium provisions, and that the Senate Finance Committee handle aspects pertaining to Medicare, Medicaid, and a cigarette tax (Wines, 1993). Senator Moynihan and his committee objected, maintaining that insurance premium provisions were *not* within the purview of the Labor and Human Resources Committee.

Under Senate rules, senators can block bills from being referred to committee simply by voice of objection. Members of the Finance Committee blocked referral of Senator Kennedy's plan for dividing responsibility of the president's health care package between the two committees. This prompted Senator Kennedy to then serve notice that he would block referral of the plan to the Finance Committee. And for good measure, he blocked committee referral of a competing health care proposal being sponsored by a finance committee member. With all plans blocked by objections, they all remained on the Senate's calendar until jurisdictional disputes could be resolved.

The House approved several changes in its rules when it convened as part of the new 104th Congress in January 1995. These included a limit of four consecutive terms a member can serve as Speaker and three consecutive terms as committee chair; a one third cut in committee staffs; a ban on proxy voting; the use of actual rather than inflation-adjusted spending levels in comparing spending proposals; a three fifths rather than a majority vote to raise income taxes; and a ban on any measure that would provide a retroactive increase in the income tax rate ("Rules Change," 1995). Also approved were rules to end closed-door hearings and to limit the power of committee chairs by prohibiting several committees from claiming simultaneous authority over important or politically popular bills (Wines, 1994). The intended effect of the latter was to avoid stalemates such as the one that occurred over health care legislation when three separate House committees wrote three separate and contradictory bills. Although rules were approved to make taxes more difficult to raise, some also were approved to make spending cuts easier.

In 1997, the House passed a Truth in Testimony rule that required anyone from a nongovernmental group testifying before the House to disclose how much money in grants and contracts the group had received from the federal government in the previous 3 years (Seelye, 1997). The rule, designed in part as a check on federal spending, affected an estimated 1,000 grant recipients and contractors whose spokespersons testified before the House each year. The political subtext of the rule was that it would disproportionately affect some liberal advocacy groups. Supporters held that the rule would force grant recipients to disclose how much they depended on the very programs for which they were seeking financing while they were offering supposedly objective testimony. Opponents objected, saying the rule could be used to selectively embarrass and intimidate certain organizations and witnesses, thereby trivializing their participation in government as being merely self-serving.

▪ Citizen Participation: An Institutional Norm

Although the effectiveness of citizen committees in influencing the family policy agencies of their states may be open to question, such committees provide opportunities for people to participate as citizens in constructing solutions to problems confronting families—and governments. Membership on advisory boards and task forces offer similar opportunities for citizen participation. The public review process requires it. In a democratic political order, citizen participation is a norm and part of the ongoing activity of government. It exemplifies the role of citizens in a democratic society as outlined in the Constitution. As one official said, if only technical expertise were required for the solution of social problems, such problems would have been solved a long time ago.

Yet, citizen participation often creates the kind of tension between public officials and citizens that characterizes the relationship between the House and Senate. Citizens often complain that public officials do not take their views seriously and that meetings are long and boring (Blake, 1993). Officials complain that citizens are uncompromising in seeking to advance parochial and uninformed concerns and use meetings to expound on issues not germane to the ones at hand. Pertinent here are former Vice President Al Gore's efforts to "reinvent government" and make it more "user friendly" and responsive to citizens' needs. A Republican proposal for a citizen legislature is similarly pertinent.

Opportunities for citizen involvement in the solution of family and public problems have increased with technological advances. Although cable television was not available to the framers of the Constitution, such technology *is* available today to public officials as a means of facilitating such involvement. City councils, school boards, county boards, and Congress all use this medium to televise sessions and keep citizens informed about their views and actions on issues. Electronic mail is another means of fostering communication between citizens and public officials. Radio talk shows, which have played such an important role in recent elections, is another medium. In some places, public meetings are scheduled in the late afternoon or early evening so that people who work during the day can attend them. Another structural modification for increasing citizen participation and involvement is prior notification of hearing and meeting agendas, so that people will know if and when issues of interest to them are scheduled for discussion. In one city, neighborhood district councils elected by neighborhood residents have been created to serve as a bridge between city government and neighborhoods. Most of the projects funded by the city were the result of the councils' recommendations, largely because city officials were interested in the thinking of neighborhood groups, and family members wanted to be involved in government and contribute to such thinking. In short, under favorable conditions, individual citizens can make a difference in policy choices pertaining to families.

■ Summary and Conclusions

From this discussion, we can see that from the institutional perspective, one of the influences on the solutions that are constructed to family problems is the way in which government itself is structured. Embedded in such structural arrangements are the values and norms that underlie them. Such values reflect our Founding Fathers' fears of government domination and the importance they attached to individual rights and freedom as a result of their experiences as subjects of tyrannical monarchs in Europe. In fashioning a government of checks and balances and divided state and federal authority, however, they also created a structure that gives rise to competition and conflict—among individual lawmakers, committees, departments, and agencies, the three branches of government, between state and federal governments, and, in some instances, between government and families themselves.

Although the family was not part of the Founding Fathers' conception of the new political order, many government committees today are responsible for addressing issues pertaining to aspects of family life. However, no one committee has overall jurisdiction for dealing with all the problems families experience in society; nor does any one of the government's administrative agencies. Specialization has contributed not only to competition and conflict among governmental committees and agencies but also to the fragmented policy approach to family problems that characterizes the family policies of the United States—which may in fact be what our Founding Fathers really wanted.

To a large extent, political, economic, and social institutions establish the range of effective options and strategies that political actors are likely to adopt while attempting to realize their ambitions (Noble, 1997). Structures are not only barriers but also openings that allow some individuals and groups access to decision makers and not others; they also encourage alliances among individuals and groups having particular interests acting under similar circumstances. As relatively fixed aspects of the political environment, such structures load the dice against certain policy solutions, such as universal federally financed health care, adequate funding for low-income family housing, and the elimination of child poverty through the tax code and other measures. As noted in Chapter 4, nations vary considerably in their social and political structures and thus in the likelihood of using government to solve family problems.

Structures are not immutable, however, and can be changed, at least in the long term. Changes could involve everything from campaign finance reform to changes in labor law to make union organization easier and thereby improve living conditions for all working families. Institutional reforms also could attempt to effect a change in the relationship between the executive and legislative branches to better approximate unitary government and also to increase public access to the electronic media. The goal of such reforms should be to increase the odds of constructing more coherent solutions to the problems of families in the 21st century.

The conceptual terms associated with the institutional framework—values, norms, institutional roles, patterns of behaviors and activities, structure and structural arrangements, continuity over time, and the legitimacy, authority, and universality of policy choices—are useful for drawing attention to some of the structural and cultural influences that may account for some of the solutions constructed to family problems in the form of family policies and programs. From an institutional perspective, such policies and programs are the outcomes of institutional arrangements and activity at all levels—federal, state, and local—governed by the norms and values that underlie such arrangements. From an institutional perspective, family policies as institutional outcomes are characterized by their *legitimacy, authority,* and *universality.*

This concludes the discussion about this very important framework for understanding some of the structural influences on government's constructed solutions to family problems in the form of family policies.

■ Some Questions for Your Reflection and Discussion

1. What three features characterize family and all government policies?

2. What are the basic assumptions underlying institutional arrangements in the United States with respect to government?

3. Explain the relevance of the issues the Anti-Federalists raised about the Constitution to debates about family policy today.

4. What are some of the institutional means for ensuring citizen participation in government?

5. What are some of the problems inherent in citizen participation?

6. What experiences have you had in citizen participation? How would you evaluate them?

7. Identify and define the major concepts associated with the institutional perspective.

8. Define family policy from an institutional perspective.

9. Find an illustration of the institutional framework in family policy from the newspaper or from actual observation. Explain your illustration, from the institutional perspective.

As useful as the institutional perspective may be for providing the language for understanding the institutional influences that could account for some policy solutions constructed to family problems, other perspectives are useful for understanding other influences. Prominent among these perspectives is rational choice theory, the topic of the next chapter.

CHAPTER 10

The Rational Choice Framework
The Construction of Family Policy as Rational Choice

☐ Whereas the institutional framework emphasizes government structures and the values and norms underlying such structures that govern institutional practices, the rational choice framework emphasizes choice in the selection of alternative solutions constructed to address family problems, family policies and such solutions taking the form of different programs. Indeed, readers may recognize that in addition to the institutional framework, the debates over the Constitution are also illustrative of many of the features of the rational choice framework. Family policy from the perspective of the rational choice framework refers to the selection of one solution constructed to a family problem over another, based on the values it maximizes. The discussion that follows outlines the central features, underlying assumptions, and concepts of the rational choice model. It draws on the health care reform debates of 1993-94 and discussions about Social Security during the later years of the 1990s to illustrate the model and inform readers about two key family policy issues.

■ The Model

The core of the rational choice model consists of the values to be maximized in the selection of an alternative that addresses some family problem. The model is based on the following assumptions:

- All values relevant to the situation are known.
- The context of the choice situation is known and understood; the context refers to all the social, economic, cultural, and historical factors that are part of the situation, including the values, attitudes, and psychological predispositions of a population, such as those outlined in Chapters 4 and 5.

- The context determines the range of alternatives that can be considered in selecting a course of action to address family problems, as for example, the context in which the Defense of Marriage Act (DOMA) was debated that determined its passage and not its defeat.
- In calculating the net value ratio, the same values are applied to each alternative.
- In selecting an alternative, some values must be sacrificed to achieve others; in relation to families, an example is the value of family privacy in order to ensure the safety of children and wives.
- The alternative with the highest net value ratio, that is, that maximizes the largest number of desired values relative to potentially negative consequences, will be the alternative selected.

Policy choice from the perspective of the rational choice model refers to the selection of the alternative with the greatest potential for maximizing agreed-upon values and goals (Dye, 1975). The concepts basic to all rational choice models include:

- The problem
- The context
- Values, goals, and objectives
- Alternative solutions, actions, and/or strategies for achieving agreed-upon goals
- Intended and unintended consequences of such solutions and actions, both negative and positive, and
- Net value ratio

Depending on the problem that has been constructed and the situation in which choices are made, the values such choices may seek to maximize include:

- Individual and family well-being
- Economic security
- Health security
- Social integration
- Independence
- Equality of opportunity
- Efficiency
- Equity or justice
- Affordability
- Freedom
- Individual rights

Based on the nature of the problem and the values to be maximized, the rational choice model requires those engaging in the process of rational choice to:

- Generate a list of alternative solutions or ways to address the problem.
- Generate a list of potential consequences for each alternative.
- Calculate a net value ratio for each alternative, based on the values each maximizes relative to the positive and negative consequences of each (i.e., benefits relative to costs).
- Rank the alternatives based on their net value ratio selecting the alternative with the highest net value ratio or the one that maximizes the greatest number of desired values in addressing a problem relative to its calculated costs (i.e., negative consequences).

Some family policy issues such as health care reform and Social Security reform illustrate the model better than others, largely because they involve alternatives that have been constructed to deal with the problems of each. Readers will be able to discern the applicability of the model to other family policy issues as well, especially those that involve alternatives from which a choice must be made in addressing a problem, such as the income maintenance alternatives that addressed the problems of Aid to Families with Dependent Children (AFDC) in the 1960s and early 1970s (Zimmerman, 1988a, 1995a). The model is particularly useful for gaining a better understanding of policy issues related to families and clarity about their substance. For this reason, readers are encouraged to apply the model whenever a number of alternatives are constructed and presented to address a family problem.

■ Health Care Reform

In 1993-94, health care as a family policy issue portended the advancement of the most sweeping policy reforms in the United States since Social Security was enacted in the 1930s. It had the potential of affecting every family, man, woman, and child in the country. Much of the debate over health care reform centered on the role of government, which tended to ignore the role it already was playing in health care. This included the funding of a privately operated health care program for federal workers; two separate medical payment systems, one for the elderly, Medicare, and the other for public assistance recipients, Medicaid; the funding and operation of a system of public health services for veterans; and the subsidization of employer-provided health benefits by virtue of their nontaxable status. The discussion below follows the rational choice model.

The Problem(s) and the Context

The problems in health care as defined in 1993-94 were that many people were underinsured and uninsured, whether they worked or not, and that the costs of health care were escalating. In 1993, 39 million people, 14% of the population, were without health insurance and did not have access to health care except in an emergency (Hamburger & Meyers, 1993). In half of the uninsured households, a person worked full time, and in another third of the households, a person worked part time or part of the year (Eckholm, 1994). Many others worked for small companies that offered no benefits or for companies in low wage or contract jobs that could not afford costly insurance premiums for employees (Snyder & Boyce, 1994).

The uninsured included many of the poorest Americans. Less than half of those living below the official poverty line of about $15,000 for a family of four in 1994 were covered by Medicaid. Minorities under the age of 65 with lower than average incomes—23% of whom were black, 35% Hispanic, and 14% white—were disproportionately represented among the uninsured.

Disparities in health insurance coverage between states were marked. In much of the South and West, where jobs without benefits were more common and Medicaid less generous, the uninsured constituted more than 20% of the population under age 65, as contrasted with only 10% in many Northern and Midwestern states.

Over the course of a year, 58 million people were temporarily uninsured as a result of losing a job with health benefits. The numbers of long-term uninsured people also were large. On any given day, about 29 million people were uninsured for a year or more, and more than half that number were uninsured for at least 2 years. In addition to the anxiety they experienced because they had no insurance, their health also suffered, and they tended to seek help less often than others, thus ending up sicker. Most found ways of getting care when it was essential, but charity often paid for it. Persons with preexisting medical conditions, whom many insurers excluded from coverage, accounted for only a small fraction of the uninsured but had the most tragic stories to tell. Millions more people were underinsured.

In addition, health care costs in many areas of the country were out of control. Between 1960 and 1990, spending for health care as a percentage of the gross domestic product (GDP) more than doubled—from 5.3% to 12.2%—and was projected to increase to almost 15% in 1993 and to almost 20% by 2000, unless health care reforms were effected (Hamburger & Meyers, 1993). The GDP refers to the total output of goods and services produced by labor and property in the United States (U.S. Bureau of the Census, 1998).

Despite rising costs, polls of consumer satisfaction and international comparison standards based on rates of infant mortality and longevity indicated that the health care system in the United States was not meeting performance expectations. The Clinton administration held hearings around the country on health care reform and learned about the problems people experienced with the present health care system. Lack of insurance coverage was foremost, but other problems were high copayments for necessary and basic health care; the exclusion of coverage for preexisting conditions; arbitrary and complicated rules; inequities of coverage for different conditions; and "job lock." Job lock or job immobility refers to being locked into a job for its health benefits (i.e., not being able to leave a job because it would mean losing health insurance benefits).

Some Case Examples

The story of one family whose 18-month-old son was diagnosed with Hurler's syndrome, a rare and fatal condition, is illustrative of the kinds of problems existing health care arrangements created for families. Shortly after the child's condition was diagnosed, the father was laid off from a job that provided health insurance coverage for his family. Hence, he could not seek insurance payment for his son's treatment. Then the mother, upon returning to work after taking leave to stay home to care for her son, learned that her employer-provided health insurance would not pay for her son's treatment because it involved a pre-existing condition. The couple accumulated hundreds of thousands of dollars worth of medical bills and were forced to give up their apartment, and the husband was forced to take a low-paying job so the family could qualify for Medicaid and Social Security disability benefits. Subsequently, the child died, leaving his parents to not only grieve over his death but also worry about medical bills they could not pay ("Clinton Applies Health Plan," 1993).

This is not the only example of the kinds of problems that existing health care arrangements created for families—and also for government. Another example is the story of a 26-year-old aspiring actor who lived in New York City and worked as a waiter or bartender to support himself (Eckholm, 1994). Like many of his friends, he was last covered under his parents' health insurance when he was in college, but since then, he had no money to pay for his own insurance. He paid for doctors as he needed them. Disaster struck when he developed a severe case of pneumonia and the fluid around his lungs became infected. He spent 18 days in the hospital with a tube inserted in his chest; his hospital bill came to more than $25,000. He also owed several thousand dollars in doctor bills, but he negotiated to pay his surgeon with his surfboard; the hospital charged his bill to charity.

■ Alternative Solutions: The Values and Goals They Sought to Maximize

True to the rational choice model, a number of alternative solutions were constructed to achieve the values or goals being sought in health care reform. These values and goals included:

- Health care security
- Individual rights, particularly the right to health care
- Choice of treatment and doctors
- Administrative simplicity
- Quality of care
- Sensitivity to diverse needs and populations
- Fairness with respect to the treatment of different conditions
- Cost containment

The criteria that President Clinton emphasized during the health care reform debates and said were nonnegotiable were universal access, comprehensive coverage, and cost containment.

Alternatives varied in their reliance on government or the market, that is, on government mandates and/or tax and market incentives and hence in terms of other goals or objectives being sought ("Health Care: Clinton's Plan," 1993; "Seeking a Cure," 1993). The alternatives debated at the time included:

- *The single payer approach,* with only one entity such as the federal government as the insurer
- Different versions of *a multiple payer approach,* involving both private insurance companies and government, one version being *employment based* and *market driven* and the other being *employment based* and *employer mandated*
- *State-based reforms,* with states (such as Oregon and Minnesota) being used as test sites for national health care reforms
- *The continuation of existing arrangements* (e.g., fee for service with minor modifications, emphasizing cost containment)

Other main features of these approaches are discussed on the following pages.

The Single Payer Plan

The single payer plan would have provided for *universal* health care coverage, that is, health insurance for everyone. The primary insurer would have been the federal government, replacing private health insurance companies. Financing for the plan could have come from a combination of income, corporate, and payroll taxes. The proposal before Congress in 1993 called for payroll taxes to finance the plan. The costs and potential savings of the plan necessarily varied with the benefit package and the comprehensiveness of its coverage. During the health care reform debates, the Canadian health care plan was presented as the model for what the single payer plan might look like in the United States.

The Multiple Payer Plan

This approach included:

- An *employment-based, market-driven* version that relied on *managed competition and tax incentives* aimed at individuals and small businesses as a way of expanding health care coverage and controlling costs.
- An *employment-based, employer-mandated* version that also relied on managed competition to expand health care coverage and control costs. However, instead of relying on tax incentives and market competition to achieve these objectives, this version was based instead on *government mandates* to ensure that employers did in fact provide health insurance coverage for employees. The payroll tax would have been used to finance the plan.

Both versions of the multiple-payer plan contained provisions for unemployed persons and for *consumer choice*. To ensure consumer choice, the market-based multiple payer approach provided for a *refundable tax credit* for individuals, based on income, to help pay for out-of-pocket health care expenses. It replaced the tax exclusions employers received for employees' health benefits. The employer-mandated version provided for consumer choice by offering one or more insurance companies from which employees could choose their coverage.

State-Based Reforms

State-based reforms as an approach to health care reform were aimed at giving states latitude to reform health care in a variety of ways, the states having become test sites for health care reform. Such reforms were made possible by waivers the federal government gave to states that allowed them to shift federal funds and/or provide new federal funding for state experimentation. Projected changes in federal spending as a result of state-based reforms were dependent on a state's reform choices.

The Ranking of Proposed Solutions

A "citizens jury," consisting of 24 people randomly selected from a list of 2,000 names representing different regions of the country, income levels, races, and degrees of health insurance coverage, received extensive information on each of these alternative approaches to health care reform. After considerable study and dialogue with Republicans, Democrats, and White House officials, the jury voted 19 to 5 in favor of the single payer approach (Howe, 1993). The jury ranked the single payer plan the highest on net value ratio, basing its assessment on the following values criteria:

- Universal access (equality)
- Comprehensiveness of benefits
- Cost containment
- Individual rights
- Equitable treatment (fairness)
- Administrative simplicity

In terms of political feasibility, however, the multiple payer approach ranked higher because it incorporated many of the values underlying existing institutional arrangements that people also wanted to achieve in health care reform—freedom of choice, market competition, and cost containment—while promising expanded access to health care. As far as state-level reforms were concerned, these were at odds with the view that primary responsibility for health care financing rested with the federal government, not the states, although many states (e.g., Oregon, Minnesota, Florida, Massachusetts, and Vermont) had already enacted health care reform legislation, and many others were following suit.

The Clinton Plan

President Clinton's Health Security Plan was the major proposal around which others developed theirs. It is presented here in greater detail than others, although it was far from the only proposal that took the form of a legislative bill in 1994. The proposal was first presented in October 1993. It was a multiple payer approach that combined both government and market-based provisions and used financial incentives to encourage individuals and families to voluntarily join low-cost health maintenance organizations (HMOs). The same inducements were proposed to encourage doctors, hospitals, and insurers to form health networks or alliances ("A New Framework," 1993). Insurance premiums for low-wage earners and small businesses were to be subsidized by the federal government. Medicare and Medicaid payments would remain essentially the same as under existing arrangements, except that they would be made through the health networks or alliances. Large corporations would have the option of negotiating directly with insurers or with the alliances for their employees' coverage. Employers would be *mandated* to contribute 80% of the cost of workers' health insurance premiums, and workers would contribute the remaining 20%.

The health alliances and employer mandates were the core of the plan. The health alliances, in effect, were regional planning and health insurance purchasing groups that states would operate under federal supervision and oversight. The alliances would manage the plan. They would be responsible for collecting premiums, making payments, certifying health plans and offering them to consumers, monitoring increases in premiums to make sure they did not exceed federally set limits, collecting and publishing data on the performance of health plans, and negotiating fees with local doctors and hospitals for services provided outside the HMOs.

The Clinton plan was universal, covering all citizens and legal residents. It offered individuals the choice of one of three types of medical plans: (1) an HMO (i.e., a prepaid health insurance plan with an organization that provides comprehensive health care), (2) a fee-for-service plan that in addition offered a choice of doctors, and (3) a combination of an HMO and fee-for-service plan. In calculating projected costs, the HMO was the least expensive of the three plans. Preliminary estimates showed that the average plan would cost $1,800 per year per individual and $4,200 for a family.

The major provisions of the Clinton plan are as follows (Pear, 1993a):

- Coverage for all Americans, regardless of medical or employment status.
- A guaranteed package of benefits, including free preventive care.

■ A choice of three kinds of health plans: a traditional fee-for-service plan, an HMO plan, and plans that combined the two.

■ The formation of health alliances or networks or health insurance purchasing pools to increase the purchasing power of consumers, generally one alliance per state or region. Companies with more than 5,000 employees would have the option of creating their own corporate alliances. The alliances would negotiate with health care providers and offer consumers a choice of plans and information about their cost and quality.

■ Employers would pay 80% of the cost of premiums for employees, who would pay 20%; the cost would vary with the plan they chose. Those who chose not to join an HMO would have higher out-of-pocket expenses.

■ The costs of premiums for small businesses and poor individuals would be subsidized by the government.

■ Insurance premiums would be capped at 3.5% of income for small companies and 7.9% for larger ones to bring increases in health costs in line with the general rate of inflation over 5 years.

■ A national health board would be created to set national and regional health care budgets.

■ A health security card would be issued to everyone and would entitle them to the following benefits:

– Preventive dental care
– Prescription drugs
– Eye and ear exams
– Nursing home or rehabilitation care for a maximum of 100 days per year
– Home care, subject to reevaluation every 60 days
– Hospice care for terminally ill people
– Hospital care (semiprivate rooms)
– Limited psychotherapy
– Office visits, including outpatient hospital services
– Prosthetics and medical equipment
– Physical, occupational, and speech therapy, subject to a 60-day evaluation
– Prevention services such as immunizations, mammograms, pap smears, prenatal care, and cholesterol screening
– Substance abuse treatment—limited inpatient and outpatient services

The plan excluded services not deemed medically necessary such as sex change surgery and fertility services. The costs of the plan were to be offset by savings from Medicaid and increases in the cigarette tax.

It may be useful to recall that policy is not policy until enacted into law. In the manner suggestive of the rational choice model, several alternatives to the Clinton plan were introduced in Congress in 1993 and 1994; almost all aimed to expand access to health care and control costs, but they varied in their administration, structure, financing, the comprehensiveness of benefits, mechanisms for ensuring consumer choice and cost control, provisions for malpractice claims and costs, and last—but, as it turned out, certainly not least—they varied in their emphasis on the role of government and the private sector in the financing, management, and delivery of health care.

■ Assessing the Net Value Ratio of the Clinton Plan/Solution

Many faulted the Clinton plan. Those who liked the simplicity and inherent fairness of the single payer plan regarded the Clinton plan as too complex. They also doubted that the Clinton plan would result in universal access to health care, that the care of poorer Americans would be the same as the care of others, and that it would effect the cost savings it promised. According to the General Accounting Office (GAO), the Clinton plan would cost $500 billion more than the single payer plan over a 5-year period—1995 to the year 2000 primarily because of higher administrative costs. Authors of other multiple payer plans rejected the idea of the employer mandates that were part of the Clinton plan partly because they thought mandates would harm small business and partly because they were mandatory and thus at odds with the individual rights and freedom of choice they thought it was important to maximize. They said Clinton's plan also called for too much government. For whatever it may be worth, however, one senator opined that the president's plan went further than any of the other plans in maximizing the values that were sought in health care reform.

Polls taken in October 1993 showed that survey respondents had other questions about the Clinton plan: Would it adversely affect their choice of doctors and hospitals? Would their personal costs for medical care increase? Would some procedures be available to everyone who needed them? Would taxes have to be raised to pay for the plan? Would abuse and fraud result from the plan? Would employer mandates lead to the elimination of jobs? Would the plan create yet another bureaucracy? Would people who needed care receive adequate care? ("Health Care: The Public Reacts," 1993). In another poll taken at about the same time, most (69%) thought passing the Clinton plan was better than doing nothing and that Congress should pass it without any or with minor modifications (52%). However, only 40% said they would support increased taxes to pay for it. By June 1994, support for the Clinton plan had clearly eroded; the percentage who thought Congress should pass the plan with minor or no changes dropped to 42%, and only 37% said that Congress should pass a health care reform bill that year ("Health Care Update," 1994).

■ Anticipated Effects of Various Plans for Family Well-Being

The anticipated consequences of the various health care reform plans for individual and family well-being—the goal of family policy—depended on the assessment measures different analysts used: infant mortality, longevity, or improved lives. Using these measures, Uwe Reinhardt, a health economist at Princeton University, expressed doubt that any of the plans would have had much of an effect on family lives. He pointed out that infant mortality was highest in the inner cities, where low-income pregnant women were covered by Medicaid and had access to free or low-cost health care at neighborhood clinics (Kolata, 1993). For people to be healthy, Reinhardt said, they had to have a way of getting out of poverty. He noted that women in Great Britain, through the national health service, have had access to free prenatal care for more than 30 years, but the infant mortality rate among poor women remained triple the rate of higher-income women. Indeed, the projected average after-tax household income of poor households in the United States, adjusted for inflation, was 12% lower in 1999 than in 1977 (Shapiro & Greenstein, 1999). During that same time period, the share of national after-tax income going to the bottom 38% of the population declined 3%, and the share going to the top 1% of the population increased 5.6%.

Medical demographers, using the average life span as a measure of individual and family well-being or improvement in lives, also were pessimistic about the effects of the alternative health plans. Medical care sometimes saved lives, they advised, but its main purpose was to help people recover from acute illnesses, which could not measurably change the average life expectancy of a nation. If relief from pain were used as the measure, then all the alternative plans were potentially useful. At the very least, they all held out the promise of greater health care security for individuals and families, although some more than others.

Summary

However incomplete and uneven this discussion about health care reform, it illustrates some of the major components of the rational choice model as it pertains to (a) the problems of uninsured or underinsured individuals and families, the high costs of health insurance, job lock, and so on; (b) the context in which such problems were being discussed; (c) the values and goals being sought in addressing such problems (e.g., comprehensive benefits, affordable costs, and universal access); (d) alternative solutions or courses of action for achieving these goals (e.g., the single payer plan; the multiple payer plan, both market-based and government-coordinated or -mandated versions; and (e) assessments of the intended and unintended consequences of the various plans (both positive and negative being based on the values being sought).

What readers should have observed from this discussion is that just as our Founding Fathers created a new institutional framework for government when they wrote the Constitution, the Clinton plan and some of the other plans—in addressing problems that both families and government were experiencing in relation to health care—attempted to construct a new institutional framework for the financing and delivery of health care in this country. The process, according to the rational choice model, involved rational, reasoned choice that was expected to lead to the selection of the alternative plan that best maximized the values and goals being sought.

As I suggested earlier, this same analytic framework can be applied to all policy choices that involve alternative solutions for dealing with problems experienced by families: welfare reform, Social Security, educational reform, tax and spending proposals, and so on. Next, I discuss Social Security to further illustrate the model and also to inform readers about the issues that were raised in discussions about reforming Social Security.

■ Social Security: A Family Protection Program

The Context

Known as a family protection program, Social Security protects individuals and families against the loss of income due to unemployment, disability, inflation, retirement, and the death of the breadwinner; preretirement protections increase with wages. Because of Social Security and Medicare, no family has to bear alone the potentially huge cost of caring for parents who are sicker than average or who exhaust their private savings. A husband and wife, 27 years old, who have two small children and earn average wages currently have survivors' protection worth $307,000 in the event of the death of a parent and disability protection of $207,000.

Today, over 90% of all couples over 65 are Social Security beneficiaries. For two thirds of those couples, their monthly Social Security check represents 50% or more of their income; only 42% have other retirement income ("Making Sense," 1998). Unlike the private pensions that some receive, Social Security payments increase each year with the Consumer Price Index (CPI), protecting beneficiaries against inflation. The CPI is a measure of the average change in prices over time in a fixed "market basket" of goods and services purchased by urban wage earners and consumers (U.S. Bureau of the Census, 1998). Such increases in Social Security payments are known as cost of living adjustments (COLAs). Because of COLA and because private pensions do not increase with inflation, the longer people live, the more they depend on Social Security.

Thousands of widows over age 80 who have outlived their savings and whose pensions have diminished with time and inflation would be destitute were it not for Social Security. Social Security has been key to bringing the poverty rate among the elderly down to about 11% in 1996; in 1967, it was 28%, which at the time was two and a half times higher than the rest of the population. It keeps some 15 million people above the poverty line and millions more from near poverty (Ball, 1996). Without Social Security, well over half of the elderly would have incomes below the federal government's rock-bottom definition of poverty. Moreover, because it is not means tested, those above the poverty level are able to add other income to their benefits and thus provide a level of living in retirement that is not much lower than when they were working. Following workers from job to job, Social Security in effect functions as a three-tier system that includes private pensions, individual savings, and Social Security.

How Social Security is Financed

Social Security is financed by a payroll tax imposed on almost all workers and their employers—6.2% each on all wages below $72,000 (Rosenbaum, 1999). Nearly 90% of the money is now used to pay monthly benefits, most of which goes to retirees and their widows and widowers. A much smaller amount is paid to the survivors of workers who died before they retired and to disabled people. Today's workers are taxed to pay retirement benefits for their parents' generation. When today's workers retire, their benefits will be covered by their children's generation, but because today's workers—the baby boom generation (those born between 1946 and 1964)—had fewer children, such coverage will impose a heavy tax burden on their children. The principle underlying the financing of Social Security is different from an investment or an insurance policy in which individuals pay premiums and the income from these premiums is used later to pay their benefits.

When the government receives more money in Social Security taxes than it pays in benefits, as is presently the case, the reserves are credited to a trust fund (Rosenbaum, 1999). The money is invested in government bonds. The interest on the bonds is credited to the trust fund. The trust fund is a bookkeeping entry, for the most part—a collection of government IOUs promising to pay benefits to future retirees. Although this obligation can be fulfilled only to the extent politicians are willing to raise the necessary money through taxes or borrowing, as a political matter, it would be difficult to ignore.

For years, the surplus in the trust fund had been used to meet part of the operating expenses of the government and to offset part of the overall budget deficit. This is no longer the case, because at least for the next 15 years, the government is expected to run a total budget surplus of 4.4 trillion dollars.

The Problem

In 1999, President Clinton unexpectedly used his State of the Union speech to propose vast changes in the way Social Security is financed. The problem was that despite the budget surplus at the time, the future of Social Security was uncertain, in part because of changing demographics both with respect to the number of workers paying taxes to retirees (which was projected to shrink) and the number of retirees drawing benefits (which was expected to grow). In 1950, there were 16 workers for each Social Security beneficiary. In 1999, there were slightly more than 3. By the second or third decade of this century, when most baby boomers will have retired, actuaries project only two people at work for each person receiving benefits.

The aging of the baby boom generation is integral to the demographic problem facing Social Security ("Making Sense," 1998). This cohort of 75 million people, the largest generation in American history, is anticipated to create severe financial pressures on the system when its members retire, the oldest of which will become eligible for full retirement benefits after the year 2011. Because baby boomers married late and had relatively few children, the Social Security tax burden for their children and grandchildren is expected to be especially heavy. The country's relatively slow rate of economic growth from the 1970s to the 1990s compounded the demographic problem, because the pool of wages from which benefits were paid grew more slowly during those years.

Estimates are that in the year 2029, the Social Security trust fund will be sufficient to pay beneficiaries only 75% of their promised benefits. Although the system will not be bankrupt, as is often claimed, an additional 25% in revenues must be found if beneficiaries are to receive their promised benefits in full. At that time, unless changes are made before then, the trust fund will have a deficit. The latest estimate is that Social Security taxes will continue to exceed benefits until 2013. Interest payments owed on the bonds are credited to the trust fund, so income in the fund will exceed payouts until 2021. After that, the trust fund will begin to shrink rapidly, year after year, until 2032, when the money will run out. Economists and politicians agree that the sooner the problem is addressed, the less painful and abrupt the solution will be.

Alternative Solutions to the Anticipated Problem

The challenge of Social Security is to secure agreement on a solution to the expected trust fund gap long before the year 2029. Although policy makers and the public face a bewildering array of proposals to reform or replace the Social Security system, most proposals take one of three approaches (Aaron & Reischauer, 1999): (a) Some would *replace* the current public system with private accounts; (b) others would *supplement* the current system with private accounts; and (c) still others would *strengthen* and *modernize* the current system. All the plans would restore financial balance to the nation's basic retirement system. Their common goal was to ease the strain on Social Security so that the country can fulfill its promise of retirement security to the baby boom generation without imposing an undue tax burden on their children and grandchildren.

The debate that was anticipated but did not happen after President Clinton talked about changing the way Social Security is financed would have given voters an opportunity to decide (a) whether they wanted to keep the current system largely intact by gradually increasing the age of retirement from 67 to 70, raising payroll taxes, bringing all government workers into the system, increasing the taxes on the Social Security benefits received by the wealthiest retirees, raising the $72,000 cap on wages from which payroll taxes presently are collected, reducing the COLA, and so on, *or* (b) whether they wanted individuals to be allowed to invest the money they presently pay into Social Security in individual retirement or personal security accounts, diverting monies from the Social Security trust fund. The latter is known as the privatization of Social Security.

Values/Criteria for Assessing Proposals of Alternative Solutions

Henry Aaron and Robert Reischauer (1999), senior fellows in the Brookings Economic Studies program, analyzed the various proposals for reforming Social Security. The criteria or values they used in doing so included adequacy, equity, a fair return, protection against risk, administrative efficiency, and increased national saving. Based on these values that they applied to seven proposals, they advised that a successful plan should (a) ensure adequate benefits and their equitable distribution, maintaining protections for low wage earners and other vulnerable people; (b) spread unavoidable risks broadly to minimize undue risks for individual workers; (c) keep administrative costs low and rules as simple as possible for private businesses, workers, and government; and (d) increase national saving by adding to trust fund reserves or individual accounts. Applying these criteria to seven plans, Aaron and Reischauer assigned an overall grade to each plan, based on the grade they assigned to the plans for each criterion. Such grades, in effect, represented Aaron and Reischauer's calculation of the net value ratio of each plan—as suggested by the rational choice model. Because of the importance of Social Security for the well-being of families, the plans that Aaron and Reischauer graded are briefly described below. In addition to the criteria Aaron and Reischauer applied in calculating grades for the plans, readers should note differences in the emphasis on choice and the role of government in each plan.

Personal Security Account

The Personal Security Account (PSA) plan would gradually *replace* Social Security with a two-tier system consisting of a *flat benefit* based on years worked and the age at which benefits are first received and *a benefit based on balances accumulated in mandated personal savings accounts*. The flat benefit would be financed by a payroll tax of 6.2% for employers and 1.2% for employees; 5% of each worker's earnings, up to a maximum subject to the payroll tax, would go into his or her personal account. The PSA plan would be phased in over many years. Retirees and workers over age 55 would remain under the Social Security system. Workers between 25 and 55 would receive a blend of benefits under the new and old systems. Workers under 25 would receive benefits only under the new system. Aaron and Reischauer gave the plan an overall grade of C: a C+ on adequacy, equity, and a fair return; a C on protection against risk; an F on administrative efficiency; and a B– on increased national saving.

Personal Retirement Account

The Personal Retirement Account plan proposed by Martin Feldstein, former chair of the Council of Economic Advisers, also would *replace* Social Security. Under this plan, each worker would deposit 2% of their earnings up to the maximum subject to the payroll tax in a personal retirement account. *The accounts would be invested in regulated stock and bond funds chosen by the worker and administered by private fund managers.* When workers begin to draw pensions from their accounts, their Social Security benefits would be reduced by $3 for every $4 withdrawn. In effect, the benefits promised by the current system would become a floor. Overall, retirees would receive about 60% of their benefits from Social Security and 40% from their personal accounts. Higher earners would depend more on their personal accounts; some would receive nothing from Social Security. Eventually, the cuts in benefits would close the projected long-term Social Security trust fund deficit. As they did in their ranking of the Personal Security Account plan, Aaron and Reischauer gave this plan an overall grade of C: a B+ on adequacy, equity, and a fair return; a B– on protection against risk; an F on administrative efficiency; and a D on increased national saving.

Individual Account Plan

The Individual Account Plan, proposed by Edward Gramlich, former chair of the Advisory Council on Social Security, would gradually cut Social Security benefits to allow the current 12.4% payroll tax to cover future program costs. *A 1.6% increase in the employee payroll tax would finance small personal retirement accounts that would be invested in a limited number of index mutual funds managed by a government agency. Balances would be converted into inflation-protected annuities at retirement.* The annuities would be small. Older workers would receive less than younger persons—$125 per month or just 13% of the benefits they would receive at age 65 under the current system—because they would have contributed to the plan for fewer years. Payroll taxes would fully finance the new individual accounts, so the plan would require no other transitional taxes or borrowing. Aaron and Reischauer gave this plan an overall grade of B: a B on adequacy, equity, and a fair return; a B on protection against risk; a B– on administrative efficiency; and a B+ on increased national saving.

Moynihan Plan

Senator Daniel Patrick Moynihan from New York proposed cutting both payroll taxes and Social Security benefits and authorizing, but not requiring, workers to set up individual accounts. *Retirement, survivors, and disability benefits would fall an average of 20%. Individuals would be allowed to invest 2% of the total 12.4% Social Security tax in 401(k)-type plans managed by private firms or in three plans managed by the federal government. Payroll taxes would be cut 2%, which workers could spend or save in either personal accounts administered by a new government board or in special individual retirement accounts (IRAs) managed by financial institutions of their choosing. Workers' contributions would have to be matched by their employers.* Withdrawal from the account at retirement would be unrestricted; it would not need be in the form of an annuity. Over time, the Moynihan plan would return Social Security to a pay-as-you-go system, with a contingency reserve sufficient to tide the system over a severe economic downturn. Aaron and Reischauer gave the Moynihan plan an overall grade of D: an F on adequacy, equity, and a fair return; a C+ on protection against risk; a D on administrative efficiency; and a D on increased national saving.

Breaux-Gregg Plan

The plan proposed by Senators John Breaux (D-Louisiana) and Judd Gregg (R-New Hampshire) would divert 2% of the current payroll tax to individual accounts, similar to the Moynihan plan. To cover that cost and to close the projected long-term deficit, *the plan would cut Social Security benefits an average of 25 to 30%. At retirement, a worker would be required to convert enough of his or her account balance into an inflation-proof annuity to ensure that the annuity plus the reduced Social Security benefit would meet a minimum retirement income standard.* The balance of the account could be withdrawn as needed by the retiree. A minimum benefit would be established equal to 60% of the poverty threshold for those with 20 years of covered earnings, rising to 100% of the poverty threshold for those with 40 years of earnings. A fail-safe mechanism would automatically keep the program in long-term balance. Aaron and Reischauer gave this plan an overall grade of C+: a C on adequacy, equity and fair return; a C on protection against risk; a C– on administrative efficiency; and a B– on increased national saving.

Ball Plan: Retain and Reform Social Security

Robert Ball, a former commissioner of Social Security, offered a proposal that *would not divert monies from the Social Security trust fund, but would allow individuals to supplement their Social Security contributions with IRAs, keeping the system intact.* He would restore projected long-term balance in the trust fund by *raising revenues and cutting benefits modestly* as well as by diversifying the assets held by the trust fund reserves. Roughly half the projected long-term deficit would be closed by investing a portion of trust fund reserves (up to 40% by 2015) in the stock market. Aaron and Reischauer gave the Ball plan an overall grade of B+: an A– on adequacy, equity, and fair return; a B+ on protection against risk; an A on administrative efficiency; and a C+ on increased national saving.

Aaron-Reischauer Plan

The Aaron-Reischauer plan relies exclusively on a defined benefit retirement system. It would *cut benefits by about 8% on average* to boost reserve accumulation and raise national saving. It would establish a *new Social Security Reserve Board, modeled after the Federal Reserve Board, which would manage all financial operations of Social Security*. With multiple institutional safeguards in place to insulate the Board from political pressure, *the Board would invest Social Security reserves in excess of 1½ years' benefits passively in a broad mix of private securities*. The two analysts gave their own plan an overall grade of A–: a B+ on adequacy, equity, and fair return; an A on protection against risk; an A on administrative efficiency; and a B+ on increased national saving.

Although readers may apply different criteria and grade each of the plans differently, Aaron and Reischauer's analyses of the various plans demonstrate (a) that, as the rational choice model suggests, some values must be sacrificed to achieve others; (b) that there is, in effect, no perfect solution to the Social Security trust fund problem; and (c) that none of the plans merited an A on the basis of the four criteria Aaron and Reischauer applied to their analyses. Their analyses also illustrate how alternative solutions to problems can be rated and ranked against each other, based on the application of the same values criteria to each: the Aaron and Reischauer plan, an A–, followed by the Ball plan, B+, followed by the Individual Account Plan, a B, the Breaux-Gregg plan, a C+, the Personal Security Accounts plan and the Feldstein plan, both Cs, and the Moynihan plan, a D.

Other policy analysts have applied other criteria to assess the different proposals, namely equality, economic security, and choice. According to Mashaw and Marmor (1996), plans for privatizing Social Security would exacerbate existing inequalities among families in the United States because higher savings are positively associated with income, and higher wage earners—who saved more and made lucky investments—would be entitled to higher retirement benefits. Low wage earners would not only be disadvantaged by such arrangements, but the imposition of market risks would threaten their retirement security. As noted earlier, Social Security is more important to low-wage earners than to high-wage earners. Moreover, because most of such plans viewed workers as investors who would be required to save a fixed percentage of their wages, individual choice was precluded with regard to savings.

In addition to trading the retirement security of most retirees for higher investment returns for wealthier beneficiaries, some plans, Mashaw and Marmor advise, traded a portion of Social Security's protections (i.e., survivor benefits) for the transfer, upon their death, of beneficiaries' accounts to heirs. Those who would benefit the most from such an arrangement would be families with two moderate-to-high-wage workers who have IRAs with no cap on expected returns. This would further reinforce the distributional shift toward high-wage, dual-earner families occurring in the economy generally. High-wage earners would on average also be able to collect benefits for a much longer time than low-income workers, because longevity, like savings, is positively correlated with income.

Such distributional effects are confounded by gender, Mashaw and Marmor go on to advise. Although Social Security has reduced poverty among the elderly, the poverty rate among women over 65 is twice that of men over 65. Women typically work fewer years than men, earn less, and, because they live longer, are more likely than men to deplete their savings and slip into poverty. In 1994, women's monthly benefits averaged almost 25% less than retired men's. Women would remain disadvantaged under most proposals for reforming Social Security, according to Mashaw and Marmor (1996), because current proposals for reforming Social Security did not address their problems.

For Mashaw and Marmor, the privatization of Social Security is an oxymoron, a contradiction of terms. They caution that partial privatization could lead to pressure for full privatization and the loss of political support for collective provision through Social Security, which in turn could lead to the destruction of the very economic security that reform is supposed to preserve. Based on their calculations and assessments of the various plans, Mashaw and Marmor conclude that workers on average would not be better off investing privately for retirement instead of through Social Security, because private investments would expose beneficiaries unduly and directly to the fluctuations of the financial markets and make many worse off. As Ball (1996) notes, the more dynamic the economy, the more individuals and families need protection against major economic hazards.

Polls showing an increase in public awareness of possible solutions to the Social Security trust fund problem also show that most people opposed investing Social Security trust funds in the stock market. Indeed, in 1999, there was more support for raising the payroll tax that funds Social Security than there was for investing funds directly in the stock market ("Public Perceptions," 1999). All the uncertainties and ambiguities inherent in the stock market gave credence to such views.

Summary

Just as the debates over health care reform in the early years of the 1990s were illustrative of the rational choice model, discussions about Social Security in the later years of the 1990s also were illustrative of the model. Such discussions occurred within the context of the institutional framework within which Social Security was constructed and alternative solutions to its problems could be considered. In highlighting the problems associated with Social Security, such discussions also highlighted (a) the values that are important to maximize in constructing solutions to such problems; (b) alternative solutions proposed for achieving and maximizing such values; and (c) the calculation of net value ratios based on the application of the same values to the different proposals. The concepts associated with the rational choice model—which include the problem; the context; values, goals, and objectives; alternative solutions; intended and unintended consequences, and net value ratio—helped to frame the analyses of both health care reform and Social Security reform proposals and also helped to clarify substantive issues in both.

Although none of the alternative solutions debated in the case of either health care and Social Security reform were selected, the underlying issues remain. Health care reform was *not* enacted in 1994, as had been anticipated. Through a variety of procedural maneuvers, it was never even allowed to come to the floor of Congress for a vote, in part because the personal needs and motivations of some lawmakers prevented them from behaving in ways consistent with rational choice norms. The same applies to Social Security, which was tied to other tax provisions about which Republicans in Congress and the president could not agree. More will be said about these kinds of stalemates in a later chapter in conjunction with the appropriate policy models.

In the meantime, it is useful to note that by 1998, the number of people without health insurance had increased by 4.5 million since President Clinton came into office in 1993 and promised health insurance for all Americans (Pear, 1999b). Over 44 million people, more than 16% of the population, were without any health insurance at all in 2000, despite a series of incremental laws that had been enacted to expand health insurance coverage. With regard to Social Security, both the President and Congress were in agreement that sooner or later a solution had to be found to the Social Security trust fund problem, but which solution it will be remains *the* question.

▪ Some Caveats

Now that I have laid out the basic framework, readers should be aware that many of the assumptions underlying the rational choice model have been questioned. For one thing, there are limits to the resources available for securing all the information needed to carry out the model and in calculating the net value ratio. Even if such information were available, its role in decision making, according to Dye (1975), is likely to be limited—given differences in the values that people think should be maximized in the selection of alternative solutions to problems and in their constructions of problems and solutions to them—as discussion of health care reform and Social Security both demonstrate. Furthermore, lawmakers, like other people, are motivated by personal needs and desires that often prevent them from behaving in ways that conform to rational choice norms. The motivation of many of the congressional authors of alternative health care plans, for example, was their desire to have been able to participate in final health care reform negotiations, whenever these might have occurred (Clymer, 1994a). The uncertainties and ambiguities surrounding the selection of an alternative solution and course of action also serve to weaken assumptions underlying the rational choice model. Cases in point are some of the questions that were raised about the Clinton health care plan and about proposals for privatizing Social Security.

This concludes the discussion of the rational choice model as it applies to the selection of alternative solutions to family problems as they relate to health insurance and Social Security. In applying the model to such solutions, readers hopefully took note of all the interrelated choices involved in selecting an alternative that maximizes desired values. As noted earlier, this same observation would apply to other reform efforts as well.

Given the questions that have been raised about the applicability of the rational choice model to everyday policy choices, it seems reasonable to ask questions about some of the alternatives to and variations of the model. What are they? These questions are addressed in the next and succeeding chapters. But before turning to them, review the questions I have listed below for you to think about and discuss in relation to the rational choice model and in selecting an alternative solution to a family problem that best maximizes the goals and values you, the reader, think are important to maximize in addressing that problem.

■ Some Exercises and Questions for Your Reflection and Discussion

1. Identify the major concepts of the rational choice model.
2. What are its major assumptions?
3. What is meant by "net value ratio"?
4. Update the discussion on health care reform in the chapter, using the rational choice model. Have any changes occurred? If so, what are they? What arguments have been made for and against them?
5. What values were the various health insurance proposals trying to achieve?
6. Update the discussion on Social Security, using the rational choice model. Have any changes occurred? If so, what are they? What arguments have been made for and against them?
7. What values were the various Social Security alternatives trying to achieve?
8. Apply the model to the analysis of another issue of your choice, such as child care or housing.
9. What values do you think are most important to maximize in the issue you have selected? Why?
10. Give examples of how this model has been used in your work setting or in any other activity in which you have been involved?

Now, let us turn to the next chapter to look at some variations of the rational choice model to see if they might fit real situations of choice any better.

CHAPTER 11

Incremental Theory and Game Theory

Variations on Policy as Rational Choice in the Construction of Policy Solutions to Family Problems

Questions have been raised in previous discussions about the degree to which the rational choice theory realistically depicts the policy-making situation. Such questions have to do with the limits of human capacity to deal with policy problems in all their complexities (Simon, 1957). Herbert Simon coined the term *bounded rationality* to describe the physical and psychological limits of human capacity to generate alternative solutions, process information, and solve problems in accordance with the model. Speaking to such limits, President Clinton, at one point in the discussions about health care reform, said he had read and thought so much about health care reform that his head ached. According to Simon, these limits mean that policy makers are required to separate problems and deal with them one at a time. Such segmentation precludes decisions based on the coordination of input from all the specialists whose views may be pertinent in addressing a problem. From this, Simon concluded that rational action requires simple models that deal with only the main features of a problem and not the entirety of all of its complexity. Such a conclusion could be applied not only to health care reform but also to welfare reform, education reform, Social Security reform, and other reform efforts as well.

In this chapter, two variations are presented of the rational choice model that address the questions critics have raised about it: incremental theory and game theory. Each emphasizes different constraints on rational choice in constructing policy solutions to family problems. Let us now examine each of these frameworks in greater detail to see what they illuminate about the processes involved in the construction of family policy.

■ Incremental Theory:
Family Policy as the Outcome of Incremental Choices

If former Speaker of the House Tom Foley was right in saying that problems of the past seemed simpler, solutions clearer, and the need to balance the interests of competing constituencies less critical (Clymer, 1993d), then incremental theory probably depicts the policy-making situation more accurately than rational choice theorists are likely to acknowledge. Policy from the perspective of incremental theory is a process of constant adjustment to the outcomes of previous actions (Lindblom, 1959). Just as health care reform is illustrative of rational choice theory, it also is illustrative of incremental theory.

Some of the assumptions that underlie incremental theory that are illustrated in the discussion that follows are that:

- Existing policies and programs provide the framework through which policy makers come to view and understand the problems that come to their attention relating to families, Social Security, and health care.

- Existing policies and programs structure situations of choice in ways that constrain and confine policy choices to relatively narrow limits.

- Existing policies and programs provide the information used to arrive at decisions in constructing policy solutions to family problems, an assumption empirically supported in one study of the information used in planning social services for families at the county level (Zimmerman & Sterne, 1978).

- Policy makers have a stake in policies and programs to which they have committed themselves in the past (e.g., Head Start, a preschool program for disadvantaged youngsters to which policy makers are committed).

- Existing policies and programs enjoy a certain legitimacy that new policies and programs do not.

- Existing policies and programs are apt to continue because of the gains and losses they represent for affected groups.

- Radical policy departures are unlikely to receive serious attention because they threaten the disruption of ongoing economic, organizational, and administrative processes.

- Policy makers prefer small incremental choices based on experience with existing policies and programs because of the uncertainties and ambiguities surrounding the adoption of a new or different set of policies and programs.

- Policy makers act to satisfy constituent demands, searching for ideas and programs likely to work and not necessarily those that might work better or best in constructing policy solutions to family problems.

Because policy from the perspective of rational choice theory is seen as a process of constant adjustment to the outcomes of previous actions (Lindblom, 1959), it also can be seen as a variation of past policies and programs involving a series of small, incremental choices (Frohock, 1979). Policy goals from this perspective are seen as *emergent* rather than predetermined, as in rational choice theory. Political considerations and the complexity of policy problems, coupled with limits on policy makers' time and intelligence, are seen as constraints on policy choice. Given the uncertainties and ambiguities surrounding policy choice and the conflict created by sharp policy departures, it is no wonder that policy makers prefer small incremental choices based on experience with existing policies and programs. For this reason, some analysts maintained that the apparent seismic political shift in the 1994 midterm elections would prove illusory in terms of dramatic policy departures (Berke, 1995). Next, we will focus on ongoing attempts to construct solutions to problems that many people were experiencing in the area of health care.

Health Care Reform 1993-94

Resistance to Radical Policy Departures

Subsequent to the nation's experience with health care reform in 1993-94, developments for solutions to family problems in the area of health care were more reflective of the incremental than the rational choice model. True to the incremental model, experience with existing health care arrangements provided the framework through which policy makers had come to view and understand the escalating costs of health care and the problems many people experienced in gaining access to it. Existing health care arrangements also served to confine the thinking of many to relatively narrow limits, such as the proposal in 1996 to extend coverage to the millions of people *without* health insurance rather than trying to reform the health care system completely, as President Clinton had proposed in 1993-94. The reluctance of policy makers to seriously attend to a policy departure as radical as the one proposed by President Clinton can be attributed in part to the threat it posed to ongoing economic, organizational, and administrative processes. One congressman cavalierly dismissed the idea of the health care alliances that were part of the Clinton health care plan almost as soon as the plan surfaced. Many more reacted the same way to the single payer plan.

Uncertainties and Ambiguities Surrounding the Clinton Plan

The uncertainties and ambiguities surrounding the costs of the Clinton health care plan were given voice when it was suggested that payment of subsidies for the insurance premiums of low-income individuals and families be delayed until projected savings from health care reform were actually realized (Ifill, 1993). Such uncertainties and ambiguities would also have pertained to any other health care plan. The ambiguities and uncertainties surrounding adoption of the plan were further evidenced in the response of Richard Gephardt, the majority leader of the House in the 103rd Congress, to a reporter, who in late August of 1994 asked him when the House would begin debate on health care reform. Exasperated, Gephardt said the answer to that question is, has been, and would be for some time that he did not know and knew of no one who did (Toner, 1994).

Winners and Losers

Whether or not the lineup of potential winners and losers in health care reform would prevent it from being enacted also was part of the uncertainty and ambiguity surrounding the situation. Those who stood to lose under the Clinton reform plan included insurance companies, small businesses that had not provided health insurance coverage for their employees in the past, drug manufacturers, cigarette smokers, medical specialists, malpractice lawyers, infertility clinics, and states that failed to act quickly on reforms.

Those who stood to gain from the plan included primary care doctors, nurse practitioners and physician's assistants, large and small businesses that currently insured their employees (their costs would go down), individuals and families with a preexisting health condition, managed-care companies and large health maintenance organizations (HMOs), generic drug manufacturers, medical schools (more federal aid would become available to train primary care doctors), the states (as a result of reductions in Medicaid costs), and individuals and families in general who would be guaranteed lifelong coverage. All the lobbying for these groups was suggestive of conditions of natural *disharmony* surrounding the construction of a solution to the health insurance problem as different groups sought to gain, or at least protect, their advantage in the process.

The Satisficing Principle

Also surfacing during the debates on health care reform in 1993-94, at least twice, was what is called the satisficing principle. This principle refers to the selection of a course of action that is "good enough" in constructing policy solutions. It is based on the assumption that policy makers act to satisfy constituent demands and search for ideas and programs that are likely to work, not necessarily those that might work better (Allison, 1971) or that achieve the highest net value ratio. Bill Clinton used just these words at the Governor's Association meeting in 1994 when he said he was looking for a health care plan that would work, claiming no pride of authorship in his plan. Just as net value maximization is central to rational choice theory, satisficing as a principle is central to incremental theory.

Senator Kennedy told a story early in the health care reform debates that also illustrates the satisficing principle. He was the Senate's foremost advocate of national health insurance. Since 1970, he supported one health care proposal after another in seeking a majority to join him (Clymer, 1993b). Announcing that, unlike earlier years, he now was more interested in practical or "satisficing" solutions to the problem, he declared that he was interested in a program that would work, not necessarily one that might work better. To illustrate his point, he told a story about three geography teachers being interviewed for the same job and a school board bitterly at odds over whether the earth was round or flat. Each job contender was asked how they would deal with this issue, that is, whether they would teach that the earth was round or flat. In response, one of them said that he could teach it either way—he could teach that the earth was round *or* he could teach the earth was flat. Making his point, the senator added that he was now ready to do the same—that if health care reform were universal, cut costs, and ensured quality, he could support it, "round or flat."

An exchange between Senator Kennedy and Senator Dave Durenburger from Minnesota, a member of the Labor and Human Resources Committee chaired by Senator Kennedy, further illustrates the concept. Like Senator Kennedy, Senator Durenburger also was a longtime advocate of health care reform, but unlike Senator Kennedy, he favored a market-based, multiple payer approach, not employer mandates, as Kennedy did. The issue they disputed were the caps on increases in health insurance premiums (Clymer, 1994b). After the committee had been meeting for more than 9 hours, Senator Durenburger urged the committee to take more time before voting on the caps, imploring that if something was going to be done on health care reform, it ought be done right. To this, Senator Kennedy rejoined that the committee had been meeting and meeting and meeting, and that although it might not have the issue right, it was as close to being right as it was going to get.

Modest, Step-by-Step Solutions: The Health Insurance Portability and Accountability Act (HIPAA) (Kassebaum-Kennedy Act) of 1996

Subsequent developments in health care—the passage of HIPAA in 1996—further illustrate the incremental model. HIPAA, in effect, is the outcome of a process of constant adjustment to the outcomes of previous actions. A relatively modest piece of health insurance legislation, HIPAA represents an adjustment to the outcome of health care reform efforts in 1993-94. Instead of restructuring the entire health care insurance system, as the Clinton plan proposed, HIPAA addressed specific issues—segmented problems—that contributed to the overall health care problem, as suggested by Herbert Simon (1957). Readers will recall that job lock and preexisting conditions were two problems families experienced in relation to health care. HIPAA addressed the job lock problem by making coverage portable, that is, by requiring insurance coverage to follow people from job to job so they can retain their coverage if they lose or change jobs (Pear, 1996). Moreover, HIPAA prohibits insurance companies from using preexisting conditions to deny people eligibility for coverage.

Although supporters of President Clinton's ambitious plan to guarantee health insurance to every American said that anything less than a complete overhaul of the health care system might cause more problems than it solved, many in 1996 saw merit in *modest gradual steps* to improve coverage. Based on past experience, when many worked hard for health care reform and nothing happened, an architect of the Clinton plan said he supported HIPAA, although in 1993-94, he said that he probably would have viewed it as too modest. With major reform highly unlikely, however, he said incremental reform had to be viewed as progress. The chief architect of the Clinton plan also said he supported the bill, although he doubted it would solve the basic problems of health care in this country: the unacceptably high and rising number of uninsured, the declining number of Americans covered by health insurance through their employment, and the high cost of health care. After 20 years of incremental changes following the passage of Medicare and Medicaid in 1965, he said, the problems just keep getting deeper. Nonetheless, he thought passage of HIPAA could restore lawmakers' confidence in their ability to deal with health care issues, their loss of confidence dating back to 1988-1989 and the failed attempt to expand Medicare to cover catastrophic illnesses.

Emergent Solutions:
Mental Health and 48-Hour Maternity Care Coverage

   HIPAA, in dealing with the problems of job lock and preexisting conditions, illustrates not only the idea of gradualism embedded in the incremental model but also the emergent nature of the constructed solutions to family problems depicted by the model. The solution took the form of an amendment to HIPAA that required insurers and health plans to provide coverage for mental illnesses equivalent to that provided for other health conditions. When Tipper Gore, the wife of Vice President Al Gore, pushed for such a requirement in 1993, it seemed politically inconceivable that Congress would accept it. But since then, lawmakers have heard many firsthand accounts of the effectiveness of mental health services and the hardships individuals and families experienced as a result of insurance policies that denied such coverage. In promoting the bill, Nancy Kassebaum, Republican senator from Kansas, and Senator Kennedy, sponsors of the bill, emphasized how modest it was, boasting that it did not strike out in a bold new direction, just as the incremental model advises. HIPAA also was amended to require health insurers to lengthen the time that mothers of newborns can remain in the hospital, from 24 hours to at least 48 hours following birth.

   Although some experts bemoaned the limitations of such piecemeal incremental steps to expand health care coverage, many policy makers seemed committed to such an approach after the earlier failure of attempts at more comprehensive reforms. Indeed, politicians had not ventured near the issue again until 1996. The cost, complexity, and political fallout of the Clinton plan were painful, lingering memories for them. No one in 1996 campaigned for health care reform on a scale of the order of President Clinton in 1993-94 (Toner, 1999b).

A Variation of Past and Existing Legal Protections:
The 1999 Patients' Bill of Rights

   The Patients' Bill of Rights of 1999 also is illustrative of the incremental model. The legislation came before the House and Senate in late 1999 to ensure the rights of patients in health care, including the right to sue health insurance plans that caused injury to patients by denying care or providing substandard treatment (Pear, 1999a). The measure was not a radically new policy departure, because it already existed at the state level and merely federalized what already existed. The issue of patients' rights highlighted the continuing tensions in a health care system that during the 1990s had been transformed from a traditional fee-for-service system in which patients were free to choose their own doctors and doctors were free to decide which services their patients needed to a managed care system in which HMOs and insurance plans tightly controlled patients' choice of doctors and doctors' choice of patient treatment (Toner, 1999a). Managed care refers to the bureaucracy of insurance companies and HMOs that has rapidly replaced the once familiar institution of fee-for-service doctors' offices.

Passed by the House and Senate in 1999, the two versions had to be reconciled in conference committee. They differed from each other in two major ways (Pear, 1999b). The Senate version applied to a much smaller number of people— only 48 million—and the House bill applied to 161 million people. The Senate version additionally provided a more limited set of rights than the House version. Whereas the Senate version did not expand patients' right to sue HMOs, the House version would have allowed patients to sue health plans in state courts. The House version also guaranteed to patients access to emergency care and medical specialists, allowed them to appeal coverage decisions to an independent board, and prohibited HMOs from retaliating against doctors who fought for the needs of their patients. It also was tied to tax breaks to help individuals and small businesses buy health insurance.

Hailed a victory by supporters, President Clinton called the House bill a major victory for "every family in every health plan." The outcome of the House-Senate conference was highly uncertain because of the tax break provision. Recall that the incremental model accounts for uncertainties in constructed solutions to family problems. Projected to cost $40 billion over 10 years, Republicans supported the tax breaks, which, according to the president and other Democrats, would go mainly to a small number of healthy affluent people. Opposed by Democrats and the White House, the bill to ensure patients' rights could easily become bogged down in negotiations with the Senate, according to House Minority Leader Richard Gephardt of Missouri, especially since the president said he would not sign any legislation whose costs were not fully offset by the conference committee.

The House bill differed from the Senate bill in that it weakened protections many HMOs enjoyed against lawsuits. Under the Employee Retirement Income Security Act of 1974, courts had repeatedly rejected lawsuits that related directly to the administration of claims under employee benefit plans. More recently, however, judges had become more receptive to lawsuits seeking damages from HMOs for providing inadequate care. Such lawsuits gave credence to claims that the House measure was not new but was merely an extension of what already existed at the state level and thus not a radically new policy departure. In fact, almost every provision in the House bill, including the right to sue, had been enacted in some form by one or more states earlier. Doctors already faced liability as a result of the decisions insurance plans forced upon them, proponents adding that it was only fair that insurance plans be held to the same accountability standards as doctors. Both House and Senate bills were alike in saying that if an HMO denied a claim, the patient could have the decision reviewed by an independent panel of medical experts. Both versions would prevent health plans from interfering with a doctor's ability to discuss treatment options with patients.

According to one of the authors of the bill, Representative Charlie Norwood, a Republican dentist from Georgia, insurance plans had enjoyed near total immunity from legal accountability for injuring and killing people in this country for monetary gain for almost a quarter of a century. He added that no thinking or feeling American could agree to allow that situation to continue. Another Republican, Representative Merrill Cook of Utah, who voted for the bill, argued that if Americans had the right to sue for a damaged fence or an unsafe toy, they should have the right to sue if their life or health has been endangered. Managed care leaders tried to make the case that opening managed care to lawsuits would raise costs that ultimately would be passed on to consumers.

Indeed, rising costs were again the most worrisome trend in health care in 1999—and the most difficult to discuss politically. Cost control was risky: the cost containment provisions in the Clinton plan had created fears of health care rationing. At the same time, the gatekeeper and referral requirements of managed care had led to one story after another on the floor of the House about dying children and heedless bureaucrats on the other end of the phone. Some experts worried that the managed care revolution had already squeezed out easy savings. At the same time, rising health care costs were directly related to the growing number of people who were uninsured; they also raised profound questions on the equity of a Medicare program that lacked prescription drug coverage just when the pharmaceutical revolution offered immense promise for many of the ills of old age.

The complex, interrelated nature of these issues is what prompted the Clinton administration—and many other health planners—to push for a grand, comprehensive health care plan in the first place in 1993-94. Working on these problems with incremental measures, step by step, was harder, some health planners said, but probably all the political system could handle.

Summary

Health care reform is an issue that probably can be used to illustrate all the policy models discussed in this book. It was mentioned in relation to the institutional framework, was a major focus of the discussion of rational choice theory and now in relation to the incremental model, all of which points to the breadth and complexity of the health care problem and solutions to it.

The incremental model, unlike the other models discussed thus far, highlights the importance of experience with past policies and programs in a desire to avoid the uncertainties associated with the construction of new policies and programs for families.

The concepts—the words, ideas—important to the incremental model in the construction of policy solutions to family problems include the following:

- Existing policies and programs as policy outputs
- Segmented problems
- Uncertainty and uncertainty avoidance
- Satisficing
- Political feasibility
- Goals as emergent rather than predetermined
- Short-term feedback and corrective action

Just as the institutional and rational choice frameworks do not preclude other ways of understanding the construction of solutions to family problems in the form of family policies and programs, the incremental model does not either. Other policy models—such as game theory, another variation of the rational choice model—call attention to other aspects involved in such constructions that also act as constraints on policy choice related to families.

■ Game Theory

Game theory, another variation of rational choice theory, views the construction of policy solutions to family problems as rational choice under competitive conditions of no authority (Dye, 1975), which means that policy makers are not required to seek the approval of party or congressional leaders or anyone else for the choices they make when they vote on particular measures. The assumptions underlying game theory are as follows:

- Family policy, as rational choice under competitive conditions of no authority, depends on the choices and actions of two or more players (Dye, 1975).
- Policy making is a game in which the interdependent moves of relevant players determine the outcomes.
- The moves of players not only reflect their desires and abilities as individuals but also their expectations of the moves of others.
- The rules of the game define the choices available to players.
- Players seek to minimize their losses and maximize their gains.
- Players are required to cooperate to achieve the outcomes they desire.
- Competition for support requires the use of persuasion, compromise, accommodation, and bargaining.

The Policy Game

In game theory, the construction of policy solutions to family problems is a *game* in which the moves of interdependent players determine its outcomes. To play the game, players must be aware not only of their own preferences, talents, and interests but also of the talents, interests, and preferences of others. The *rules of the game* define the choices available for playing the game, including the possibility of bluffing and the deliberate misrepresentation of facts and attitudes. A set of moves aimed at achieving the payoffs players are seeking is called a *strategy*. A strategy takes into account the possible moves of other players, given their desires and goals. A strategy that aims to protect a player against an opponent's best play is known as *minimax*. Minimax is a strategy that attempts to minimize maximum losses and maximize minimum gains. Rather than seek maximum gains at the risk of greater losses, minimax looks for minimal gains as a protection against maximum losses. Cutting one's losses is one expression of this strategy. Players can be any goal-seeking entity capable of rational action— individuals, groups, organizations, political entities (e.g., states, cities), and even insurance companies.

From the perspective of game theory, the construction of policy solutions to family problems takes place under competitive conditions of no authority, which means that players are required to *cooperate* to achieve the outcomes they desire—on the vote on a desired measure, for example—even in situations of competition and conflict. From this same perspective, *policy may be seen as a process of conflict and consensus building that requires the use of persuasion, accommodation, and bargaining in the competition for support*. This sometimes also requires the exchange of side payments and favors. All these processes were in evidence in the passage of the North American Free Trade Agreement (NAFTA) and in the support the Clinton administration sought for the passage of health care reform and an anticrime bill in 1993. Although NAFTA was not a case of explicit family policy, its passage in 1993 was thought important for job growth for American families. Knowing that cooperation was required to enact the legislation Republicans desired, Speaker of the House Newt Gingrich (R-Georgia) announced after the 1994 midterm elections that he would co-operate and work with the president and the Democrats to achieve his goals, qualifying his intention by saying that he would not compromise his principles to do so. Both the president and the Democratic leader of the House, Richard Gephardt, said the same thing—they would cooperate with the Republicans but would not compromise their principles.

The Rules of the Game

The rules of the game determine how the game is played. In the Senate, the opposition party often uses the filibuster rule to delay or stop action on bills the majority party wants to pass, as in the case of health care reform. It is the rule that many hold responsible for congressional gridlock and the inability of the

Congress to complete its work in a timely fashion. The rule allowing senators to block referral of legislative proposals to committee simply by voice of objection enables them to delay committee action on bills until their objections are met. Both Senators Kennedy and Moynihan employed this rule as part of their strategy to win concessions from the other regarding committee jurisdiction over the president's health care package in 1993.

A change in the filibuster rule was proposed in the Senate when the 104th Congress convened in 1995. The change would have prevented members who felt strongly about a measure from being able to delay a vote on it indefinitely ("Time to Retire," 1995). The measure did not pass. Democratic senators in addition proposed a rule change to end congressional gridlock in the Senate, which encouraged senators to use their time on the floor to debate the substance of a measure rather than engage in procedural maneuvers and obstruction, as some Republicans in fact did in the case of health care reform in 1993-94.

The House also proposed rule changes for playing the game in the House when the 104th Congress convened in 1995, many of which passed: a ban on proxy voting, a three fifths rather than a simple majority vote to raise income taxes, a ban on closed door hearings, and others ("Rules Change," 1995). Although rule changes were approved that made taxes more difficult to raise, some also were approved that made spending cuts easier.

Strategies for Achieving Desired Outcomes

The Case of the $792 Billion
Tax Cut Bill and Moderate Republicans

Strategies for achieving the outcome players desire in constructing solutions to family problems include cooperation, competition, compromise, negotiation, accommodation, and bargaining. In this regard, the $792 billion tax cut bill that the House proposed in 1999 is instructive. In July 1999, after adamantly opposing a 10% tax cut written into the bill, the largest in 18 years, and forcing a minor change in the tax bill, moderate Republicans were pleased (Dao, 1999a). Assuming victory, they withdrew their opposition to the bill at the last moment, even though the size of the tax cut was not reduced by the language they had negotiated. The language made part of the reduction in tax cuts contingent on reducing government debt payments, a bargain many economists said was unworkable.

Many moderates viewed the concession as a glowing demonstration of their increased strength and stature relative to conservative Republicans and Republican leaders, but most Democrats and some moderates saw the concession as illusory. To them, it underscored moderates' weakness and lack of negotiating skills and unity on the issue. Although some favored a deep across-the-board income tax cut, others worried that a large tax cut would divert money from other priorities such as building new schools, shoring up Medicare and Social Security, and reducing the national debt. The moderates introduced a more modest array of tax cuts of $100 billion over 5 years; for weeks, it appeared that their proposal would prevail over the 10% tax cut plan.

To their dismay, however, the Republican leadership revived the 10% tax cut plan. Angered because they had not been consulted, several of the moderates vowed to join Democrats in killing the Republican bill unless it was scaled back. Over the next few days, House Speaker Dennis Hastert argued that his leadership was on the line and that the party needed a big tax cut to win the 2000 congressional and presidential elections as the payoff all House members were seeking. Moreover, Speaker Hastert argued, because the tax cuts were almost certain to be scaled back in negotiations with the White House, they involved minimal losses for moderates, with the potential of maximum gains for Republicans in terms of voters' approval in the 2000 elections.

Similar moves were observed when health care reform was an issue in 1993-94 and in many other instances involving other policy issues related to families. Some senators introduced health care reform plans in 1993-94 to compete with the president's as part of their strategy for ensuring a place for themselves at the table when negotiations on health care reform were finally scheduled to take place—which was the outcome they were seeking. As part of *his* strategy for achieving the payoff *he* was seeking—the passage of health care reform—the president delayed introducing his health care plan well beyond its announced date in order to accommodate the preferences and objections of political supporters. These objections pertained to lifting the funding caps on insurance premiums for low-income individuals and workers and also spending caps on health care. Similarly, when lobbyists created a fuss over his proposal for an alcohol tax to help finance the plan, the president dropped the tax, calling it yet another distraction from the game's primary objective—health care reform. Some people thought he should have used this strategy when he became embroiled in the controversy with congressional leadership over gays in the military.

Players need not interact directly with each other to win support for their positions. They instead may bargain with the electorate to win their support. President Clinton used television as the medium in trying to *persuade* the electorate to support his budget reduction plan in 1993. Bob Dole, the former minority party leader in the Senate, used the same strategy and the same medium in trying to win the electorate's support for Republican opposition to the plan and in relation to many other issues pertinent to families. By not interacting directly with each other in these particular instances, each in effect was acting on those conditions that would help him secure the outcome he was after, each trying to persuade and cajole (Frohock, 1979) the electorate into supporting his position on the budget reduction plan, a strategy commonly used for such purposes. In this respect, game theory differs from power and control theories (that are part of conflict theory), which view participants as bargaining and negotiating in direct interaction with each other.

Confusion and Uncertainty as Part of the Game

Allison (1971) advised that to understand and explain a particular construction of a policy solution to a family problem, the game, the players, the coalitions, and the bargains and compromises must first be identified. Here the story of the Republican moderates and leadership in trying to win support for their tax cut plan in 1999 is again illustrative. The confusion of the process, which includes not only the moves of individual players but also their interests, power, and skill, also must be appreciated—the story of Republican moderates in 1999 again is illustrative. Deceit and the misrepresentation of facts add to the confusion. Certainly such confusion could be observed in the health care reform game in which administration officials tried to remain vague and ambiguous for as long as possible, preferring generalities over details, using horror stories and dire predictions that illustrated the need for change, repeatedly saying that the only nonnegotiable features of the Clinton health care plan were its overarching principles: comprehensive coverage, universality, and cost savings. Although his friends were trying to build support for the president's insistence on universal, or 100%, coverage, the president himself added to the confusion when he later said in a speech to the governors at their meeting in July 1994 that 95% or 98% coverage might do (Jehl, 1994). Articulating his apparently long-standing but unspoken position that although he and his wife repeatedly talked about universal coverage, the model they were using was Social Security, which covered about 98%, not 100%, of the population. Another way of adding to the confusion of the game includes the presentation of similar but competing agendas by political leaders who label them as different. Pat Robertson did this in 1992 when Bill Clinton was running for president, and Newt Gingrich did it when he called for streamlining government and cutting government spending, both having been set in motion by the Clinton administration earlier. Bill Bradley and Al Gore, both Democratic presidential candidates in 2000, did it when they were competing to be their party's nominee for president, as did George W. Bush and Al Gore in competing for the presidency in 2000.

The Game of the President's Budget Proposal 2000

The 1999-2000 budget talks offer many good examples of how policy solutions are constructed under competitive conditions of no authority and the compromises that have to be made and bargains that have to be struck to effect a particular policy solution to a family problem. In February 1999, President Clinton sent a budget proposal to Congress in the form of a spreadsheet that was a political document for a new fiscal era (Stevenson, 1999b). Presidents always have used their budget proposals to present their wish lists, but President Clinton was particularly adept at using the annual budget cycle not just to win attention and support for new and recycled programs but also to portray himself as active and engaged in his last year in office.

Yet, the president had a broader goal. He was eager to seize the high ground in a fast developing and fundamental debate over how the nation should capitalize on its newfound prosperity in constructing policy solutions to family problems. For example, should the country invest its anticipated fiscal windfall in preparing for the aging of the baby boom generation and the strains it will create on Social Security and Medicare? Fiscal prudence, the president argued, would allow succeeding generations to deal with the unforeseen and unknowable challenges of the next century "unburdened by the unfinished business of the 20th century, unshackled by our profligacy in the latter part of the 20th century" (Stevenson, 1999b). Republicans declared they were equally dedicated to shoring up Social Security, and like Democrats, also believed more money should go for education—and to the military as well. Although the budgetary math did not support their calculations, they wanted in addition a 10% tax cut.

The two parties were in tacit agreement about some things. One was not to aggressively question the assumption that the trillions of dollars in anticipated surplus would actually materialize, and the other was that nearly two thirds of the surplus should go to dealing with Social Security. However, they were not in agreement on the best way to shore up Social Security or how to use the money left over once the future of Social Security was ensured.

The stakes of the game were high. The Republican congressional leadership and President Clinton had strong reasons for finding some accommodation and enacting legislation on Social Security and dividing the surplus. No longer able to use the specter of unending deficits to impose limits on the growth and power of the federal government, Republicans returned to the approach Ronald Reagan championed two decades earlier: big tax cuts to stimulate the economy, with the corollary of starving the bureaucracy.

The Democrats, having worked hard to refashion themselves as the party of fiscal responsibility, now had to find a strategy for promoting what Clinton called "a prudent but progressive" approach to governing. The question was whether they could use government to construct solutions to family problems without opening the floodgates to new spending. The fact of the matter, according to Democratic Senator Frank Lautenberg from New Jersey and senior Democrat on the Senate Budget Committee, was that the United States would be spending *less* as a percentage of the American economy on government than at any time since 1973, and that the public debt, projecting 10 years ahead, would be at its lowest point since 1917.

Nonetheless, Senate Republicans, over the opposition of President Clinton and congressional Democrats and moderate Republicans, kept moving closer to passage of a $792 billion tax cut over 10 years (Stevenson, 1999c). Seeking to make political points and win the support of the electorate, Democrats offered a series of amendments in constructing their solution to the budget problem, including one that would have postponed the tax cuts and another that would have put aside enough money for a prescription drug benefit for the elderly as part of Medicare. All the amendments were defeated, largely on party-line votes.

Republicans had no higher priority than passing a tax cut in 1999—even though they knew the president would veto it. However, passing the bill would not be so easy. The House bill was more appealing than the Senate bill to conservatives in both chambers. The House bill was constructed around a gradual reduction in all income tax rates, a provision that Republicans said would benefit those who paid the most in taxes. but Democrats said would disproportionately reward the wealthy.

The Senate version provided a smaller income tax cut and directed a greater share of it to middle-income households. But it also went further in addressing the marriage penalty, a quirk in the tax code that forces many two-income couples to pay more in taxes than they would as singles. A primary goal of social conservatives, the Senate plan would have almost eliminated the penalty by eventually allowing married couples to file taxes as if they were single. The House plan would have limited its marriage penalty provisions to people who used the standard deduction and thus would do little for higher-income couples, who almost invariably itemize their deductions. The House bill also contained a provision for a reduction in the capital gains tax in the top rate from 20% to 15%; the Senate version had no such provision.

House and Senate negotiators had to maintain a delicate political balance to retain the appeal of the package to both the conservative and moderate wings of the Republican party. Vetoing the $792 billion Republican tax cut in September 1999, the president called upon a skeptical Congress to reach a bipartisan compromise with him on taxes, domestic spending, and the long-term financing problems facing Medicare and Social Security (Stevenson, 1999d). With Congress and the White House headed for a showdown over spending priorities for 2000—and with time running out for this legacy-minded administration to make substantive progress on big issues—the president urged both parties not to throw in the towel before trying to reach a broad budget agreement.

Although he said he was flexible, the president made no specific new offers and did not call for direct negotiations. Republican leaders kept him at arms length in efforts to engage Congress, asserting they would not be lured into last-minute budget negotiations. The fiscal dueling illustrated how increasingly intent both parties were on reaping political gain by blocking the other's initiatives rather than compromising and passing legislation, despite the opportunities created by projections of a mounting budget surplus.

The president vetoed the tax cut bill, as he had promised. The veto was staged with all the fanfare of a victory ceremony. The Marine Corps band played, Cabinet secretaries and senior administration aides gathered in the Rose Garden, representatives of interest groups attended, and the president sat behind a desk on a platform to wield the veto pen with the same flourish he might have used in signing a favored bill into law.

A package of routine tax provisions that the House Ways and Means Committee had drawn up was the vehicle for progress on tax measures in 1999. The provisions included an extension of a tax credit for corporate research and development costs, tax credits for companies that hired workers from welfare rolls, and rules that limited the effect of the alternative minimum tax on low- and middle-income taxpayers.

Although some members of both parties thought there was room to expand the package to include provisions with bipartisan support (e.g., a cut in the marriage penalty and estate tax), White House officials thought their best chance for bipartisanship rested with efforts of the Senate Finance Committee to draft legislation shoring up Medicare and adding a prescription drug benefit to the program. But an effort to develop a bipartisan approach to Medicare had collapsed earlier in the year, and the issue was so complicated that prospects for a deal before Congress adjourned later in the year were slim. Chances of reaching a compromise on shoring up Social Security were even slimmer. Despite nearly 2 years of efforts to find a middle ground, most Democrats remained committed to keeping the current system of retirement benefits intact, and most Republicans wanted to move toward a system under which workers could invest part of their payroll taxes in the stock market.

With regard to both the Patients' Bill of Rights (which was presented here as an example of the incremental model) and the tax and budget bills (which were presented as examples of game theory), readers may have a better appreciation for the confusion that reigns in constructing policy solutions to family problems, the uncertainties involved in doing so, the importance of players' interests and negotiating skills in playing the game, and the stakes of the game in terms of what stands to be lost or won and who stands to win or lose it.

The standoff over tax cuts in 1999 was repeated in the summer of 2000, when the Senate, with the help of seven Democrats who broke with their party on the vote, backed a Republican plan providing $292 billion in tax breaks for married couples over the next 10 years (Lacey, 2000). President Clinton vetoed the measure, calling it too costly and accusing Republicans of advancing a series of "tax giveaways" that abandoned the fiscal discipline that helped produce the longest economic expansion in the country's history. Although both parties advanced plans to remedy the so-called marriage penalty, the Republican plan was more broad, giving an election-year tax break to nearly all married couples, even those who do not pay a marriage penalty. The president urged a more modest tax relief package intended to benefit people of low and middle incomes. Earlier, he said he would agree to the Republican tax reductions for married couples if Congress would back his proposal for a Medicare prescription drug benefit. Republicans who had their own less sweeping prescription drug plan refused. The president's veto of the tax cut plan in 2000 set the stage for resuming the tax cut game when Congress returned to Washington after a late summer break.

Summarizing Assumptions

Following Allison (1971), a list of summarizing assumptions underlying the construction of policy solutions to family problems from the perspective of game theory that can be applied to both the examples presented here and others is given below:

- Actors are players in positions (e.g., the president, senate majority leader, etc.).

- Actors' perceptions, characteristics, and personalities are influencing variables, as are the personal and organizational goals and the interests of individual actors (e.g., the motivation for some in the health care reform game was to prevent the majority party from moving health care reform forward, as was true in the Patients' Bill of Rights and tax and budget games).

- The stakes of the game are the result of overlapping personal, organizational, and policy and program interests and consideration for the welfare of others.

- Deadlines and events raise issues and force busy players to take stands on issues at appointed times (e.g., the vote on the Budget Act in July 1999, the vote on NAFTA in November of 1993. Although health care reform was scheduled for a vote in the fall of 1994, the 103rd congressional session drew to a close before it could be enacted).

- The effective influence of individual players is:
  - A blend of their bargaining advantages, their skill and will in using their advantages and other players' perceptions of these ingredients of influence.
  - Their bargaining advantages, stemming from formal authority, organizational position, control over resources, including information and expertise that allow players to define the problem, identify the options, and determine whether and in what form decisions are to be implemented.
  - Their effectiveness and ability to affect other games—that is, their personal persuasiveness on positions and issues that have a high probability of being supported (see examples above).

- Action channels are the regularized means by which governments act on issues and structure the game through the preselection of major players and the distribution of the game's advantages and disadvantages.

- The rules of the game—the Constitution, laws, court decisions, executive orders, conventions, and culture—define the game, create the positions, distribute the power, establish the procedures for taking action, and sanction moves such as bargaining, coalition formation, persuasion, deceit, bluffs, and threats while defining others as illegal, unethical, or inappropriate (see examples above).

- The action, or choice, is the outcome of political processes in the context of shared power and individual judgments about important choices.

- The game itself is played in an environment that reflects uncertainty about what must be done, the necessity of doing something, and the critical consequences of what is done (e.g., health care reform).

- The structure of the game, the confidence with which it is played, the rewards of the game are important in influencing its outcomes (e.g., the president, House Speaker Dennis Hastert, and House moderates).

- Once the decision is made, the game is not over, since it always can be ignored or reversed (e.g., the reversal of the 1988 Catastrophic Health Care Act after its passage and the failure of some welfare agencies to inform TANF recipients and their families of their continued eligibility for Medicaid and food stamps.

The important concepts for family policy as rational choice under competitive conditions of no authority—the words, ideas—are as follows:

- The game
- Payoffs or rewards
- Competitive conditions of no authority
- Influence and power
- Actors as players in positions
- Conflict and competition
- Rules of the game
- Cooperation and compromise
- Stakes of the game
- Negotiation and negotiation skills
- Strategies and tactics
- Bargaining, accommodation, persuasion
- Minimax

The above concepts and their accompanying assumptions are invaluable for the insights they provide into the processes by which solutions to family problems are constructed in the form of policies and programs for families. The model directs attention to the many influences that are critical in affecting such solutions: the interests, motivations, and skills of individual players and their ability to cut deals—to negotiate and compromise—in order to attain the objectives and payoffs they seek under competitive conditions of no authority. The model helps to explain why the game often produces solutions and outcomes that do less to address the problems of individuals and families than what was anticipated before the game first started.

■ Summary and Conclusions

This concludes the discussion on two variations of rational choice theory. Once you are sensitized to their distinguishing features, you undoubtedly will find other examples of both incremental and game theories. Both theories do much to illuminate the constraints underlying policy choices. In addition to these two variations of rational choice theory, other frameworks (which will be discussed in Chapter 13) highlight other kinds of constraints on the construction of policy solutions to family problems. In the meantime, Chapter 12 focuses on political culture theory as a leading alternative to rational choice theories. Although presented in Chapter 8 as the framework for the analyses of the family policies that selected states constructed in the 1990s, in Chapter 12 it is presented as part of the discussion of policy frameworks or models. It is presented here both because it is a policy framework—and thus belongs in the discussion—and also to demonstrate its applicability to cross-national comparative analyses of the values and attitudes people from other countries hold to government and other people and the policy solutions different countries construct to family problems. Before turning to Chapter 12, however, think about and discuss the questions listed below for you, the readers, in relation to incremental and game theories as they relate to health care reform, tax and budget bills, the Patients' Bill of Rights, and many other matters of consequence to families.

■ Some Questions for Your Reflection and Discussion

Incremental Theory

1. What does "bounded rationality" mean?
2. How does the incremental model address some of the limitations of the rational choice model?
3. Give some examples of policies that have been shaped by past policies and programs, other than those presented in this chapter.
4. Why are existing policies and programs likely to continue?
5. What are some of the advantages of the incremental model? Give examples from the chapter.
6. What are the major concepts associated with the incremental model? Apply them to some family policy issue of interest to you (look to newspaper articles, TV, news magazines, etc.).
7. What are the assumptions underlying incremental theory? How do they apply to health care reform?

Game Theory

1. Why can policy making be viewed as a game?
2. Define policy choice from the perspective of game theory.
3. What are the major concepts associated with game theory? Apply them to some family policy issues of interest to you (look to newspaper articles, TV, news magazines, etc.).
4. Compare and contrast the construction of policy solutions to family problems from the perspectives of game theory and rational and incremental choice models.
5. How does game theory apply to health care reform, the budget, the Patients' Bill of Rights? What insights does it provide about the construction of policy solutions to family problems, as illustrated by the examples in the chapter?

And now, let us turn our attention to the next chapter for insights into the constructions of policy solutions that other countries construct to family problems, using political culture theory to illustrate differences.

CHAPTER 12

Political Culture Theory
An Alternative to Rational Choice Theory

Government structures and the values that underlie them are viewed as key to explaining constructed solutions to family problems from the institutional perspective; net value maximization is key from the perspective of rational choice theory; past policies and programs are key in such constructions from the perspective of the incremental model; and competitive conditions of no authority are key from the perspective of game theory. But the attitudes and values that people hold toward government and other people are seen as key to such constructions from the perspective of political culture theory. Because the framework was presented in some detail in Chapter 8, I will not discuss it in as much detail here. Therefore, you are advised to review Chapter 8 for a more complete discussion of the model. You may recall that Inglehart (1990) argued that because rational choice theory failed to take into account the linkages between culture and economic and political phenomena, it was limited as an explanatory model. Taking a leaf from Inglehart (1990), it may be useful to review the assumptions that underlie political culture theory, which are as follows:

- Certain basic attitudes, values, and habits of behavior characterize the populations of different societies.
- Although attitudes and values may change, they are relatively stable.
- Such change, though perceptible, occurs gradually in relation to specific causes, such as long-term economic development.
- Though related to the political economy, political culture incorporates a distinct set of variables oriented around attitudes toward government.

To these assumptions, I have added the following:

- Such attitudes shape the construction of family problems in relation to government.

241

■ Such attitudes determine the policy solutions constructed to address family problems.

The discussion that follows is meant to illustrate the relevance of these assumptions to family policy through examples of policy solutions other countries have constructed to family problems. To facilitate intercountry comparisons, the discussion is first set in the context of the political culture of the United States.

■ The Cultural Traditions of the United States: Democracy and Capitalism

The two cultural traditions that have dominated American political and economic life since the country's founding are capitalism and democracy. The values central to democracy are freedom and equality; the values central to capitalism are freedom and private property or free enterprise. The tensions between these two traditions, which are the bases for sharp ideological divisions within American society, are a definitive feature of American life and are reflected in two different conceptions of the political order (Elazar, 1984). In the one, the political order is viewed as a marketplace in which the primary public relationships are seen as products of bargaining among groups and individuals acting in their own self-interest. In the other, the political order is viewed as a commonwealth in which people hold undivided interests and cooperate as citizens to create and maintain government at its best and to effect shared moral principles.

You will recall that according to Elazar (1984), these cultural traditions have evolved into three ideal types nationwide: *individualistic, moralistic,* and *traditionalistic.* According to this typology, the *individualistic* political culture emphasizes private over public concerns, placing a premium on the restriction of outside intervention—governmental *and* nongovernmental. It stands, as you will recall, in opposition to even minimal intervention in activities considered private and holds that government is best that governs least. In contrast, the *moralistic* political culture emphasizes the use of community power—governmental *and* nongovernmental—to intervene into private activities and constrain individualism whenever the public good is at stake. The *traditionalistic* political culture, on the other hand, while also viewing government in a positive light, seeks to restrict its role to maintaining the existing social order. Although applied to the American states and not fully extant in the real world in that most states, according to the typology, represent different mixes of the three (Elazar, 1984), the typology is suggestive in terms of its applicability to different countries. For that reason, it frames the discussion here for the insights it might provide into the policy solutions constructed by other countries to family problems.

As noted earlier, because attitudes central to a culture are learned early in an individual's socialization experiences (Inglehart, 1990), and because differences in cultural learning help shape what people think and do, political culture is held to be important. It is seen as important for shaping not only the attitudes people hold toward government and the problems of families but also for the policies that are enacted, here as they apply to families in different countries. For this reason, Inglehart (1990) maintained that policy choice cannot be interpreted as simply the result of rational choice in selecting an alternative that maximizes desired values or such external factors as the state of the economy. Rather, he says, choice is shaped by the culture in which it occurs. Thus, reflecting on the attitudes and values central to the political culture of the United States, culture helps to explain why, in the United States, market-based rather than government-based approaches to health care reform are preferred. Reflecting a more egalitarian approach to policy solutions and holding a more positive view toward government, it also explains why countries such as Sweden and Canada have national health insurance plans in which government plays a central role. In this discussion, case illustrations of Norway, Sweden, France, and Japan, drawn from news articles, are presented to illustrate the main features of political culture theory—values, the attitudes people hold toward government and other people, and habitual patterns of behavior. Readers should pay particular attention not only to the attitudes people in these countries express toward government and other people but also to how such attitudes are expressed in the policy solutions that have been constructed to family problems by these countries. The discussion begins first with Norway.

■ The Case of Norway

Plagued by rapidly rising budget deficits, governments everywhere in the 1990s, from Europe to Africa to Latin America and even to once very wealthy Arab oil countries, embraced the free market doctrine preached by President Ronald Reagan and Prime Minister Margaret Thatcher of Great Britain in the 1980s (Ibrahim, 1996). Norway was an exception. Buoyed by an unending supply of oil revenue and guided by a national commitment to egalitarianism, Norway's 4.25 million people strongly supported their welfare state. A welfare state is defined as one in which government assumes a relatively large role in the social and economic affairs of the country. Even business people—including those in the business of exporting manufactured products and raw materials to the globalizing world of competitive capitalism—joined in their nation's adherence to social democracy. Inflation in Norway in 1996 was below 2%; its unemployment rate was the lowest in Europe. Economic growth in the 1990s ranged between 3% and 5%. Oil exports ran at 3 million barrels a day, second only to Saudi Arabia's, and the petrodollars fed a budget surplus of $6 billion more than the government's $61 billion it spent, suggesting that policy solutions to family problems in Norway were not constrained by a shortage of money.

Individual tax rates in Norway could climb above 50%, but the country's welfare state is among the most generous in the world today. It provides annual stipends of $1,620 for every Norwegian child under 17—which increases slightly for each additional child as a family grows and increases—and still more if the family lives in a remote part of the country; retirement pay equivalent to industrial workers' pensions for all homemakers, even those who have not worked outside the home; 42 weeks of fully *paid* maternity leave; and reimbursement of all medical costs exceeding $187 a year per person.

Although these benefits are financed by oil and high taxes, as earlier discussion suggests, they also are supported by the Norwegian national character. Norwegians, profoundly proud of their egalitarian orientation, disapprove of wide disparities in income, such as those that characterize the United States. Their strong sense of solidarity permits one of the highest personal tax rates in the world and provides vast latitude to government in social engineering. As one diplomat explained, high taxes enjoy a great national consensus because, he said, it's a way for people to be saved from themselves.

Norwegians have a word for their antielitist views—*Jantslaw*—which means no one should think they are better than anybody else. Politicians have lost their jobs for failing to remember this. Disdain for the trappings of wealth and power is reflected in restrictions on executive pay and mandates for extensive workplace rules that have met little opposition from business. In contrast to the multiples of 50 or even 100 or more in the United States, the owner and president of a transport company said his after-tax annual pay in 1996 was about double that of his workers' average. Norway has a 23% sales tax in addition to high personal income taxes. Gasoline costs $6 a gallon, and a glass of beer in a bar costs $8. According to one company owner, money does not have to change hands more than two or three times before going back to the government and the welfare state.

Although business leaders sometimes complained about short workweeks, high overtime raises, and paid sick leaves of up to 2 weeks, they have accommodated themselves to the situation. According to the director general of the Confederation of Norwegian Business and Industry, some businesspeople would like to fine-tune attitudes on sick leave, working hours, and the minimum wage, but many did not think radical change was worth the social risks and disruption that would result. In fact, labor in Norway, defying a world trend, continued to squeeze concessions from management. Having won agreement to lower the retirement age from 67 to 64, the unions were pushing to lower it to 62—at full pension.

Norway's Parliament was dominated by the Labor Party, which in 1996 was expected to approve legislation for a "lifelong learning" program that would give Norwegians a year of leave at full pay from their jobs every decade or so to sharpen their work skills. The cost of employee salaries was to be shared by employers and the state.

Even with so many social programs, Norwegian businesses were doing well, largely because of having one of the best educated and technologically advanced

workforces in the world. The reduction in Norway's corporate tax rate from
50% to 28% in 1992 also helped.

In an ultramodern office building just outside Oslo, pots of free coffee and
plates of free fruit and cakes were placed at strategic locations as an extra benefit
for employees who worked in a setting surrounded by fine paintings and sculp-
tures. Reciting familiar business complaints about high costs and extensive regulations in Norway, the chief executive of Norway's largest supermarket chain,
when asked if he would favor abandoning his country's approach for a British-
or American-style model, said no. He explained that Norway was a very social
democratic society and that Norwegians were not familiar with any other system, which speaks to the importance of both habitual patterns of behaviors and
early socialization experiences for the attitudes that people hold toward government and each other. It may be expensive, he said, but there were no poor people
in Norway, and he himself did not want to see any. There were no strikes and no
high demand for salary increases. He said he wanted adjustments to be made in
Norway's system in order to preserve it.

The health minister said the country would never abandon its social programs—even if it did not have oil, it would not want to rethink its notion of the
welfare state. Protecting workers against the vagaries of the marketplace was
only part of it, he said. In his view, the state's investment in workers' health,
financial security, and education paid big economic dividends. He scorned
worldwide union busting and Britain's experiment in downsizing government
over the last quarter century, saying such practices produced great dissatisfaction and enormous strains on British society that would come back to haunt it.
According to a leading member of the Conservative Party and Parliament's
social affairs committee, the good side of Norwegian society was that whether
people had or did not have money, it made no difference; everyone went to the
same doctors and received the same services and would continue to do so as long
as people were willing to give back to the community. Clearly, the attitudes Norwegians hold toward government and other people help to explain the country's
egalitarian approach to family policy in which government plays a major rather
than a minimal role, having all the hallmarks of the moralistic political culture in
the Elazar typology.

■ The Case of Sweden

The same can be said about Sweden to further illustrate the role that attitudes
toward government and other people play in the construction of policy solutions
to family problems. At a time when world leaders were fascinated by the United
States's economic success and its credo of less government and low taxes, Sweden seemed to be defying them. Sweden was still a country where government
consumed nearly 60% of the national economy, far above the 32% consumed in
the United States (Andrews, 1999). Taxes and wages in Sweden were among the
world's highest. Firing a lazy worker in most cases was legally nearly impossible,

a situation in which Swedes take great pride. When the prime minister introduced his budget plans, promising that Sweden would consolidate its position as a leading welfare nation, he pledged to create another entitlement: the right of every person who turned 65 to retain a personal assistant.

At the end of the 20th century, this largely *unreconstructed* welfare state had one of Europe's most vibrant economies. Although Sweden's recent prosperity was part of a cyclical recovery from back-to-back recessions, it also reflected a wider pattern in Europe and a particularly nuanced reaction to the United States's robust economy of the 1990s. For even as Sweden, like other countries in Western Europe, continued to preserve traditional European social programs, it also embraced entrepreneurship and unrestricted competition. Continuing to finance health care, education, and many social services, Sweden also had deregulated industries from telecommunications to airlines and banking. As a result, new companies and high technology have flourished, much of the growth coming from companies that did not exist 10 years ago. Information technology and service companies eclipsed traditional manufacturers as main sources of new jobs.

Economic growth in Sweden in 1999 was projected at 3.8%, which was faster than Europe as a whole and close to the recent growth rate in the United States. The government that 5 years ago carried a deficit equivalent to 11% of the gross domestic product now had a budget surplus. Unemployment had declined from 8.2% in 1993 to 6.1% in 1999, with estimates for the year as low as 5.3%. Stockholm had shortages of computer specialists, sales representatives, teachers, and also caterers.

Sweden was not the only country to challenge some central tenets of the current American-British model. France, where the Socialist Cabinet had mandated a workweek of 35 hours, was growing by nearly 3%, and its double-digit jobless rate was coming down. Finland, where personal taxes were high and job rules were rigid, had become a world leader in the mobile phone industry. The Netherlands still had generous welfare programs even though corporate taxes were low. Sweden's boom was arguably the most unusual. Besides clinging to a cradle-to-grave system of security, Sweden was one of just a few countries that refused to join 11 European nations in adopting the euro as a common currency. Yet, Sweden was growing faster than most of its euro zone neighbors.

What was behind Sweden's recent rebound? For one, Swedish political leaders had finally put the country's economic house in order. After staggering deficits in the mid-1990s, the Social Democratic government rejected most demands to cut back the welfare state, raised personal taxes, imposed tough spending limits, and deregulated its markets to foster an entrepreneurial culture. It also loosened its job rules, permitting companies to hire temporary workers who could be laid off at will; the result was a dramatic expansion of temporary employment companies.

Unlike the German economy, which slowed to a standstill in 1997 and 1998, Sweden's economy accelerated. Worried that a slowdown would generate new budget problems, the prime minister rejected the idea of tax cuts. But later, with tax coffers overflowing, he promoted modest tax cuts and spending increases for health care, pensions, job training, and higher education, all directly affecting families.

A cafe owner in Stockholm who was no better off financially at the end of the 1990s than she was at the beginning of the decade said that as the mother of a son with a hearing disability, the Swedish government had eased her burden. Her son, 20 years old at the time she was interviewed, had received special instruction from kindergarten through high school, and the government paid for soundproof insulation in their home to make the use of his hearing aid easier. "All such things were free," she said, adding that she would not have been able to afford all that her son received if "we did not have the social system that we have in Sweden."

■ The Case of France

Just as the attitudes held by people in Sweden and Norway toward government and other people find expression in the policy solutions those countries have constructed to family problems, the same is true of the French. In 1991, a French woman discovered she was pregnant and filed a form to begin collecting $150 a month beginning in her fourth month of pregnancy. Such a subsidy is extended to every mother in France, regardless of economic or marital status. When the woman became pregnant again 2 years later, the subsidy doubled; she would continue to receive it until her two boys are 18 (Ibrahim, 1995). Throughout her pregnancy, all her medical needs, checkups, and medications were free of charge and free of burdensome paperwork or delays at a government-financed clinic not far from her upper-middle-class neighborhood. In 1994, when her live-in companion, a photographer, was seriously wounded covering a conflict in Chechnya, he was flown back to France, where he was treated in a specialized war wounds hospital in Paris for 2 months, incurring no expenses; he recuperated at home for another 2 months with full pay guaranteed by the state.

When the woman went to the Office of Family Allocations in her neighborhood to request domestic assistance to help her cope with the care of her children and convalescing companion, in addition to her job as a freelance writer, she was assigned a housekeeper for a few weeks. She paid the housekeeper $3 an hour, and the Social Security fund paid the remaining $7 an hour. As the woman explained, such assistance was the foundation of the French Republican system that could be traced back to the French Revolution. "Equality and fraternity are not mere slogans here," she said, adding that the engagement of the state "is an expression of solidarity that gives us values."

The message that people mattered more than the bottom line was at the heart of a 3-week strike by public workers and hundreds of thousands of demonstrators who filled the streets of every major city in France in 1995. The strike, the country's most serious labor unrest in a decade, was called to protest the prime minister's proposal to slash medical, social welfare, and benefit payments in an effort to contain a widening budget deficit. But the attitude of the French, like those of the woman with two children and a live-in companion, multiplied a million times over, demonstrated why more confrontations could have been in the offing. According to the woman, most French people wanted France's values to be decided in the spirit of solidarity, not in terms of budget deficits and economic competition at cold, remote economic summits. People were worried, she said, that France's austerity plans and talk of a balanced budget could signal government's retreat from the spirit of solidarity that she said imbued France, and they demanded that another way be found.

Larger, poorer families benefited from an amazing array of government-financed benefits that included paid yearly holidays and transportation to a sea or mountain resort. The government pays for moving expenses, care at home for older people, subsidized apartments, and even dishwashers and washing machines for those who cannot afford them and have large families. In the greater Paris region, where people are encouraged to use mass transit, employers are required to pay half the commuting costs of their employees. Tenants unable to pay rent during the winter months are protected from eviction and get a tax break to reduce the financial burden of heating bills.

Welfare extends to issues like the right of each office employee to have a window from which the person "can see either sunset or sunrise." Five weeks' vacation is mandatory. In high-stress jobs like medicine or journalism, vacations extend to 9 weeks and are complemented by tax breaks. Throughout France, citizens are entitled by law to free schooling, including university education. From day care through high school, subsidized meals are included. These benefits and many others constitute a form of subsidy that allowed people of limited means to stretch their income.

The woman with the two children and live-in companion said that as a result of France's safety net, she enjoyed considerable peace of mind. More important, she believed the safety net fulfilled an essential social purpose. One worker who joined the strike revolted because government cutbacks meant that he could not go to the theater anymore, a comment that a sociology professor applauded, saying that it showed the sophistication of the French people, that even simple workers believed it was their right to go to the theater and eat at a decent restaurant occasionally.

Polls showed a surprising amount of sympathy for the strike on the part of those who did not participate in it and suffered the paralysis of mass transit and essential services. Many people explained that they supported the strike because the government's austerity programs were stripping away layer after layer of subsidies that permitted French families of even the most modest means to sample the cultural and culinary treasures that only the rich could afford. The strike and the protests were a defense of a way of life that had brought cohesion and social peace to France for decades. Living in a more egalitarian society than most Western industrialized countries, children of disadvantaged families living in France had a good chance of moving into a middle-class status in just one generation.

Sociologists and political scientists alike argued that French politicians were increasingly the product of an elitist system, charging that they had become cold machines disconnected from the reality of taxi drivers and cleaning ladies. That message seemed to have registered even with hardened right-wing French politicians, including the former interior minister, a conservative. "What's more important is not the confidence of the market," he said, "but the confidence of the French people," adding that a country could not be run without the support of the people.

■ **The Case of Europe in General**

The attitudes that people in France, Norway, and Sweden expressed toward government were pretty much the same all over Europe. Europeans in general accept relatively high taxes in exchange for governments that provide vibrant cities, first-rate public transportation, free universities, and bountiful social services (Stanley, 1999). A manager of three clothing factories in Milan, Italy, who supervised 300 employees and led a national trade group of fashion manufacturers, arrived at his office at 9:30 a.m. and left no later than 6:30 in the evening, limiting his workweek to 5 days, and never on Saturday or Sunday (Stanley, 1999). An executive in the United States with similar responsibilities could expect to work 60 hours a week plus a frequent weekend. Indeed, few Americans object to working overtime if it meant a bigger paycheck. Those in the United States striving for more prosperous lives willingly endure long hours and short vacations. But in Europe, millions of Europeans shared the Milan manager's unwillingness to give up free time, even if it meant missing out on an economic boom that enriched so many Americans in the 1990s.

In Europe, dinner each day with the family and a month on the Mediterranean each summer are part of a lifestyle most think is too precious to sacrifice for the mixed rewards of American-style capitalism. A market analyst in Italy said that she did not think industry suffered as a result, that people who are content and happy in life did their jobs properly.

According to the World Bank, the United States's per capita gross domestic product (GDP) averaged $29,080 in 1987; the French per capita GDP averaged $22,210, which was followed in descending order by Germany, Britain, and Italy. The higher GDP in the United States was attributed to the longer hours that Americans work. Americans averaged 1,966 hours of work in 1997, 235 hours more than the British (the hardest-working Europeans), and 310 hours, or nearly 30 working days more than the French.

Even so, Europe was closing its productivity gap with the United States, although most Europeans worked fewer hours. In France, businesses were beginning to cut their workweek to 35 hours in response to a new law introduced by the Socialist-led government. By contrast, Americans worked almost 3 days more in 1997 than in 1990, according to the International Labor Organization (ILO). These data suggest that although Americans may own more cars and bigger homes, they had less time to enjoy them, begging the question as to who was really richer. Work habits in Britain were somewhat closer to those of the United States, especially in internationally competitive industries like banking.

■ The Case of Japan

If the favorable attitudes people in Europe hold toward government and other people are embedded in the policy solutions European countries have constructed to family problems, such attitudes, which are far less favorable in Japan, are similarly embedded. The case of Japan is included here not only because it, like the European countries and the United States, is an industrialized country, but because of the contrast its policy solutions offer to the discussion. Recounting the day he welcomed a visitor into his "home," which consisted of a piece of cardboard on which he slept in the train station, Mr. Kawagoe, drawing deeply on a cigarette, recalled the times he had applied for public assistance from the government. They were not helpful, he said (Kristof, 1996). The only way a person could get aid, he said, was to be over 65 or so sick that hospitalization was necessary.

Japan's welfare system in some ways makes even the newly dismantled American system seem like a model of generosity. As was the case in the United States under English Poor Law in the 18th and 19th centuries, applicants in Japan are obliged to get help first from their families; a poor person physically able to work is not eligible for help—whether the person has a job or not. From some perspectives, the Japanese system works well. Japan's main safety net is the family rather than government, which some say has strengthened family ties. Since 1946, as people have become better off and accumulated savings, the number of Japanese in the basic welfare program has declined sharply. In 1996, just 0.7% of the population received benefits, compared with almost 5% who received Aid to Families with Dependent Children (AFDC) or the almost 10% who received food stamps or the over 2% who received Supplemental Security Income (SSI) benefits in the United States.

The context of Japan's welfare system in 1996 was very different from that of the United States. Only 1% of Japanese births were to unwed mothers, in contrast to 30% in the United States. Japan also had a far lower percentage of drug addicts than the United States, a much more egalitarian distribution of wealth, a greater sense of family obligation, and an abiding sense of shame that colored almost every aspect of Japanese life. Scholars say the Japanese system, with its emphasis on work and the importance of family ties, almost never breeds welfare dependency.

Caseworkers in Japan rigorously check applicants, dropping by their homes regularly to make sure they do not have prohibited luxuries like cars or air conditioners; fraud is especially rare. For these reasons, the welfare system seems to enjoy broad public support in Japan. In fact, instead of complaining about welfare mothers in Cadillacs, people sometimes complained about the harshness with which authorities treated the poor. Although the absence of a broad public safety net reinforces the attitude that people need to walk a straight line, when some people slip (as they inevitably do), there often is nothing to protect them.

In 1995, a 77-year-old woman and her disabled son starved to death in their Tokyo apartment. Although they had not formally applied for welfare, local authorities apparently knew that the family was having trouble getting food. After their bodies were found, the authorities discovered a diary kept by the woman whose last entry read, "Every day is a struggle, and I want to die soon."

In another case, a 79-year-old widow was threatened with loss of welfare benefits unless she got rid of her air conditioner. She did and then collapsed in her apartment during the next heat wave and had to be taken to the hospital, where she spent 6 weeks recovering. An 80-year-old man who had run away from his wife and children because "they picked on him" and since then was living in a cardboard box said Japan was a very cold society. Like many homeless people, he had not applied for welfare benefits because he said he would never get them anyway.

Japan has constructed two solutions to family problems that far surpass such solutions in the United States: universal medical care and comprehensive day care. Everyone has access to doctors and hospitals at affordable prices, and services are free for the poor. Neighborhood nurseries throughout Japan provide excellent care for children from 5 months old to school age for a modest fee if mothers work, but the fee is waived for low-income families. Unlike the United States, though, Japan has no food stamp program and relies principally on a single program of cash grants. Eligibility is income and family based, so anyone who is poor is eligible for the grants, provided the person has no family or assets and is unable to work.

Because able-bodied people are excluded on grounds that they can find work if they want to, the largest group of recipients is the elderly—many of whom are bedridden widows; they account for over 40% of all households getting aid. Households with a sick or handicapped person account for another 40%. About 9% are single mothers, but in Japan, most of them are divorced or widowed, rather than never married. Most single mothers in Japan do not get benefits, because they have parents or other family members who can support them. Because of this, single mothers are likely to live with their parents, which means that children grow up under the supervision of several adults. Mothers are reluctant to apply for or accept welfare. According to one welfare official, shame and stigma are a part of the costs of receiving welfare in Japan. To avoid the embarrassment of getting off a crowded elevator at the welfare floor, applicants take a separate hidden elevator to the welfare office. Many people eligible for welfare do not apply for it because of the stigma and shame it involves.

Interviews with homeless people, who rarely qualify for welfare, were revealing in the attitudes that people in Japan hold toward welfare. Unlike the French, the Swedes, the Norwegians, and Europeans in general, the Japanese express little sense of entitlement to help. Even those who said their neighbors should be getting help quickly added they did not deserve it. Based on the Elazar typology, the political culture Japan represents would appear to be a mix of individualistic, moralistic, and traditionalistic: individualistic in terms of the negative attitudes people express toward welfare as a government program; moralistic in terms of the positive attitudes they hold toward universal health care and day care as government programs related to families and also with respect to a more egalitarian distribution of income; and traditionalistic in terms of their attitudes toward the family's role in social provision.

■ Summary and Conclusions

As the cases of Sweden, Norway, France, Europe, and Japan demonstrate, political culture acts to constrain or support some constructions of policy solutions to family problems and not others. The case illustrations highlight the attitudes and values that people in Japan, Norway, Sweden, France, and Europe in general hold toward government and other people and how such attitudes and values are embedded in their countries' constructions of solutions to family problems in the form of their policies and programs. Political culture theory—unlike (a) the institutional perspective, which emphasizes structures and structural arrangements as constraints on policy solutions to family problems; (b) rational choice theory, which emphasizes the net value maximization in the selection of an alternative solution to family problems; (c) incremental theory, which views policy choice as a process of constant adjustment to the outcomes of past policies and programs; and (d) game theory, which talks about policy choice as occurring under competitive conditions of no authority—focuses instead on the values and attitudes people hold toward government and other people as an explanation for policy solutions constructed to family problems.

The concepts central to political culture theory as a framework include:

■ Values
■ Attitudes
■ Habitual behaviors as all three pertain to government and other people

Thus, from the perspective of political culture theory, values, attitudes, and patterns of habitual behaviors with respect to government and other people constitute the political culture of a community, state, or nation. Although political culture theory may be the leading alternative to rational choice theory, as Inglehart says, it also might be regarded as a complement to other perspectives. Two of these other perspectives are interest group theory and elite theory; these two theoretical frameworks offer different language for understanding and thinking about the construction of family policy. But before turning to these frameworks, consider the questions listed below about *this* chapter.

■ Some Questions for Your Reflection and Discussion

1. What attitudes do people in Western European countries hold toward government?

2. How are these attitudes expressed in their family policies?

3. Compare and contrast the attitudes of people in Norway, France, and Japan toward government. Compare and contrast the family policies constructed in these three countries.

4. How do such attitudes and constructions compare with those in the United States?

5. How would you characterize Japan's political culture, using Elazar's typology? Why?

6. Scan the newspaper for articles in which political culture seems to play a key role in the construction of some policy solution to a family problem and explain its role in that situation.

7. Inglehart (1990) maintains that political culture theory is a leading alternative to rational choice theories. Why?

Now it is time to turn to Chapter 13 to see how interest group and elite theories can contribute to the understanding of family policy as a constructed solution to family problems.

Interest Group Theory and
Elite Theory

☐ Interest group theory and elite theory frameworks, unlike the policy frameworks presented in previous chapters, focus less on the processes directly involved in policy choices related to families than on some of the factors external to such choices that nonetheless influence them. These frameworks stand in contrast to the institutional perspective, which focuses on government structures and regularized patterns of activity and the values that underlie them. They also contrast with rational choice theory, which focuses on the systematic assessment of alternative solutions and the net value ratio of each. They similarly contrast with models that emphasize the constraints of policy choice such as (a) political culture theory, which focuses on the attitudes people hold toward government; (b) incremental theory, which focuses on the uncertainties and ambiguities that surround the construction of policy solutions to family problems; and (c) game theory, which focuses on the competitive nature of the policy game in the construction of policy solutions to family problems.

Interest group theory and elite theory also contrast with each other in important ways. What brings them together in this chapter conceptually is that they provide a way for thinking about influences that, although impinging on policy choice, are both internal and external to it. Now let us look at these two frameworks to see what they highlight about the construction of solutions to family problems, beginning first with interest group theory, again drawing on news articles for case illustrations.

■ Interest Group Theory: Family Policy as the
Equilibrium Reached Among Competing Interest Groups

Policy from the interest group perspective is defined as the equilibrium reached in the struggle among contending interest groups to influence government action (Dye, 1975).

254

The assumptions underlying interest group theory are the following:

- The group is the mechanism through which individuals influence government on matters pertaining to families.
- All meaningful political activity is characterized by group struggle and conflict.
- The important determinants of group influence are membership size, wealth, organizational strength, cohesion, and access to decision makers.
- Group equilibrium is maintained through compromise, negotiation, bargaining, overlapping memberships, and the formation of coalitions.

Within this framework, the group is the mechanism through which individuals exert influence on government. Organized for the purpose of making demands on government and influencing government actions, interest groups are comprised of individuals who share similar interests and views on issues. Mothers Against Drunk Driving is an example. So is the American Association for Retired Persons (AARP), the National Organization of Women, the Christian Coalition, the Pharmaceutical Manufacturers Association, the American Dental Association, the American Medical Association (AMA), and the National Association of Social Workers. The groups supporting President Clinton's health care plan included the American College of Physicians, the American Academy of Family Physicians, the Catholic Health Association, and the National Education Association. Individuals from this perspective are seen as important only as they act on behalf of group interests. The perceptive reader also will recognize the central role of interest groups in the social change model as described in the Notes in Chapter 7 in the discussion of DOMA and also will recall reference to them in the discussion of incremental and game theories. Interest groups have been an institutional feature of the political system in this country from the very beginning, as evidenced by the number of congressional committees that represent the interests of different groups (e.g., business, labor, agriculture, energy, the environment).

The Political Nature of Interest Groups

The distinguishing feature of interest groups is that unlike other groups that also are organized around the shared interests of members, interest groups are political in nature. A group becomes political if and when it makes a claim through or upon government at whatever level—local, state, or national (Truman, 1971). The Million Moms who marched on Washington on Mothers Day 2000 to demand that Congress take steps to limit gun access is illustrative. Although the role of groups is to articulate demands for policies and programs that address the problems of families in relation to society, and government's role is to respond to them, the process can be reversed: government can propose solutions to problems and groups can respond to them, as when different groups were invited to comment on President Clinton's health care plan in 1993-94. However, groups with technical expertise also may develop policy proposals to which they then may invite government officials to respond (Ziegler & Huelshoff, 1980). Examples are the Jackson Hole, Wyoming, group that introduced the concept of managed competition into the health care reform debates and the Center for Budget and Policy Priorities, which routinely analyzes and testifies before Congress on budget and policy choices in relation to economic trends, particularly as the latter relate to the growing wealth and income gap in the United States. Other groups, such as the Children's Defense Fund and the Child Welfare League of America, have developed proposals that address issues related to adoption, child care, foster care, homelessness, and education. Such groups are organized not just at the federal level but at state and local levels as well.

Key determinants of group influence include membership size, wealth, organizational strength and cohesion, leadership, and access to decision makers. AARP is an example of an organization that meets all of these criteria, as is the National Rifle Association (NRA) and Tobacco Growers Association, which for so long blocked legislation to curb the use of tobacco. Changes in the relative influence of groups can be discerned by changes in public policy that shift influence away from the interests of groups losing it and toward groups gaining it, such as the Children's Defense Fund and labor unions, which gained a small measure of influence when President Clinton was first elected to office and President Bush out of office. In 1993, the passage of the Brady Bill, which provided for a 5-day waiting period for the purchase of a hand gun, signaled a decline in the influence for a time of the NRA, a strong opponent of gun control. One reason President Clinton did not champion the single payer health care plan was because of the strong influence of the insurance lobby and its opposition to that plan.

Group Struggle, Conflict, and Compromise: Some Case Examples

From the perspective of interest group theory, all meaningful political activity is characterized by group struggle and conflict. Policy makers within this context are seen as responding to the competing demands of various groups for government action. Examples of groups competing for government action in relation to the Clinton health care reform plan were abortion rights and antiabortion groups: abortion rights groups demanded coverage for abortion services for low-income women under the plan, and antiabortion groups demanded the line be held against it (Toner, 1993). The demands of competing interest groups like the AFL-CIO and the National Association of Manufacturers (NAM), combined with the Investment Company Institute (ICI), which represents the interests of the mutual fund industry in the privatization of Social Security are more examples: the AFL-CIO was against it, and the NAM and ICI supported it (Wayne, 1996). The political system attempts to manage group conflict by seeking a balance among competing groups through compromise—arranging for it, enacting it, and enforcing it—as the Clinton administration attempted to do in the case of health care reform, the North American Free Trade Agreement (NAFTA), the Family and Medical Leave Act (FMLA), welfare reform, all tax and budget bills, and so on. To prevent the abortion issue from becoming a center of focus in the health care reform debates, for example, the administration sought to effect such a balance when abortion rights advocates attempted to capitalize on the first president sympathetic to their cause in 12 years (Toner, 1993).

Contrary to game theory (which depicts policy as the culmination of negotiation, bargaining, and compromise among competing individuals), interest group theory depicts constructed policy solutions as the culmination of negotiation, bargaining, and compromise among competing groups. One of the reasons President Clinton delayed the introduction of his health care reform plan for so long was because in addition to trying to accommodate the preferences and interests of individual congresspersons, as in game theory, he also kept trying to effect compromises with different interest groups on different parts of the plan (Pear, 1993b). For example, when the director of the National Health Law Program protested that funding caps on subsidies to pay the insurance premiums of low-income individuals and small businesses could disadvantage these groups in the competition for funds, the president agreed to change the provision, placing a cap on the percentage of income that low-income individuals and families and small businesses would have to spend on insurance premiums instead.

Managing Group Conflict: Coalitions

One strategy politicians use to facilitate compromise among competing interest groups is the formation of a majority coalition of groups. Coalitions are groups that join together for a common purpose such as to advance a particular construction of a policy solution to a family problem. The main objective of forming coalitions is to mobilize and channel groups' goal-seeking efforts in the redress of perceived problems. The coalition that was formed to sponsor the 1980 White House Conference on Families is an example. Other examples of coalitions are the one to promote intergenerational equity, housing for homeless persons, President Clinton's health care reform plan, and the school prayer amendment in 1998.

Families USA is a coalition of groups that was organized in support of President Clinton's health care reform plan to counter the influence of insurance companies and lobbies that worked to defeat its passage. Families USA sought to create a constituency for the president's plan in the form of a movement, using the family as its symbol. It held that health care was a matter of concern for the entire family, cutting across all age groups—children, young adults, the middle aged, the elderly, parents, grandparents, and siblings. Having gained influence during the 1992 presidential campaign, the group was credited with helping to make health care reform the number one concern of the public and also of political candidates—constructing it as a family problem in dire need of solution.

A coalition of women's groups was formed in 1993 to launch a drive to pass the Equal Rights Amendment, even though the deadline for ratification had expired 12 years earlier; they argued that the deadline was arbitrary and Congress had the authority to lift it. Thirty-five of the 38 states that were needed to ratify the measure had already done so, which meant only 3 more states were needed. Lifting the deadline would have made ratification of the amendment by the 3 states possible.

The factors that determine the selection of groups for inclusion in a coalition include the size of their constituency and the diversity of interests that need to be represented. Diversity often undermines the ability of coalitions to achieve their goals (Ziegler & Huelshoff, 1980). The more diverse the groups that make up the coalition, the greater the difficulty in maintaining the cohesion that helped to create the coalition in the first place. Doron (1992), in fact, warns against oversized coalitions, saying that the political costs of support from oversized coalitions are usually higher than warranted. He writes that unless policy makers seek the support of everyone, the beneficiaries of their activities probably would not be the public at large but the groups on which they rely the most for support.

The coalition the Carter administration formed to sponsor and build support for the White House Conference on Families in 1980 is illustrative of the political costs of an oversized, diversely representative coalition. The coalition was comprised of many diverse organizations, some of which were the National Conference of Catholic Charities, the American Red Cross, the National Urban League, Planned Parenthood, the Synagogue Council of America, and the National Christian Action Coalition. Conservative groups that were part of a National Pro-Family Coalition dominated state-level meetings that were organized to elect delegates to the White House Conference. Polarized over the abortion issue—which for antiabortion groups symbolized family and for abortion rights groups symbolized freedom of choice for women—the meetings became embroiled in controversy and conflict that spread to the conference proceedings themselves.

Balancing Group Conflict: Overlapping Memberships

The formation of coalitions is only one way of effecting balance and compromise among contending interest groups. Overlapping memberships that involve shared as well as conflicting interests also serve to moderate group demands. Because groups try to avoid alienating members with multiple affiliations, they are reluctant to move too far in directions that clearly diverge from other groups. Since no single group constitutes a majority, group equilibrium is maintained by countervailing centers of power and influence. The influence of one group counters that of another, just as Families USA had hoped to do in the case of health care reform. Such countervailing influence also applies to the efforts of a coalition of nearly two dozen groups that included the Christian Coalition, Focus on the Family, and the Family Research Council, which joined forces on the school prayer amendment in 1998 (Seelye, 1998).

Political Parties as Coalitions of Interest Groups

Within the interest group model, political parties are perceived to be coalitions of interest groups. The Democratic Leadership Council (DLC) was one of the coalitions within the Democratic party that supported President Clinton's candidacy for president. A centrist group within the Democratic party, it vowed to challenge those within the administration who wanted to convert provisions in the 1993 National Service Bill into an entitlement, welfare reform into a handout, health care into a government bureaucracy, or who worked to weaken the DLC's agenda (Berke, 1994). When Clinton became president, however, he had to win the support of more liberal members of Congress and thus depart somewhat from the DLC's more centrist positions. Just as members of the DLC were uncertain of how aggressively to promote their position on issues without jeopardizing their relations with the White House, White House officials were concerned about jeopardizing their relations with the DLC, wanting to maintain its loyalty.

The Christian Coalition constitutes a group within the Republican party that represents a similar challenge to Republican party leaders. To capture the support of other party members, the Coalition has had to go beyond abortion as the issue with which it was most closely identified, in recognition of the fact that taxes, health care, and government were also important to party members ("Christian Group," 1993).

Interest group theory views the political system as a large interest group system maintained in equilibrium by many forces. These include a large, latent, almost universal, not generally visible group in American society that supports the Constitution and the ways in which the political system works (Dye, 1975). This amorphous group is comprised of people who tend to observe rather than participate in politics and who are unlikely to sustain participation in an organized interest group. They constitute a "potential group," in Mancur Olson's (1974) terms. An underlying assumption is that all groups have a common interest in maintaining the institutional framework within which group conflict occurs and is resolved.

The Case of the Clinton 1997 Budget Proposal and Medicare

Illustrative of interest group theory are the different groups that attempted to influence the outcome of the debates over President Clinton's 1997 budget proposal that included cuts in Medicare. Reductions in spending in Medicare were scaled back in the 1997 budget proposal from the Medicare cuts in 1995, when President Clinton vetoed the Republicans' budget balancing bill. Although he listed 82 reasons for his veto, starting with the extreme cuts in Medicare, Republicans still wanted to make major changes in the structure of Medicare modeled after the 1995 budget balancing bill (Pear, 1997). In the 1995 showdown, the political stakes were higher. Democrats charged Republicans with undermining the Medicare program, and some Republicans lost their seats in the 1996 elections as a result.

Leading experts for the Democrats on Medicare shared the Republicans' conviction that the program, created in 1965, had to be updated to keep pace with revolutionizing changes in the health care industry. Most people on Medicare—88% of the 38 million beneficiaries—were in the traditional program, which paid a separate fee for each doctor's service and each hospital admission. Although HMOs were readily available to the elderly in cities like Minneapolis, Phoenix, and Los Angeles, there were no Medicare HMOs in 12 states and in some cities.

To solve the problem, congressional leaders wanted to reduce huge regional disparities in payments to HMOs. This would mean less money or smaller increases for very large cities such as New York, Los Angeles, and Miami but more money for rural areas and cities like Des Moines, Milwaukee, Minneapolis, and Seattle. Such reductions also would mean less money for many health care providers.

As both houses of Congress endorsed the budget deal that included reductions in Medicare, lobbyists, representing the interests of various health groups, prepared for battle. Hospitals designed a strategy to stave off a freeze in Medicare payment rates, which had been recommended by the president and a federal advisory panel that found that since 1982, hospital profit margins on Medicare patients had increased at a rapid rate.

The National Association for Medical Equipment Services, in denouncing Clinton's budget proposal that cut Medicare payments for home oxygen therapy by 40%, threatened to flood Congress with 100,000 letters from the industry and patients who needed the therapy to treat their respiratory illness. AARP lobbied Congress and scheduled 100 events around the country to tell legislators that they must not impose financial burdens on beneficiaries beyond the modest increase in Medicare premiums envisioned in the budget agreement. Nursing homes complained that under the Clinton budget proposal, they would be absorbing a disproportionate share of the cuts to the projected growth in Medicare spending. The AMA ran newspaper ads protesting "deep, unfair cuts to physicians." The American College of Surgeons asserted that its members would bear almost all the cuts among doctors. HMOs, fighting Clinton's proposal to slash their payments, negotiated with Congress on ways to achieve more modest savings.

The Case of Managed Care

The campaign waged in 1999 by the country's largest organization of managed-care firms, the American Association of Health Plans (AAHP) (Hamburger, 1999), is another example of the role that interest groups play in trying to influence government action. In an unprecedented investment in the early presidential primary and caucus states in election 2000, AAHP attempted to deter attacks on managed care by national candidates and help fight against the enactment of the federal legislation it opposed. As noted earlier, managed care refers to the medical bureaucracy of insurance companies and HMOs that has rapidly replaced the once familiar institution of independent, fee-for-service doctor's offices. The growth of managed care was credited with having improved efficiency and quality in health care—which reasonable people might dispute.

The AAHP showed its determination to influence the initial rhetoric of the 2000 presidential contest by infusing more than $1 million into the Iowa and New Hampshire primaries, even before some of the presidential candidates had spent any money. Altogether, the organization had budgeted $7 million to $9 million for public affairs in 1999, a substantial part of which was spent in the early caucus and primary states to which serious candidates were drawn. The AAHP called legislation to protect patients' unnecessary government interference that was counterproductive and expensive. Hoping to raise voter fears and thus mobilize opposition to the Patients' Bill of Rights legislation that was pending (to which reference was made earlier), the AAHP ran ads in Iowa suggesting that the regulatory cost of patient protections would increase insurance costs to the point where more than 28,000 Iowans would lose their health coverage. House Representative Greg Ganske, a Republican physician from Iowa, defused the charge, saying the effect would be minimal and that in fact premiums would increase by only a few dollars. Both doctors and patients were unnerved by the rapidity with which managed care had transformed the health care system. Taken seriously, their concerns were at the core of the political debate about managed care at the end of the 1990s, about which more will be said in later discussion.

The Case of Social Security

The debate over Social Security is yet another example of the role of interest groups in seeking to influence the actions of government. In 1996, when Congress and the nation were gearing up for a huge debate on the future of Social Security, labor, Wall Street, corporate America, and organizations of the old and young were quietly marshalling their forces for one of the biggest lobbying battles in decades (Wayne, 1996). Although there was broad consensus that Social Security needed reform, there was little agreement about what should be done to reform it. The battle was joined in public relations campaigns and in maneuvers for position in Congress. As noted earlier, the central issue in the debate was whether Social Security should be shifted toward the private markets or left largely intact, with modifications in the age of eligibility, the payroll tax, and benefits. The federal panel studying the issue was divided between wanting to privatize Social Security, at least in part, and allowing the government to invest Social Security monies in the stock market.

Wall Street's big brokerage firms were inescapably at the center of the debate. They viewed changes in Social Security as an opportunity to sell billions of dollars in financial products directly to the government or to individuals. Fearful, however, of setting off a backlash that would weaken its position in Congress, Wall Street was reluctant to play a prominent role in the debate.

The AFL-CIO nonetheless focused on Wall Street as an adversary, believing that the government should retain its central role in ensuring retirement benefits and in providing a financial safety net for low-income workers. Although the AFL-CIO also favored investing Social Security money in the stock and bond markets, it wanted the money to be controlled by the government, not private investors.

Business, large and small, was primarily interested in containing the growth in payroll taxes to free up capital for business expansion and favored putting Social Security money into the private markets. In the vanguard of privatization was the Cato Institute, a libertarian research organization based in Washington, D.C. The Institute favored full privatization, putting the entire 12.4% Social Security payroll tax into individual 401(k)-style accounts that would be invested and managed by workers themselves. Under the Cato plan, the $400 billion that go into the Social Security trust fund from payroll taxes each year would be redirected through the new investment accounts into the stock and bond markets. The money would be available for businesses to draw on to expand, which Cato said would improve the health of the nation's economy. The Institute, which favors and promotes minimal government, rejected proposals of government-purchased stocks, because it said such proposals implied government ownership of private corporations.

At the opposite end of the spectrum, the AFL-CIO said it would join other unions in opposition to any privatization plan. The Federation, with 13 million members, said Social Security was one of its prime lobbying priorities. It wanted Social Security to stay just as it was, but with a major difference: allow the government to put up to 40% of the money in publicly traded stocks and bonds. Union lobbying included education programs as well as lobbying in Congress. The Federation was afraid individual investment accounts would lead to a total unraveling of the Social Security program and would undermine what the unions saw as the strength of Social Security— that the government, not the individual, carried the risks. The head of governmental affairs for the AFL-CIO said this was a battle between those who see government as having a role in Social Security and those who believe it should have none. According to the president of the Securities Industry Association, a Wall Street trade group, Social Security is the most successful of all government programs. A spokesperson from the Third Millennium, a lobbying group in New York that works on issues affecting people younger than 35, likened the skirmishes to a presidential campaign, but it was nothing compared to what would be necessary to enact true reform with older workers wanting to maintain existing Social Security benefits and younger workers fearing they would have none.

Each case example of Medicare, managed care, and Social Security illustrates the assumptions underlying interest group theory mentioned at the beginning of this chapter. Not illustrated by the examples was the assumption pertaining to group equilibrium: that group equilibrium is maintained through compromise, negotiation, bargaining, overlapping memberships, and the formation of coalitions—largely because the struggle over the construction of policy solutions to the family problems that were represented is not over yet.

Summary

Given the ubiquitous nature of interest groups and the role they play in American politics and society, the interest group framework probably is more familiar to most readers than some of the others. The importance of membership recruitment and fund-raising for maintaining and increasing group influence means that groups are always searching for new members, constantly approaching nonmembers to join. They also continually solicit members for funds to influence Congress, state legislators, or county commissioners to enact legislation they support; they also continually exhort members to contact their congressional and legislative representatives to express their support for or opposition to issues. In engaging in these activities, interest groups sometimes convey the impression that they seek to promote the public's interest, not their own, in making recommendations about policies of importance to families. *Sometimes* some interest groups *do* promote the public's interest, but certainly not all of them and not all of the time.

The key concepts—language, words, ideas—of the interest group model include:

- Demands
- Politics as the struggle between competing groups
- Policy as the equilibrium reached among contending interest groups
- The group as comprised of individuals organized around shared interests
- Group conflict, negotiation, bargaining, and compromise
- Coalitions
- Group influence

This concludes the discussion of interest group theory and its application to policy issues related to families. Questions for readers to think about in relation to the theory are listed at the end of the chapter. Now let us turn our attention to a different theoretical framework: elite theory.

■ Elite Theory: Family Policy as Elite Preference

If interest group theory views the world horizontally, elite theory views it hierarchically. The concept of elites conveys the idea of ranking—that individuals and groups rank higher or lower in relation to one another in terms of influence, wealth, status, and power (Frohock, 1979). The positions elites occupy within the structure as well as their interests as individuals help shape their perceptions of the problems families experience and what should be done about them. Because the positions and interests of elites differ, their perceptions about such matters also differ and often conflict, despite their agreement on basic institutional values (e.g., freedom, equality, opportunity). From the perspective of elite theory, constructions of policy solutions to family problems are seen to reflect elite preferences, not interest group influence.

The basic assumptions underlying elite theory are that:

■ Policies and programs reflect the values and interests of elites in a hierarchically arranged society.

■ Elites share a consensus concerning existing institutional arrangements and the values underlying them.

■ The size and complexity of modern society and organizational life preclude the active and full participation of everyone in the political process, requiring some division of labor in the political process.

■ The division of labor creates a class of *ruling* or *governing* elites.

Found in any society, political system, or organization, elites are seen to predominate when there is little or no countervailing organized political interest and activity, ruling almost by default. The conditions that encourage the formation of elites—the absence of organized political activity and interest—may help to explain why voter participation in public affairs is essential to a democratic political order that depends, at the very least, on voter interest and participation in the election of political candidates for its survival. Congressional members, state legislators, and county commissioners all constitute *ruling or governing* elites within their respective spheres. However, because of the large sums of money that large corporations and big business contribute to political campaigns, some hold that policy reflects the preferences of the financial supporters of governing elites as much as the preferences of governing or political elites themselves—maybe more.

Elite Preferences and Money: The Case of GOPAC

GOPAC is illustrative of how elite preferences influence the construction of policy solutions to family problems. GOPAC, a political action committee led by former Republican Speaker of the House Newt Gingrich, was an interlocking set of organizational entities that helped Gingrich raise money and shape an ideology while operating largely out of public view sowing the seeds for the 1994 midterm elections (Engleberg & Seelye, 1994). Along with GOPAC, there was the Progress and Freedom Foundation, a think tank directed by some of Gingrich's closest intellectual advisers. The Foundation raised money for a college course that Gingrich taught called Renewing American Civilization. Each entity—GOPAC, the Foundation, and the college course—raised money from an overlapping pool of businesspeople, investment bankers, and longtime Gingrich supporters.

The amount of money that GOPAC raised was difficult to determine, but it spent $2 million on direct mail appeals, tapes, candidates' training, and office expenses to nurture an energetic and forceful generation of new Republican politicians that Gingrich hoped would one day parade from statehouses to Congress. The spadework GOPAC did, together with the campaigning Gingrich did in 127 congressional districts, was credited with winning the elections of 47 Republican candidates in 1994. According to Paul Weyrich, a conservative thinker who founded National Empowerment Television (NET) (which carried Gingrich's TV course), GOPAC provided the ideological framework around which many candidates built their campaigns, something the Republican party had always avoided. Many readers may think GOPAC is as illustrative of interest group theory as it is of elite theory—and indeed, they would not be wrong. However, the point being illustrated here is the role that elite preferences play in the construction of policy solutions through the large sums of money financial supporters contribute to political campaigns on behalf of particular issues and candidates.

Elite Consensus on Institutional Values

From the perspective of elite theory, the range of issues over which governing elites compete is relatively narrow. Indeed, part of the confusion surrounding policy choices related to families is that such differences are often matters of degree rather than substance, as earlier discussion has shown. Elites, in general, share a consensus concerning institutional norms and values with respect to constitutional government, democratic procedures, freedom of speech, and others (Dye, 1975; Frohock, 1979). Indeed, such consensus is considered essential for the stability and survival of society. Thus, it is not surprising that in a survey of one group of governing elites, state legislators, Republicans and Democrats alike agreed that government should help families when necessary (Zimmerman et al., 1979). This should not be construed to mean, however, that elites agree about the problems of families and what should be done about them.

The Concept of Power: The Cases of Dan Rostenkowski and Tom DeLay

Central to elite theory is its emphasis on *power* (Dye, 1975). Power is defined as a one-sided transaction between two or more actors. The central action of the transaction lies in getting others to act in some preferred way. This, as will be recalled, is what President Clinton and Senator Mitchell tried to do in relation to the president's budget deficit plan in 1993, NAFTA, and later in relation to health care reform, the crime bill, and many other issues.

Dan Rostenkowski's name comes to mind when we talk about power . In his position as chair of the House Ways and Means Committee, Rostenkowski skillfully influenced members to vote as he preferred and was considered key to the passage of difficult legislation such as the 1986 Tax Reform Act, the 1990 and

1993 budget bills, and NAFTA (Rosenbaum, 1994a). He lost his power when he lost his position and was no longer able to make deals and dispense favors to influence votes. When Newt Gingrich ascended to the position of Speaker of the House in 1994, he too was in a position of power to influence committee votes, later losing his position and thus his power and finally his membership in Congress.

Tom DeLay, House majority whip and the most powerful member of the House in 1999-2000, was not shy about displaying his power (Mitchell & Lacey, 1999). Though he was technically the third-ranking member of the Republican leadership, he eclipsed Speaker Dennis Hastert, whose election to that position he helped engineer. Although DeLay enjoyed moments of showmanship, he had acquired his power by quietly building a political machine that many experts called the most formidable organization of any member of Congress. As a measure of his strength, he was the only House leader to go unchallenged in the 1998 midterm elections, when the loss of seats by Republicans forced the resignation of Newt Gingrich as Speaker of the House and instigated a struggle for every other position in the House Republican hierarchy. One congressional analyst called DeLay the most powerful majority whip in the history of the House of Representatives. Almost every member of the House was somehow indebted to him. He won praise for his skill, energy, and willingness to help a colleague, but much of his power was rooted in his unabashed devotion to political money, having emerged as the chief fund-raiser for the National Republican Congressional Committee, the campaign arm of House Republicans.

Elites as Revolving: The Case of George Mitchell

The show of power by Tom DeLay is at odds with the concept of power in the revolving version of elite theory. In the *revolving* version, power is seen as being widely dispersed. It is based on a pluralistic view of the American political system, similar to interest group theory. Power is seen not only as being widely dispersed but also as being fluid, with one group of individuals or groups exercising power for a period of time followed by another, depending on the issue. Just as game and incremental theories emphasize bargaining and compromise as strategies for winning the cooperation of others and persuasion as a strategy for involving the general public in face-to-face transactions, the revolving version of elite theory does too.

When George Mitchell, Senate majority leader from 1985 to 1994, announced his intention not to run for reelection in 1994 and therefore to relinquish his position as senate majority leader (Seelye, 1994), he articulated his understanding of power and position from the perspective of the revolving version of elite theory. Having been senate majority leader for 9 years, he said the position should not be regarded as permanent to the person but merely an opportunity for someone to *temporarily* act on behalf of the larger common good and public interest. In that sense, all elected positions in a democratic political order are revolving, all being temporary, with one person holding a given position for a period of time, followed by another.

Concentric Circles of Elites

Allison (1971) thinks of elites as being positioned within a series of concentric circles that consist of:

- *The general or inattentive public,* or "potential group," in Mancur Olson's terms: persons who sit at the outer ring of the circle because of their indifference to most policy issues.
- *The attentive public,* who sit one ring closer to center stage, such as the media, interest groups, and interested, informed citizens who constitute the audience of governing elites.
- *The policy and opinion elites,* who structure public discussion of issues and provide access to social and political groups surrounding the center stage, such as key presidential, gubernatorial, or mayoral advisers.
- *The real actors in the situation,* as, for example, the president and vice president, congressional leadership, governors, mayors, and their respective cabinets, and legislators—the governing or revolving elites.

The president's White House staff are policy and opinion elites. They serve as adviser to the president, who occupies center stage. One task the White House chief of staff performed during the early years of the Clinton White House was to provide access to the president for the social and political groups surrounding center stage. Such access allowed a range of viewpoints to enter the Oval Office as a way of encouraging debate about policy issues that interested the president (Devroy, 1993). Seen as a White House ambassador to the diplomatic and power-centered social world, the White House chief of staff's functions ranged from organizing and managing the White House staff to frequent liaison work with congressional members and other constituencies and frequent representational appearances at lunches and dinners (Devroy, 1993).

Another member of the White House staff having the reputation of being a first-class, behind-the-scenes political tactician was key to bringing closure to difficult and important issues. Another, widely portrayed as a master manipulator of the media and responsible for developing a broad communications strategy, served as a senior counselor in helping to make policy, not simply sell it. That adviser was almost always present at domestic policy-making meetings with the president and vice president. The vice president also played a key advisory role to the president as one of the policy and opinion elites, the cast changing with the issue—in the manner suggested by the revolving version of elite theory.

Both the positions they occupied within the Clinton administration and their interests as individuals helped shape their perceptions as policy and opinion elites with respect to the problems families were experiencing and their constructions about what should be done about them. Because their positions and interests differed, however, their perceptions about such matters often conflicted, despite their agreement on basic institutional values.

Policy and Opinion Elites: The Case of Welfare Reform

The case of welfare reform is a good example of how the position and interests of policy and opinion elites shape their constructions of policy solutions. On the issue of welfare reform, for example, presidential aides in 1994 were bitterly divided over a proposed provision that would drop families from both a welfare *and* a work program after 2 years in order to force parents to find work in the private sector (DeParle, 1994a). The issue was argued with particular fervor because it struck at the heart of the philosophy underlying welfare. Senator Moynihan, along with advocates for the poor, vehemently opposed the move, charging that it could punish well-intentioned families and start the nation down the slippery slope of abolishing welfare. Bruce Reed, a White House aide who led the White House faction that wanted to limit the program, argued that government assistance was never meant to be forever and that a cutoff was needed to change a system everyone regarded as a failure. In closed meetings, he also raised political concerns, arguing that unless time limits were applied to the work program as well as to financial benefits for welfare families, opponents would accuse the president of failing to keep his pledge to "end welfare as we know it."

Mary Jo Bane and David Ellwood led the faction that objected to cutting families off from the work program. Both were assistant secretaries in the Department of Health and Human Services, Bane for Children and Families and Ellwood for Planning and Evaluation. They argued against the time limits, maintaining that plenty of incentives were available for welfare mothers to find jobs, such as tax credits for low-income workers that could increase their incomes by as much as $3,400 a year; such credits were not available to people in the work program. Moreover, allowing states to drop people from both welfare *and* work, even if they had no job offers, they argued, would throw them deeper into poverty and violate the idea that people who play by the rules should not be left stranded. Both Ellwood and Bane also argued against a family benefit cap on welfare benefits. Without evidence to support it, the assumption underlying a family benefit cap was that larger benefit checks encouraged welfare mothers to have more babies and stay on welfare longer ("The Harm," 1994).

The president, as a former governor, tended to favor state experimentation, giving states options to experiment with their welfare programs. Others within his administration argued that welfare policy was the wrong place for such options. Mario Cuomo, former governor of New York, reacted by saying that cutting willing workers off from assistance could happen only in a moment of madness, adding that it would be bad for our soul as a nation (DeParle, 1994b).

According to Bob Woodward (1994), who wrote about the early years of the Clinton administration, the contest over welfare reform among top Clinton aides reflected the deep ideological differences that existed among the policy and opinion elites serving in senior positions in the administration. They represented both sides of the deficit reduction and government spending dilemma and both sides of Clinton's thinking. The result, Woodward said, was a never-ending contest between the two sides for the definition of the Clinton presidency: the investment populist, tax-the-rich side and the deficit reduction, cut-government-spending side. Clinton later refuted that characterization, contending that he had never been ambivalent about the role of government in people's lives, that government was neither good nor bad but could be used to help make life better for people. With the 1994 midterm elections, he planned to change the membership of the policy and opinion elites that surrounded him.

Strategic Elites: Some Examples

The concept of strategic elites is pertinent here. Strategic elites refer to those who occupy roles that place them in the center of the action, such as presidential advisers, formal and informal. They are the people who possess information, make major decisions, especially with regard to alternative policies and strategies, and help facilitate the implementation of these decisions. Examples from earlier administrations include Senators Kennedy, Mitchell, and Moynihan and Congressman Dan Rostenkowski (before he fell from power), whose actions were viewed as a function of the assumptions structured into their roles as well as the assumptions they as individuals brought to their roles. In the Clinton administration, they also included Bruce Reed, Mary Jo Bane, and Dave Ellwood with respect to welfare reform.

After the 1996 presidential election, many members who were part of the Clinton administration's first strategic team resigned. When Clinton first came to Washington, his top aides were people he had known for years: a kindergarten classmate, a graduate school friend who steered him to his future wife, and a longtime friend of the First Lady who ran his campaign (Shogren, 1997). Four years later, he was more experienced and more comfortable with people in the government bureaucracy, some of whom he selected to be part of his team of strategic elites in his second term, although his history with them was more recent.

The Strategic Role of Revolving Elites:
Charlie Norwood, the Real Actor in the Patients' Bill of Rights

As part of the revolving and governing elite, Representative Charlie Norwood, Republican from Georgia, played a strategic role in policy solutions to family problems—namely in the battle over the Patients' Bill of Rights in 1998 and 1999. A small-town dentist with a dislike for "big" government, he plunged into politics in 1994 in large part to fight President Clinton's plan for national health insurance (Alvarez, 1998). Three years later, he found himself at the center of one of the year's fiercest and strangest political storms, one that not only joined him with his old enemy, Mr. Clinton, but that divided his own Republican political "family," as he called it, and infuriated his party's leadership. Promoting more government regulation of the managed care industry, Mr. Norwood suddenly found himself siding with liberals like Senator Edward Kennedy of Massachusetts in an unusual coalition that conveyed the depth of the backlash against managed care.

Although the struggle put Mr. Norwood on the side of more, not less, government, he insisted that he had not changed. "I couldn't stand Clinton Care." He said (referring to the Clinton health care plan of 1993 and 1994) that he liked freedom and could see that "we would lose our ability to choose" as a result. Corporate care, though, was not any different, and "that is what we've got right now," he said. Saying he wanted to make managed care more accountable and flexible in effect meant that he wanted to impose federal regulations on HMOs and give people the right to sue them.

Amassing 224 cosponsors for the Norwood bill, from urban liberals to rural conservatives, almost equally split between Republicans and Democrats, Senator Alfonse D'Amato, Republican from New York, sponsored the measure in the Senate; he was supported by Senator Kennedy, a Democrat from Massachusetts. Other Republican leaders, however, contended that Mr. Norwood's bill was too far reaching. Even some of his allies, conservatives who said they agreed with him in principle, began to distance themselves from the bill. But the most adamant opponents of the bill by far were Dick Armey, House Republican from Texas, and Trent Lott, Senate majority leader from Mississippi. Mr. Norwood knew that he had to work out his differences with Mr. Armey and other leaders, which also at the time meant working them out with House Speaker Newt Gingrich. Clearly, Charlie Norwood, a small-town dentist and part of the revolving and governing elite, emerged as the real actor in the issue of patients' rights in seeking to construct a solution to the problems many families were experiencing with managed health care.

Elites' Characteristics: Personal Skill, Family Life Cycle Stage, Gender

In elite theory, the characteristics of elites, whether strategic, governing, or revolving, are considered critical in the construction of policy solutions. George Mitchell's characteristics as Senate majority leader are what made him invaluable in occupying that position early in the Clinton years. He had the stamina, patience, and endurance, being both conciliatory but firm, to hold Senate Democrats together, not by telling them what to do but by appealing to their sensibilities (Seelye, 1994). When he noticed that Senate sessions were likely to extend beyond midnight, he would ask his colleagues whether they wanted to make statements and prolong adjournment or pass laws and go home. The importance of elite characteristics in constructing policy solutions also emerged in the survey of state legislators' attitudes toward family policy to which reference was made earlier. In that survey, the family life-cycle stage emerged as a correlate of their attitudes toward family policy (Zimmerman et al., 1979).

As far as gender is concerned as a characteristic of elites, it should be noted that except for Hillary, President Clinton's wife, few women were a part of the strategic elite in the first term of the Clinton administration or privy to the thinking that went into strategic planning meetings with the president. And despite their increased representation in both the House and Senate in 1993, women had difficulty penetrating the inner circles of congressional power. In a speech to the White House press, Dee Dee Myers, the first woman to hold the position of White House press secretary, noted that although women held important cabinet positions—for example, Attorney General Janet Reno, Secretary of Health and Human Services Donna Shalala, Surgeon General Joycelyn Elders, and Secretary of State Madeleine Albright—women did not chair any of the congressional committees ("With Wit," 1994). It was Myers's view that the political world was male dominated and that as a consequence, women in that world had greater difficulty in commanding authority than men.

Still, as a characteristic, gender was important in family policy developments. When women in Congress were heard, they brought a perspective that male senators in the past heard only from their constituents and sometimes from their wives. When Senators Kerrey and Danforth, chair and vice chair of the newly formed Federal Bipartisan Commission on Entitlement and Tax Reform, stated, for example, that the trend in government spending on benefit programs was not sustainable and that it would grow automatically year after year until by the year 2030, interest on the federal debt would consume all federal revenues, the women on the commission challenged the implications of their assertions (Pear, 1994). Eva Clayton, House member on the Democratic side from North Carolina, said that antipoverty programs were not to blame for the growth in government spending on federal benefits, and cutting programs like AFDC was not the answer. Carol Moseley-Braun, senator from Illinois, urged members to remember that the charts and graphs that were shown were about the lives and livelihoods of thousands of American people and their families. Furthermore, although Bob Kerrey was credited with having saved the 1993 Budget Reduction Act from defeat, analysis of the votes of male and female senators showed that it could have been the votes of the women as a group that saved it from defeat. With only 6 women in the Senate, 3 voted for the bill, 2 against it, 1 abstained. With 94 men in the Senate, 46 voted for the bill, 47 against it, 1 abstained, proportionately more women voting for the measure than men (Zimmerman, 1993a).

Current and former female congressional members complained about a sense of paternalism that prevailed in Congress, a sentiment that became more pronounced whenever women's health issues, especially those involving reproduction, were discussed. In the 104th Congress, the abortion issue came up 53 times. As Representative Constance Morella, Republican from Maryland, observed, "It's very interesting the issues they select to work on or promote," adding, "They don't want to intervene in the bodily functions of men" (Stolberg,

1997). Patricia Schroeder, former Democratic representative from Colorado, said that it all seemed to go back to women's reproductive organs, because women evidently were not smart enough to deal with their bodily functions by themselves. Mockingly, she said, "We need Congress's help. Now if we did this on their health, they would be nuts."

According to an expert in women's health, the nation's mostly male legislators seemed increasingly inclined to intervene in the way doctors and private health insurance companies conducted themselves when the patients were women. Wondering why they seemed to give women's issues all the attention while ignoring men's, she speculated that maybe it was because most of the legislative assistants were women. With female members making up just 9% of the Senate and slightly less than 12% of the House, women were still vastly outnumbered in the nation's legislature but nonetheless effective in bringing women's health issues to the fore.

One Senate staff member who tracked health legislation called women's health issues "family friendly." All that friendliness, she said, made some women's advocates suspicious. They suggested that it was politically expedient for members of Congress to tell insurance companies what to do—at no cost to the government—while at the same time ignoring other issues of critical importance to women, like child care and flexible work hours. They also complained that some of the same legislators who jumped on the women's health bandwagon were among those fighting to restrict women's right to abortion.

In the 1997 debate over late-term abortion, Senator Patty Murray, Democrat from Washington, implored her colleagues not to ban it (Stolberg, 1997). She pressed instead for a compromise offered by Senator Tom Daschle of South Dakota, the minority leader, that would have barred women from terminating their pregnancies at the point when the fetus could survive outside the womb. Republican Senator Alfonse D'Amato from New York was among those who ignored Ms. Murray's plea; he voted for the ban, pointing to Democratic Senator Daniel Moynihan, also from New York, who also voted for the ban.

Perhaps the most outrageous example of how gender as a personal characteristic can manifest itself was when Senator Jesse Helms, chair of the Foreign Relations Committee, ordered Capitol Hill police officers to remove 10 female House members from a Senate hearing he was holding, saying they were disrupting the meeting by trying to present him with a letter supporting an international treaty eliminating the discrimination against women (Schmitt, 1999). The uproar began when Representative Lynn Woolsey of California led the group of women, all House Democrats, from a Capitol Hill news conference, to Mr. Helms's Senate office and then to a nearby hearing room. The group entered the hearing room quietly, seeking to give Mr. Helms a placard-size letter signed by 100 congressional members in support of the Convention on the Elimination of All Forms of Discrimination Against Women, which has been ratified by 165 countries but not the United States.

Taken aback, Mr. Helms gaveled the hearing to a halt and scolded Ms. Woolsey—"Please be a lady"—before ordering uniformed officers to escort them out of the room. Afterward, the women expressed shock at the treatment they had received from Mr. Helms, who, though notoriously tough, also assumes a courtly air with women who appear before his panel. "While he was asking us to be ladies," Representative Nancy Pelosi of California later said, "he could have been more gentlemanly in treating us like colleagues in Congress." After the women filed out, Mr. Helms turned to a Republican male House member testifying at the hearing and chortled, "Heh, heh, some of your colleagues."

■ Summary and Conclusions

Elite theory, in general, directs attention to the importance of hierarchy (i.e., position, influence, and power) in the construction of policy solutions to the problems of families and the importance of elite characteristics such as gender. Concepts such as revolving, governing, and strategic all call attention to the different roles elites play in such constructions; concentric circles of influence call attention to the overlapping positions elites occupy within the structure. Although elite theory incorporates many of the same process concepts—language, words, ideas—associated with interest group and game theories, such as bargaining, persuasion, compromise, competition, it also includes concepts unique to it. These include:

- Hierarchical ranking of individuals and groups
- Attentive public and general public
- Revolving elites and revolving power
- Governing or ruling elites
- Strategic elites
- Concentric circles of influence
- Negotiation, bargaining, persuasion, competition, compromise
- Policy as elite preference

In most respects, elite theory is contrary to democratic norms and values that presumably underlie institutional norms and practices in this country. To the extent that constructed solutions to family problems do in fact represent elite preferences, it is important in any analysis of family policy to find out whose solutions they represent and the values and interests they represent. The cases of health and welfare reform are all too illustrative.

In the next and final chapter of Part III, a systems approach to the construction of policy solutions to family problems is presented to complete the discussion of policy frameworks that can be used to better understand family policy as substance and process. Whereas interest group theory focuses on interest groups and elite theory on elites as influences in such constructions, systems theory conceptualizes such influences in terms of demands and support. But before concluding our discussion of interest group and elite theories, readers should attend to the questions below.

■ Some Questions for Your Reflection and Discussion

Interest Group Theory

1. How is policy defined from an interest group perspective? Why?
2. What is an interest group? How does it differ from other groups?
3. Give some examples of interest groups in your community that are organized around some family policy issue. What makes them an interest group?
4. What are some of the determinants of group influence?
5. What is one of the major assumptions underlying interest group theory?
6. How is group equilibrium maintained? Give examples from the chapter.
7. Identify the interests of the interest groups involved in Social Security and health care reform.

Elite Theory

1. Define policy choice from the perspective of elite theory.
2. Identify and define the major concepts associated with elite theory.
3. What are some of the assumptions underlying elite theory?
4. What distinguishes elite theory from interest group theory?
5. Analyze some policy situation related to families from the perspective of elite theory.
6. Based on elite theory, why do you think the income gap between the rich and poor in the United States has been allowed to widen?
7. In what ways has gender influenced the construction of policy solutions to family problems?

And now to the last chapter of Part III and the final policy framework presented in this discussion.

CHAPTER 14

A Systems Perspective

Policy from a systems perspective, being more abstract than the other policy models that have been presented in this discussion, takes on a different cast, in part because of the abstractness of systems language itself. Just as political culture theory holds that the political culture of a population is distinguishable from other aspects of the culture, systems theory holds that as a system of human interactions, the political system is distinguishable from other kinds of interactions (Easton, 1979). It refers to that set of interactions through which the values of the society are authoritatively allocated (Dye, 1975).

As Easton defines the term, *authoritative allocations* refers to the distribution of something that is valued among persons or groups in one or more of three possible ways: An allocation may deprive someone of something that is valued that another already possesses (e.g., adequate housing); it may obstruct the attainment of values that would have been otherwise obtained (e.g., reproductive choice in the case of low-income women); and it may give some persons access to values and deny them to others, as eligibility criteria for health and income benefits in fact do.

An allocation is authoritative when people consider themselves bound by it. Policy from a systems perspective is defined as system outputs that represent values authoritatively allocated for the society (Dye, 1975). At the end of the 20th century, these values in the United States included personal responsibility, freedom, competition, family, and the free market.

The boundary of a political system consists of those interactions that differentiate the political system from its environment and determines what it does and does not include. The environment is everything external to the system, such as the conditions that surround and affect it—the economy, culture, climate, geography, technology, the educational level of the population, and so on. According to findings from a study undertaken by David Pimentel, an ecologist from Cornell University, the rapid disappearance of the earth's land, water, and cropland ("Study," 1994) is one of the environmental conditions affecting political systems all over the world. Paul Ehrlich (2000), honorary president of Zero

Population Growth, wrote that the United States is adding the population equivalent of four Washington, D.C.s, every year, another New Jersey every 3 years, and another California every 10.

The boundaries of a political system can be empirically determined by:

- The extent to which political roles can be differentiated from the roles that people play as members of other systems (e.g., the family, church or synagogue, and school)

- The degree to which persons performing political roles form a separate identifiable group and possess a sense of internal solidarity and cohesion (e.g., the governors of the 50 states when they meet semiannually at the Governors' Association conferences or as state legislators do when they meet at the National Association of State Legislators' conferences)

- The degree to which political roles take the shape of a hierarchy distinguishable from other hierarchies (e.g., mayors and city councils or governors and state legislators or presidents and congressional members)

- The degree to which the criteria for the recruitment and selection of persons for political roles differ from the criteria used in the recruitment and selection of persons for other professional and life roles, which in the case of political roles pertains mainly to the ability to win elections.

Much of the following discussion is based on David Easton's work (1979), *A Framework for Political Analysis*. Although his analysis includes all elements of systems theory as it applies to the political system, here the focus is confined to policy as system outputs, and system inputs and withinputs because of their immediate relevance to the construction of policy solutions to family problems.

The basic assumptions underlying Easton's version of systems theory as it applies to family policy as system output are as follows:

- Political life is a system of behavior.

- A system is distinguishable from the environment in which it exists and is open to influences from it.

- A political system is goal setting, self-transforming, adaptive, and comprised of human beings who are capable of anticipating, evaluating, and acting constructively to prevent disturbances in the system's environment.

- System authorities (persons elected to allocate values and their designees) seek to correct disturbances that might be expected to cause system stress in relation to system goals.

- Variations in system processes and structures represent alternative efforts by system members to regulate or cope with stress flowing from sources internal and external to the system.

- The capacity of a system to survive in the face of system stress is a function of the information and feedback that return to system authorities and other influences.

Death w/ Dignity

■ Family Policies and Programs as System Outputs

In this discussion, system outputs take the form of family policies and programs that link the political system to the environment. As outputs, they represent the authoritative allocation of society's values as defined above. Outputs include statutes, administrative decisions and actions, decrees, rules, and other policies articulated by political authorities that are reflective of basic system values. An example of a presidential decree as a form of system output was the Clinton administration's announcement in 1999 allowing states, for the first time, to use a pool of unemployment insurance money to pay for paid time-off for up to 12 weeks for mothers or fathers who choose to stay home after the birth or adoption of a child.

Other outputs of the political system in the 1990s were identified in Chapter 6. They included the Family and Medical Leave Act (FMLA), guaranteeing family members up to 12 weeks of unpaid leave for medical emergencies and the birth or adoption of a baby; the National Service Act, providing living allowances and up to $10,000 in educational grants to service volunteers; a measure making it a federal crime to bomb, burn, or block access to abortion clinics or threaten with violence doctors and nurses who perform abortions; increases in the minimum wage; funding for breast cancer research, job training programs, child care, and all the other state and federal legislation discussed in earlier chapters. Such outputs are viewed as transactions that flow from the political system to the environment. Figure 14.1 is a depiction of the policy process from the perspective of the political system based on Easton's (1979) model of policy as system output.

Ex. OUTPUTS

■ System Inputs: Demands and Support

If system outputs are transactions that flow from the political system to the environment as family policies and programs, system inputs (which flow from the environment to the system) are demands and support for the construction of particular policy solutions. Both system outputs and inputs connect the political system to the environment but in opposite directions (Easton, 1979). Inputs refer to everything in the environment that has the potential of altering, modifying, or affecting the political system in any way. They take a variety of forms: information, money, and energy (human and nonhuman). Inputs can come in the form of parent demands for better schools, school safety, and better instruction for their children. They can come in the form of parent support for schools, as evidenced by their willingness to campaign for more money for schools and volunteering their time for school projects. Inputs also can take the form of information and feedback about system performance, about which more will be said in subsequent discussion.

Ex. INPUT

Inputs reflect, summarize, and communicate information about changes in the environment to which the system is required to respond and adapt. System

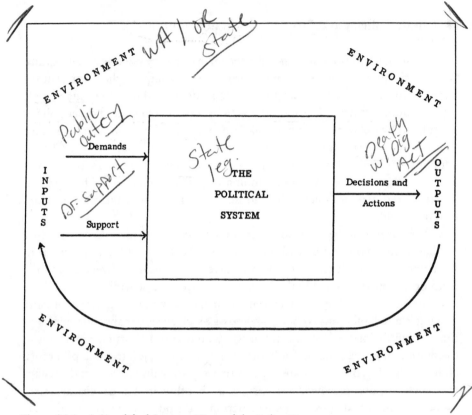

Handwritten annotations on figure: "WA / or State", "Public Outcry", "State leg.", "Pr. Support", "Deaty w/ Dig Act"

Figure 14.1. A Simplified Systems View of the Policy Process
SOURCE: Easton (1979, p. 112, Diagram 3). Copyright © 1979 by University of Chicago Press.
Reprinted with permission.

response to change and demands is a measure of system performance. Such change could pertain to changes in consumer confidence ratings, unemployment rates, citizen satisfaction ratings, demographics, family structures, crime rates, poverty rates, marriage and divorce rates, geographic mobility, and so on.

Demands as Inputs and System Stress

By definition, demands are articulated statements directed toward system authorities, proposing some kind of authoritative allocation or decision to address perceived family problems. As system inputs, demands can affect a political system by fostering states of discontent and dissatisfaction unless authorities are able or willing to address them, at least to some degree. One organization that tried to raise awareness and discontent about environmental conditions is Negative Population Growth Inc. It wrote a letter demanding that Congress and President Clinton set as a national priority the achievement of a negative rate of population growth for the country until the scale of economic activity was reduced to a sustainable level. It urged leaders of other countries to do the same ("NPG Statement," 1994). Periodic reports on the ever-widening gap between the rich and poor in the United States are similarly aimed to foster the degree of dissatisfaction necessary to lead to demands for a more equitable distribution of income in the United States.

The failure to meet system demands can have important consequences for system inputs in the form of support and also for subsequent system performance. In challenging the AFL-CIO's opposition to NAFTA, President Clinton risked losing the support he needed from labor on health care reform. By neglecting to attend to the demands of middle-class families, he and Democrats in general lost constituent support in the 1994 congressional elections, resulting in system stress. System stress refers to conditions that threaten the system's ability to respond to demands from its internal and external environment and thus its performance and capacity to even survive. This was a worry for the Clinton administration following the 1994 midterm elections.

The Case of HMOs: The Loss of System Support

The failure of managed care insurance companies to contain the costs of health care and to adequately address and respond to the health care needs of individuals and families is illustrative of a condition that leads to the loss of system support and threatens system survival. One after another, constituents told their congressional representatives of their experiences with managed care; their representatives in turn gave testimony about what they had heard (Rosenbaum, 1999). Representative Ron Kind, Democrat from Wisconsin, told the story of a young family in western Wisconsin whose little girl was denied treatment for brain cancer and subsequently died. Representative Sheila Jackson-Lee, Democrat from Texas, told of a little boy who could not have a CAT scan he needed.

At the end of the afternoon, Representative Greg Ganske, Republican from Iowa, trumped them all. He brought a 7-year-old boy from Georgia who had artificial legs and no hands onto the House floor. With the boy seated in the front row in shorts and a tank top, Dr. Ganske told the boy's story. When the boy was 5 months old, he developed a high fever. His mother called the family's HMO and was told to go not to the local hospital, but to another one 70 miles away. Halfway there, the boy went into cardiac arrest. He was revived at the hospital, but because gangrene had set in, he lost both hands and both feet. As Dr. Ganske constructed the problem, the boy was not an anecdote and the problem needed to be fixed so these kinds of cases did not happen.

At one town meeting held by Charlie Norwood of Iowa, at least a dozen people spoke about their ordeals with managed care (Alvarez, 1998). A husband told about his wife's death after being denied a bone marrow transplant. Another described how he came home to find his wife sprawled on the floor with a broken hip and was then informed that the managed care company would not pay for an ambulance to transport her to the hospital. Richard Gephardt, House minority leader from Missouri, described how in the 1970s, before managed care became so widespread, his young son was diagnosed as having terminal cancer, but an experimental treatment prescribed by a doctor saved the boy's life, causing Mr. Gephardt to wonder aloud whether an HMO would even permit such treatment in today's environment.

System Stress: A Case of Too Many Demands

Demands may produce system stress independent of their impact on system support if they result in demand overload, that is, if too many demands are placed on the system at one time. Environmental change can create a major but fundamentally neglected type of stress for political systems by not only increasing the volume and variety of demands coming into the system but also broadening them. The increasing numbers of refugee families seeking asylum in the United States as a result of political and economic upheaval in their countries of origin is illustrative. These families have broadened the variety of demands on the political system for medical care, jobs, housing, schools, and so on, resulting in stress for the political system in those states that have experienced an influx of large numbers of people from other countries: Florida, California, Texas, and New York. System stress also may result from the simultaneous expression of these and other demands on the system simply because of the energy and effort required for processing them. Such demands are in addition to constituent demands for increased funding for AIDS research, reproductive health research, affordable housing, financing federal mandates, foreign aid, health and welfare reforms, and better schools.

Withinputs: Within-System Demands and Supports

Many influences affecting the ability of political systems to respond to demands come from *within* the system itself. The concept of withinputs, or within-system influences, sensitizes observers to the need to look *within* the system as well as in the environment for sources of system stress. Within-system demands in 1993 and 1994 took the form of demands by congressional leadership for a balanced budget amendment to prevent the political system (i.e., Congress and the president) from responding to external demands for increased spending. Within-system influences also led to the removal of Dan Rostenkowski as chair of the House Ways and Means Committee, depriving the president of an able strategist to shepherd health care reform through committee to passage in the House. Within-system influences also led to the resignation of Newt Gingrich both as Speaker of the House and as an elected member of the House of Representatives. Within-system demands also took the form of congressional hearings on Whitewater, a complicated Arkansas land development scheme in which President Clinton and the First Lady were involved. The hearings served to distract congressional attention from important legislative matters on the authoritative allocation of values in relation to health care and welfare reform and other policy solutions to family problems.

Despite the widely held perception that President Clinton lacked support from Congress in 1994, as a form of system withinput, evidence shows that Congress backed him on over 86% of the votes on which he took a position (Langdon, 1994). Since Lyndon Johnson, whom Congress supported on 93% of the votes on which he took a position in 1965—the year Medicare, Medicaid, the Voting Rights Act, federal aid to elementary and secondary education, and the student loan program were enacted, and the Department of Housing and Urban Development was established—no president has matched Clinton's score as a second-year president. Even Republicans acknowledged that Clinton was remarkably effective in winning victories on 121 of the 140 votes in the House and Senate. With a Republican majority controlling Congress in 1995 and beyond, however, withinputs in the form of system support for his agenda weakened.

In 1997, pressure from within the system—Congress, including the women among its members—drove the National Cancer Institute to reverse itself and recommend breast x-rays for women in their 40s, even though evidence that the procedure saved lives was inconclusive. Just as the Senate debates over late-term abortions in 1997 were illustrative of elite theory, they also were a form of withinput from a systems perspective, as, for example, when Senator Patty Murray—within the system—implored her Senate colleagues not to ban late-term abortions (Stolberg, 1997). Similarly, it was a delegation of congresswomen in the late 1980s who demanded that the National Institutes of Health include women in clinical trials. At that time, women were routinely excluded from studies financed by the Institutes because of concerns about pregnancy, birth defects, and menstrual fluctuations. The result was that an entire body of medical literature had developed based solely on how new drugs and therapies worked for men. It was only when congresswomen declared, "This can't continue; we can't continue to treat women's health as if women are just men without a certain organ," that the practice stopped, according to the president of the Center for Women Policy Studies, a feminist research group in Washington. Such withinputs in the form of within-system demands offered a very positive way of getting women's health issues on the policy agenda to increase funding for basic research as one policy construction to a family problem.

Disturbances and System Stress

Just as demands that exceed system response capacities can create system stress, disturbances can as well. A disturbance is a change resulting from occurrences affecting the way a system operates. Disturbances refer to all activities that disrupt the pattern of system operations. An example might be Anita Hill, the woman who in 1991 came forward with charges of sexual harassment against Clarence Thomas during Senate confirmation hearings on his nomination for the Supreme Court. Her charges created a disturbance in the pattern of Senate operations with regard to the treatment of women by men in both the public and private sectors. Similarly, the realignment of political power in 1994 that gave Republicans a majority in the House and Senate represented a disturbance that portended a disruption in the patterns of operations that had evolved over the 40 years the Democrats were in the majority, in this case, in the House. In 1998, it was the Clinton-Lewinsky affair, leading to the president's impeachment by the House of Representatives, that created a disturbance in the pattern of operations in both the House and Senate for over a year, preventing the construction of any meaningful policy solutions to family problems that year.

System Response to Input Demands

The system may employ a variety of responses to manage demand overload and avoid system stress. One such response is the synthesis and homogenization of demands in order to develop a plan of action and broaden the base of support for proposals. This is what coalitions do. Another kind of response is the expansion of the system's capacity to carry demands. Taken to the point where it becomes output, expanded channel capacity reduces stress by providing a way for the system to respond to demands; expanded channel capacity, in fact, *is* one response to demands. Expanded channel capacity can take the form of electronic mail, fax mail, voice mail, and larger numbers of phone lines coming into the system. Call-in TV and radio talk shows that allow people to voice complaints or to speak to the president are still other channels that can be used for communicating demands—and support—as forms of inputs into the system, including those related to families. Information and referral services of different kinds also are forms of expanded channel capacity.

Expanded channel capacity, however, is not the same as expanded *system* capacity to respond to demands in the form of family policies and programs. Illustrative is the report of the director of health care studies at the General Accounting Office, an investigative arm of the Congress, indicating that despite President Clinton's announcement to improve the quality of care in nursing homes a year earlier, problems continued to persist in many states a year later, with complaints about serious harm to nursing home residents often ignored for months (Pear, 1999c).

Political Management of System Stress

The degree to which stress threatens the ability of the system to respond to demands, and thus to persist and survive, is seen to depend on the ability of political leaders to manage the conditions causing the stress. Some think increasing rates of poverty and income disparities present such threats. In 1999, the top one fifth of American households with the highest incomes earned half of all the income in the United States, *four* fifths of American households earning the other half (Johnston, 1999). Income in 1999 for the top 1% of households averaged $515,600, and for those in the poorest one fifth of households, it averaged $8,800. In the past, threats included the Great Depression, the race riots of the 1970s, the Viet Nam War and its aftermath, and Watergate. In 1994, it was said such threats in the future could come from the interest owed on the federal debt, which Senator Bob Kerrey from Nebraska, who chaired the Bipartisan Commission on Entitlements and Tax Reform, said would consume all federal revenues unless Congress intervened in the meantime (Pear, 1994). But by 2000, with the reality of budget surpluses and prospects for paying down the national debt, that threat appeared to have evaporated.

Support and System Stress

Support—declining support or lack of support—like demands, is another indicator of system stress. Support can exist for various aspects of a system, such as for system authorities, the regime, constitutional order, or for certain parts of the political community itself, such as Democrats or Republicans. When support threatens to fall below a minimal level, whatever the cause, the system must take measures to revive it, according to Easton.

Polls are a major source of input for gauging system support, both for the system as a whole and its component parts. According to surveys by various polling organizations, George Bush's approval ratings as a measure of presidential support ranged from a high of 87% after the Gulf War in 1991 to a low of 32% in July 1992, just before the 1992 presidential election ("Things Have Always," 1993). Bill Clinton's approval ratings fluctuated from a high of 56% when he first took office in January 1993 to a low of 41% 6 months later ("Clinton's Job Ratings," 1993). By 1999, 62% of those surveyed approved of the job Clinton was doing as president: 77% thought his presidency had been a success, and 56% thought his accomplishments outweighed the failures ("Profiling the Clinton Presidency," 2000). Approval ratings are not the only measure of system support, however. The payment of taxes and the participation of citizens in the political process, including voting in local, state, and national elections, are also.

System Responses to Declining Support

Generating Diffuse Support

System responses to declining support may take three forms: structural modification, the stimulation of diffuse support, and/or the stimulation of specific support. Structural modification is a regulatory response that includes efforts to change the structure of the system through, for example, measures to include women and minorities in policy-making positions, to change the rules of the House and Senate to minimize or reduce Congressional gridlock, or to create ways for citizens to participate in the political process through town meetings and public forums. Diffuse support is expressed in terms of citizen loyalty. Citizen loyalty may be generated by encouraging sentiments of legitimacy, attitudes of compliance, feelings of community, and the notion that the common good takes precedence over the private good of particular individuals and groups. Such support is independent of the specific rewards people acquire as system

members. Polls showing that 90% of those surveyed in 1993 did not want to settle in another country are indicative of the widely diffuse support the United
States as a country enjoys; the comparable percentage for Great Britain was only
51% ("Even Governments," 1993). A 1996 General Social Survey (GSS) similarly showed that almost all Americans (89%) would rather be citizens of the
United States than any other country (McLean, 1999).

Generating Specific Support

Specific support refers to members' satisfaction when they perceive that their
demands have been met. A measure of their well-being, it results from the specific benefits and advantages the system provides as outputs for members, such
as tax benefits that accrue to families with children, or Head Start for preschool
children of low-income families. To affect its level of specific support, the outputs of the political system must alter existing conditions such that the latter
would not have changed if not for the outputs. Improvements in school readiness and achievement in the case of low-income children attending Head Start
might be one such example. Another might be improvements in the quality of
care in nursing homes.

The 1994 midterm elections reflected a lack of support for the outputs of the
political system that year, particularly among men and middle-income families.
Later, to generate such support, President Clinton proposed middle-class tax
cuts comprised of tax-deductible college tuition, tax exemptions for each child
up to $500 per child for families with incomes less than $75,000 per year, the use
of savings in tax-free individual retirement accounts (IRAs) for purposes other
than retirement, and education and training vouchers that people could use as
they saw fit. To generate the specific support of seniors in 2000, President
Clinton proposed covering the cost of prescription drugs under Medicare.
Allowing states to use unemployment insurance money to pay for paid family
and medical leave for parents of newborns and adopted babies also was a way of
generating specific support for his regime.

■ System Requirements for Information and Feedback

The essence of all systems is their self-regulating, self-directing sets of behaviors.
The capacity of a system to respond to stress is derived from two central processes: feedback and response. All systems are required to have information
about conditions in their environments as well as information from within the
systems themselves in order to be able to anticipate circumstances that could
lead to the withdrawal of system support, diffuse or specific. In this discussion,
such feedback as a form of system input pertains to whether such outputs effectively address some of the problems that families experience and meet system
goals. Indicators might be an increase in the number of children completing
school as a result of mandated parent involvement in the education of their

children, an increase in the number of families covered by health insurance as a result of health care reform, a reduction in the number of families living in poverty as a result of more job training programs and better paying jobs, or fewer babies born out of wedlock as a result of the campaign the federal government has been waging to discourage out-of-wedlock births. To survive, a system must be able to modify system goals or transform them entirely in response to information and feedback about its performance—whether with respect to its external environment or internal component parts—or change its internal structures and processes accordingly. Bill Clinton's speech outlining a Middle Class Bill of Rights following the election of a majority of Republicans to Congress may be seen in this light.

In this regard, the history of system response to feedback in the form of research findings about the effects of specific system outputs is not entirely encouraging, particularly when such findings portend a withdrawal of support for specific outputs (Zimmerman, 1999). Illustrative is feedback about boot camps for youthful offenders and Wisconsin's Learnfare program. When, for example, research findings indicated that Learnfare had no effect on the school attendance of children from AFDC families, the findings were discredited by system authorities. Similarly, although available 6 months before Congress passed an anticrime bill funding the expansion of boot camps, research findings were largely ignored that indicated that boot camps for youthful offenders did not measurably reduce recidivism and that marginally lower recidivism rates tended to diminish over time (Nossiter, 1993). Also ignored was a letter signed by 80 social science researchers in 1994 refuting the claim that welfare programs were among the primary reasons for the rising number of out-of-wedlock births (Hopfensperger, 1994).

System response to feedback about the family cap in New Jersey was similar. The family cap is a measure that New Jersey enacted in 1992 that eliminated extra welfare payments for mothers who have babies while on welfare (Lewin, 1998). When researchers reported that their findings did not show the cap was a determinant of New Jersey's falling birthrate but *was* in fact associated with widened differences in the abortion rates of welfare and nonwelfare mothers, neither the state nor the federal agency would accept their report, criticizing the research methodology on which it was based. Subsequently, despite the evidence presented to the contrary and the demands of some legislators, women's groups, and opponents of abortion rights to repeal the family cap, the governor of New Jersey declared she was persuaded to continue the family cap because of the state's declining birthrate (Preston, 1998).

On all these issues—Learnfare, boot camps, the family caps—the feedback threatened support for specific system outputs. It also was contrary to the solutions policymakers had constructed to family problems, most congresspersons intuitively believing boot camps, in particular, ought to be expanded and the opposite for welfare. Although political systems may need information and feedback as inputs for policy, acceptance of such feedback does not necessarily follow.

■ Summary and Conclusions

As goal setting, self-transforming, and adaptive, the political system consists of an identifiable set of institutions and activities that function to transform demands into authoritative allocative decisions (Dye, 1975), as the case examples in this chapter illustrate. In this discussion, policy solutions to family problems are seen as system outputs that flow from the system to the environment. System inputs in the form of demands and support for system outputs flow from the environment to the system, both system outputs and inputs connecting the system and environment to each other. The environment refers to everything external to the political system. As an open system, the political system must have information about its environment and feedback about its performance if it is to adapt to the needs and demands of its environment. Indeed, the emphasis on information and feedback for effective system performance is one of the distinguishing features of systems theory. For this reason, it is a good complement to incremental theory, which emphasizes small gradual steps in the construction of policy solutions to family problems based on experience with existing policies and programs, implying the need for information and feedback about such experience. Of all the policy frameworks presented in this discussion, systems theory is unique in this regard.

The basic concepts underlying the systems approach to the construction of policy solutions to family problems include the following:

- Policy as system outputs
- Environment
- Inputs
- Boundaries
- Withinputs
- System stress
- Demands and support
- Information and feedback
- Specific and diffuse support
- Demand overload

Systems theory may be more abstract than most of the other policy frameworks presented in this discussion, but its terminology provides interesting conceptual tools—inputs, withinputs, and system outputs—for analyzing constructed solutions to family problems. Indeed, its abstraction makes its application appropriate to almost all policy situations related to families, regardless of issue or level of analysis—federal, state, or local—although its lack of specificity can obscure as much as disclose about such situations.

Given that family well-being, from the perspective of family policy, is the goal and value to be maximized in constructing solutions to family problems—and also for assessing the consequences of such constructions—it is now time to engage in a discussion of family well-being and some of the family frameworks that might be used for determining if particular policy constructions achieve it. These frameworks are the subjects of Part IV.

This concludes the presentation of the policy frameworks discussed in these last four chapters. This discussion does not preclude the myriad of other ways of thinking about how and whose solutions to family problems are constructed into policies and programs. Among these are social capital and social integration theories, which are not presented here. Nevertheless, whether policy is defined as

1. The outcome of institutional arrangements and norms, distinguished by its legitimacy, authority, and universality;

2. Rational choice in the selection of the alternative solution with the highest net value ratio;

3. Rational choice constrained by political culture (i.e., the attitudes that people hold toward government);

4. Variations of past policies and programs, with goals being emergent rather than predetermined;

5. Choice under competitive conditions of no authority that reflects the interests and motivations of interdependent players and their ability to bargain, negotiate, and compromise to achieve the goals they are seeking;

6. The equilibrium reached among contending interest groups organized to influence and make claims on government;

7. Elite preference, the size and complexity of modern society precluding the active and full participation of everyone, thus creating a class of ruling or governing elites; or

8. System outputs, linking the political system to the environment, and inputs in turn linking the environment to the system;

they each provide many clues for understanding how and why some solutions to family problems are constructed in the form of family policies and programs and others are not. They also provide many clues for guiding behaviors in constructing policy solutions to family problems, which could include yours, the readers, depending on the role you come to assume in that process. More will be said about the implications of the policy frameworks for policy practice in Part V, the book's conclusion.

In the meantime, some additional questions are provided below to help you, the reader, reflect upon the implications of the systems framework for family policies and programs.

■ Some Questions for Your Reflection and Discussion

1. Define policy choice and constructed solutions to family problems from a systems perspective.

 2. Identify and define the major concepts associated with policy from the systems perspective.

 3. What are the major assumptions of systems theory as they relate to family policy?

 4. Based on systems theory, why do you think the income gap between the rich and poor in the United States has been allowed to widen?

 5. Scan recent magazines or newspapers for examples of policy from each of the perspectives presented in Part III. Analyze and discuss them in terms of what you think they imply for the construction of family policies and programs.

 6. Which of all the policy perspectives do you think is the most useful for thinking about the construction of policy solutions to family problems? Why? For which policies and under what conditions?

Now let us turn to Part IV, which focuses on family well-being as the goal of family policy and family frameworks that can be used to assess its consequences for families—or anticipate them.

PART IV

Family Frameworks: Implications for Families and Their Well-Being

□ Given the nature of the processes involved in the construction of policy solutions to family problems, what are the implications of policy solutions to families and their well-being? How can family well-being be conceptualized? What are the ways in which it can be determined or assessed, either in anticipation of or after such policies have been enacted and implemented?

Webster defines well-being as "the state of being healthy, happy and free from want." As noted earlier, in the family and sociological literature, it has been operationalized along economic, social, psychological, and interpersonal dimensions based on such indicators as income, unemployment, satisfaction, self-esteem, and affect balance. It also has been defined in quality of life terms. Herzog, Rodgers, and Woodsworth (1982) regard it as the outcome of long-term socialization and developmental processes and concurrent environmental conditions and processes. To Campbell, Converse, and Rodgers (1976) and Andrews and Withey (1976), it is a composite of satisfactions in such life domains as marriage, job, leisure, family, and housing. Others have conceptualized the term similarly (Rettig & Bubolz, 1983). Inglehart (1990) refers to life satisfaction as part of a broad syndrome of positive or negative attitudes that people hold about the world in which they live. To Griffin (1986), well-being connotes the degree to which basic needs are met—basic needs referring to that which is essential for survival, health, the avoidance of harm, and proper functioning. Sen (1980, 1985) says that the primary feature of well-being can be seen in terms of how a person can "function," in the broad sense. Although most definitions of well-being refer to individuals rather than families, if individuals are viewed as interdependent and interacting members of family systems, whereby what affects one member affects all, then such definitions may be extended to family units as well. Indeed, personal well-being and the quality of family life have been shown to be related (Rettig, Danes, & Bauer, 1991).

Although I have addressed family frameworks to some degree in earlier discussions, in the three chapters that follow, I present some family frameworks that offer conceptual tools that can be used in assessing how well family policies address family problems and advance the goal of family policy: family well-being. These include:

- Family systems theory
- Exchange and choice theory
- Symbolic interaction
- Family stress theory
- Conflict theory
- Feminist theories
- Cultural theory, as it applies to race and ethnic minorities

As you review these frameworks, you will find that many of the concepts paramount in the policy frameworks also are salient in the family frameworks. Their differences, as noted earlier, are to be found in their configuration and application.

Discussion of the family frameworks will begin where discussion of the policy frameworks ended—with systems theory, as it applies to families. The frameworks are presented in the order in which they appear above. Family systems theory and exchange and choice theory are presented together in Chapter 15; symbolic interactionism and family stress theory are presented in Chapter 16, and the remaining frameworks are in Chapter 17. The purpose of presenting a variety of family frameworks is to familiarize readers with the different ways in which family well-being can be conceptualized in analyzing policy solutions to family problems. By knowing about them, readers can choose the one that seems the most applicable to a particular policy construction and assess it accordingly. Note that references to the implications of family policies and programs as constructed solutions to family problems for families and their well-being are meant to draw attention to their linkages. For the sake of brevity, such linkages may not always be stated in their entirety; they are implicit throughout, however.

Family Systems Theory and Exchange and Choice Theory

■ Family Systems Theory

As noted earlier, systems theory can be applied to almost any phenomena of interest. Appearing in a number of different versions, it frequently is applied to the study of families in the family field, often in conjunction with ecological theory (Bronfenbrenner, 1986; Bubolz & Sontag, 1993). Family ecology theory conceptualizes the interactions and relationships between families and their environment as constituting an ecosystem of interdependent parts and wholes. Similarly, family systems theory sees families as systems of interdependent component parts interacting with each other and their environment, the whole being greater than the sum of its parts.

The family systems perspective that guides the discussion here is based on Reuben Hill's (1971) paper titled, "Modern Systems Theory and the Family: A Confrontation." Because it is more structural than other versions of family systems theory such as Broderick's (1993) and Kantor and Lehr's (1975), the data to support it are more readily available through public sources like the U.S. Census Bureau. Not surprisingly, it employs many of the same concepts as Easton's political/policy model. The difference between the two, as noted earlier, lies in their focus—Easton's on political systems and Hill's on family systems—the two levels of social phenomena interacting with one another through their respective input and output processes.

Hill begins with the assumption that all systems are characterized by four basic properties:

1. The tasks they perform to meet the needs of their members and the larger environment

2. The interdependence of their component parts

3. Boundaries and boundary maintenance tendencies that serve to differentiate systems from one another and also from their environment

4. Equilibrium and adaptive propensities for ensuring system viability

Focusing on the environment as an object of study and analysis, Shirley Terreberry (1972) emphasized the increasing importance of the environment for effective system performance, which from the perspective of families includes the economy and the political system and the latter's outputs in the form of family policies and programs. The four system properties outlined by Hill are discussed below, followed by Terreberry's conceptualization of the environment, the focus being on the implications of constructed policy solutions to family problems for family well-being.

Families as Social Systems: Their Tasks and Functions

The task-performing property of families pertains to the functions families are expected to perform. These include (a) the physical maintenance and care of family members; (b) the addition of new members through procreation or adoption and their relinquishment when they mature; (c) the socialization of children for adult roles, such as those of spouse, parent, worker, citizen, neighbor, community member; (d) the social control of members to ensure the maintenance of order within the family and groups external to it; (e) the maintenance of family morale and motivation to ensure task performance both within the family and in other social groups; and (f) the production and consumption of goods and services needed to support and maintain the family unit. Thus, if the capacity to function (Sen, 1980, 1985) defines well-being, then the capacity of families to perform their functions defines family well-being.

However, the ways families perform their tasks vary and change over the life cycle, depending in part on the age and sex of family members and the family's ethnic and socioeconomic background. The urgency with which family development tasks are performed during specific family life-cycle stages—such as the establishment, childbearing, school age, adolescent, launching, postparental, or retirement stages—also varies. Because the sequencing of family life-cycle stages has blurred in recent years, the performance of the tasks associated with these stages has shifted as well. For example, childbearing often precedes the establishment stage, having implications for many parents in the retirement stage who are grandparents of children whose parents remain nonestablished (unmarried) and unable to assume responsibility for their children. Cultural variations in the performance of family developmental tasks also should be underscored. For example, because adolescence does not exist in the Hmong culture (Mydans, 1994), the concept of teenager is alien to Hmong families, whose children traditionally go to work when they are 13 or 14 years old, either as farmers or soldiers. The task-performing property of families as systems suggests that family well-being could be assessed in terms of the support they provide for the performance of family tasks at different life-cycle stages, taking culture into account.

Interdependence of Family Roles and Positions

The concept of interdependence or interrelated positions also has application to the assessment of family well-being. This concept refers to interacting and reciprocal positions and roles that make up the family system, such as husband-wife, brother-sister, father-son, father-daughter, mother-son, and mother-daughter roles. Implicit in such positions are roles that must be performed if the family as a system is to fulfill its functions for its members and society. Based on shared values and normative expectations, a network of family relationships develops that serves to unite members in ways that distinguish them from other groups. These relational networks, which vary with social class and culture, are likely to persist unless or until they are disrupted by members who challenge basic system values and norms. Such disruption might occur when new members come into the system—such as daughters- and sons-in-law who have different values and norms from the focal system—or when members temporarily or permanently withdraw from the family socially, psychologically, and/or physically. Today, relational networks are able to continue even when members are geographically dispersed, largely because of technological advances in communications and transportation that make meaningful family exchanges and the retention of family identity and ties possible (Litwak, 1985). Even in banking, technological advances permit families to perform essential caregiving roles for members who become ill and require care in another community.

The case of Marcelino Corniel is illustrative of a disrupted family relational network. As a young man with a history of gang violence and imprisonment who was fatally shot by police outside the White House for wielding a knife at people, he disrupted his relational network of family and friends when he gradually turned away from his reportedly stable family and toward the streets. Also illustrative is the case of Lorena Bobbitt, who in self-defense and protest, challenged the basic system norms and values of her family—male domination and abuse—when she cut off her husband's penis while he was sleeping because he repeatedly raped and beat her.

The greater leadership content contained in parent roles lends particular significance to the provision of supports for their performance. When Al Gore unveiled his antipoverty agenda, emphasizing responsible fatherhood, he in effect was calling attention to the leadership content in the father role. Similarly, when a dozen experts in child development urged parents to take control, based on their observations of their children's disorderly behaviors, they in effect were advising parents to exert their leadership role in disciplining their children (Iovine, 1996). Although almost all parents of 13- to 17-year-olds surveyed in a nationwide poll by the *New York Times/CBS News* said they set rules for the time their children come home at night, and almost all said they did not want their children to smoke marijuana, less than half (40%) told their children not to do it (Goldberg & Connelly, 1999). Yet, findings from student surveys showed parental influence was key in discouraging children from experimenting with drugs and alcohol. For this reason, the executive director of a drug treatment center for youth and families was prompted to advise parents to use their parental leadership influence and give their children a clear message about not using drugs and alcohol (Cummins, 1999a).

Structural Deficit

Because the tasks associated with family roles are important for family functioning, the tasks associated with unoccupied family positions must be allocated or reallocated to those that remain. The remaining positions then tend to become overburdened with too many tasks to perform, as heads of single-parent families, both male and female, and grandparent-only families frequently report. Families with positions that have never been occupied, as in the case of families headed by never-married mothers or fathers, or with positions that later become unoccupied, as in the case of family breakup, are characterized by structural deficit. In 1998, single parents maintained over one fourth (27.3%) of family households with children under 18, of which a little over 2 million were maintained by fathers and almost 10 million by mothers (Casper & Bryson, 1998a). Between 1992 and 1997, grandfather-only families with no parent present grew by an astonishing 39%, grandmother-only families by 27% (Casper & Bryson, 1998b).

In addition to the burdens associated with unoccupied family positions, some positions may become overburdened by having *new* tasks to perform (e.g., the care of a frail and elderly parent, a new infant, a grandchild, or stepchildren in addition to one's own) or having more of the same tasks to perform (e.g., working multiple jobs to compensate for declining real wages or working longer hours to meet workplace demands). Americans now surpass every other industrialized nation in the time spent on the job, according to an analysis undertaken by the International Labour Organization (Grimsley & Salmon, 1999). Limits on work hours, with accompanying income supports, might be appropriate to compensate for such deficits and burdens.

Structural Excess

An excess of structure, in contrast to structural deficit, may occur when too many occupants are available for given family positions, as could happen in (a) families with twins, triplets, or quadruplets, (b) families in which adult children live in the same household with parents, (c) families in which grandparents live in the same household with adult children and their children, or (d) stepfamilies. In families maintained by both grandparents, a parent was present in almost one third of the families with children under 18 and in almost 30% of those maintained by a grandmother only (Bryson & Casper, 1998).

With regard to stepfamilies, dual problems of underfilled and overfilled positions often can be observed: underfilled for adults who are both parents and stepparents of two or more sets of children and overfilled for children who may suffer from loss of position and patterns of interaction with which they were familiar in their families of origin. One consequence of such loss may be internal family conflict about issues pertaining to overcrowded positions, which may require outside help to resolve. Such conflict may manifest itself not only in heightened stepsibling rivalry (Hetherington & Jodl, 1993; Zill, Morrison, & Coiro, 1993) but also in ambiguous and divergent role expectations (Anderson & White, 1986; Bray & Berger, 1993; Hetherington & Jodl, 1993; Zill et al., 1993). In 1990, 11% of all married couple households were stepfamily households; 16% of all children under 18 lived in such households (U.S. Bureau of the Census, 1993). New census data undoubtedly will report an increase in these arrangements.

Boundaries and Boundary Maintenance

As noted earlier, the boundary of any system, or another system property, can be conceptualized as the demarcation line that separates the system from its environment. An empirical test of family boundaries might be differences in the intensity, frequency, and content of the interactions that take place within families from those that take place between families and other systems in their environment such as schools, social service agencies, churches, hospitals, and workplaces. In recent years, e-mail, voice mail, cell phones, and portable computers have blurred the boundaries between families and work, fostering expectations of instant responses and 24-hour-a-day availability.

Despite such blurring, the family is perceived to be a *semiclosed* system that opens selectively to engage in transactions with the outside world through *liaison roles* built into family positions (Hill, 1971). Hence the family is viewed as a *semiclosed, semiopen* system. Examples of liaison roles built into family roles are parents who appeal to the authorities of the political system for regulations to allow their severely retarded children to be mainstreamed into regular schoolroom classes, parents who advocate for bus safety measures to protect the safety of their children, and adult children who seek home services for elderly parents. Liaison roles linking families with other systems are more generically performed by children as students and consumers and parents as consumers, citizens, and workers, often with the encouragement of public officials and specific family policies. Grandparent mentoring programs in the schools are illustrative, as is the 1993 Educate America Act, which calls for parent involvement in the education of children, directly and explicitly linking parents to schools. Similarly, when the Minneapolis School superintendent sent a letter to parents warning them of an impending deficit and urging them to press their legislators for more funding (Draper, 1999), she in effect was encouraging and supporting them in the performance of their liaison roles in relation to both the schools and state legislature. Many other examples could be given. As in the education of children more generally, school-family linkages via parent involvement was found to be characteristic of quality day care (Wilgoren, 1999) and hence supportive of family well-being.

The implications of family and policy linkages for family well-being became apparent during the debates on health care reform in 1993-94. One of these exchanges involved the chair of the House Ways and Means Subcommittee, who wondered out loud where one of the members on the committee got her "medical degree," saying he presumed she got it through "pillow talk" with her husband, who was a physician ("House Health Debate," 1994). With the election of more women to Congress, the implications of such linkages for family well-being have become much more pronounced, in part because women legislators tend to join their family experiences with their policy roles more than men, as for example when California's Senator Dianne Feinstein argued during the debates on FMLA that she learned about the reluctance of employers to hire women with small children when she divorced a few years after her baby was born (Clymer, 1993a). Patty Murray, senator from Washington state who also argued for the bill told how she had to quit her job after her baby was born because although she worked out of economic necessity, no other options were available at the time.

Family Boundaries and Family Privacy

Because of the intimate functions that families perform for their members, families are protected from public view by the legal sanctions that can be imposed when their sanctity and privacy are threatened by outside intruders. For this reason, the family as a boundary-maintaining system probably is more closed than other systems. Consider O. J. Simpson's statement when the police were called to his home on one of several occasions to stop him from beating his wife. A celebrated football player charged with murdering his wife, O.J. indignantly protested that the altercation was a *private* family matter the couple could handle themselves, wondering why such a big deal was being made of it in the first place (Rimer, 1994).

Family boundaries supported by privacy laws help to explain why situations involving child and spouse abuse often go undetected for so long. For example, authorities did not know the two children they caught shoplifting were virtually imprisoned in a locked attic room and allowed to come out only for meals that they ate by themselves in the basement; they had not attended school for months (Hanley, 1993a). To go to the bathroom, they had to knock on the door to have it unlocked. Neighbors reported that the parents kept to themselves and had no listed phone number, symptomatic of just how closed their family system was.

Similarly, until the oldest of four children—ages 4, 8, 11, and 17—wrote to an aunt pleading for help, no one knew they were being deprived of food and water, made to sleep on the living room floor in shorts under a plastic sheet in the winter, and not allowed to go outside ("Teenager," 1999). Charging the parents with four counts of nonsupport of a minor, the authorities removed the children from the home and placed them with another aunt. In these and similar instances, when the health and safety of children or other family members are at stake, the state is required to protect vulnerable members—at least when such instances come to its attention—child protection taking priority over the protection of family boundaries and privacy rights in such instances.

Family Boundaries and the Juvenile Court System

A controversy over family boundaries and privacy erupted in Minneapolis when a proposal was made to open juvenile court proceedings to public scrutiny—in effect, to lift the veil that served to hide the deeds of abusive families from the public's view. Behind the curtains, the following deeds were cited as having been committed (Toogood, 1997):

- One father kept his daughter out of school for a year, repeatedly tying her up and using a stun gun to rape her.
- A mother sold her 9-year-old daughter for cash for drugs to a 60-year-old man so that he could sexually abuse her.
- A mother's drunken boyfriend bashed her head against the kitchen table while her children were eating, took a knife, and began cutting her throat.
- Several children were found living in what authorities described as "a garbage house" in the midst of rats and cockroaches, with adults coming and going and dealing drugs and guns day and night.

The case for opening up the court system was argued on the basis of the following:

- Closed systems are inclined to rot.
- The public has a compelling interest in knowing how the court system deals with threats to the lives of children by their parents.
- The media has a right to information about state power, based on the First Amendment.
- There is an importance and a need for minimal community standards with regard to adequate parenting.

Counterarguments to opening up the court system were based on concerns for the vulnerability of abused children and their revictimization as a result of exposing their identities and family problems to the shaming gaze of a scornful public. Leading child psychotherapists also argued that certain rights—parental autonomy, a child's right to autonomous parents and privacy—were essential to family integrity, an argument that Toogood said also was used by men who opposed state intervention in spousal abuse situations. By opening up the courts and allowing the public to see inside, Toogood maintained that the lives of children who might otherwise die at the hands of their parents would be saved.

Going Outside the Family

Although families may be more closed than other systems and often seem to exclude the outside world when coping with their internal family problems—

like the teenager whose parents denied him and his siblings food and water— evidence suggests they are much more open than in the past. Members at least seem more willing to involve persons outside the family's boundaries, such as lawyers, psychotherapists, and family counselors, to help them deal with internal family problems or to use outside support groups, such as Parents Anonymous, Alcoholics Anonymous, or caregiver groups for a similar purpose. They are even willing to appear on TV talk shows such as Oprah Winfrey's to share intimate family matters with the nation's viewers. Among them are Bill and Hillary Clinton, who, during the 1992 presidential campaign, appeared on national television to share information with all the American public about earlier marital problems. The same is true for Lorena Bobbitt, whose spousal rapes and beatings went undetected for years until she cut off her husband's penis and became front page and prime time news.

One mother took her case to the public when she shared the story of her son with the local newspaper. When the boy was 4 years old, he hid steak knives under his pillow "to cut off your legs when you're asleep," he told his mother (Cummins, 1999b). One night, the boy set her bed on fire while she slept. That year, he alarmed his Head Start teacher with drawings of fires, guns, dead people, and blood. By age 13, he had racked up 9 years of vandalism, marijuana use, school expulsions, and a suicide attempt. After the efforts of two case workers and two treatment centers, the boy's mother believed he was finally getting better and had a chance of turning his life around—provided the county paying for his treatment would allow him to stay in residential treatment a while longer. The county, however, refused to do so, declaring that after a year's worth of treatment, the boy had to leave. In appealing the county's decision and going public with it, the mother exposed not only the workings of the county system but the workings of her own family as well to secure the help her son needed.

Equilibrium and Adaptive Propensities

The notion of equilibrium assumes a range of possible states within which a system can function and to which it presumably can adapt (Hill, 1971). In terms of the family, if patterns of interactions develop in conformity with the range of norms that members share, it probably can continue to function and survive as a system. The point at which this range is exceeded becomes manifest by the behaviors of family members. Illustrative are youth who run away from home and parents who abandon their children. When Mia Farrow sought to deny Woody Allen visitation rights after their longtime cohabiting relationship broke up because of Allen's affair with Farrow's adopted daughter, she revealed the point at which the range of norms she deemed acceptable for their systemic relationship to continue had been exceeded. Because of its variable size and rapidly changing age composition, families may be more vulnerable to internally induced disequilibrium than other organizations and groups, as evidenced at major life transitions such as the birth of the first child, retirement, or other major turning points in life.

Negative and Positive Feedback Processes

States of equilibrium and adaptation are made possible through negative and positive feedback processes, which can be either negative or positive in their consequences for families (Hill, 1971). Families as systems need information and feedback about their performance in relation to their external environment and internal component parts—that is, their members. Information and feedback incongruent with established family goals become the basis for modifying family behaviors and operations and are used as inputs into family decision-making processes. Thus, the implications of policy solutions to family problems for family well-being can be assessed in terms of the extent to which such solutions include the information and feedback families need to guide their behaviors and decisions. Families, for example, require information about changes in the Social Security program as input into decisions about retirement and the coordination of such information with other information pertinent to their situation. In this manner, they attempt to arrive at decisions that will ensure the maintenance of family stability and viability after their income from current earnings ends. Given that the Social Security Administration now annually informs workers of their estimated retirement benefits, such decisions should be somewhat easier for preretirement families. Information, aggressively provided, that they could still be eligible for Medicaid and child care even after going to work guided the behaviors and decisions of many TANF mothers in one county in Illinois seeking to change their employment status (Pear, 2000).

Feedback about family task performance can be both positive and negative, neither necessarily being negative or positive in their consequences. Both negative and positive feedback begin with error or a mismatch between system behaviors and internal and external standards or criteria. Negative feedback processes differ from positive feedback processes, however, by operating so as to *reduce* the mismatch between information about a system's performance and basic values, triggering behaviors to bring the two into convergence when they diverge. In this sense, negative feedback is a *change-resistant* set of operations geared toward *system sameness* or the status quo or *morphostasis*.

Positive feedback, on the other hand, is a *deviation-amplifying* rather than deviation-reducing process. Viewed as instructive and system enhancing, positive feedback is considered essential to the morphogenic process through which systems change and grow. Change that occurs as a result of positive feedback processes is referred to as *morphogenesis*. Morphogenesis can take many forms. From the perspective of families, one is a change in the work behaviors of welfare mothers following the enactment of the Personal Responsibility and Work Opportunity Reconciliation Act (PRWORA) and also the work behaviors of older family members following the elimination of the earnings test in Social Security. Another is a change in the work and nonwork behaviors of disabled family members following the enactment of the Americans With Disabilities Act in 1990, which required government and businesses to make their facilities and services accessible to people with disabilities. Another form that morphogenesis can take is a change in system values, purposes, and standards, such change being evident in many of the positive statements of mothers who formerly received AFDC and now do not. As one mother said, the transition to work after 12 years on welfare was "scary," but having more confidence now, she said she "wished she had gotten off public aid a long time ago" (Pear, 2000). Changes in system values, norms, goals, and behaviors often occur during periods of economic downturn when family members are out of work—or economic upturn when family fortunes improve. They also occur when families move to a different country and adopt its culture as their own, as many refugee families in fact do after coming to the United States.

In addition to changes in system values, purposes, and standards, morphogenesis may take the form of a change in internal and external input operations, such as changes in the way parents communicate with children—or with each other at different family life-cycle stages—and consequent changes in members' attitudes and behaviors. Illustrative is a mother who said she learned how to parent better as a result of her participation in group programs in which parents and children met with social workers and talked about how to manage their problems. Finally, such change may take the form of the ascendance of components with new and different properties and attributes in the governance and management of the system. Here again, fatherhood programs that teach fathers how to parent are illustrative.

Integrally related to the concepts of positive feedback and morphogenesis is the idea of "mapping for variety" and the necessity for a continuous flow of varied information, experience, and input into the system. Here, computer technology and the Internet, by making information on a wide variety of subjects instantaneously and readily available to families, is relevant. Also relevant are the disparities in access to such technology that exist among families at different income levels in the United States, accentuating disparities in family well-being.

The Environment

The environment refers to conditions or influences external to the system that are both system-specific and general in nature (Hall, 1972). General environmental conditions affecting all systems include climate, natural resources, cultural norms and values, the globalization of the economy, technological advances, violence, and others, as discussed earlier. Examples of environmental conditions specific to families as systems would be support for child care subsidies for working parents, support for coverage for prescription drugs for elderly family members, and support for gun control to ensure the safety of family members.

Terreberry (1972) has characterized the environment in which families are embedded as highly complex, interactive, and turbulent. Maintaining that the environment has become increasingly important for effective system performance, she holds that it constantly presents families and other organizations with sudden and unpredictable changes that continually threaten to upset their equilibrium and adaptive capacities and their ability to predict the future and control the consequences of their actions. Thus, families as systems are vulnerable to disequilibrium not only because of changes internally induced by their members and their own developmental processes but also because of the turbulent and changing nature of their external environment. The ongoing restructuring of the economy and the uncertainty that continues to surround health care costs and Social Security, or any major policy change, are examples. Terreberry's conceptualization of the environment in terms of a focal organization's actual and potential transactional interdependence underscores the importance of the input-output processes that connect families to their environment and vice versa. Here, the obvious implications for family policies would appear to reside in attempts to stabilize the environment, as the Federal Reserve Board attempts to do when it increases and reduces interest rates to control inflationary pressures that erode family income.

Family Well-Being: Concepts for Assessing It From a Family Systems Perspective

As readers may have observed in this discussion, family well-being can be used as a standard for both assessing and constructing policy solutions. From a family systems perspective, family well-being might be assessed in terms of the effectiveness with which policy solutions facilitate the performance of family tasks or functions at different life cycle stages, *family task performance* being one of the hallmarks of newer definitions of the term *family*. An example might be an analysis of the effects of recent increases in the minimum wage on the task performance of young families who often are low-wage earners and the elimination of the tax on Social Security benefits of retired couples.

The implications of policies and programs for families and their well-being also might be analyzed and assessed in relation to the *positions* and *roles* that make up the family's structure—the parent role, for example—and the *supports* such policies and programs provide for effective role performance. Supports can come in a variety of guises—parent education, child care, nutrition education, respite services in the case of families with a disabled child, education, job training, financial management counseling, housing, transportation, and others. To this might be added the supports such policies and programs provide for the caregiving role that adult children often perform for elderly parents and that now are being sought for grandparents in their caregiving role of grandchildren.

In terms of *overburdened* family positions, the implications of such policies and programs for family well-being might be assessed in terms of the extent to which such policies and programs _add to_ or _alleviate_ their burdens. An example might be foster care reimbursement policies that pay grandparents and other relatives less than nonrelatives for the care of grandchildren at risk, which could be assessed in terms of the extent to which they add to or alleviate grandparent burden. Medicaid reimbursement caps could be similarly assessed. The same applies to many of the provisions of PRWORA. A federal appeals court judge in California, ruling on cuts in welfare benefits approved by the Bush administration in 1992, said that because the cuts put families at increased risk of homelessness, inadequate nutrition, and a variety of physical and emotional problems, adding to the burdens they already had, the cuts were detrimental to their well-being—and therefore invalid.

In terms of *structural excess,* which also has implications for family well-being, policies and programs could be assessed in terms of their contribution to the *positive resolution* of problems arising from such excess, whether these pertain to multigenerational or blended families. Examples are rulings on visitation rights, child custody arrangements, child support, and court-mandated courses for divorced couples that deal with the impact of divorce on children, conflict resolution, and the challenges of stepfamily relationships.

In terms of *family boundaries,* the implications of policies and programs for families and their well-being might be considered in terms of their provisions for protecting family boundaries and the rights and safety of individual members at the same time. Because *liaison roles* are integral to the role performance of family members, which in turn is integral to family task performance and intersystemic relationships, family policies and programs could be assessed in relation to the support they provide for a family's liaison roles and function. The Educate America Act, calling for parent involvement in children's schooling, is an example. Another is a reimbursement provision for out-of-pocket expenses that family members incur when volunteering their services in nursing homes, schools, parks, and libraries, or as advocates.

Because *family equilibrium* and *adaptation* are critical for family task performance, and hence for family well-being, family policies and programs might be assessed in terms of the extent to which they contribute to family equilibrium and adaptation or their opposites: family instability and disequilibrium. The 2-year time limit for families receiving financial assistance under TANF or PRWORA is an example of the latter, as are the current minimum wage and the scarcity of affordable housing. Such policies also could be assessed in terms of the extent to which they enable families to adapt to changes in their external environment. This might include the widespread distribution of *information and feedback* about changes in their external environment—changes in family policies, or information pertaining to school closings, road construction, taxes, weather conditions, college costs, and so on that could trigger family behaviors and decisions accordingly.

Summary

If the objective is to take a more or less comprehensive approach to the assessment of the implications of family policies, then a family systems perspective clearly offers language that provides a host of conceptual tools for doing so and an overarching interpretative framework in which to place them. Although this is the most comprehensive and challenging of the frameworks presented in this discussion—and a framework that provides for linking families to the environment and the environment to families—some may prefer to work with a more parsimonious and less abstract framework. With this in mind, let us turn our attention to exchange and choice theory, which provides different concepts and a different interpretative framework for this task.

■ Exchange and Choice Theory

Exchange and choice theory, although based on a different set of assumptions and concepts, offers another way of conceptualizing the input-output processes associated with family systems theory. From the perspective of exchange and choice theory, exchanges are forms of inputs, and outputs are based on choices. Such choices here refer primarily to the choices made by families and their members, but the concept of exchange necessarily implies and involves the choices of systems with which families interact. Such exchanges and choices are at the heart of exchange and choice theory.

One of the basic assumptions underlying exchange and choice theory is that families are made up of people, who as humans are rational, make decisions, and initiate actions (Blau, 1964; Ekeh, 1974; Gouldner, 1960; Heath, 1976; Levi-Strauss, 1966; Nye, 1979; Thibaut & Kelley, 1959). Applied to individuals and families, this framework is similar in many respects to the rational choice model as it pertains to policy. In addition to the above assumption, the other core assumptions underlying exchange and choice theory as they apply to families are that

- Within the limits of the information they possess and their ability to predict the future, families are able to assess the rewards and costs of alternative choices (Sabatelli & Shehan, 1993)
- Based on their assessment of the costs and rewards of alternative choices, families choose the alternative that promises the greatest rewards for the least cost
- Families seek to maximize the rewards and minimize the costs of their behaviors and choices
- By engaging in one set of behaviors rather than another, families incur costs in the rewards they seek; they also forego the rewards of alternative choices
- Unless no other viable alternatives are available and the costs are low, behaviors not rewarded in the past will not be repeated
- The values and standards that people hold determine the rewards and costs of alternative choices
- If rewards exceed expectations, they will be valued less in the future
- In assessing the costs and rewards of various exchanges, norms of reciprocity and fairness take precedence over profitability

The concepts embedded in these assumptions are discussed below. Readers will recognize the applicability of many of the concepts associated with these frameworks to family well-being.

Rewards

Rewards from the perspective of exchange and choice theory are defined as pleasures, satisfactions, and gratifications that may be derived from particular relationships, interactions, experiences, and statuses (Nye, 1979). They are almost synonymous with family well-being as defined here.

Rewards may include any of the following:

- Social approval in the form of respect, prestige, and admiration
- Autonomy in being able to choose activities, positions, relationships, and/or locales that offer gratification and satisfaction without entailing costs
- Physical security having to do with food, clothing, shelter, health care, physical safety, and so on
- Money for purchasing goods and services that provide pleasure or satisfaction or satisfy needs
- Agreement with values and opinions or support for positions, psychologically reinforcing feelings of self-worth and competence
- Equality in terms of what the respective parties can offer each other

Illustrative of such rewards and their relevance for family well-being is legislation enacted in at least a few states requiring employers to give nursing mothers "break time" and a sanitary, private room for breast pumping "as long as it does not disrupt business operations." In advocating for the legislation, proponents explicitly referred to the rewards of breast feeding for babies, mothers, and even employers: healthier, happier children and women, fewer sick days, and reduced health insurance claims. Breast milk, some studies have suggested, also increases intelligence later in life, making way for additional rewards in terms of smarter parents and employees in the future (deFlebre, 1998).

Also illustrative of rewards embedded in policy solutions that enhance low-income families is the earned income tax credit (EITC) for low-income parents who work. A bill in Minnesota is similarly illustrative: It reduces marriage license fees from $70 to $20 as a reward for couples who complete a 12-hour premarital education program that includes discussion of the seriousness of marriage, the teaching of conflict management skills, and the desirability of seeking marital counseling in times of marital difficulties ("Marriage License," 2000).

Costs

In exchange and choice theory, costs are the opposite of rewards. They are statuses, relationships, interactions, situations, or feelings that individuals and family members regard as unpleasant, distasteful, or uncomfortable, representing in effect family *ill*-being. Here, a provision in Minnesota to increase the cost of dissolving a marriage from $122 to $172 and thus make divorce more costly financially, psychologically, and socially is relevant. Costs also can take the form of rewards foregone as a consequence of choosing a competing alternative. For an adoptive father of a 4-month-old Paraguayan baby, the cost implications of his taking a 4-month parent leave for his family's well-being was the loss of his job, his salary, life and health insurance coverage, and reprimands from superiors because some of the projects on which he had been working were late (Hillbery, 1994). For some single mothers, the costs of taking time off to care for sick children under FMLA may be too high, given the income they would have to forego as a consequence, with obvious implications for the well-being of the families involved.

Uncertainty as a Cost

Uncertainty is inherent in the calculation of costs and rewards; therefore, exchange and choice theory holds that the costs and rewards of alternative choices cannot be fully known in advance. For this reason, families often experience considerable ambivalence and anxiety as additional costs when faced with the uncertain outcomes of alternative choices. This includes midlife executives who, in the face of company downsizing, lose their jobs and then are confronted with the uncertainties of finding alternative employment. Choices with regard to retirement also are of this nature, involving, as they do, uncertain calculations concerning life expectancy, the future growth of accumulated resources (including Social Security), the costs of health care and housing, and so on. Because of all the information and treatment possibilities that new technology provides, family members as patients or parents of patients increasingly are required to make highly uncertain life and death choices. For example, should a woman 21 weeks into her pregnancy abort the fetus or give birth to a baby who is likely to need dialysis and die shortly after birth in any case? On a similar note, should children be told they have inherited a defective gene that could, but might not, manifest itself later in a serious illness?

In general, unpredictability, ambiguity, uncertainty, and anxiety all represent costs that individuals and families must bear when making choices. Residents of three community nursing homes were faced with just such costs upon learning that their nursing homes were closing and not knowing where they would go (Wolfe, 2000). "Almost every conversation turns into a discussion about who's going where and what's going to happen next," one of the nursing assistants said.

Such costs often prevent families from seeking alternatives that may offer rewards exceeding those of their present situation, status, or relationship, as for example, Mayor Jan Jones's decision not to pursue congressional office as an alternative to the position she held as mayor of Las Vegas. Uncertainty about the costs and rewards of moving to a community where jobs are more plentiful and the pay is better may prevent some unemployed parents from making the choice to move. Similarly, despite the high costs of their situation, the uncertainties involved in leaving husbands who abuse them prevent many abused wives from doing just that. In the past, the high costs of taking a low-paying job with no health benefits prevented many AFDC mothers from making that choice. Today, they have no such choice.

Uncertainty about the costs of the Clinton health care reform plan as a constructed solution to a family problem prompted many families to oppose it, fearful their taxes would increase if it should pass, placing their health and household economy and thus the future well-being of their family at risk. Indeed, premiums for a managed care plan for a family of four with earnings of $40,000 in 1994 were projected to *increase* from 8% to 10% of its income by 2000, based on projected earnings of $50,000 (Meyers, 1994). For a 60-year-old single woman earning $35,000 per year who would be relying on Social Security and pension income upon her retirement, premium costs were projected to increase from 5% of her income in 1994 to 22% when she retires. For a 25-year-old single man, premiums represented almost 13% of his income in 1994; by the year 2000, they were projected to increase to over 15%.

Profitability

The idea of profitability in exchange and choice theory also has implications for family well-being. Profitability strives for the most favorable reward-to-cost ratio, similar to rational choice theory, which strives for net value maximization. The profitability of alternative choices can be determined by assessing the potential rewards and costs of possible actions. A profitable outcome is one that not only absorbs the uncertainty of an alternative choice but, in addition, compensates for it. Although no longer a choice, mothers receiving financial assistance in states that guarantee families access to health care and subsidies for child care are being helped to absorb the uncertainties they face as they enter the workforce, although whether such provisions actually compensate them for the costs they incur as a result remains to be seen. At the same time, according to some polls, when families anticipate profitable outcomes, they are willing to pay more in taxes for quality education, universal health care, and better police protection—with obvious implications for family well-being.

Depending, however, on the values families and their members hold relative to particular relationships, statuses, experiences, and objects, perceptions of the rewards and costs of alternative choices vary. The costs and rewards of particular choices can be determined empirically by asking individual members what they like and do not like and by observing their behaviors. Thus, the relative rewards and costs of parenthood can be determined for the couple who left their two young daughters home alone while they vacationed in Mexico and later terminated their parental rights voluntarily ("Couple Who Left," 1993). Similarly, the relative rewards and costs of health insurance and private schooling for their children were possible to determine for the parents, who chose the latter. They said they could not afford to pay $300 a month for an insurance plan with a $2,500 deductible and send their children to a private school at the same time (Eckholm, 1994).

The increase in the number of top company executives and political figures who said they were resigning so they could spend more time with their family is indicative of their assessment of the relative rewards and costs of their occupational and family positions. As one father who quit one of Wall Street's top-paying jobs explained, he used to see his children mostly in the dark. They knew him by his silhouette—at bedtime. Now he was part of their day-to-day lives. In some sense, he said, his decision was a way of reordering his priorities, of reassessing the relative costs and rewards of the choices he had made in the past (Shellencharger, 1998).

It is similarly possible to determine the relative costs and rewards of sexual intimacy for one 45-year-old homosexual, who though fully informed about the transmission of AIDS, became infected with it. Conveying his understanding of his choice, he said he would rather have sexual intimacy and a shorter life than a longer life without it (Gross, 1993). In another instance, a 15-year-old boy who had undergone two liver transplants won a judge's permission to stop taking the medicine that could have prolonged his life. The medicine caused the boy so much pain that he chose to have a shorter but more comfortable life without the medicine than a longer life with it in excruciating pain ("Behind a 15-Year-Old's Decision," 1994). The boy died 2 months after the court ruled in his favor. The same observation, although different in nature, might apply to low-income expectant mothers for whom barriers to prenatal health care, such as the lack of transportation and a phone, are so formidable and hence costly that they are willing to forego the rewards of good prenatal health care.

Comparison Level and Comparison Level Alternatives

According to Thibaut and Kelley (1959), comparison level refers to a *standard* by which families evaluate and compare the costs and rewards of their situation. Individuals make such comparisons intuitively. The assumption is that those who perceive they are less well off than they think they deserve to be will be angry, and those who perceive they are better off than they think they deserve to be will feel guilty. Both anger and guilt represent costs. A spouse laid off from a job that supported a middle-class lifestyle and could not find one to replace it or workplace shootings by laid-off employees might be examples of the former. Illustrative of the latter might be workers whose jobs are retained while those of co-workers are cut when companies downsize. Newspaper accounts are replete with stories about the anxiety and guilt employees experience as a result of company downsizing and layoffs. The same could hold true for those who suddenly become millionaires in the stock market while their friends become impoverished.

Individuals and families intuitively compare the costs and rewards of alternative situations and choices, aided sometimes by computer simulations that make more precise comparisons possible. Illustrative are computer analyses of the costs and rewards of alternative tax and health care reform plans for families in different circumstances or the costs of health insurance premiums in 1994 compared with the year 2000. The concept of comparison-level alternatives as applied to family policy and family well-being might be defined in terms of the comparison of the rewards and costs associated with alternative constructions of policy solutions to family problems. Paul Krugman (2000), an economist who writes for the *New York Times,* noted that although making more money does make people a bit happier, its influence is swamped by being married. Similarly, having a job was more important to people than how much the job paid. What such findings could suggest for family policies that enhance family well-being are generous health and unemployment benefits, long mandatory paid vacations, a limit on working hours, high taxes, and government policies that limit work hours—in the manner of France and other European countries, whose family policies were discussed in Chapter 12. Such comparisons speak to the differences in values that make assessments of family well-being so situationally contingent.

Reciprocity

In exchange and choice theory, reciprocity as a norm takes precedence over the norm of profitability, or striving for the most favorable reward-to-cost ratio (Nye, 1979). Reciprocity implies interdependence, a spirit of mutuality, of taking other people into account in making choices, and is based on the assumption that *people should help, not hurt, others, especially those who have helped them in the past.* According to the reciprocity principle, individuals and families make choices, aware of the rewards and costs their choices entail for others and what others might anticipate as a result. Reciprocity, for example, may prompt some family members to seek treatment for alcohol abuse, aware of the costs their addiction entails for other members. Reciprocity also may prompt some members to comply with no-smoking ordinances and the 55-mile-per-hour speed limit because they are aware of the costs of noncompliance for others. The willingness of families to pay more in taxes in return for quality education, universal health care, and better police protection also could reflect such awareness.

Reciprocity often is expressed in gifts of philanthropy and the statements of donors who say they want to give back what they have received from others. Walt Disney's housekeeper of 30 years left her multimillion-dollar estate to poor and disabled children ("Disney's Maid," 1994). Her only son, in his mid-50s, lived in a home for the developmentally disabled persons. Her wealth was attributed to gifts of a few shares of stock for Christmases and birthdays that she saved, whose value in the 1990s skyrocketed.

A one-time welfare recipient who fought in World War II left $5,000 to the Hennepin County Department of Economic Assistance when he died (Brunswick, 1998). Commenting on the unusual nature of the gift, saying that no one ever gives money back to the government, his attorney said the man held deep convictions about the help he had received from the county earlier in his life. A widower with no children, he also left $5,000 each to his alma mater, South High School in Minneapolis, and to the alumni association of the Civilian Conservation Corps. He also left $5,000 to the Minnesota Department of

Veterans Affairs to pay back the bonus check he received after the war, saying the money should be used to help indigent veterans who did not qualify for other assistance.

Similarly, although on a much grander scale, one businessman secretly gave more than $150 million plus a business enterprise worth billions of dollars to Cornell University, saying he had never set out to create a fortune, only to make a good living for his family. As his fortunes grew, he said he never forgot that the reason that he, a poor boy from Elizabeth, New Jersey, made it through Cornell University was because of the G.I. bill and a scholarship he received when he was in school in his senior year. In addition to gifts of philanthropy and a willingness to pay more in taxes, reciprocity also finds expression in the willingness of people to expend considerable time and energy in working to improve policies and programs for families.

The case of Oseola McCarty, who died in 1999, warrants discussion here. Quitting school in the sixth grade to go to work, she never married, never had children, and never learned to drive. All she ever had was her work, which she saw as a blessing (Bragg, 1995). Comparing her situation to others, she knew that too many other black people in rural Mississippi did not have even that. Spending almost nothing, over the years her money—mostly dollar bills and change—grew to more than $150,000. More than she herself could ever use, Ms. McCarty gave her money to the University of Southern Mississippi to finance scholarships for black students. The first young person whose life was changed by her gift informally adopted Ms. McCarty. She visited her regularly and filled the empty space in the tiny woman's life—exemplifying what reciprocity is all about.

Indeed, the principle of reciprocity is now built into the social contract of American family policy, as readers may recall from previous discussion. People receiving benefits are now expected to provide some kind of community service in exchange for the help they presently receive or have received in the past, with potential multiplier effects for family well-being as defined here.

Family Well-Being:
A Standard for Constructing Policy Solutions to Family Problems and Assessing Their Implications

The concepts—the language, words, ideas—associated with exchange and choice theory are:

- Costs
- Comparison levels and comparison level alternatives
- Rewards
- Profitability
- Satisfaction
- Reciprocity
- Expectations

All can be used as conceptual tools to assess the implication of family politics for family well-being and also for constructing policy solutions that meet the standard of family well-being. The most obvious application of rewards and costs is that they can be used to assess the *relative rewards and costs* associated with a specific family policy or program. The greater the rewards associated with a particular policy or program and the lower its costs, the more likely it is to meet the family well-being standard. As noted earlier, this kind of assessment could be applied to the EITC for low-income families, to the subsidies some states provide to enable families with severely disabled children to care for their children at home, to the subsidies available for family members who take time off from work to care for a sick family member at home, to threats to cut off all assistance for families whose mothers do not comply with TANF work rules, and so on. It also could be applied to the analysis of the relative rewards and costs of the choices that face many workers and their families—whether to take higher pay *without* health benefits or lower pay *with* them.

The concept of *comparison level alternatives* might be used to compare the costs and rewards that alternative family policies and programs might entail for families and their well-being. Foster care reimbursement payments and TANF payments are examples. Others might be a comparison of the relative rewards and costs associated with the Supplemental Security Income (SSI) program for low-income adults and the TANF program for low-income families with children. The concept was illustrated in a comparison of the income gains of the richest American families with the rest of American families over time. In 1999, the richest top 1% of the American population had as many after-tax dollars to spend as the bottom 100 million (Shapiro & Greenstein, 1999). Because unfavorable comparisons tend to create dissatisfaction (which is the nemesis of a democratic society, as noted throughout this discussion), such comparisons could lead to a policy solution that would address the problem of such disparity. One small step in that direction was the legislation that Congress enacted in 1993 that limits corporate tax deductions for the compensation of executive officers to $1 million annually.

Profitability also might be used to assess family well-being. In terms of health care reform, for example, one of the conclusions that many reached was that the Clinton health care plan would *not* be profitable for them. From their point of view, it did not promise to provide rewards that exceeded its costs and absorb the uncertainties associated with it at the same time, and therefore did not meet the standard of family well-being.

And finally, *reciprocity* might similarly be used to assess the implications of family policies and programs for family well-being—in terms of their embodiment of the principle that they should help, not hurt, families. The principle could be applied to an assessment of specific policy solutions, like health care reform, welfare reform, crime, education reform, and others. Of all the concepts associated with exchange and choice theory, the implications of reciprocity for the construction of family policy are the clearest—based on the case examples in this discussion. People return the help they received earlier.

Summary

These are only some of the ways in which the concepts from exchange and choice theory can be used to assess family well-being. They elicit provocative questions within an interesting interpretative framework. The framework has the additional advantage of being parsimonious and easily understood. Viewing choices as situational, the framework incorporates the variety of situations in which individuals and families are required to make choices and in which family policies and programs may play a part. I used this framework to interpret the inverse predictive relationship between states' AFDC payments and teen birth-rates in the context of high poverty and unemployment rates and a sex ratio unfavorable to women (Zimmerman, 1988b). In this context, the rewards of teen parenthood were interpreted as being greater for teen mothers than its costs, including the cost of low AFDC payments. The framework seems to underlie many state welfare reforms, many of which seem to be based on the assumption that by upping the costs of welfare and making them ever higher, welfare mothers will take a job at *any* cost—which is almost, in fact, what has happened.

This concludes the discussion of exchange and choice theory. Before turning to Chapter 16 and a presentation of symbolic interactionism and family stress theory as frameworks that also can be used to assess family well-being, please review questions listed below pertaining to this chapter.

■ Some Questions for Your Reflection and Discussion

Family Systems Theory

1. According to Hill's formulation, what are the four properties that characterize systems?
2. What is the major underlying assumption of family systems theory?
3. What are the major tasks that families are required to perform?
4. What is the significance of the concept "role" in family systems theory?
5. What is negative feedback? Give an example.
6. What is positive feedback? Give an example.
7. What is meant by family boundaries? What are the implications of this term for family policy?
8. What is meant by "environment"? What are the implications of this term for families and family policy?
9. Identify some of the ways in which family well-being might be assessed from a systems perspective.
10. Analyze and interpret a newspaper article related to families and policy in terms of family well-being from a systems perspective.

Exchange and Choice Theory

1. What are the major assumptions underlying exchange and choice theory?
2. What is meant by rewards?
3. What is meant by costs?
4. Give examples of policies that represent both costs and rewards for families. Explain.
5. What is meant by reciprocity? How does it differ from profitability?
6. What are the implications of reciprocity for family policy? Give examples from the chapter.
7. Analyze a newspaper article related to families and policy from the perspective of exchange and choice theory. What conclusions do you draw from it with regard to family well-being, using the concepts from the framework?
8. What are the concepts that make possible the joining of family systems and exchange and choice theory? Explain. Give some examples.

Now let us turn to Chapter 16, where you will find other interpretative frameworks that also offer interesting ideas and concepts for thinking about family well-being and the construction of policy solutions to family problems.

Symbolic Interactionism and Family Stress Theory

Interpretative Frameworks for Thinking About Family Well-Being

☐ This chapter presents additional interpretative frameworks for assessing the implications of constructed solutions to family problems for family well-being. It focuses first on symbolic interactionism and then on family stress theory. Although persons working from a symbolic interaction perspective tend to focus on internal family relationships, the framework itself also speaks to the connections between families and the larger society. That it has not been used much for this purpose speaks not to the limitations of the framework but to the limitations of its adherents, including family policy scholars, who have not extended it to the realm of family policy. A similar statement could be made about the other family frameworks.

■ Symbolic Interaction

Symbolic interactionism deals with subjective experience within the context of *objective reality*. Both its assumptions and major concepts offer conceptual tools that can be applied to an assessment of family policies and programs. The major assumptions of the model as they apply to families are as follows:

- Individuals and society are two sides of the same phenomenon, each being dependent on the other (Cooley, 1902).
- People live in a symbolic as well as physical environment and acquire complex sets of symbols in their minds and cognitive frameworks (Burr, Leigh, Day, & Constantine, 1979).
- If people define their situation as real, it is real in its consequences (Thomas & Thomas, 1928).

- Interaction as a principle of social life applies not only to internal family relationships but also to the relationship between families and their environment (Burgess, 1926).

- Through such interactions, families and their members form a conception of themselves and become units with ties to the community and the larger society and, by extension, to political systems as well.

These assumptions underlie the foci of symbolic interaction as a family framework. Its central foci are socialization and personality organization as they pertain to the problems of individuals in society (Stryker, 1964), which here is extended to families. The concepts embedded in these assumptions are discussed below.

Socialization and Anticipatory Socialization

Socialization refers to (a) the interactional processes by which individuals acquire characteristic ways of behaving and (b) the values, attitudes, and norms of the larger society and the groups of which they are a part. The children of a homeless couple who returned a wallet with all its valuable contents to its owner were in fact being socialized by their parents about the values and norms their parents regarded important—in this case, honesty. Seen as developmental in nature, socialization occurs over time as individuals assume different roles and, through their interactions with others, learn the rights, obligations, expectations, and attitudes associated with their roles. As readers may recall from the introduction to Part IV, well-being is associated with early socialization experiences in families, schools, religious institutions, and the culture at large.

Parents are the primary socializing agents in a child's early life, so the role of parent is central to the socialization of children. Most parents learn parenting skills when they become parents. They bring to their role the values and attitudes they acquired earlier as members of their families of origin and also the larger society. For parents who do not develop parenting skills, they may learn them retroactively through programs designed to teach them how to parent, often as a consequence of policies mandating that they do so. Illustrative is a woman who, when her boyfriend was murdered, turned in despair to the Brooklyn Bureau of Community Service for counseling (Dugger, 1995). Scarred by severe abuse and relational instability, she was afraid her daughters, 1½ and 3, would be caught in the same cycle of violence. She said she used to spank her daughter and "mess" with drugs and probably would have given her daughters away, because she thought she would never be a good enough mother for them. Through group sessions at the agency, she learned how to be a better parent. To illustrate her newly acquired parenting skills, one recent afternoon when her older daughter started to whine for her favorite television program, the mother, instead of yelling at her to shut up, quietly flipped through the channels to show her that the program was not on. The daughter then climbed onto the mother's lap and, with her head down, drifted off to sleep.

Individuals who have not been socialized into the ways of the larger society inevitably experience difficulties in getting along in the society. Had the mother of the two daughters not gotten help, for example, she said she probably "would have kept on spanking them and doing drugs"—and her daughters in turn "would have done it to their children." In addition to families, other socializing institutions include day-care centers, schools, churches and synagogues, youth serving groups, work settings, the media, voluntary organizations, and associations of all kinds, including political parties. Readers may remember that one of the polls cited earlier indicated that respondents thought such institutions could do more to help families and teach family values.

Anticipatory socialization refers to the processes whereby individuals learn the norms, values, attitudes, and other aspects of a role *prior* to assuming the role. It also includes the processes by which individuals are taught what to expect when they enter a new situation, such as the first day of kindergarten or college, or marriage—or Congress. It functions to ease the strain and tensions that attend role transitions and first-time experiences. Examples of anticipatory socialization are classes in death and dying, birthing classes, infant care classes, parenting classes, and job skills training. Pertinent here is a proposal that people be licensed before becoming parents to show they have the requisite child-rearing knowledge. Take Your Daughter to Work days to acquaint daughters with what their parents do at work and with what the world of work is like also is illustrative of anticipatory socialization.

Some anticipatory socialization experiences have not succeeded in providing parents the skills and attitudes they need to perform their roles effectively (Iovine, 1996). Many child psychologists, for example, acknowledge that a lot of their "nothing but positive reinforcement" advice has paralyzed parents into believing that any kind of punishment will indelibly mark a child for the worse, failing parents and children miserably (Iovine, 1996). Although many parents were all too aware of the need to impose discipline at home and were desperately searching for some clarity on the subject, parents today, one psychologist said, acted more like amateur psychologists than authority figures. Here, readers will recognize the earlier discussion of family systems theory, using a similar example to highlight the leadership aspects of the parent role.

The Importance of Early Socialization Experiences

Socialization, as a principal means for transmitting the culture, is important in shaping attitudes and behaviors acquired early in life that persist throughout adulthood. Indeed, some of the attitudes people express related to family policies can be better understood by knowing something about their childhood experiences. One senator, who in early discussions on welfare reform suggested doing away with AFDC and placing children in orphanages instead, based his suggestion on childhood impressions: he said his grandfather had grown up in an orphanage and described it as a "wonderful" place (DeParle, 1994b).

The policy constructions of other political leaders can be similarly understood. Illustrative is Robert Reich's preoccupation with issues pertaining to unemployment and employment and the attitudes and values he holds about job security, economics, and politics. Secretary of labor in the early years of the Clinton administration, the roots of Reich's preoccupations lay in his early childhood experiences (Manegold, 1994) during the Great Depression when he and his family moved from one economically depressed city to another, living through the kinds of economic disruptions and convulsions he later would analyze and try to do something about.

Bill Clinton also underscored the importance of early socialization experiences when he called upon parents to become more involved in their children's education. Referring to his own mother and childhood, he said in his 1994 State of the Union speech that by turning off the TV, getting to know their children's teachers, helping their children with their homework, and teaching their children right from wrong, parents could make all the difference in their children's lives. Then he added he knew this was so because he himself had such a parent—his mother (Clinton, 1994).

Indeed, findings from a 12-year study showed that coaching parents and teachers on how best to encourage young children to become involved and interested in school and to teach them how to interact socially can have a significant long-term effect on their later behaviors and academic achievement (Brody, 2000). Parenting programs show parents how to reinforce desirable behavior, provide consistent discipline, and how to help their children succeed academically. By starting early—in grades one through six—to foster an interest in school and learning among children and to enhance their self-esteem, the study showed that many risky behaviors in adolescence could be averted and school performance and attendance all the way through high school could be improved. Such findings as indirect and direct measures of family well-being are indicative of the implications not only of early socialization experiences but also of this particular solution to a family problem for family well-being.

Role and Its Derivatives

Implicit in the concept of socialization are other concepts associated with symbolic interactionism: role and all its derivatives, which it shares with family systems theory. Role is defined as a relatively integrated set of distinguishable norms and behavioral expectations. This pertains to behaviors associated with positions such as father, mother, daughter, son, grandparent, sibling, partner, and worker (Stryker, 1964). This definition explains why it is said that people tend to view their social situation as a set of structurally created statuses or positions. Although roles, by definition, are shared expectations of behaviors associated with family positions, how they are enacted is the result of interactions that develop among persons in related roles and positions—in this case, among persons in related family positions.

Role expectations pertain to the rights and duties that give both form and content to family relationships, like parents and children. These are reinforced by a broad cultural consensus as to the rights and duties associated with different family roles and the sanctions that can be imposed if and when behaviors deviate too far from norms, as illustrated by the couple who left their two girls home alone while they vacationed in Mexico, leading to the girls' removal from the home by state authorities. A Wisconsin woman was jailed on suspicion of child neglect after taking her emaciated 15-year-old daughter, who weighed only 15 pounds, to an emergency room, where the girl was pronounced dead ("Wisconsin Woman," 1998). According to the grandmother, the girl never weighed more than 23 pounds and was about the size of a 6-year-old. The cultural expectation that parents provide financial support for their children and protect and guide them is codified into law. A man in Wisconsin, charged with a maximum penalty of 2 years in prison for every 6 months of missed payments, was sentenced to 24 years in prison for failing to pay more than $50,000 in child support ("Man Sentenced," 1999).

Role Taking and Role Making

Role behaviors may be culturally prescribed, but cultural prescriptions for role behaviors are subject to change. For this reason, role behaviors are also subject to change. Traditional views of family and child rearing, for example, have been challenged by the view (a) that children are autonomous beings, (b) that socializing children and attempting to mold their character are wrongful uses of parental power, and (c) that children should develop independently of the prevailing culture and even in opposition to it (Taffel, 1999). Thus, according to some experts, parents at both ends of the political and economic spectrum often are ambivalent about their leadership role and how to enact it. This is the consequence of cyclical waves of often contradictory advice they have received over the past 30 years. Trying out the latest one-size-fits-all theory, only to find it superseded a little later by a new popular orthodoxy, they have swung back and forth between permissiveness and toughness in their role behaviors.

Family role behaviors also are subject to variation, because within broad parameters, individuals have considerable latitude in how they perform their family roles. Persons enact their roles in ways that fit their interests and personality. Thus, it is not unusual to think of roles in terms of role taking and role making, whereby a person takes on a role as culturally prescribed and shapes it to his or her own situation and personality. The different ways people perform their parent role are illustrative.

Instructive with respect to role-making and role-taking is the role Elizabeth Dole played as president of the American Red Cross and wife of former Senate majority leader Bob Dole during the last half of the first term of the Clinton administration. Originally a Democrat, she became a Republican when she married Bob, a presidential candidate in 1996. Described as a woman of force and power, she was admired for *making a role* for herself as a strong, effective, nonthreatening leader (Chira, 1993a).

The role of Hillary Clinton as First Lady also is instructive. Except for a few feminist diehards, no one argued that she ought to discard the title of First Lady for that of First Spouse, but everything else was up for debate when she as the wife-mother-lawyer first assumed the role of First Lady (Barringer, 1992). The debate divided into two camps: one talked about the opportunities open to the country's most visible professional woman, and the other talked about the constraints on the country's most visible political wife. Others pleaded that she be left alone to ease into her job and *shape* it her own way. Becoming less visible after the failure of the health care reform effort she led, Hillary nonetheless continued to make speeches on matters of substance (Dowd, 1994). Having taken on the role of First Lady, she shaped it to fit her personality and interests—within the limits the culture allowed. The same was true of Eleanor Roosevelt and other First Ladies—and many other women as well—who took on a role as society prescribed it and, within limits, shaped it to make it fit them (Caroli, 1987).

Identities and Roles

LaRossa and Reitzes (1993) frame their discussion of roles in terms of identities, context, and interactions. Identities associated with roles are hierarchically arranged in terms of the salience they hold for persons, whether in relation to parents, children, or presidents. Salience suggests that people are motivated to excel in behaviors central to their role identities (McCall & Simmons, 1978), such as facilitating the deliberative processes that might have led to policy change in the case of Hillary Clinton in her role as First Lady and a leader of health care reform in 1994. Identities refer to the self-meanings of roles, as exemplified by the 77-year-old adopted woman who undertook a search for her 98-year-old birth mother—and identity. After an exhaustive records search, she found her identity and also her mother, who was alive in a nursing home and not buried in a cemetery, as she had expected. Some hold that adopted children are more likely to suffer from identity problems than children raised by biological parents, although others disagree.

Context here refers to culture. As an encompassing expression of a person's life, culture is seen as both the subjective and objective expressions of self, subsuming racial and ethnic rituals, symbols, language, and general ways of behaving (Geertz, 1973). It places individuals and families in a society with others on the basis of characteristics distinctly unique to certain people. Culture, in symbolic interaction, is seen to influence and shape behaviors, just as behaviors are seen to influence and shape culture (Stokes & Hewitt, 1976). A 98-year-old birth mother, who in 1913 had decided to give her baby up for adoption because the culture did not provide a viable alternative, is a decision the culture does not require of young birth mothers today, at least not as of this writing. Similarly, when a man was told by his attorney that he could probably collect alimony from his former wife, he was dumbstruck. That a man could collect alimony was not even an idea when the couple married in 1954.

Definition of the Situation

Another construct central to symbolic interactionism is definition of the situation, which also is central to many other frameworks, the social change framework presented in Chapter 7, for one. Definition of the situation refers here to the subjective meanings a situation has for families and their members, the situation referring to a number of stimuli that relate to each other in some special way (Stryker, 1964). Such stimuli here refer to family policies and programs. Because family members live in a symbolic as well as physical environment, the subjective meanings they attach to such stimuli are part of a complex set of symbols that have formed in their minds and cognitive frameworks (Burr et al., 1979). Decisions about what and what not to do—such as what policies and programs should be constructed to address family problems—are based in part on the symbols that make up the cognitive frameworks people acquire in their interactions with others. One- and two-parent families represent such symbols, as do "welfare," the Fourth of July, and Christmas.

The proposition that the definition of the situation influences its effects such that the two are congruent is associated with the proposition that if people define a situation as real, it is real in its consequences. As earlier discussion indicates, definitions and perceptions of situations prescribe how problems such as poverty and family dismemberment are constructed and addressed. Thus, during the Reagan years, poverty was redefined so that it no longer existed as a problem for families, justifying cutbacks in the funding of programs that dealt with it (Schorr, 1984). During the Clinton years, the problem was defined in terms of welfare dependency, justifying the elimination of entitlement to public financial assistance, the imposition of a 2-year time limit on such assistance, a strong work requirement, and a 5-year limit on such assistance over a lifetime. At the same time, the official definition of poverty has not changed in any substantial way since 1965, at the onset of the war on poverty. Under present guidelines, a family of four that earned less than $16,600 in 1999 was officially defined as poor. Under a proposal for new guidelines, a family of four that earned less than $19,500 would be officially defined as poor. Should the new guidelines take effect, the poverty rate would increase to 17%, almost 5% higher than the 12.7% that was officially announced as the lowest level in nearly a decade (Uchitelle, 1999), underscoring the fact that definitions do matter. The different definitions that people attach to the family and policy trends discussed earlier also speak to this phenomenon.

The debate over whether health care in this country represented a crisis, as President Clinton said it did, or was simply a problem, as Senator Dole said it was, similarly speaks to the concept of definition of the situation. Along this same vein, many college graduates in the early 1990s redefined the meaning of success to be consistent with their job-seeking experiences and prospects and lowered their job expectations accordingly (Berg, 1994). By the late 1990s, employers, desperate for staff, were offering job hoppers 10% to 20% raises over their current salaries, changing the meaning and definition of job quitting entirely (Clark, 1999). Although their mothers may have told job quitters that quitters never prosper, their children were redefining the meaning of job quitting in light of the job situation in the late 1990s.

Satisfaction

Satisfaction, another concept associated with symbolic interactionism, often is used as a measure of individual and family well-being (Andrews & Withey, 1976; Herzog et al., 1982; Zimmerman, 1992a). Satisfaction refers to subjectively experienced feelings of pleasure, contentment, or happiness, similar to the concept of rewards in exchange and choice theory. It is important to note that blacks typically report lower levels of satisfaction than whites, low-income unmarried women lower levels of satisfaction than high-income married women, and unemployed persons lower levels of satisfaction than employed persons (Zimmerman, 1992a). Given the trends reported in Chapters 3, 4, and 5, such associations are of particular relevance to this discussion. Also, in light of the contradictory views about HMOs, studies showing that the elderly poor in Medicaid-HMO plans were as satisfied with the care they received as those in fee-for-service plans (Slovut, 1994) are similarly relevant here.

Satisfaction also has been defined as the congruence between expectations and rewards. The story of Ms. McCarty, who had few expectations for the "good" life, is pertinent here. She derived great satisfaction just knowing that her gift of $150,000 to the University of Southern Mississippi to which reference was made in the previous chapter would help support the education of young black people with whom she wanted to share her wealth (Bragg, 1995).

The experiences of many refugee families coming to the United States speak to the lack of congruence between expectations and rewards and the dissatisfactions they have experienced as a consequence. One Chinese refugee came to the United States expecting to find what he heard everyone else had: a big car and house and a wonderful life. The reality, instead, was that having left his wife and 10-year-old son behind in China, he was homesick. He also was deeply in debt, having borrowed $27,000 and enduring a dangerous, 52-day sea voyage to come here (Kleinfield, 1993). Unable to find work, and with little hope of seeing his family for years into the future, he felt betrayed, and regretted his decision to leave his family and country. Some of the dissatisfactions expressed about existing health care arrangements are attributed, in addition to rising costs, to false expectations about the miracles that modern technology can perform in further extending life.

Relative Deprivation

Relative deprivation, which also is integral to symbolic interactionism, conveys the idea that how people evaluate their situation is partly a function of how they view it in relation to significant others, groups, or points of comparison in their lives. Its meaning is similar to comparison level, which is a part of exchange and choice theory. Families that view their situation less favorably in relation to others are likely to suffer from relative deprivation. Young parents in the early 1990s often compared their economic situation with their parents' situation in the 1960s and 1970s and evaluated their situation accordingly, namely as deprived, relative to their parents' situation at a comparable life-cycle stage. The situation was reversed in 2000. On the other hand, grandparents and great-grandparents who lived through the Great Depression often compare conditions of that period with those of the 1990s and may or may not conclude that they are deprived, relative to that period of their lives. Consider, for example, some data from Minnesota comparing aspects of family life in 1900 with aspects of family life in 2000, when divorce was seven times greater than in 1900, more women were in the paid workforce, and families were smaller (Peterson, 1999).

Language for Conceptualizing and Assessing Family Well-Being

All the concepts central to symbolic interactionism could be applicable to assessing the implications of policy solutions to family problems for family well-being:

- Socialization and anticipatory socialization
- Definition of the situation
- Role and all of its derivatives

  - Role performance or enactment (the ways roles are carried out)
  - Role behaviors (the behaviors associated with given roles)
  - Role competence (the effectiveness with which a role is performed)
  - Role ambiguity (the lack of clarity about a given role)
  - Role dissensus and consensus (agreement and disagreement about roles)
  - Role conflict (incompatible roles, conflicting role norms)
  - Role compatibility (congruence of role with personality and experiences of individuals performing it)
  - Role rewards (the satisfactions individuals derive from the role)
  - Role strain (the psychic tension associated with a role)
  - Role identities (the person's identification with a role)
  - Role salience (the importance of the role to the person)
  - Satisfaction and relative deprivation
  - Culture as context

Using the above listing, family policies and programs might be assessed in terms of the extent to which they socialize family members for roles they must perform to meet the requirements of the larger society. The better such policies and programs do in this regard, the more they can be said to promote family well-being. This includes school readiness programs and education of all sorts on all kinds of subject matter—reading, writing, and arithmetic; culture, society, history, political theory, family, computer usage, health, the environment—that prepare people for a long life of learning to help them move out of and into new and changing roles. Early socialization experiences might be assessed in terms of their influence on the attitudes and values people hold later in life with respect to family policies.

The importance of culture as context for assessing family well-being was evidenced in the strongly predictive relationship of past state teen birthrates on later state teen birthrates in a lagged dependent variable multiple regression analysis of state teen birthrates for 1970, 1980, 1985, and 1990 (Zimmerman, 1992a; 1994). This relationship was indicative not only of the strong feedback effects of the past on present behaviors (Phillips, 1988) but also of the cultural context in which such behaviors occur. To the extent such feedback effects are present, they contribute to the teen birthrate phenomenon. In short, teen birthrates, like divorce rates, are a part of the culture in which they exist. Culture and cultural sensitivity increasingly are recognized as important for family well-being, whether in relation to adoption, teen births, health care, education, elder care, or any other policy and program pertaining to families.

The concepts that probably can be used most directly and immediately for assessing family well-being from the perspective of symbolic interactionism are definition of the situation and relative deprivation. Particularly relevant for hypothesizing about family well-being is the assumption that the *outcomes of a situation are congruent with the ways they are perceived and defined.* Thus, in seeking to determine the consequences of the solutions that are constructed to deal with family problems in terms of family well-being, symbolic interaction directs observers to the ways families affected by the programs perceive and define them. If families do not perceive and define family policies and programs as fostering their well-being, they in effect do not. That so many mentally ill homeless persons seem to prefer living on the streets to living in a shelter could be viewed as a statement of their definition of the situation relative to housing policies in the United States. The same holds for determining the satisfactions that people experience by participating in specific programs or as a result of specific policies. It also holds for relative deprivation. The obvious implication with regard to relative deprivation is to either change people's expectations relative to family policies and programs or put into place policies and programs that match their expectations—or both.

Summary

The primary aim in using the conceptual tools associated with symbolic interaction would be to assess the extent to which family policies and programs promote individual and family well-being. Because of the failure to apply a symbolic interactionism perspective to the connections between families and family policies, analysis of their connections has suffered accordingly. Many so-called policy failures might have been averted had some consideration been given (a) to the ways in which families *themselves* perceived and defined their situation; (b) to the meanings *they* attached to their roles as defined by different policies; and

(c) to the satisfactions *they* derived from such roles, rather than always focusing on how policy makers, interest groups, and political elites perceive and define the situation. Proposals for health care reform incorporated cultural sensitivity as an evaluative criterion, suggesting that the subjective as well as objective aspects of policy, as experienced by families of all racial and ethnic backgrounds, were finally being taken into account in policy design. Such sensitivity seems to have become more widespread in other policy arenas as well.

Based on a different set of assumptions and emphasizing different aspects of family phenomena that also have relevance for assessing family well-being, family stress theory incorporates many of the concepts associated with symbolic interactionism but configures them differently.

■ Family Stress Theory

The family stress framework could be discussed under the rubric of symbolic interactionism because of the concepts they share, but the term *family stress* is of such common reference that it is being presented as separate from although related to symbolic interactionism.

The original family stress model, called a crisis model, was developed by Reuben Hill (1949, 1958), who saw demands arising from a stressor event as interacting with the family's resources for meeting them and the family's definition of the situation as determinants of a family crisis. This model is known as the ABCX model whereby:

- A is the stressor event that creates demands.
- B is the family's resources for meeting the demands arising from stressor event.
- C is the family's definition of the situation.
- X is the crisis.

The basic assumption of the model is straightforward: Depending on the resources available to families and their definition of the situation, the demands arising from a stressor event may or may not result in a crisis. Each of the concepts incorporated in this assumption offers a way of operationalizing family well-being in relation to family policy and other policy efforts. These concepts are discussed below and are illustrated by examples drawn from news articles.

The Stressor Event

Normative stressors

Not surprisingly, the stressor event is paramount in the family stress model. It is the A factor that is thought to create the demands that induce change in the family system that families are required to meet. The stressor event may be normative or nonnormative. A normative stressor is an expectable, taken-for-granted occurrence in the life cycle of the family, such as marriage, the birth of a child, the entry of the child in kindergarten, and so on. Although the sequencing of events (such as getting married and having children) may differ for individual families, such normative life-cycle events induce changes in families' roles, goals, values, and patterns of family interaction. Because of its increased frequency, some may view divorce as a normative family life event, and because of its decreased frequency, marriage a nonnormative family event.

Parent care, which is coming to be more pervasive, also is coming to be a normative family life experience and stressor, according to Robert Binstock, professor of aging, health, and society at Case Western Reserve University (Toner, 1999c). Indeed, two thirds of all women aged 40 to 59 participating in a survey conducted by the National Partnership for Women and Families said they expected to be responsible for the care of an elderly parent or other relative in the next 10 years. Generally perceived as a personal problem, a part of the life-course problem, Senator Patty Murray from Washington state said the difficulty of caring for parents was hard to talk about in public because of fears that parents would think they were a burden to their children. According to an expert in long-term care at the Urban Institute, people simply did not understand that the delivery and financing systems for long-term care could be improved. As Senator Russell Feingold, Democrat from Wisconsin, said, "It is something everybody can relate to—it involves their loved ones; it involves guilt, it involves their fears for the future, it involves the very heart of family values." Readers may remember from Chapter 2 that in order for an undesirable condition, like the demands of long-term parent care, to be considered a problem, a sizable proportion of the population must accept not only the depiction of the condition as a problem but also the solutions proposed to remedy it. Although a sizable portion of the population may accept the depiction of long-term parent care as a problem, it has not so far accepted solutions that have been proposed to remedy the problem.

Overburdened family positions in general are sources of psychological stress and familial stressors and strains. Based on telephone interviews with 170 parents and children and with 605 other working parents, Ellen Galinsky (1999) found that parents in the Washington and New York City areas experienced heightened levels of family stress as a result of long commutes, traffic congestion, the high cost of living, and heightened expectations for personal achievement. According to one father of four, life was 100% more stressful than it used to be, stating that in his firm, people worked 365 days a year, 24 hours a day (Grimsley & Salmon, 1999). One 7-year-old girl recalled that when her mother, a single parent, managed a retail store, she sometimes came home in the middle of the night and yelled at the cat.

Nonnormative stressors

Nonnormative stressors are unexpected and unanticipated life events such as car accidents, catastrophic illnesses, the birth of a severely retarded child, tornadoes, fires, car jackings, robberies, kidnappings, murders, earthquakes, job layoffs, and winning big-time in the lottery. Normative and nonnormative stressor events can coincide, such as when the birth of a baby occurs at the same time the baby's father is transferred to a job in a different city, or when a family member dies prematurely, or when a young father with a pregnant wife is paralyzed from the neck down after hitting the pavement head first when he descended a utility pole and was sent flying by a jolt of electricity (Johnston, 1997). Whether normative or nonnormative, such events necessarily create demands that induce changes in families' boundaries, roles, goals, values, and patterns of family interaction. Depending on the resources available to them, such demands have the potential of upsetting the balance that families require in order to function effectively. According to military experts, the primary reason for the increased violence among military families in the early 1990s was the increased stressfulness of military life, attributable to the downsizing of the military after the cold war ended, more frequent deployments, and ongoing uncertainty about life careers among military families.

Boss's (1999) work on boundary ambiguity as a source of family stress should not go unnoticed here. Although the term *boundary* is a systems concept, boundary ambiguity, which refers to uncertainty as to who is and is not in the family unit, has been found to be a family stressor. Boss measured the concept in terms of the physical presence but psychological absence of family members or, vice versa, their psychological presence but physical absence. As a concept, it can be usefully applied to constructed solutions to family problems in child custody and child support cases, as earlier trend data suggest. It also has application for stepfamilies and grandparent-maintained families, regardless of the absence or presence of parents. Depending on the situation, boundary ambiguity could be classified as either a normative or nonnormative stressor.

The situation of grandparent-maintained families is pertinent to the discussion of nonnormative stressors (Gilbert, 1998). One 68-year-old woman sobbed as she spoke of the trouble that she and her husband had in raising their 17-year-old grandson since he was 3. Their grandson had been caught stealing and was in danger of failing in school. The boy's parents were in the Marines; his mother used drugs and left his father for another Marine when the boy was 2. The father took care of the boy for awhile, but then the grandparents took him into their home. The grandmother attributed the boy's problems to the physiological effects of his mother's drug abuse during pregnancy and the emotional fallout of his abandonment. The grandparents took him to psychiatrists—her doctor, who said she was on the verge of a nervous breakdown, wanted her to go to a psychiatrist too, but she did not have the money. Even when money is not a factor, however, many grandparents deny their own symptoms, particularly when they are seeking custody of a grandchild whose parents are drug addicts, fearful that if they admit to problems, they will be denied child custody.

Family Resources

Family resources, the B factor, are those material and nonmaterial assets families can draw on to meet the demands of their situation. Such resources include:

- Family integration or cohesion that develops out of common interests, shared values, mutual affection, and financial interdependence
- Family adaptability, which refers to families' ability to overcome difficulties and change direction (Olson, Sprenkle, & Russell, 1979)
- Satisfactions families derive from meeting the needs of members and moving toward collective goals (Cavan & Ranck, 1938; Koos, 1946)
- The psychological and physical health of family members
- A structure organized to meet the needs and demands of members
- Time, energy, and money
- Negotiation skills
- Knowledge and information
- Friends and community

Readers may recognize from earlier discussion that such resources are the very ingredients of family well-being. Other resources include policies and programs families can draw on to meet particular demands, such as health insurance to meet demands arising from the illness or failing health of a family member, financial assistance to meet demands arising from spells of unemployment or a low-paying job, or child care to meet demands arising from parents' employment outside the home.

Whatever the resource, it must be relevant to the demands of the situation and for maintaining or restoring the necessary demand/resource balance for individual families. Grandparents, for example, were reported to be desperate for information and emotional support as resources for raising their grandchildren, according to the director of a Washington, DC-based national resource service (Gilbert, 1998). Some grandparents also said they would like more help and support from their doctors. One woman reported that when she suffered two minor strokes, her internist never discussed their possible connection to the problems she experienced in caring for her two grandchildren ever since her daughter was killed in a car accident several years earlier. In recent years, the biggest source of help for grandparents raising grandchildren has come from support groups. These groups, which have exploded in number, provide grandparents with a wide range of information, including updates on discipline techniques and the legal aspects of custody and guardianship as well as a place to vent their feelings—clearly resources for grandparent families.

The observations of Jonathan Kozol (2000), a journalist, are relevant with respect to the resources needed by families of persons suffering from Alzheimer's disease, as his 94-year-old father did. Expressing his gratitude for the $50 million research program that had been put in place to advance the disease's early diagnosis and investigate its possible prevention, Kozol reflected on his good fortune. He did not have to worry about suffering the serious financial worries that most children of Alzheimer's patients face, because his father's savings were sufficient to support the cost of his superb care—more than $100,000 per year—

and to allow his mother, who was 96 years old, to live with dignity in her own home. However, most families facing this dilemma were not as fortunate, he said. Medicare, a federally supported program for the elderly and a potential resource, cannot be used to pay for long-term care beyond 100 days and only in the aftermath of medical emergencies. Medicaid, which is means-tested and also a potential resource, cannot underwrite the costs of chronic care in nursing homes unless a family first exhausts its savings and the wife or husband reduces himself or herself to indigence. The solutions Kozol constructed to deal with these family stressors called for revising Medicare and Medicaid rules to cover long-term care for all who suffer from Alzheimer's without compounding the stressors their families experience by adding indigence to their grief and fear to their loneliness.

Definition of the Situation

The C factor, families' definitions and perceptions of the situation, is integral to family stress theory, just as it is integral to symbolic interactionism. This factor is based on the meanings families assign to the stressor event, the demands of their situation, and the resources they have available for meeting such demands, as well as their values and previous experiences in dealing with change. Persons testifying at congressional hearings about their families' experiences with HMOs were, in effect, giving their definition of the situation to congressional members vis-à-vis present health care arrangements. Here, Kozol's statement above is relevant.

The Crisis Situation

The crisis, the X factor, refers to (a) the incapacity of families to function as a result of a stressor event, (b) their lack of resources for meeting the demands of the stressor event, and (c) their definitions and perceptions of the situation. If families have the resources necessary for meeting demands and do not perceive or define the situation as a crisis, they may never experience a stressor event in crisis terms, despite the structural or operational changes it may impose on them. This is what is meant by the model: A, the demands arising from a stressor event interacting with B, the family's resources for meeting such demands interacting with C, the family's definition of the situation, and X, the crisis that may or may not occur as a result of the interactions between A, B, and C. Thus, whereas the 1994 California earthquake was not experienced as a crisis by one Los Angeles family, whose home was on the verge of collapse, many older people who lost treasured photos from their earlier lives experienced the 1993 floods in the Midwest as a crisis.

Laotian Refugee Families and Welfare Reform

As a constructed solution to a family problem, the passage of welfare reform in 1996, which denied food stamps and other federal assistance to the almost 2 million legal immigrants in the country, created a crisis for many Laotian families who came to this country as refugees after the Vietnam War (Weiner, 1997). From 1961 to 1974, the Central Intelligence Administration (CIA) had enlisted the mountain tribes of Laos as guerrillas in the Vietnam War to carry out U.S. foreign policy. As the Personal Responsibility and Work Opportunity Reconciliation Act (PRWORA) took effect, many refugees despaired; some committed suicide. Most were members of the Hmong tribe, migratory slash-and-burn farmers with only the rudiments of a written language. Left behind when the United States left their country in 1974, thousands of them, many physically or mentally wounded by war and exile, walked through jungles to refugee camps in Thailand, settling in California, Minnesota, Wisconsin, and a few other states where they have tried to overcome barriers of skill, education, language, and culture, far from their roots. Two Hmong women in California, one in Fresno and one in Sacramento, who committed suicide in 1997 left messages blaming the welfare cutoff for their actions, which pretty much told how they perceived and defined the policy solution that had been constructed to address a family problem. In Wisconsin, a Hmong elder also committed suicide that year. Despite strong cultural taboos, social service providers said suicide threats among refugees were common.

Thus, solutions like welfare reform can create demands that some families simply are unable to meet. By threatening the demand/resource balance that families require to function, such demands can overwhelm their adaptive capacities and result in a crisis. At the same time, in the case of the floods in the Midwest in 1993, the infusion of federal resources like low-interest government loans and housing, however inadequate, may have been sufficient to bring into balance families' demands and resources and thereby prevent a crisis for some. The same would apply to families living through the 1994 earthquake in Los Angeles or any other natural disaster.

A Minneapolis family of an 8-year-old boy born with extensive disabilities is another example, along with the Laotian refugees, of how the failure to provide the resources families need for restoring their demand/resource equilibrium can overwhelm the adaptive capacities of families. The boy required a variety of technological devices to assist him in breathing, moving, eating, and talking—in short, in living. In a letter to the editor, his mother wrote that because their insurance no longer would cover the costs of home health services for children with chronic conditions, an impending crisis was looming that threatened to destroy the family. Although the family had used its own resources before seeking outside help, the parents learned that without certain kinds of supports and resources, they could not meet the basic needs of their son and two daughters. Nothing prepared them, the mother wrote, for the realization that they would not be able to do everything parents needed to do to support a family and provide 24-hour medical care for their son at the same time (Westendorp, 1994), a problem for which a solution has not yet been constructed.

The Double ABCX Model

McCubbin and Patterson (1981) elaborated on Hill's original ABCX model by extending it over time to bring a postcrisis, longitudinal perspective to the framework. The Double ABCX model, like the original family stress model, has implications for the construction of policy solutions to family problems and family well-being. According to McCubbin and Patterson, four additional factors seem to play a role in influencing the course of a family's adaptation to a stressor event. These are:

1. The AA factor: additional stressors that impinge on the situation, called stress pileup
2. The BB factor: family efforts to generate new or additional resources to bring to bear on the situation
3. The CC factor: modifications in families' perceptions and views of their situation
4. The XX factor: family adaptation to the situation

In this formulation, family coping strategies are viewed as the BB factor—or AA factor—since particular coping strategies, such as alcohol abuse, would contribute to existing family strains and tensions and thus act as added stressors. Other coping strategies, such as therapy or volunteer work, might alleviate such strains and tensions, in which case they would generate additional resources—the BB factor. Illustrative are grandparent support groups that in the manner of the BB factor enable grandparents to tap into their strengths and cope more effectively with the demands of their situation and overcome the obstacles they face in their determination to do a good job bringing up their grandchildren. In an era of funding cutbacks for social services, coping strategies that rely on such resources could act as additional stressors that compound the problems and stress families experience, or the AA factor.

Case Examples

The story of a 49-year-old grandmother who became the mother of four of her grandchildren is illustrative of the Double ABCX model. One of the children, a 6-year-old girl, was born with cerebral palsy and additional motor damage to part of her brain, and a second, a 4-year-old girl, suffered from behavioral problems and hyperactivity, both because their mother was addicted to crack. The oldest child, a 7-year-old boy, was born before his mother's addiction and therefore had no behavioral problems associated with it (Holloway, 1993). When the mother no longer was able to care for the children, they became the grandmother's responsibility. Taking time off from work to care for the children, the grandmother subsequently lost her job. Then a second daughter, who had a

13-year-old daughter, was killed in a car crash. Multiplying the stressors the grandmother was experiencing, none of which was expected, the granddaughter also became the grandmother's responsibility. Together—in the language of the Double ABCX model—such stressors clearly represented a severe case of stress pileup.

Faced with these multiple stressors, the grandmother coped with them by contacting a community agency to bring the demands of her situation into better balance with her resources. The agency brought multiple resources to bear on the situation, arranging for a homemaker to help with the children, plan low-cost nutritious meals for the family, and escort the children to school every week-day morning. The homemaker's presence also helped the grandmother cope with the grief surrounding the circumstances that suddenly made her the mother of four grandchildren, shoring up her adaptive and coping capacities. Before receiving such support, she reported being on the verge of losing her mind and also the children—in short, on the verge of a crisis. The infusion of community resources helped restore her sense of confidence and control over her life, con-tributing to her decision to adopt her four grandchildren—the XX factor, bonadaptation. In redefining and reassigning meaning to her situation, the grandmother said that although she thought she had done all right the first time around, God had given her a second chance to be a mother.

Examples of both the ABCX and Double ABCX models are not hard to find. The story of Ms. Bowman began when she was living with six housemates and earning her keep by having conversations with male callers to a telephone sex line (Jay, 1995). Her daughter, Catey, was living in an unofficial foster home. The crisis in her life was precipitated by a paranoid depression, sparked, she said, by two puffs from a cigar wrapper filled with marijuana. She spent 17 days in the psychiatric ward at a Harlem hospital, an unpleasant experience except for a moment of clarity in which she decided to become a photographer. Taking charge of her situation—coping with it—she bought a camera, sought therapy, compiled a portfolio, and applied for public assistance and a 2-year photogra-phy program. Envious of her coping capacities, motivation, and energy, her housemates took her jewelry and clothes and then left her furniture on the side-walk, defacing it. After an accumulation of such stressors—stress pileup—she moved in with a high school friend, who sexually assaulted her. Taking only her camera, photographs, and two pairs of underwear, she slept in a chair at a drop-in center for the homeless, where she caught the attention of the director of a center for mentally ill homeless women.

An important resource, the director, Ms. Steele, invited Ms. Bowman to live at the transitional living center, which proved to be a stable nurturing place. In defining her situation to Ms. Steele, the mother said that if she did not do some-thing now, she could just end up spiraling down. She stayed at the center and commuted to the photography school for a summer program, where she learned how to draw, sculpt, and talk about art. Late in the summer, she felt secure and confident enough to leave. The center paid for her first month's rent. Then she received a $3,000 windfall from the IRS upon verification of her earned income tax credit (EITC), an additional resource. Other resources she brought to bear on her situation included a student loan of $8,550 and a $5 an hour work-study job. As evidence of her ability to effectively cope with her situation, her daughter was allowed to return home and enroll in an experimental public school near the school her mother attended.

October was difficult, because the tax refund was gone and because welfare workers said that anyone who could afford to attend a photography school could also buy food, although Ms. Bowman and Catey often went hungry. Their refrigerator contained only a vegetable or two. Strangers who passed through the student lounge which had become Catey's second home sometimes paid for her meals. Once, a school friend took Ms. Bowman to the supermarket and bought her $80 worth of food. November was better, because they finally received emergency food stamps and were able to celebrate Thanksgiving. Ms. Bowman, praised by her teachers for her creative eye and assured that once she mastered the techniques of the darkroom, her photographs would be good enough to sell, took stock of her situation. Defining it as pretty good, she told herself that she should be pretty proud of herself, that she had said what she was going to do and she did it, and furthermore she was good at it, loved it, got her daughter back, and had an apartment.

Empirical evidence for the coping effects of community resources comes not only from these examples but also from two different studies, one that examined the coping effects of adult day care on families with an elderly disabled member, and the other, the coping effects of a family subsidy program on families with a severely retarded child. In both cases, the coping effects of the programs as resources were significant, although they were greater for families experiencing multiple stressors (Zimmerman, 1988a). Other evidence of the coping effects of such resources comes from the Minnesota Family Investment Program (MFIP), a program that provides transitional cash assistance and child care and medical benefits on a sliding fee scale for up to 6 months for families until program participants find a job that pays a living wage (about $7.50 an hour for a full-time job for a parent with one child) (Schimke, 1995). According to one mother whose young child developed asthma following his parents' divorce and required around-the-clock attention, resulting in the loss of her $22,000 a year job, MFIP gave families a chance to start over in life, a chance to catch up, a chance to restore their balance—in short, a way of coping with and adapting to their situation. In defining her experience as a participant in the program, the mother said that although she knew it was not government's responsibility to save people from their mistakes, MFIP made the state a better place in which to live—and hers a better life to live—consistent with family well-being as the goal of family policy.

Language for Conceptualizing and Assessing Family Well-Being

The basic assumption of the family stress framework is that depending on the resources available to families and their definition of the situation, a stressor event may or may not result in a crisis situation. The Double ABCX model extends this basic framework over time. The concepts that are integral to the basic ABCX model are as follows:

- Demands or stressors
- Normative and nonnormative
- Resources, material and nonmaterial
- Definition of the situation
- The crisis situation

The concepts integral to the Double ABCX model also include:

- Stress pileup (multiple stressors or demands)
- Additional resources
- Redefinition of the situation
- Coping and adaptive strategies

Thus, to the extent family policies and programs represent stressors, as in the case of welfare reform and Laotian refugee families, they can be seen to diminish family well-being. To the extent they represent resources, they can be seen as enhancing family well-being. But much depends on how families themselves define what is a stressor and a resource for them. In the case of health care reform, existing health care arrangements clearly act as a stressor for many—of crisis proportions for some, for others, a resource. The questions that then arise are: What characterizes those policies and programs that serve as resources for which families? How can the resource potential of such policies and programs be strengthened, particularly for families for whom they may have served as stressors in the past?

■ Summary and Conclusions

As with all the frameworks, assessment of the implications of family policies and programs for family well-being, from the perspective of family stress theory, needs to be policy and program specific. Although generalizations might be made about the implications of broad policy trends for different groups of families, family policies and programs—like families themselves—are not all the same. They have different objectives and functions. Family stress theory adds to the perspectives that can be used for identifying which family policies and programs promote family well-being, which do not, and for which families, and under what circumstances

This brings the discussion of symbolic interactionism and family stress theory to an end. In the next and final chapter of family frameworks, the discussion turns to conflict theory, an underutilized framework in general and, to date, a neglected framework for thinking about the implications of family policies and programs for families and their well-being. Included in the chapter is a presentation of feminist and cultural theories both as they relate to conflict theory, but more important, as they relate to family policy and family well-being. But before turning to Chapter 17, as in all the preceding chapters, please review the following questions.

■ Some Questions for Your Reflection and Discussion

Symbolic Interaction

1. What are the major assumptions underlying symbolic interactionism?
2. What are the major concepts associated with symbolic interactionism?
3. Context in symbolic interactionism is similar to what concept in systems theory?
4. What is the significance of *definition of the situation* for family policy?
5. What are the different derivations of role in symbolic interactionism? Give some examples.
6. What is the meaning of socialization?
7. Define "satisfaction" as used in symbolic interactionism. What is its significance for family well-being—and also family policy?
8. Define "relative deprivation." What is its significance for family well-being and family policy?
9. Analyze a newspaper article related to families and policy from the perspective of symbolic interaction. What conclusions do you draw from it about the implications of the policy for family well-being? Why?

Family Stress Theory

1. What are the major assumptions underlying family stress theory?
2. What are the major concepts embedded in family stress theory?
3. What is the significance of *definition of the situation* in family stress theory?
4. In what other frameworks is definition of the situation important?
5. What are the implications of family stress theory for family well-being?
6. What is the relationship of family stress theory to family systems theory?
7. What are the similarities between family stress theory and exchange and choice theories?
8. What is the major difference between the ABCX and Double ABCX models for family well-being?
9. Explain the relevance of both stress frameworks for family policy.
10. Analyze a newspaper article related to families and policy from the perspective of family stress theory. What conclusions do you draw from it about the implications of the policy for family well-being? Why?

CHAPTER 17

Conflict Theory, Feminist Theory, and Cultural Theory

◻ Although conflict theory is seldom used as an analytic or interpretative framework in family policy, it incorporates many concepts that are relevant for these purposes—substantively and practically. Thus, although the term *conflict* may connote nothing but problems for families, other terms incorporated in the framework such as *negotiation* and *bargaining* speak to ways of resolving such problems. As a conceptual framework, conflict theory probably is a more accurate depiction of the family/policy connection than nonconflict models. In any case, I offer it here in this final chapter of family frameworks for readers to consider in thinking about the implications of constructed policy solutions for families and their well-being. Because both feminist and cultural theories offer interpretative frameworks that contribute to a fuller understanding of some of the substantive issues underlying conflict theory, they will be discussed after conflict theory.

■ Conflict Theory

According to many conflict theorists, conflict occurs and exists because parties to the conflict differ on matters they regard as important and are motivated to act in ways to protect and promote their interests (Farrington & Chertok, 1993). This observation applies to conflict not only within families but also between families and the systems families interact with, much of the latter arising from the policy outputs of these other systems. The assumptions that underlie conflict theory and call attention to facets of family and social life that other family frameworks do not are as follows:

- Family members differ in interests, motivations, and preferences.
- Hierarchical structures of family relationships are the basis of differences among family members.

- Hierarchical structures of family relationships are based on age and sex.
- Hierarchy connotes differentials in power, authority, and privilege.
- Conditions of scarcity create a competitive zero-sum structure whereby gains for one party result in losses for other members.
- A competitive zero-sum structure produces behaviors of confrontation, threats, promises, and appeasement.
- Because the relationship of family members is symbiotic, family members are willing to compromise on matters of difference.
- For conflict to end, parties to the conflict must find a solution that all the parties will accept.
- Solutions for ending such conflict require negotiation, bargaining, compromise, and persuasion.
- Rules are required to protect the interests of contending parties.

The concepts embedded in these assumptions are discussed below and again are illustrated by examples drawn from newspaper articles.

Conflict and Competition

Differences Among Members

Conflict is defined in terms of differences among members—whether these pertain to differences in values, attitudes, or interests. Conflict may manifest itself in a variety of intrapsychic, emotional states and specific conduct behaviors (Farrington & Chertok, 1993). Behaviors may range from expressions of mild disagreement to hostile verbal exchanges or the physical abuse of one family member by another. Conflict may occur over any number of issues. For one couple, it involved the medical treatment of their 11-month-old baby girl, who was born with most of her brain missing and who therefore would never grow up to be able to think or feel ("Mom Fights," 1993). The mother wanted to keep the baby alive by using extraordinary measures to keep her breathing during life-threatening emergencies; the father did not, viewing such measures inappropriate on both ethical and medical grounds. Differences over medical treatment for the baby arose not just between the mother and father but also between the mother and hospital staff, who, like the father and for the same reasons, opposed the treatment the mother wanted.

Differences reported between Elizabeth and Bob Dole over the 1993 National Service Act, which provides 2-year education awards for persons volunteering in national service, also are illustrative. Ms. Dole, as president of the American Red Cross, favored the measure, but her husband, as Senate minority leader, portrayed it as a threat to the American taxpayer (Clymer, 1993c), referring to it as yet another example of Democrats' tax-and-spend philosophy. Ms. Dole, however, in a letter of support to sponsors of the measure, wrote that it would enlarge the means by which individuals could make a difference in their communities and renew the ethic of civic responsibility.

As has been noted, just as differences can arise between members within families, they also can arise between families and the systems external to them that families interact with. Illustrative is the conflict that arose between the mother and hospital staff over the application of extraordinary medical procedures to prolong the life of the baby in the example cited above. The sources of such conflict are the same as they are for internal family conflict: differences with respect to the respective parties' goals, values, and interests. Like intrafamilial conflict, there is no paucity of issues over which such differences may arise intersystemically: abortion, euthanasia, religious practices, school prayer, child discipline, school dress codes, school curriculum issues, the treatment of severely defective newborns, parents' rights, sexual orientation, domestic partnerships, and so on. Such differences, like differences that arise within families, may manifest themselves in a variety of behaviors and emotional states: the bombing of family planning clinics, the harassment of gay and minority families, the sexual harassment of women and young girls, and altercations between parents and school authorities over such school-related matters as school curricula, sports, student attendance, school safety, and so on.

Intersystemic Conflict:
The Case of Mr. Manning and Workers' Compensation

Illustrative here is the case of Mr. Manning, the young father who had been paralyzed from the neck down ever since a jolt of electricity sent him flying head first onto the pavement as he was descending a utility pole (Johnston, 1997), whose story readers may remember from Chapter 16 as illustrative of nonnormative stressors. Thirty-five years later, Mr. Manning, at age 60, was still trying to collect workers' compensation benefits for the accident. Requiring around-the-clock medical care for 35 years, his was the longest unresolved workers' compensation case that most people could remember. Although the state workers' compensation board had granted him awards, the largest of which was $1.2 million, these had been tied up in litigation. At the heart of the matter was the refusal of Utilities Mutual Company to pay for the care that Mr. Manning received from his wife; a registered nurse, her time was consumed with his care. Although Utilities Mutual voluntarily paid Mr. Manning $350 a week for almost 30 years, it stopped payment for around-the-clock medical care. When he asked for an explanation, he was told that the nonpayment was a mistake that would be corrected with a check sent to him by overnight mail. A week later, he still had not received a check. Already deeply in debt, the Mannings said they faced imminent bankruptcy and the loss of their house, which was built especially for them.

Charging the insurance company with knowing that if he did not get the medical care he needed, he would die sooner rather than later, Mr. Manning asserted that "they" wanted him to die; his lawyers agreed with his assessment. The company's lawyer, however, denied the charge, saying the issue of whether the insurance carrier was obligated to make any payment at all was a legitimate legal issue. The issue centered on whether Mr. Manning could count the value of the nursing services his wife provided as part of Utilities Mutual's award (i.e., whether the value of the services she provided, for which Mr. Manning testified he did not pay and had no legal obligation to pay, thereby reduced the company's award). As Mr. Manning's wife pointed out, had she worked outside the home as a registered nurse all these years, the company would have had to pay other nurses for her husband's care, although, as she went on to add, even when outside nurses were needed, the company still refused to pay. The court in resolving the conflict ruled in favor of Mr. Manning, saying that because he could no longer afford the physical therapy he needed, his health had deteriorated as a result, and the company's objections were without merit.

Contemporaneous Intra- and Intersystemic Differences

Sometimes conflict may characterize intra- and intersystemic relationships simultaneously, as in the case of the mother of the 11-month-old baby whose treatment plan for the baby was opposed by both her husband and the hospital staff. A very different case, also illustrative of simultaneously occurring inter- and intrasystemic conflict, highlights the role of power differentials in situations of conflict. In Atlanta, almost a year after commissioners in one suburban county passed a resolution condemning homosexuality, the commission chair's daughter announced she was a lesbian and called for the county to rescind the resolution (Applebome, 1994). Referring to the resolution as a source of unnecessary pain and division within her family and the county, she said that because of it, she felt unwelcome and afraid to come into the county that was her home. Her father, the chair of the commission, said in response that though he loved her and admired her courage, he did not approve of her lifestyle and would not ask the commission to reconsider the resolution. He added that as her father, he was aware of the impact his position on the issue would have on the family.

Also illustrative of contemporaneous intra- and intersystemic conflict involving hierarchical relationships and power differentials is a child custody case in Texas involving a child of Mexican parents (Verhovek, 1995). The custody hearing that followed a tangled divorce case concerned the father's request for unsupervised visitation rights. The father's complaint was that their daughter could not speak much English. The mother, who was bilingual, said she spoke Spanish to their daughter at home to help her be bilingual. Court transcripts showed that though the daughter could understand English, she was more proficient in Spanish. The transcripts also showed that the mother and the judge clashed on several matters. The mother, an American citizen, charged at one point that the judge was against her because she was Mexican. The judge retorted that the father also was Mexican but spoke English. He said, "Now listen to me and listen to me good. That child must speak English," and added that because the child did not speak English, the mother was "relegating the child to the position of housemaid" when she grows up, charging the mother with child abuse.

Just as conflict and competition can occur contemporaneously within families and between families and other systems on an individual family level, they also can occur between different groups of families on a community level. One of the assumptions underlying conflict theory is that conditions of scarcity create a competitive zero-sum structure in which gains for one member constitute losses for others (Sprey, 1979). The situation pertaining to day care in the United States is illustrative. Nationally, the number of children whose parents need subsidized day care for their children far exceeds the number of subsidized day care slots, creating a zero-sum competitive structure whereby one group of families wins and another loses access to subsidized day care. Although changes in welfare law requiring welfare mothers who receive benefits to work have greatly increased the need for child care, these welfare mothers are not the only mothers desperate for day care. In one New York neighborhood where most parents lack financial and family resources, the city gave welfare parents priority over working parents for day care slots at city-financed centers (Sexton, 1997). Existing tensions between poor welfare mothers and poor working mothers, who at best coexisted in a state of ambivalence characterized by resentment and sympathy, were exacerbated by the competition for scarce child care assistance.

Symbiosis and Symbiotic Relationships

Conflict theory assumes that conditions of scarcity create a competitive zero-sum structure such that gains for one member constitute losses for others, and that situations are structured such that members can either gain at one another's expense or win or lose as a group (Sprey, 1979) (as for example, in disputes over an inheritance). It also assumes that symbiosis—members' need for each other—creates a willingness among members to compromise on matters of difference.

Symbiosis is seen to reduce and minimize competition among family members. Illustrative is a conversation overheard between two brothers, ages 10 and 8. The older brother was irritably complaining to the younger one that the younger one followed him around wherever he went and wanted whatever he had. The older brother then explained to a third person who was with them that whenever one or the other got in trouble, each would cover for the other (Wilkerson, 1993).

Mother-daughter relationships also are illustrative of symbiotic relationships in competitive situations. According to family therapists, competition between mothers and daughters is an integral part of family life, especially at holiday time (O'Neill, 1993). An example is the mother who, after declaring pride in her daughter's achievements, added that of course the daughter did things on a far different scale with her two children than the mother had done with her nine. Helping the mother and daughter involved helping them reconcile differences arising from the competitive structure of their relationship and the two different worlds in which they lived. The daughter had more disposable income and less disposable time than her mother, who, like others of her generation, was less likely to have worked outside the home when she was raising children.

The story of Jermal is illustrative of the strength of the influence of symbiotic relationships in situations of conflict. Jermal was an 11-year-old boy who had been abandoned as a baby and placed in several foster homes before finally finding a foster mother who promised to make him her son (Swarns, 1998). He loved her so much that he told no one until months later that she had begun to beat him, slamming his head against the wall if he did not bring his books home and his father beating him with a belt more times than he could count. Although the boy begged not to be taken from his foster parents, the authorities took him from them anyway. Trying to find his way back to them and his best friend, an 18-year-old tabby cat, Jermal ran away from four foster homes. Although he had no actual memory of his birth mother, he said that ever since he first saw his foster mother, she reminded him of his mom.

Conflict Resolution

According to conflict theory, in order for conflict to end, a solution must be found that the parties to the conflict will accept, even when the underlying competitive structure of their relationship remains. One of the ways of resolving conflict in such situations is through the redefinition or restructuring of their relationship, thereby allowing the parties to manage it better. In the case of Jermal, it was competition from the birth of his foster parents' new baby that created havoc in the household and caused Jermal to steal and curse in order to reclaim his foster parents' attention (Swarns, 1998). If competition is to be completely eliminated, however, one of the competing parties must remove himself or herself from the situation—or be removed from it. Many child custody cases are of this nature. A former husband who abducted his two children from his former wife's home and flew with them to Algeria was convicted of depriving his former wife of her parental rights. He was released on condition that he end all contact with the children, removing him from the situation entirely (Duchschere, 1993).

In another case involving adoptive and unmarried birth parents, the birth father, after waging a successful court battle to take his biological son away from the adoptive parents, moved out of the family home without his son (Johnson, 1997b). Although he, not the biological mother, was awarded custody of their son, the boy lived with his biological mother, baby sister, and grandmother. In fact, the mother had surrendered her parental rights to the boy when he was born, and she had put him up for adoption without consulting the father; she had told the father the baby had died. The father said the separation was amicable and the couple was cooperating in raising their children, adding that although it was painful for him not to be with his children, he believed the separation—his removal of himself from the situation—was the best way of resolving the couple's apparent differences.

Persuasion, Negotiation, and Bargaining

Conflict theory focuses not only on conflict per se but also on the ways order is created and maintained within families—and society—whether through co-ercion and constraint or through persuasion, negotiation, bargaining, and compromise. Readers will recognize these terms from several of the policy frameworks discussed earlier. All—negotiation, bargaining, compromise, persuasion—represent ways of trying to influence the direction and outcome of contested decisions and issues. The attorney involved in the case of Jermal per-suaded the court to have the boy returned to his foster parents (Swarns, 1998), explaining that the father had been raised by parents who relied heavily on cor-poral punishment. Although the foster mother said she tried to persuade her husband not to hit Jermal, he insisted it was the only way to make him behave. The boy's lawyer said the boy should go home, that the foster parents had learned their lesson, and that Jermal desperately needed them. The city, in agree-ing that keeping Jermal from his foster parents would only further harm an already emotionally fragile child, effected a resolution to the conflict.

Persuasion is considered appropriate for resolving differences among mem-bers sharing similar world views. Family members often use persuasion to gain agreement on matters they may disagree on, such as vacation destinations and schedules. Persuasion involves getting others to accept one's point of view. Children use persuasion to get parents to do what children want all the time. Counseling is a form of persuasion (Gross, 1993) that was recommended as a way of addressing the resurgence of unsafe sexual behaviors among gay men. Lawyers use persuasion in pleading the cases of their clients before juries. In arguing the case, the lawyer representing the two Menendez brothers charged with the first-degree murder of their parents tried to persuade a California jury that the brothers should not be held accountable to the cold standards of a legal system that lagged behind psychological and social theories of behavior.

Negotiation and bargaining usually precede overt conflict, although they sometimes are concurrent with it. Negotiation, which includes all forms of bar-gaining, is an exchange process designed to effect agreement between contend-ing parties on matters of dispute and disagreement. In the case of two-career couples involving husbands who retire before wives, retirement prompts the renegotiation of marital roles, with husbands taking on more of the cooking and housework and wives taking on less (Lewin, 1993). However, if the parties in a bargaining situation view themselves as adversaries, each will seek to gain advantage over the other, as many divorcing couples in fact do.

Rules for Protecting the Interests of Contending Parties

Rules are viewed as necessary to protect the interests of parties involved in conflicts. Although rules too can evoke conflict, they also can help bring conflict to an end. One family, in challenging the rules of aesthetics of their housing asso-ciation, painted their house a color that violated the rules of the association, whereupon the association took them to court. The issue at stake was not so much the aesthetic correctness of the color, according to association officials, as the enforcement of the agreement the family and all other homeowners signed when they moved into the development. To terminate the conflict, the judge in the case ordered the family to submit a new color scheme, basing his ruling on the rules of agreement the family had signed at the outset.

The Special Case of the Thomases

The case of the Thomases also is illustrative of the use of persuasion in conflict resolution. For more than 20 years, Mr. Thomas, a 68-year-old former smoker, begged his 65-year-old wife to stop smoking and then sued her to get her to stop (Johnson, 1997a). He went to the U.S. District Court in Chicago, contending that his wife violated the Clean Air Act. Seeking an injunction to make her stop smoking, Mr. Thomas said he wanted the government "to protect me against having to grow old alone, to protect me against the loss of the love and support and companionship of the woman I love." The public nature of his plea mortified his wife, who had smoked for almost 50 years. The suit evoked negative feelings in the community. His car was vandalized and scratched with the words "Stop trampling on our constitutional rights." But Mr. Thomas stuck to his legal guns, using the Clean Air Act as leverage. He told the court that his mother, who had been a heavy smoker, died of heart disease; his father, who also smoked heavily, suffered a stroke that left him bedridden for 7 horrible years, unable at the end to "even hear me tell him I loved him." Before a decision had been reached on the injunction, however, Mr. Thomas returned to federal court asking that his suit be withdrawn, saying his wife agreed to stop smoking. Having persuaded her to stop smoking, the Thomases left the courthouse holding hands, their conflict resolved, thanks to the Clear Air Act as a constructed solution to the problems of many families.

Power, Authority, and Privilege

Power as a concept is as central to conflict theory as the concept of conflict itself (Farrington & Chertok, 1993). Concepts such as *power system* (Goode, 1971) and *structure of dominance* (Collins, 1975) suggest that family systems are characterized by significant differentials in power (Farrington & Chertok, 1993). The result is a stratification system characterized by the differential treatment of family members, an unequal distribution of resources, and the organization of activity around the interests of those family members with the most power, namely fathers and husbands. Readers will recognize that stratification and differential treatment based on position are characteristic not only of families but also the larger society, age and sex being the structural foundations of both stratification and the differential treatment of family members. Illustrative are curfew laws requiring teenagers to be home by a designated time. Civil libertarians traditionally condemn curfews as an unconstitutional denial of the right of assembly, one attorney likening curfews to house arrests based on chronological age (Hanley, 1993b).

Power connotes the ability to effectively control the situation, whether the situation involves people, information, services, or material goods. Illustrative is the case of the father cited earlier who, as chair of the county commission, refused to rescind a resolution condemning homosexuality, as his daughter had requested. Parents increasingly complain about their loss of control over negative influences such as violence and drugs impinging on the lives of their children. Many refugee parents complain about their loss of authority and control of their children as the latter become assimilated into American society. One Laotian father in fact said his children did not respect or listen to him (Mydans, 1994). A murder charge facing his 19-year-old son was indicative of just how much control the father had lost. The boy dropped out of high school after the ninth grade, worked off and on at odd jobs, and traveled out of state. The parents lost track of him until the police knocked on their door one day, telling them their son was wanted for murder.

Demands for compliance imply potential, not actual, control of the situation, such as when parents march to demand an end to violence in their neighborhoods. It is only when demands are met and their potential realized that actual power or the ability to control the situation becomes known. Power in essence frames the relationship between governments and families in areas such as taxes and child protection, governments having the power to secure parental compliance with laws pertaining to the payment of taxes and the education and protection of children (as evidenced in the case of the bilingual mother) and indeed in many of the examples included in this discussion. Because governments have such power, the court's ruling on the case involving the recalcitrant family and the housing development association strengthened the latter's authority to determine and enforce prior agreements pertaining to rules of aesthetics. State truancy laws are similarly used to strengthen the authority of school officials to enforce parent responsibility for ensuring their children's school attendance on a regular basis (Smothers, 1994).

Generally viewed as a resource, power is associated with both authority and privilege. According to news accounts, Elizabeth Dole was said to view power as a resource to be used for positive purposes and important for making a difference and having a seat at the policy table (Chira, 1993b). However, because the term is associated with authority and privilege, and also abuse, it has negative connotations. This has led to what some perceive as the weakening of power derived from authority that stems from hierarchy and position, such as the relationship between parent and child, teacher and student, doctor and patient, and so on, and a general undermining of respect for all authority. This was discussed earlier in this chapter in relation to the tensions between a democratic political order and authority associated with hierarchical position.

Although authority based on position connotes hierarchical relationships, such as the case of the judge in relation to the bilingual mother, privilege, on the other hand, refers to competitive advantages that some members in families enjoy and others do not. Privilege connotes special access to scarce resources, such as information or money or both. Prior to the enactment of the 1993 Family and Medical Leave Act, which treats mothers and fathers alike, maternity leaves often were cases of contested privilege because they allowed one class of worker, women, to be treated differently from others—men. The same applies to couples *without* children who have contested what they perceive to be a privilege awarded to couples *with* children following passage of the Act. In some sense, the husband of the bilingual mother was privileged in the contest for custody of their child.

Confrontation, Appeasement, Threats, and Promises

Just as conflict connotes power, it also connotes confrontation and appeasement. Confrontation involves aggressive, assertive behaviors aimed at getting others to behave as the aggressor desires, often taking the form of punishment or deprivation when the aggressor's demands are not met, as in abusive situations. Illustrative is the woman who was forced to marry her first cousin and try to bear his children, despite doctors' warnings that inbreeding would have genetic consequences (Sontag, 1993). After eight pregnancies and the loss of five children with major birth defects, she had two blind sons and one healthy son who survived. Although practically a prisoner in her own home and subjected to repeated spousal rapes, she did not feel she could appeal for help from her family, who had made plans to have her murdered when she tried to date another man prior to her marriage.

Also illustrative is the story of a 26-year-old Dominican woman whose husband in fits of rage would beat her and throw her out of their home in Manhattan, then apologize and ask her to return, always under the veil of a threat that made it impossible for her to refuse (Thompson, 1999). He told her that if she did not come back, he would call the police and have her deported, that he as a legal immigrant had more rights than she did because she was not a legal immigrant, and that he could take their son away. Advocates in cases involving immigrants say spousal abuse is a serous problem for women who do not have legal residency in the United States but are married to someone who does, making them especially vulnerable to their husband's threats. The situation was worsened when immigration laws were tightened, making permanent residency in the United States more difficult to obtain. The problem was compounded in 1998 when Congress allowed the law permitting immigrants entitled to permanent residency to stay in this country while waiting for green cards to lapse (a green card certifies that an immigrant is a permanent resident). One proposed solution to the problem was the Violence Against Women Restoration Act of 1999, allowing battered immigrant women to stay in this country while waiting for their green cards.

Although both threats and promises are coercive and rely on shared understandings to be effective, threats are different from promises in that threats convey some type of punishment while promises are regarded as constructive, positive reinforcers of behaviors. The judge who ruled on the case of the family that challenged the housing association's authority to determine the development's rules of aesthetics, for example, threatened the parents with imprisonment or fines of up to $2,000 a day unless they complied with their prior agreement. The judge in the case of the bilingual Mexican mother threatened that if the girl did not do well in school, he could remove her from her mother's custody, saying it was not in the child's best interest to be ignorant.

Summary

Conflict theory is useful as a framework for understanding the hierarchical structure of family conflict and its bases: differences in interests, values, and goals. Differences among members are seen as attributable in part to hierarchical structures that motivate members to act in ways that advance or protect their interests. Conflict theory provides the conceptual tools not only for understanding the structural roots of family conflict but also for understanding the processes involved in its resolution—whether such conflict is internal to families or between families and other social systems with which they frequently interact: schools, insurance companies, businesses, social agencies, hospitals, workplaces, and so on.

As noted at the outset, conflict theory as it applies to families and policy provides ways of interpreting and defining facets of family and social life that otherwise might not be identified, or if identified, not defined in ways that would necessarily allow for the satisfactory resolution of differences within families and between families and the systems with which they interact in a manner consistent with family well-being. The concepts that conflict theory incorporates:

- Conflict and competition
- Differences in interests, values, and preferences
- Hierarchy
- Zero-sum competitive structure
- Power, authority, and privilege
- Assertive behaviors (confrontation, appeasement, threats, promises)
- Symbiosis
- Conflict resolution
  - Negotiation
  - Bargaining
  - Compromise
  - Persuasion

Readers will remember these concepts as also part of some of the *policy* frameworks discussed earlier, particularly game, interest group, and elite theories. Conflict theory, as it applies to families, differs from these policy frameworks in terms of its focus on *families* and the hierarchical structure of family relationships, including family relationships with other systems. Conflict theory highlights conditions of scarcity as part of the context in which conflict is apt to occur in families and between groups of families and points the way for the resolution of such conflict. Through the resolution of conflict surrounding hierarchy and conditions of scarcity—namely through processes of negotiation, bargaining, compromise, and persuasion—it further suggests how the goal of family policy—family well-being—might be furthered. Many family policies and programs, such as marital rape laws, child custody rulings, surrogate parent rulings, the expansion of marital property to include the education of a spouse in divorce settlements, and no spanking laws in fact embody rules and procedures needed not only for protecting the interests and safety of contending parties but also for effecting the resolution of conflict.

■ Overriding Issues:
Gender, Race, Ethnicity, Social Class, and Culture

Although I have referred to issues of gender, race, ethnicity, social class, minorities, and culture in my presentation of conflict theory, I discuss them here specifically in relation to feminist and cultural theories, both of which provide additional and complementary concepts for thinking about the implications of family policies for family well-being. They also act to further sensitize readers to the structural roots of conflict within families and between families and other systems.

Feminist and Marxist theories are rooted in many of the same intellectual foundations as conflict theory. Marxism focuses on the hierarchical nature of class relationships and consequent location of individuals and families in the socioeconomic-political structure. Feminist theory, on the other hand, focuses on the hierarchical nature of male-female relationships and the subordinate position of women in families and the larger society. The women's movement has helped to sharpen awareness of the conflict between the interests of women as autonomous beings and the interests of families as collectivities. The women's movement also heightened awareness of the contradictions in intimate family relationships within hierarchical family structures. A gender-based hierarchical structure was the context of one couple's differences over how strictly to observe the Sabbath, the husband insisting his wife accede to his wishes on the matter and the wife refusing to do so.

Feminist Theories: Liberal, Socialist, Radical

Feminists have raised questions about concepts most family scientists take for granted—marriage, roles, family, and power—thereby demonstrating that the deep ideological division between public and private is at its foundation a division based on gender, in which men are equated with public institutions such as the market and the state, and women with the private family. Feminists assert that the boundaries between public and private are social constructions of the mind, charged with the politics of social class, gender, and race.

Just as family is the central organizing concept of family frameworks, gender is the central organizing concept of feminist theory (Osmond & Thorne, 1993). Although social and political thought is important in feminist theory, feminist theories use gender to demonstrate the social construction and exaggeration of differences between women and men and the use of such distinctions to legitimize and perpetuate power relations between women and men—often through some of the solutions constructed to address family problems, namely through family policies and programs that disadvantage women. Feminist theories, which see women as agents, actors, creators, and participants in the making of culture and history, at the same time see gender as a social structure and a fundamental basis for social inequality and stratification; they regard gender relations as power relations, with women devalued and subordinated to men. Recall the cases cited earlier of the Hispanic mother who was ordered by the male judge to speak only English to her child at home, the women legislators who were not allowed to be heard at a hearing chaired by Senator Helms, and the immigrant women held hostage to the demands of their husbands.

Empirical support for feminists' interpretation of gender as social structure and a fundamental basis for social inequality comes from the differences that were found between states with higher and lower teen birthrates. These differences were in part based on sex-gender. In states where there were more women relative to men, poverty rates were higher, educational levels lower, and teen birthrates higher (Zimmerman, 1992a, 1994, 1997b). Interpreting the teen birthrate phenomenon in part as a function of gender as social structure and a basis for social inequality finds support from a study of women and education in developing countries showing similar patterns (King & Hill, 1993).

Despite the centrality of gender to all streams of feminist thought, the different streams—liberal, radical, socialist, cultural—have different emphases. Liberal feminists argue that because women and men are endowed with the same rational and spiritual capacities, gender should not be a basis for denying women full citizenship rights or access to the same educational and economic opportunities as men. Women's rights advocates also argue that women have the same right to insurance coverage for contraceptives and fertility drugs as men have for Viagra (Goldberg, 1999a). In this regard, liberal feminism shares the perspective of this discussion, which holds that the two spheres, families and the polity, are integrally and inextricably related, both empirically and conceptually. Given its emphasis on gender equality, it may be assumed that liberal feminism would assess the implications of family policies and programs as constructed solutions to family problems for family well-being accordingly.

In this regard, gender differences in the treatment of irregularities surrounding the citizenship and Social Security status of domestic help hired by three nominees for public office during the early years of the Clinton administration— two women for attorney general and one man for secretary of defense— provided grist for feminist arguments that women are treated differently from men. In this case, feminists argued that the women were held to a higher standard and subject to an additional layer of questioning during the nomination process (Manegold, 1993).

Radical feminists, in contrast, emphasize patriarchy as the source of women's oppression (patriarchy being defined in terms of male power, dominance, and claimed authority over women) (Osmond & Thorne, 1993). Male power, they argue, lies at the heart of the social construction of gender. In contrast to liberal feminists, who look to reforming the patriarchal system, radical feminists hold that the patriarchal system cannot be reformed and therefore must be destroyed, pointing to pornography, prostitution, sexual harassment, rape, heterosexuality, abortion, contraception, sterilization, and new reproductive technologies, such as Norplant, as examples. Whether or not the case of Lorena Bobbitt, who sliced off her husband's penis after what she said were years of sexual and other abuse, is illustrative of radical feminism may be an open question, but symbolically, at least, it gets to the heart—or bottom—of the patriarchal system. According to a spokesperson from the National Center for Men, the Bobbitt case was a direct result of feminist teachings that men are the natural oppressors of women ("Spousal Assault," 1993). In the case of the male judge who admonished the bilingual mother who spoke Spanish to her daughter and whose husband spoke English that she had better listen and listen good—that the child must speak English—the assumption is that the views of both the judge and father as oppressors prevailed, based in part on male dominance and position in the socioeconomic-political structure.

Socialist feminism draws on Marxist frameworks to emphasize the material basis of women's subordination and the organization and exploitation of women's work. In contrast to liberal theorists, Marxist feminists believe that equal opportunity is not possible in a class-based society. Socialist feminists emphasize social class as a fundamental source of oppression but have revised and expanded Marxist theories to demonstrate the interaction between capitalism and patriarchy, or the sex-gender system in producing women's subordination. It may be assumed that all streams of feminism would assess family well-being in terms of gender equality, with radical feminists assessing it also in terms of women's values and the freedom of women from male domination and socialist feminism in terms of the reduction or elimination of the gross gender-based income disparities resulting from current political-economic arrangements.

Cultural Theories: Race, Ethnicity, Minorities

Race, ethnicity, minorities, and culture are the organizing concepts of cultural theories, just as gender is the organizing concept of feminism. In fact, black scholars take issue with the core assumption of feminism with regard to female oppression (Dilworth-Anderson, Burton, & Johnson, 1993). Arguing that feminists' definition of oppression is really suppression, they hold that oppression represents almost totally restricted access to the benefits, rights, and privileges that a society provides for its people, whereas suppression does not. Thus, these scholars conclude that the agendas, priorities, and relationships of suppressed and oppressed people are different. They also raise questions about the constructs of marriage and family, which they say are infused with moral and religious meanings that create dissension with regard to the forms and functions of marriage and family and the latter's contribution to the well-being of individuals and the larger society (Aboud, 1987).

Seen as a cultural reality (Gossett, 1965), race is defined as a cultural construction of identity based on a set of descriptors (Dilworth-Anderson et al., 1993). It is a social, not a scientific concept, Dr. Craig Venter, head of a genome corporation in Maryland, said, adding that, genetically speaking, there is only one race—the human race (Angier, 2000). Traits most commonly used to distinguish one race from another—such as skin and eye color or the width of the nose—he went on to explain, are controlled by a relatively few number of genes that have been able to change rapidly in response to extreme environmental pressures during the short course of human history. And so, Dr. Venter continued, equatorial populations evolved dark skin, presumably to protect against ultraviolet radiation, and people in northern latitudes evolved pale skin so as to better produce vitamin D from pale sunlight. Dr. Douglas Wallace, a professor of molecular genetics at Emory University School of Medicine in Atlanta, added that because our whole social structure is based on visual cues, the criteria used for race are based entirely on external features that humans have been programmed to recognize as a way of distinguishing one individual from another—for purposes of oppression and domination, some might add.

Ethnicity, on the other hand, is defined as an experientially-based identity that is always in process as part of the social self and the means by which individuals and families develop a sense of peoplehood and community with others in the same group (Gelfand & Barresi, 1987). According to Dr. Sonia Anand, an assistant professor of medicine at McMaster University in Ontario, ethnicity is a broad concept that encompasses both genetics and culture. Ethnicity, rather than race, she says, offers a way of joining questions about biology, lifestyle, language, diet, and customs that allows for a valid way of looking at group differences (Angier, 2000).

The term *minorities* is defined as a collectivity of people assigned or relegated to a lower social position than others in society. It connotes oppression, suppression, and discrimination as phenomena that individuals and families who make up the collectivity experience in almost all aspects of their lives. Illustrative again is the case of the bilingual Mexican mother, who, after the judge threatened her with the loss of her parental rights for speaking Spanish rather than English to her child, charged that he was against her because she was Mexican. Her case aroused fear among other Mexican immigrants in the community who also spoke Spanish to their children that their children could be taken from them too.

Culture represents the encompassing expression of a person's life (Dilworth-Anderson et al., 1993). It is an expression of self that is both objective and subjective, subsuming racial and ethnic rituals, symbols, language, and general ways of behaving. Culture based on those characteristics that are distinctly unique to certain people places a family in a society with others. Cultural approaches to the study of minority families include the *cultural equivalence* approach, the *cultural deviance* approach, and the *cultural variance* approach. The cultural equivalence approach emphasizes the features that minority families share with mainstream white families; the cultural deviance approach emphasizes variations that distinguish minority from mainstream families, interpreting these as negative and pathological (much as the judge in the case of the bilingual Mexican mother did); the cultural variance framework emphasizes the cultural basis for interpreting such qualities from the perspective of the particular cultural group, and calls for culturally and contextually relevant interpretations of the family lives of blacks and others (Dilworth-Anderson et al., 1993). The latter lends itself to a *cultural equity* frame of reference, whereby people are seen as having the right to maintain, choose, and create cultural alternatives (Lomax, 1968). A cultural variance or equivalence frame of reference could serve as a basis for assessing the implications of family policies from the perspectives of different cultural groups.

A cultural approach to the assessment of the implications of constructed solutions to family problems is particularly useful for better understanding the behaviors of families from other countries whose cultural norms may be at odds with those in the United States. When these are written into law, the transgression of such norms can be serious for transgressing families. The cases of three families from other countries—one of which were tourists—are illustrative here (Ojito, 1997). The one involved a Russian couple who left their 4-year-old daughter home alone to go out dancing. Another was a Danish mother who left her 14-month-old daughter in a stroller outside a restaurant while she was inside eating. The third was a Russian emigré who left her 7-year-old son to play in a park while she went to work. The parents all told the police they only were doing what was the norm in their country. Their lawyers claimed theirs were not criminal cases but incidents of cultural differences that required understanding, not punishment.

In New York, where the three incidents occurred, people in the community were not persuaded that a cultural variance or cultural equity frame of reference applied. They said the behavior the parents exhibited was called child endangerment and was therefore illegal. As one social worker said, "Cultural differences are beautiful, but they have nothing to do with the law," adding that there could not be one set of laws for Americans, another for immigrants, and a third for tourists. She also pointed out that the context for behaviors is different in the United States, explaining that in many places in Europe, children go out to play by themselves because of the basic trust among adults that no one would want to harm a child. The societies in which they live are safer, she added, and more community oriented than in the United States. Separating a child for a small cultural transgression may be extreme, she said, but people new to this country should adapt to its laws.

■ Summary and Conclusions

Feminist theories and cultural theories, as interpretative frameworks, offer interesting and important concepts for assessing the implications of constructed solutions to family problems, making more pointed some of the bases for such constructions and implications. They both offer concepts that can be used to assess the implications of family policies and programs for family well-being, either in conjunction with conflict theory or with some of the other frameworks included in this discussion—or by themselves. These include:

- Gender and gender relations
- Subordination, oppression, and suppression
- Social stratification
- Patriarchy (i.e., male power, dominance, and claimed authority)
- Feminists: liberal, radical, socialist, and cultural
- Race and ethnic minorities
- Cultural relevance
- Cultural deviance
- Cultural variance
- Cultural equivalence

This concludes the discussion of conflict theory, feminist and cultural theories—and also the presentation of family frameworks that can be used to guide readers' thinking about the implications of family policies and programs as constructed solutions to family problems for family well-being. Chapter 18 is a summary of where we've been in this journey of family policy and where the journey seems to be taking us as a nation. Chapter 19 talks about the application of the frameworks as guides for policy practice. But before turning to these chapters, please review the following set of questions about this chapter.

■ Some Questions for Your Reflection and Discussion

1. What are the major assumptions underlying conflict theory?
2. Identify the major concepts associated with conflict theory.
3. What is one of the major dilemmas of competitive structures for family members?
4. What role does government play in conflict theory in relation to families? Give examples.
5. What are some of the major tools of conflict resolution?
6. What are the implications of conflict theory for family well-being and family policy?
7. What are the bases for conflict, whether between family members or between families and the larger society?
8. How does such conflict theory relate to feminist and cultural theory?

9. Analyze a newspaper article that is relevant to both families and policy from the perspective of conflict theory. What conclusions do you draw from it about family well-being?

Issues: Gender, Race, Ethnicity, Minorities, and Social Class

1. What are the major assumptions underlying each of the streams of feminist thought?
2. Contrast liberal feminism with radical feminism.
3. How might family well-being be operationalized from the perspective of liberal feminism?
4. How might family well-being be operationalized from the perspective of radical feminism?
5. What are the assumptions underlying cultural theory?
6. What is the meaning of cultural equity?
7. What is the meaning of ethnicity? How does it relate to symbolic interactionism?
8. What are some of the criticisms that black scholars have expressed about family science?
9. Taking these criticisms into account, how can they be used to inform family policy?
10. How can understandings derived from feminist and cultural theories be used to inform other family frameworks? Give examples from the perspectives of men, women, African Americans, Native Americans, and people from other ethnic groups.

PART V

Summary, Conclusions, and Policy Practice Implications

☐ Part V concludes the discussion of this book. Chapter 18 presents an overall summary of the preceding 17 chapters and suggests future directions for family policy in terms of the democratization of family well-being. Chapter 19 talks about the implications of the preceding chapters for family policy practice, drawing from the conceptual frameworks presented in the discussion and also from experience-based observations and research. It notes that although many challenges confront family policy practitioners—such as public disengagement from policy issues and the decline in social capital—family policy practitioners are in the strategic position of being able to increase engagement in policy issues related to families and the nation's social capital at the same time. The chapter concludes by suggesting that by linking the concerns of individual families with the concerns of the larger society, government plays an integrative role that can be seen as a form of social capital that is necessary for the construction of policy solutions to family problems that enhance family well-being.

CHAPTER 18

Adding It All Up

Family Policy Past, Present, and Future

☐ Having come this far in the book, readers know that despite the earlier doubts of some policy scholars about the applicability of the term *family policy* to the United States, family policy as a concept and field of legislative activity, law, study, programs, and practice is alive and well in this country today. As a term, it has moved from being for all practical purposes nonexistent just a few decades ago to being the basis for full-fledged academic programs in the 1990s and keywords for at least two Internet Web sites. Its application as a term has helped to expose the family dimensions of the policies that governments enact, making clear that although most policies may not be explicit as to their family objectives, probably all policies affect families directly and indirectly, intentionally or not—regardless of jurisdictional level. If anyone should choose to challenge these assertions, he or she has only to consider the frequency with which presidential candidates in the 2000 election connected the term *family* to such policy issues as prescription drugs, health insurance premiums, education, safe communities, violence in TV programming, abortion rights, family leave, and child care. Al Gore used the term 29 times in his speech accepting his party's nomination for president. Definitions that illuminate different aspects of family policy include:

- A perspective for thinking about policy in relation to families
- Everything governments do that affect families
- A series of interrelated choices designed to achieve some family goal or objective
- A temporarily settled course of action related to families and their problems
- An agreed-upon course of action related to families
- Collective choice with regard to the achievement of family goals and objectives

Regardless of definition, the goal of family policy is family well-being.

Given the value traditions that have guided policy development in the United States since the country was founded—minimal government, private property, and individualism—the emergence of words such as *family* and *family policy* in policy discourse may be surprising to many and offensive to others. Factors contributing to the emergence of family policy in policy discourse and also to its development as a field of activity and study in United States today include:

- Alva Myrdal's work in the 1960s warning that any country that leaves to chance or mischance an area of social reality as important as family exposes it to the untrammeled and frequently undesirable consequences of policies enacted in other areas
- Daniel Patrick Moynihan's advocacy in the 1960s of a national family policy for the United States
- The expansion of government programs pertaining to families from the 1960s onward (and of course Social Security in the 1930s)
- The burgeoning interest of family scientists and scholars in the 1970s in evaluating the impact of government programs on families
- Political events such as the Mondale hearings on the state of American families in the 1970s and the 1980 White House Conference on Families
- An ever-expanding literature on the topic
- The efforts of advocacy groups interested in different aspects of family life and family policy

As earlier discussion of the White House Conference on Families served to highlight, family policy as a domain of knowledge producing and legislative activity is constituted of many hotly contested issues. In contrast to the 1960s, when the term *family policy* first emerged in policy discourse and problems such as poverty were unlikely to be couched in family terms, by the 1990s, they often were. Moreover, although such discourse in the 1960s was premised on the assumption that government had a responsibility for helping individuals and families meet their needs, by the late 1990s and into the new decade of the new century and new millennium, such discourse was premised on the assumption that individuals and families were responsible for meeting their own needs. The context of such discourse in the 1990s also was different from the 1960s—it was taking place in a new wired economy of highly integrated global markets. Moreover, the country was experiencing a budget surplus rather than a budget deficit, as had been the case in the past. Thus, family policy discourse, like family policy itself, was different in the 1990s from what it had been earlier in the country's history. What remained the same were the contradictions and ambiguities embedded in family policy and family policy discourse and the ambivalences such activity and discourse evoked.

In a very real sense, government itself—by its funding of academic training programs in family impact analysis, the White House Conference on Families, the research endeavors of family policy scholars, and an ever-increasing number of family and family-related programs—fostered the development of family policy as an increasingly differentiated field of study and activity. It spans the life cycle from birth to death in the areas of health, education, social services, housing, employment and manpower, income maintenance, family law, and taxation, keeping in mind its historical roots—Elizabethan, or English, Poor Law—which, though not recognized at the time as being a family policy, in fact was, and not a supportive one at that.

As a subcategory of social policy, family policy is a product of modernity, which rests on three conceptual foundations: progress, universality, and regularity/predictability. Increasingly, however, the domain of family policy has come to reflect features that characterize postmodernism, which in contrast to modernity emphasizes difference, particularity, irregularity, and diversity. Such characteristics are increasingly embedded in family policy discourse and in family policy itself, as evidenced by the latter's increasingly differentiated organization, structure, and practice. Indeed, if it is true that family policy is nothing less than social policy except for its focus on the family dimensions of social policy, then the differentiation of family policy from social policy, like many of the programs and practices that constitute family policy, is itself a postmodern turn.

Postmodern family policy analysis emphasizes language and discourse in subjectively shaping institutions and the politics surrounding families. Like policy discourse in general, family policy discourse is embedded in the politics of family policy and in the knowledge-producing activities that constitute and accompany it as well as in the everyday practices of many institutions. Family policy discourse refers to the written and verbal communication of thoughts and ideas about the problems families experience in relation to society and policy solutions to them. In this discourse, the problems of families are paramount themes (problems here refer to troubling conditions related to families). Because focus on a name for a troubling condition that threatens family well-being signifies a problem, the naming of family problems in family policy discourse is symbolically important.

Problems come into discourse in family policy largely because they reinforce ideologies about their causes and the role of government in addressing them. If diversity is a hallmark of postmodernism, a diversity of meanings is inherent in every policy solution constructed to address a family problem. Meanings are a function not only of the context in which discourse related to families and policy occurs but also of the disparate needs of interested individuals and publics. The contradictions embedded in constructed solutions to family problems and the chronic inability to resolve them are made tolerable by the ways in which language, cognition, and social conditions shape and reinforce each other.

In a paradoxical way, the diversity that postmodernism symbolizes and that threatens to jeopardize a shared view of the common good and family well-being as the goal of family policy could help to effect, in diversity, the universality that has eluded public and family policy for so long in this country, particularly as distinctions become increasingly finer along with efforts to address them.

Just as the meaning of family policy and the issues associated with it are hotly contested, so is the meaning of the term *family*. Notable here too are the diversity of constructions available for depicting families and the diversity of perspectives that underlie such constructions: historical, organizational, sociological, cultural, feminist, economic, psychological, biological, and so on. As an institution, family has evolved over time from what has been characterized as a "little commonwealth" to "separate spheres" to "companionate" to isolated "togetherness" to an expression of personal freedom and autonomy and, finally, to diversity, suggesting that like the world in which it is embedded, family life is always in flux, evolving and changing over time. Although such change has evoked fears and worries about the family and its future—which in fact have been present since the country was founded—such change is attributed to many factors, among which are changes in the economy, technology, demography, and the role of women. Regardless of which explanation of family change readers accept, all explanations connect family instability to postmodern conditions of instability, fluidity, and impermanence. Nonetheless, because of the high value most people place on families, most scholars believe the family as an institution will survive into the future, just as it has in the past, although in different forms.

As noted earlier, the United States today is a society without a clear set of family ideals and values. As a result, many Americans, confused and fearful about the changes that have occurred in family lives and uncertain about the policy solutions that should be constructed to address conditions they are unsure are problems, are groping for a new paradigm of American family life. Given the changing meanings of family, the changing context of family life, and the profound meanings most people assign to families, it is not surprising that the term *family values,* like the term *family policy,* has emerged in policy discourse related to families.

Despite being subject to political use and misuse, the term "family values" has meanings for people that go beyond family to encompass relationships, feelings, and ideas that people associate with family but are not confined to family. The feeling that family is primary as one definition of family values has been operationalized in nationally representative surveys as respecting one's parents, taking responsibility for one's actions, having faith in God, respecting authority, being married to the same person for life, and leaving the world in better shape. Such traditional family values were blended with newer expressive family values, such as giving emotional support to family members, respecting one's children, becoming more skilled at communicating feelings, respecting people for themselves, and living up to one's potential as an individual.

Contributing to the newer expressive values are the social movements of the 1960s and 1970s, major historical developments like the Vietnam War, Watergate, the assassinations of John F. Kennedy, Robert Kennedy, and Martin Luther King Jr., technological developments, and the affluence effect, which has led to expanded choice and greater personal freedom. The affluence effect refers to people's definitions and interpretations of their material situation—that is, their constructions of their newfound prosperity. People have been predisposed to effect a value synthesis of older, more traditional values and newer, more expressive ones because values of personal freedom and expanded choice as products of the affluence effect have proven to be at odds with their need for enduring commitments. With respect to family policy, the affluence effect has manifested

itself in changing conceptions of fairness as a value/goal in the case of both welfare reform and taxes—as discussion below will show.

Embedded in the term *family values* as a well-entrenched culturally determined sentiment that is produced and reinforced by societal institutions—
family, schools, religion—and major historical and economic developments are
deeply held beliefs about family. Although almost evenly divided about whether
government should or should not promote traditional values, most survey
respondents thought the country would have fewer problems if traditional family values were emphasized more. Despite historical traditions that promote
other values—individualism, private property, and minimal government—and
liberal political theory that ignores family—and the ideological meanings the
term *family values* connotes to some—to most it simply means that family
comes first.

Attitudes that people hold toward the economy, government, and family as
more specific expressions of values provide the impetus for action and thus, like
values, are important in the construction of policy solutions to family problems.
In the context of greater prosperity at the end of the 20th century, the affluence
effect also could be seen in survey findings showing that most people in the late
1990s defined *the good life* in terms of making money, not in terms of a satisfying job, as they had in the past. Being more materialistic, they also thought our
economic system was basically fair and provided plenty of opportunity for people to get ahead and "make it," despite the widened income disparities to which
reference has been made throughout this discussion. Indeed, most survey
respondents were not disturbed about such disparities and did not think government should redistribute wealth and income by imposing heavy taxes on the rich
to address a condition they did not name as a problem. The percentage of survey
respondents holding such attitudes, which pertained regardless of income, race,
and ethnicity, was the same in 1998 as in 1939. Although most survey respondents were aware of the prevalence of poverty in the United States in 1998, an
increasing number thought people were poor not because of circumstances
beyond their control but because they did not do enough to help themselves.
However, the world clearly looked different to white and black respondents
with regard to these matters. Most survey respondents nonetheless thought government had a responsibility to take care of those who cannot take care of themselves, despite the emphasis they placed on self-reliance.

Paradoxically, more people regarded themselves as lower class/lower income
in 1998, when times were prosperous, than in 1939, when the country was just
emerging from the Great Depression, and a smaller percentage identified themselves as rich, suggestive of the potentially operative influence of relative deprivation, a concept in symbolic interactionism, or comparison level alternatives, a
concept in exchange and choice theories.

Coinciding with the increased emphasis on self-reliance in the 1990s was a
loss of confidence in government's capacity to solve problems. Such loss of confidence was attributed to the series of traumatic events the country experienced

since the 1960s identified above and polarizing attacks by politicians who regularly denigrate government, and a mass media that thrives on scandals, in addition to government wrongdoing and incompetence. Nonetheless, despite the negative views they held toward government, people in the 1990s demanded more from government and an expanded public agenda.

As to family matters, survey findings show that almost everyone in the 1990s claimed to hold old-fashioned ideas about marriage and family for themselves. Married men and women reported being happier than those who were divorced or never married and had fewer emotional and health problems, marriage seeming to act as a prophylactic, protecting people against such problems. Yet, almost everyone agreed that marriage as an institution has grown weaker, attributing increased divorce primarily to the failure of couples to take marriage seriously. Although most thought divorce created a problem for children, an increasing percentage of people in the 1990s did not think couples should remain married if they were unhappy with each other. Men more than women favored divorce as a solution to unhappy marriages.

Challenging critics who charge parents with self-centeredness and parenting failure are survey findings showing that most people in 1997 said that having children was important to them, that watching children develop and grow was one of life's greatest pleasures, and that being a parent was more important to them than it was to their parents when they as children were growing up. Still, most thought parents needed help in raising their children. Also contrary to prevailing assumptions about the isolation of contemporary families, most said that grandparents, other relatives, and friends were very involved in their children's lives.

Because attitudes toward government, family, and the economy are central to family policy and its constructions, providing an impetus for action in concrete situations, I did a content analysis of congressional roll call votes on legislative provisions related to families for selected years in the 1980s and 1990s (1983, 1985, 1991, 1993, 1995, 1996, 1997) to determine (a) whether they in fact reflected some of the attitudes expressed in the survey findings reported here, (b) whether more family conditions were constructed as problems in need of solutions in the 1990s during the Clinton years than in the 1980s during the Reagan years, and (c) whether the nature of such solutions may have changed over time. Using the term *family* and words associated with it to identify such provisions, the analysis was in keeping with postmodernism's emphasis on language.

As hypothesized, in both the House and Senate, many more family conditions were constructed as problems in need of solutions in 1993-95 than in 1983-85, as people in fact demanded. Moreover, the nature of the family problems such solutions addressed differed markedly, also as hypothesized. For example, the number of votes taken on Medicare and Medicaid funding and health insurance was much greater in the 1990s than in the 1980s, as was true of the number of votes taken on income security—welfare reform, social security, unemployment insurance, and so on. Over the observational period as a whole, the number of explicit family measures on which roll call votes were taken clearly increased over the observational period, reaching their highest number in 1995, followed by 1996. The largest number of legislative solutions to family problems in the 1990s were sought in the categories of health and income security.

With respect to votes on particular measures, none exceeded those restricting access to abortion as a reproductive choice for women, with obvious implications for the reproductive and membership functions and tasks of families. Such restrictions permeated policy measures related to families in the areas of defense, foreign affairs, and income security (welfare reform), and even policy measures in the area of health involving Medicaid and insurance plans for federal employees. Many roll call votes on explicit family measures represented alternative scenarios of family problems and their solutions. Examples include votes prohibiting federal funds from being used to provide information about abortion in 1991 (the gag rule), votes in 1993 calling for the revocation of the gag rule and for both the expansion of the EITC and cuts in the EITC.

The influence of cultural and technological change and developments that have impinged on family life in recent years also could be discerned in many of the roll call votes related to families. Examples include the vote on DOMA, which was unique in terms of its subject matter at the federal level and reflective of cultural change and developments, whereas votes on breast cancer research, fetal tissue research, assisted suicide, family privacy protections, and partial birth abortions were primarily reflective of technological developments but cultural change as well. Some roll call votes—and the increased number of explicit family roll call votes—undoubtedly were attributable to the increased presence of women in Congress and in politics and society in general. Such votes included longer hospital stays for mothers of newborns, domestic violence prevention, home health care, breast cancer research, and related measures. Viewed against the health reform efforts of 1993-94 that never came to fruition, however, congressional solutions in the area of health in the latter part of the 1990s were relatively modest and did not extend to the larger problems of health care financing and affordability, unless cuts in Medicare and Medicaid spending are considered solutions to the federal government's budget problems. They certainly are not solutions to family problems.

Whether the solutions lawmakers constructed to family problems during the 1990s represented progress, regression, or the status quo vis-à-vis family problems depends on how such solutions are appraised—whether in the case of welfare reform, for example, the problem could be constructed as welfare dependency or the persistence of child poverty in the United States. If appraised in terms of the former, welfare reform could be seen as a needed solution. If appraised in terms of the latter, however, then welfare reform, together with tax measures favoring higher-income over lower-income families, would be viewed not as solutions but as problems in need of solutions. Although the number of roll call votes on explicit family measures clearly increased over time, suggesting a shift from a more passive government role to a more activist and responsive one, albeit conservative, the number and share of explicit or manifest family legislation remained small relative to all the roll call votes taken each data year over the observational period. Nonetheless, the growing number of such votes is indicative of a shift in attitudes regarding the role of government in the construction of policy solutions to family problems.

Unlike the content analysis of congressional roll call votes in the 1980s and 1990s documenting the increase in the number of votes on explicit family measures (from which a shift in attitudes regarding the role of government was inferred), a content analysis of the congressional debates over the 1996 DOMA revealed the attitudes that were actually embedded in the construction of same-sex marriage as a problem and DOMA as its solution. Enacted by wide margins in both houses of Congress, the passage of DOMA reflected the overwhelming acceptance of existing institutional arrangements for heterosexual marriage and the rejection of same-sex marriage on the part of the nation's lawmakers; this was consistent with attitudes expressed in nationally representative surveys.

DOMA was important not only because it was a constructed response to challenges to institutional norms with regard to heterosexual marriage as the foundation of family life but also because it created the circumstances for the first of its kind congressional debate, providing insight into the many meanings contained in its construction. The debates also demonstrated how proponents and opponents of different constructions of DOMA and same-sex marriage used language to present and defend their position while casting the position of others in a negative and unfavorable light. In doing so, the debates highlighted the attitudinal differences between individual congresspersons as Republicans and Democrats on the subject. For example, Democrats tended to construct DOMA as the problem, and Republicans tended to construct it as the solution. Not surprisingly, many of the claims made during the debates with regard to marriage and the family were at odds with historical research showing the evolving nature of family as an institution and its changing meanings over time.

Evidence of gender differences in the debates appeared in the overrepresentation of women who participated in the debates—in both the House and Senate—and evidence of regional differences appeared in the themes emphasized in the debates by individual congressional members. Two thirds of the House members participating in the debates, who represented states in the South, emphasized the theme of marriage as the foundation of society. Such regional overrepresentation in theme emphasis was suggestive of the attitudes that characterized the political culture of the states these members represented, which could also have been embedded in their construction of DOMA as the solution and same-sex marriage as the problem. (Political culture refers to the distribution of attitudes toward government and other people in a population.)

Other themes emphasized during the debates and reflecting the diversity of meanings assigned to DOMA included (a) same-sex marriage is a threat to marriage and society, (b) same-sex marriage is not a moral equivalent of heterosexual marriage, (c) marriage is private and personal, (d) DOMA usurps states' rights, and (e) DOMA does not usurp states' rights. Despite such diversity, the vote was clear: no diversity with respect to legal marriage in terms of its heterosexual basis.

Going from the national to the state level, findings from an analysis of the explicit family policies enacted by six states with different political cultures provided partial support for the hypothesized influence of political culture in constructing legislative solutions to family problems in the 1990s, using the term *family* and related terms to identify such legislation. Using Daniel Elazar's typology of states' political cultures, the six states represented the following:

- The moralistic political culture, as typified by Minnesota
- The individualistic political culture, as typified by Nevada
- The traditionalistic political culture, as typified by South Carolina
- The moralistic/individualistic political culture, as typified by California
- The individualistic/moralistic political culture, as typified by New York
- The traditionalistic/individualistic political culture, as typified by Florida

In the cases of states with mixed political cultures, the first of the pair is thought to predominate. The legislative solutions constructed to family problems by Minnesota, Nevada, and South Carolina in the 1980s that were examined earlier provided a basis for comparing their solutions in the 1990s with their solutions in the 1980s.

The influence of political culture on constructed solutions to family problems in the case of Minnesota, a moralistic state, was clear. Of the six states, Minnesota enacted the largest share of family legislation over the observational period. However, in terms of absolute frequencies, California enacted the most but proportionately the same as Nevada and South Carolina. Proportionately, New York and Florida also enacted the same amount of explicit family legislation and the least of the six states. Indeed, except for New York and Florida, the share of explicit family legislation the other four states enacted increased over the observational period. For the three states included in the 1980s analyses—Minnesota, Nevada, and South Carolina—the increase was dramatic. The six states also differed in terms of the breadth and substance of their family legislation, Minnesota's being the most proactive (education), but Nevada's the broadest in terms of the number of substantive categories in which explicit family legislation was enacted.

Despite the increase in the explicit family legislation four of the states enacted over the study period, relative to all the other legislation they enacted, it would have to be said that just as at the federal level, most of the legislation they enacted was implicit rather than explicit with regard to families and their problems. As noted earlier in the discussion, because most policies in the United States are implicit rather than explicit with regard to family, recognition of their family dimensions arrived late in this country, which helps to account for the delayed awareness of the policy/family connection more generally—and the myriad of ways in which governments might better support families. However, the increased frequency with which the term *family* appeared in the legislative summaries of four of the six states over time suggests a change in this regard on the part of state lawmakers, just as it does in the case of congressional roll call votes at the federal level on the part of the nation's lawmakers.

Although Elazar's typology of their political cultures did not characterize the family policies the six states constructed as solutions to family problems on each and every dimension on which they were analyzed—quantity, breadth, and foci—the analysis not only offered a way of analyzing states' constructed solutions to family problems within an interpretative framework but also provided partial support for that framework.

The diversity of meanings embedded in every constructed family problem and solution calls for (a) a diversity of conceptual frameworks to aid in understanding and explaining why some constructions of family problems and their solutions are accepted and supported and others are not and (b) a different set of frameworks to aid in explaining the consequences of such constructions for families in all of their diversities. To illustrate their real-world applications, throughout the discussion I included examples of many of the major concepts associated with the various conceptual frameworks—both policy and family—that I drew primarily from news articles on a range of issues. By applying the different frameworks widely to diverse issues, I tried to demonstrate not only the applicability of the frameworks across issues but also the breadth and complexity of family policy. Now, you, the reader, can apply the conceptual language embedded in the frameworks to do your own analysis of developments in Social Security, taxes, and welfare and health care reform or of any other family policy issue of interest to you and arrive at your own conclusions as to their implications for family well-being, drawing on the family frameworks in doing so. Both health care and welfare reform highlight the highly uncertain nature of the outcomes of the processes by which policy solutions to family problems are constructed. Indeed, with regard to health care, the 1990s ended as they began—with complaints about its ever-increasing costs.

The policy frameworks presented in this discussion included the institutional framework, rational choice theory, political culture theory, incremental theory, game theory, interest group theory, elite theory, and systems theory. Together, the frameworks are informative as guides for policy practice, the subject of Chapter 19. Providing insights into some of the factors that come into play in the construction of policy solutions to family problems in the form of family policies and programs—and that undoubtedly came into play in the cases of the congressional votes on explicit family measures and the policies enacted by the six states discussed above—each framework emphasizes some unique aspect of family policy as substance and process. The fact that the realities of the policy process sometimes deviate from these models says less about the frameworks themselves than about the complexity of family policy and the processes it involves.

Although all the policy frameworks may come into play in some policy issues, such as welfare reform or health care reform or Social Security, what distinguishes the *institutional* model from the others is its emphasis on values, norms, roles, patterns of behaviors, structural arrangements, and continuity over time. Policy choice as a constructed solution to family problems from an institutional perspective is defined as the outcome of the ways in which government as an institution is structured, its distinguishing features being characterized in terms of legitimacy, authority, and universality. What distinguishes the construction of policy solutions to family problems from the perspective of the *rational choice* model is its emphasis on net value maximization, based on (a) the application of all values considered important to achieve with respect to families with family well-being ranking the highest, (b) the calculation of a net value ratio for each alternative course of action and its consequences, and (c) the selection of the alternative solution with the highest net value ratio. Family policy as rational choice is defined as the selection of the alternative solution that maximizes those values considered most important in addressing a family problem, the highest ranking value here being family well-being.

In contrast to rational choice theory, the *incremental* policy model emphasizes the emergent rather than the predetermined nature of policy choice. A variation of rational choice theory, the incremental model sees policy choice as a process of continual adjustment to the outcomes of previous actions with policy makers seeking to satisfy constituent demands by finding an alternative that is "good enough" instead of the one that tries to maximize all possible values, as the rational policy model does. The idea underlying the "good enough" alternative is called *satisficing*. The model highlights the uncertainties and ambiguities surrounding policy choices related to families and the conflict inherent in sharp departures from existing solutions.

Policy from the perspective of *game theory,* as another variation of rational choice theory, emphasizes the competitive conditions under which policy solutions to family problems are constructed. Policy from this perspective is defined as choice under competitive conditions of no authority. The outcome of the game that is the constructed solution is seen to depend on the actions, skills, and choices of two or more interdependent players having a stake in the outcome. Using a strategy called *minimax,* players—that is, policy makers—seek to minimize maximum losses and maximize minimum gains. Minimax is a strategy that involves compromise, bargaining, negotiation, and persuasion.

Political culture theory, a leading alternative to rational choice theory, looks at the constraints of the choice situation, emphasizing in particular the values and attitudes that people hold toward government as influences on policy choices. Distinctions among political cultures in the 50 states are captured by such terms as moralistic, individualistic, traditionalistic, and different mixes of the three, as described earlier.

Interest group theory differs from game theory in its emphasis on groups rather than individuals. It sees policy choice as the equilibrium reached in the struggle among contending interest groups in their efforts to influence government action. Action is seen to occur because of interest group demands on government, group influence varying with membership size, wealth, cohesion, leadership, and access to policy makers.

Whereas interest group theory emphasizes groups and the pluralistic nature of society, *elite theory* sees the world hierarchically, ranking people and groups in terms of influence. Elite theory defines policy not in terms of the equilibrium reached among contending interest groups but in terms of elite preferences. The size and complexity of modern society, which are seen to require some division of labor, also are seen to preclude the full and active participation of everyone in the construction of policy solutions to family problems and to give rise to elites. From this perspective, the construction of policy solutions to family problems in the form of family policies and programs is seen to reflect the preferences of elites—fixed and governing—who negotiate, compromise, bargain, persuade, and compete to influence policy choices.

Policy solutions to family problems in the form of family policies and programs from a *systems perspective* are defined as system outputs that flow from the political system to the environment or systems that make up its environment, such as families. Outputs are seen as responses to environmental demands for some kind of authoritative decision that addresses some identified family problem. Demands in turn are seen as inputs that flow from the environment, that is, families, to the political system. In order for the system to be able to respond to such demands, however, it must have support for its outputs in the form of family policies and programs. Thus, support is another type of system input. Such inputs can take a variety of forms: money, information and feedback, constituent votes and approval. The exchange of system inputs and outputs occurs through intersystem transactions at system boundaries; boundaries serve to demarcate one system from another.

Given the confusion and complexity of policy processes, however conceptualized, there is good reason to be concerned about the implications of policy solutions for family well-being. Many of the influences that come into play in such constructions can be identified from the conceptual frameworks outlined above and discussed in detail in earlier chapters—individual motivations, competing interests, special interests, players' skills and understanding of policy and family problems, interest group influence, the attitudes and values of individual players, the political cultures of the political jurisdictions players represent, political ideology, government structures, elite preferences, the availability of relevant, timely, and necessary information—to name only a few. All these influences together provide little assurance that troubling conditions pertaining to families will be seen as problems in need of solutions, or that if they are that such solutions will do much to advance the well-being of families and their members.

Indeed, such solutions may have little to do with the conditions that presumably give impetus to their constructions in the first place. Therefore, the task of monitoring the consequences of family policies and programs for family well-being falls to those who believe that regardless of their shape or form, families and their well-being are important not only for individual members but for society as well. *Well-being,* which Webster defines as "the state of being healthy, happy, and free from want," has been operationalized in the family literature along social, economic, psychological, and interpersonal dimensions. The family frameworks presented in this discussion provide the conceptual language that can be used for thinking about and assessing family well-being—conceptually—and in framing questions that need to be asked with regard to the policy/family connection. They also provide the context for assigning meaning to and interpreting the implications of policy solutions in policy practice and a basis for formulating hypotheses for testing in family policy research.

The family frameworks presented in this discussion included family systems theory, exchange and choice theories, symbolic interactionism, family stress theory, conflict theory, feminist theory, and cultural theory. Thus, just as systems theory can be applied to the analysis of the construction of policy solutions to family problems, it can also be used to assess the implications of such constructions for families and their well-being. From a *family systems* perspective, families are systems that interact with other systems in their environment, such as the political system, including governments, through their respective input-throughput (or withinput) and output processes. The implications of policy solutions for family well-being can be assessed in terms of family task performance (functions), the role performance of family members, including family liaison roles, family boundaries and boundary maintenance, and family equilibrium and adaptive capacities, and all the concepts embedded in these broad conceptual categories outlined in Chapter 15. If family policies and programs support and promote (a) family task performance and functions, (b) the role performance of family members, (c) family stability and adaptation, and (d) the integrity of family boundaries, they can be said to promote family well-being.

The implications of constructed solutions to family problems may also be usefully assessed from the perspective of *exchange and choice theories*. This framework is based on the assumption that family members are rational and they make decisions based on their expectations of the costs and rewards of alternative choices, the information available to them about alternative choices, and their values and standards. Rewards and costs are two basic concepts of the framework; others include profitability, reciprocity, and comparison-level alternatives. The implications of constructed solutions to family problems might then be assessed in terms of the relative costs and rewards such policies and programs entail or create for families and their members, given their values and standards. If family policies and programs provide rewards that exceed their costs for families, and if they exemplify the principle of reciprocity, they can be seen as promoting family well-being.

From *symbolic interactionism* come such concepts as socialization, role and all of its derivations, expectations, satisfactions, relative deprivation, and the family's definition of the situation. Symbolic interactionism shares with family systems theory concepts such as socialization, role, and role performance. Unlike most of the other family frameworks, symbolic interactionism takes into account the subjective meanings of the situation in which families find themselves. This pertains to *their* perceptions of policies and programs that have been constructed to address family problems. Thus, the implications of constructed policy solutions to family problems from the perspective of symbolic interaction can be assessed in terms of families' expectations, satisfactions, sense of relative deprivation, and definition of such constructions in relation to their situation. If families perceive and define such policies and programs as promoting their well-being, however they might define it, then such constructions in fact do. The same holds for families' expressions of satisfaction with and expectations of family policies and programs, keeping in mind the phenomenon of relative deprivation as a potential influence.

Just as the definition of the situation is central to symbolic interactionism and the social change model outlined in Chapter 6, it also is central to the *family stress framework*. Underlying family stress theory is the assumption that depending on the resources available to families and their definition of the situation, the stressors or demands that families are required to meet may result in a crisis such that families are unable to function. The basic concepts of the framework include stressors or demands, resources, families' definitions of the situation, and crisis. The implications of constructed solutions to family problems for families and their well-being might then be assessed in terms of the resources they do or do not provide for families, the demands or stressors they create or alleviate for families, the ways in which families perceive and define their situation, and the demand/resource balance such solutions provide to avert family crises. If family policies and programs provide the resources families need to cope with the demands of their situation and facilitate family adaptation, they can be said to promote family well-being.

Conflict theory, in contrast to the other family frameworks, calls attention to the hierarchical nature of family relationships. Resulting in power differentials based on age and sex, hierarchy is seen to create a structure for conflict and differences among family members in terms of their motivations, interests, and preferences. A zero-sum structure of scarcity whereby gains for one member result in losses for others is seen to exacerbate such differences. Thus, the implications of constructed solutions to family problems vis-à-vis family policies for family well-being might be assessed in terms of (a) their support for the democratization of family structures and relationships; (b) the tools and mechanisms such policies and programs provide for resolving family conflict—such as negotiation, bargaining, compromise, and cooperation—or for preventing family conflict in the first place; and (c) their support for the creation of a win-win structure for resolving conflict in contrast to a zero-sum structure, whereby one party wins at the other's expense. As case examples illustrated, conflict theory with regard to family policy applies to intersystemic relationships involving families and the systems with which they interact—schools, businesses, governments—as well as to intrasystemic family relationships themselves. If family policies and programs structure the situation in ways that portend to avert family conflict or provide for tools for constructive conflict resolution, while protecting the interests of the parties involved, they can be said to promote family well-being.

Permeating the construction of policy solutions to family problems and their implications for families and their well-being are issues of gender, ethnicity, race, and social class. Here, terms such as *liberal feminism, socialist feminism,* and *radical feminism* come into play from the perspective of feminist theory, each with an emphasis unique to it. In general, if a feminist perspective is taken, gender equality would be used to assess the implications of solutions to family problems. If a cultural perspective is taken, the implications of such constructions might be assessed in terms of family diversity—whether such solutions construct culturally diverse families as culturally relevant, culturally deviant, culturally variant, or culturally equivalent. If such constructions approach culturally diverse families and families of color as culturally variant or equivalent, they can be said to enhance family well-being.

Throughout this discussion, I have emphasized the importance of language. As noted earlier, the conceptual language of the policy and family frameworks can serve as guides to the construction of policy solutions that foster family well-being rather than ill-being. Language, attitudes, and social conditions, being mutually reinforcing, serve to shape each other in ways that lead to the acceptance of some troubling conditions as family problems but not others, as in the case of dependency and welfare reform captured by the phrase "ending welfare as we know it." By providing the language for assigning meaning to such conditions from a family perspective, the family frameworks can be useful in this regard. More diverse, the kinds of family problems finding their way on the public agenda at both state and federal levels suggest a change in attitudes regarding the role of government in addressing such problems. More targeted and flexible, perhaps, such diversity makes more difficult the construction of solutions to large, overriding, troubling family conditions as problems, such as growing income disparities among families, which some also might frame in terms of diversity but are more appropriately framed in terms of justice and fairness.

Indeed, the perception of unfairness resulting from a number of strategic choices in the past has served to erode popular support (Noble, 1997) for many programs in the family policy domain. According to Charles Noble (1997), scholars who focus on political institutions suggest that much of what governments do can be explained by institutional and policy legacies. According to this view, social and family policy have been shaped by the organization and dynamics of political institutions themselves. Decentralization, for example, not only has made it easier for business interests to veto social legislation unfavorable toward business but also has encouraged jurisdictional competition among states and localities for investments. Such "competitive federalism," Noble says, has given business interests "structural" power over social reform by discouraging governors and state legislatures from imposing high costs on geographically mobile firms. Similarly, the structure of the American electoral system (including single-member districts and winner take-all elections) has affected the balance of power among competing interests by discouraging demands for structural reforms and penalizing political forces that enter the political system from the opposite side.

Such choices with regard to decentralization and the marketization of public business reinforce and support postmodern tendencies toward differentiation that threaten the achievement of a shared view with regard to family policy and family well-being as its goal. Such choices, as legacies of the past, include the decision in the Progressive era to create targeted materialist programs rather than universal programs; that decision made it more difficult for middle-class individuals and families to identify with a widely shared public interest in economic security that in turn might have simultaneously guided and legitimated state intervention into the market. In the 1930s and 1940s, such choices included the decision to create a federalized system of public welfare and pursue full employment as a policy goal, thereby institutionalizing the economic foundations of corporate power and leaving American workers unusually dependent on market sources for income and the decisions of private employers while reproducing political divisions among workers. In the 1960s, the decision to launch a war on poverty and to extend social protections to the aged without substantially increasing the states' redistributional or regulatory capacities left many programs that pertained to families—and others—vulnerable to political attack. In the 1970s, the failure to do more to protect working and middle-class living standards in the new global economy worsened matters, feeding the backlash against the government, to which reference was made in an earlier chapter. The legacy of the 1980s, the Reagan era, according to Brennan (1996), lay in establishing individualism in the public sphere and convincing people that self-interest was the only viable operative principle in life.

Even when large political and economic shocks temporarily lowered political institutional barriers to change, the choice was made to extend rather than supplant market principles and institutions (Noble, 1997). Brennan (1996) advises that although markets in theory may efficiently translate preferences into outcomes by rewarding businesses that satisfy preferences for the least cost, the reasons market choices do not have to reflect social values—many of which pertain to families—point to the need for a public sphere to at least complement markets in some cases and substitute for them in others. Moreover, as Esping-Anderson (1996) (who maintains that a favorable institutional environment may be as capable of nurturing flexibility and efficiency as free markets) points out, fragmented political institutions lack the capacity to negotiate binding agreements among contending interests. The assumption that the market should supplement the basic public safety net—and in some cases supplant it—has, she says, resulted in the privatization of risks rather than the means to confront them.

Elsewhere I have written that family policy as a measure of political and social integration reflects the legitimacy accorded to political institutions to make decisions that further the well-being of individuals and families, and that such decisions serve to mediate connections among individuals and families so as to better meet their needs (Zimmerman, 1992a). Regardless of how they are measured, political and social integration affects the distribution of well-being in a population when some persons are excluded from the benefits that others receive through networks of reciprocal aid and support, such as governments (MacRae, 1985). As noted throughout this discussion, growing disparities among families in terms of their well-being are attributable in part to the weakening of social integration as represented by descendance of the public sector and the ascendance of markets in an increasingly competitive global technological economy.

Here it is useful to recall Tom Friedman's (1999) admonition about the country's stake in the sustainability of globalization if the country is to be able to generate the incomes necessary for ensuring rising living standards—and the well-being of *all* families—in all of their diversities. This means addressing the new economic insecurities and risks faced by working-age families because of a rapidly changing labor market, high divorce rates, and single parenthood while simultaneously sustaining traditional social/family programs that now support a rapidly expanding elderly population (Esping-Anderson, 1996). The much greater occupational and life-cycle differentiation that characterizes contemporary society implies more heterogeneous needs and expectations. With greater career uncertainty, demands for more flexible adjustment and changing family arrangements, not to forget greater female employment, citizens also face more diverse risks.

Just as the implicit nature of the family dimensions of so many public policies delayed recognition of the policy/family connection in this country for so long, the blurring of public and private, jurisdictional competition, and the increasing diversity of family problems that come to the attention of lawmakers could exacerbate existing tendencies toward differentiation, specialization, and fragmentation in constructing policy solutions to family problems and obscure recognition of their shared domain—family policy—and common aim—family well-being.

The fact that individual and family well-being varies so widely among families and that the gap in well-being has widened so dramatically among families over the years has serious implications for the kind of society we in the United States live in. It is serious if for no other reason than that families *ideally* do what no other collectivity can: provide individuals with a sense of belonging and continuity based on affective relationships of love and reciprocal caring that can carry them through life. To the extent that their well-being suffers, families are less able to do what society expects them to do, especially those less favorably positioned in the socioeconomic-political structure of society. But wide disparities in individual and family well-being are important for other reasons too. Threatening the civic and social underpinnings of our society, they also threaten our democratic institutions. These require more, rather than less, equality of conditions among individuals and families. Just as welfare may be the antithesis of our value traditions of minimal government, individualism, and private property, gross disparities in the well-being of individuals and families are the antithesis of a democratic political order. Indeed, the latter calls for the democratization of family well-being as a policy goal.

If Arac (1989) is correct in saying that the personal has become political because of public agitation for public remedies in areas long considered private, the same may be said with respect to families: the family has become political because of public agitation for public remedies to family problems. Since the 1960s, the United States has become a permissive society not merely in the sense of becoming more open and tolerant of diversity but also in the sense of becoming more reluctant to accept responsibility for the economic and social consequences of social and economic change—increasing numbers of divorces, working mothers, teenage pregnancies, homelessness, and so on. Individuals, families, and society have been hesitant to accept collective responsibility for the care of young children, the elderly, the poor, the handicapped or mentally ill, or birth control and human reproduction (Mintz & Kellogg, 1988). Such reluctance in the face of our changing economy does not bode well for the future, given the country's penchant for achieving public purposes through private means and the latter's preoccupation not with families' needs or the fallouts of the new economy but with the bottom line. For family well-being to be advanced in our rapidly changing world, family and family policy discourses need to be placed in broader context and incorporated into the larger discourse of the new economy, which includes stemming the erosion of our democratic political order that gross disparities of wealth and income have encouraged.

What does all this mean for readers who would like to be involved in constructing policy solutions to family problems that advance family well-being in the years ahead—in family policy practice? For some suggestions, readers should turn to Chapter 19.

Implications for Family Policy Practice

■ Family Policy Practice: What Is It?

Before answering the question "What does this book mean for readers who would like to be involved as family policy practitioners in the construction of policy solutions that advance family well-being?", the question "What is family policy practice?" should be answered first. If policy practice includes efforts to influence the development or construction, enactment, implementation, or assessment of public policies (Jansson, 1994), then family policy practice might be defined in similar terms: as efforts to influence the development, enactment, implementation, or assessment of constructed solutions to family problems that have the greatest potential for advancing family well-being.

■ Guides to Family Policy Practice: The Conceptual Frameworks

As noted throughout this book, the policy frameworks presented offer clues for family policy practice. The institutional framework, for example, calls attention to the importance of government structure, roles, and norms for policy outcomes. In Chapter 18, Noble (1997) explained our country's fragmented policy approach to problems in institutional terms. Within this context, family policy practitioners would be required to understand organizational structure, inter-organizational relationships, the roles of people in different positions within the structure, the legislative process, and institutional procedures and rules, so that they can work their way through the structure to effect necessary changes in the construction of policy solutions to family problems and perhaps work with others to change the structure within which such solutions are constructed and the rules and procedures for constructing them.

If the rational choice framework is used as a guide for policy practice, then the emphasis would shift to the need for technical and analytic skills that would help to ensure the selection of the alternative solution to family problems that promises to advance family well-being the most and the later evaluation of its outcomes for families. Here, the family policy practitioner would need to be skilled at data analysis and interpretation from a family perspective and in communicating the results of such analyses and interpretations to others in both oral and written forms, or they would need to arrange for such analyses and data interpretations by others who do have such skills. Regardless, such skills are important for bringing a sense of rationality to the process of selecting the alternative that has the highest net value ratio with respect to the achievement of family well-being as a policy goal.

If the incremental policy framework is the practitioner's guide for practice, he or she would focus on the political feasibility of a particular policy solution to a family problem, aware of the pitfalls inherent in effecting dramatic departures from existing policies. Rather than trying to effect sweeping changes in solutions that have already been constructed to family problems, the family policy practitioner would want to work to effect small changes that promised to bring about higher levels of family well-being, if only marginally, taking cues from past policy experience. Working from the incremental model in helping to effect changes in a particular policy requires knowing the history of policy efforts to address the problem and a willingness to *satisfice* rather than *maximize* family well-being, and change direction as a result of experience-based feedback about that particular solution.

If game theory is used as a guide for family policy practice, the family policy practitioner would be required to think strategically and in suppositional and "what if" terms in anticipation of what others might think or do in the competition for acceptance of a condition as a problem and its accompanying solution. Knowing how to persuade, negotiate, and compromise to effect bargains and agreements and being willing to lose some points so as to avoid losing others are all a part of the repertoire of skills required of the practitioner operating from the perspective of game theory.

The family policy practitioner operating out of the political culture framework would seek to effect positive changes in attitudes that populations in different jurisdictions hold toward government so that policy solutions can be constructed that show promise of advancing family well-being in that jurisdiction. The practitioner here would be required to know about the political and social history of that jurisdiction and how to create support for desired solutions, which again speaks to the need for oral and written communication skills and the ability to persuade others to accept a particular family condition as a family problem and the role of government in addressing it.

If interest group theory is used as a guide for family policy practice, and depending on where the family policy practitioner is located in the policy structure, he or she may represent the position of an interest group in working to influence the development and enactment of family policies or, in the manner of an advocate, work to persuade other groups to adopt a position on a particular family issue that converges with the interest group's or provide them with the information they need about the problem and its solution so that they can arrive informed at their own position. He or she also could be involved in creating a coalition of like-minded groups to increase the strength of their individual efforts to influence policy.

If elite theory is used as a guide for family policy practice, then the practitioner might want to consider Allison's (1971) conception of elites, which is constituted of a series of concentric circles consisting of the following:

- The general or inattentive public (a potential group) who, because of its indifference to policy issues, sit at the outer ring of the circle.
- The attentive public, comprised of the media, interest groups, and informed and interested citizens, who sit one ring closer to center stage as the audience of governing elites.
- The policy and opinion elites who structure public discourse on family policy issues such as presidential, gubernatorial, or mayoral advisers.
- The real actors in the situation—the president, governors, mayors, their respective cabinets, legislators, and agency administrators.

Here, the family policy practitioner would work to inform elites about the problems of families for which policy solutions are needed, capturing their attention through various forums and debates (about which more will be said in later discussion). The practitioner would be required to have analytic, public speaking, and organizational skills in addition to skills in effecting bargains and negotiated agreements among the various parties involved in the issue.

Finally, if the practitioner is guided by systems theory, he or she would seek to anticipate and evaluate disturbances in the system's environment that could affect the construction of policy solutions to family problems and families in negative ways, like oil shortages leading to escalating fuel costs for families and strains on governments' budget in addressing that problem. He or she also would provide information and feedback about general and specific environmental support and demands for particular solutions to family problems, such as subsidies to help meet the higher fuel costs of low-income families. Such a feedback function requires practitioners to transmit the information they receive and interpret it from a family perspective through system channels. It also implies securing feedback from diverse constituencies about their problems, including problems with presently constructed solutions to their problems, and what they may see as appropriate solutions to them. It also implies an understanding of the informational needs, motivations, and concerns of system authorities. For system authorities as family policy practitioners, the idea of feedback requires that they be open to it and take it into account in policy deliberations.

Unlike other policy practitioners, the *family* policy practitioner would be required to be knowledgeable about particular family policy issues and to be able to explain and interpret such issues to others from a family perspective, using any one of the family frameworks. Such interpretation can occur at all stages of the policy process: formulation or development, enactment, implementation, and evaluation. Thus, guided by family stress theory, if a particular solution is anticipated to enhance the well-being of families with mentally disabled children by providing resources that would alleviate the stress such families experience, the family policy practitioner would argue for the solution accordingly and work for its enactment. Guided by exchange and choice theories, if the rewards of a particular solution were anticipated to outweigh its costs for families (e.g., EITC), the family policy practitioner would work for *that* constructed solution.

From the perspective of symbolic interactionism, if parents' role performance and satisfaction were anticipated to be diminished as a consequence of, for example, cutbacks in funding for job training programs that can advance their job skills based on the assumption that government is not responsible for improving workers' job skills, the family policy practitioner might work to correct that assumption and to increase the funding for such programs. Obviously, an economic argument could also be made for such a solution.

Guided by family systems theory, if the failure to construct a solution to a family problem, like affordable housing, upsets the equilibrium and adaptive capacities of low-income families, the family policy practitioner would interpret the family implications of such failure to lawmakers and the general public in an effort to effect a policy solution that promised to stabilize families' housing conditions and thereby restore their equilibrium and adaptive capacities.

Guided by conflict theory, if a constructed solution to a problem such as standardized testing for school children were a source of difference and contention between school authorities and parents, the family policy practitioner might seek to interpret the implications of such contention for school, family, and child relationships to boards of education and attempt to negotiate and transform their differences into a win-win situation for everyone. From a feminist perspective, the family policy practitioner might interpret a policy of equal pay for equal work in terms of gender-based hierarchical differences for men and women as heads of families that should be eliminated. If guided by a cultural perspective, the family policy practitioner would seek to protect the religious rights of culturally diverse families in all settings (e.g., the schools and workplace) in recognition of their cultural equivalency.

In each of these and most other instances, the family policy practitioner is required to understand the political and economic context in which family policies are constructed and the family implications of such constructions conceptually and to acquire the necessary analytic, political, interactional, and value-clarifying skills to engage in such practice. This includes (a) engaging in family policy discourse to develop family policy agendas and define programs and (b) helping to enact, implement, and assess family policies (Jansson, 1994) from a family perspective. What should be clear is that family policy practice is not a solo but a collective practice that involves practitioners engaged in complementary activities at all levels in the policy structures of family policy domains. It also should be clear that institutionally sponsored family policy practice is governed by the rules and regulations of the work setting, and that as guides for practice, the policy frameworks are more suitable for some practice roles than others.

■ The Tasks Associated With Family Policy Practice

Jansson (1994) outlines the following tasks and activities common to all policy practice, which here pertains specifically to family policy:

- *Agenda development*, which describes what policy practitioners do when they work to persuade lawmakers to place particular family policy items on their policy agendas.

- *Problem definition*, which depicts what policy practitioners do when they analyze specific conditions they define as problems, together with the latter's causes and prevalence, drawing from theory and research to interpret the implications of such conditions for families and their well-being and society at large.

- *Proposal writing*, which includes developing solutions to specific problems, examining alternative policy solutions to such problems, identifying and weighing the criteria to be applied in selecting the alternative that promises to yield the highest net value ratio with respect to the achievement of family well-being.

- *Policy enactment*, which describes what family policy practitioners do when seeking approval for a specific family policy solution (e.g., meeting with legislators, encouraging constituents to write letters to legislators and to the editor, and speaking to groups to secure support for the enactment of the policy).

- *Policy assessment*, which involves the collection, analysis, and interpretation of data about a policy's performance and its effects, from a family perspective.

When family policy practitioners succeed in persuading lawmakers to place items such as the expansion of FMLA or the marriage tax penalty on their policy agendas, they help to shape the direction of policy deliberations. In agencies, practitioners are sometimes able to propel specific issues to the forefront of policy deliberations by making timely presentations, talking about them with other staff or with public officials—in short, by engaging in family policy discourse with policy actors.

As Jansson (1994) points out, because the tasks associated with family policy practice are often performed simultaneously and sometimes by the same person, they are not easily distinguishable from one another. Moreover, because of the fluidity of the policy situation and process, these tasks are rarely accomplished in a sequential or predictable order. Such fluidity reflects in part the shifting context and phases of the policy process involved in specific family policy issues (e.g., the estate tax or marriage tax penalty) and external developments that may affect the process (e.g., the advent of budget surpluses or deficits or the mobilization of strong opposition to proposed solutions to problems, or armed conflict within or between nations, as in Kosovo and the Middle East).

▪ The Context of Family Policy Practice

The mobilization of opposition to proposed solutions is suggestive of the contested nature of many constructed solutions to family problems and, by extension, of family policy practice itself, whether with respect to the technical aspects of measurement and sampling or definitions and conceptualizations of family problems and solutions to them; different experts and groups view such matters differently. Competing to have their definitions and perceptions of such matters accepted by lawmakers and the general public, spokespersons for different positions and groups are unlikely to be swayed by data that do not support their position on issues. Illustrative is the adamant denial of the executive director of the National Rifle Association (NRA) on a recent television news program with Peter Jennings that under existing law, 600 cases of gun violations had been federally prosecuted in a recent 3-year period. The executive director insisted that only 1 case had been prosecuted as a way of buttressing the NRA's opposition to federal gun control laws. Moreover, because the causes of problems experienced by diverse families and groups of families vary over time, generalized statements about family problems for which policy solutions are sought often are open to challenge.

▪ What Knowledge and Skills Are Required for Family Policy Practice?

Although the knowledge and skills required for family policy practice were incorporated in the discussion of the conceptual frameworks as guides for policy practice and the tasks associated with such practice, they are being discussed as topics in their own right here to underscore their importance. As has been suggested, family policy practitioners need analytic skills (a) for evaluating family problems and their severity, (b) for identifying barriers to policy enactment and implementation, and (c) for developing strategies for assessing programs and writing policy proposals. Family policy practitioners also need political skills (a) to gain and use power and (b) to develop and implement political strategies to increase prospects for a proposal's enactment or to prevent its enactment, as the case may be. Power with reference to family policy practitioners would derive from their expertise and knowledge about families and particular problems confronting them, such as homelessness, the position they hold in the policy structure or the group(s) they represent, and their interactional skills. Policy practitioners need interactional skills (a) to participate in task groups, committees, or coalitions; (b) to persuade others to support or not support specific policy proposals; and (c) to deal with the controversies surrounding family policy issues and practice. They also need value-clarifying skills to identify and help others identify and rank values in analyzing alternative policy solutions to a family problem and the selection of one. Each of these skills is associated with the different policy frameworks as guides to family policy practice outlined earlier in the chapter. Although analytic and value considerations usually dominate policy deliberations, political and interactional factors often supersede them (Jansson, 1994). In summary, family policy practitioners should know or know about the following:

- The actors in key positions in government settings
- The motivations of public officials
- The legislative process
- Social agencies, health clinics, and schools in their political and economic context and the policies that govern their programs
- Community organizations that influence agency policies, local governments, state legislatures, and Congress
- Organizational structures and charts, budget priorities, persons who perform important boundary-spanning liaison roles, informal networks of relevant organizations and people, and community and cultural factors that may affect the development, enactment, and implementation of different family policies
- Cultural and political factors that shape perceptions of problems
- Both qualitative and quantitative analytic approaches to problem identification and classification, and measurement of the prevalence, severity, location, and causes of family and family policy problems
- The diversity of family problems or problems associated with diverse groups of families

In short, family policy practice requires the application of a broad range of knowledge and skills and a variety of perspectives and analytic approaches. It also implies a large network of practitioners in different policy positions in a variety of family-related settings working toward the same broad goal.

■ Family Policy Practitioners: Who Exactly Are They?

Given that family policy practice broadly refers to efforts to influence the development, enactment, implementation, and assessment of family policies, the more appropriate question might be, Who is not a family policy practitioner or at least minimally involved in family policy practice, such as lending support or withholding support for particular constructions of family problems and their solutions, such as PRWORA? Just engaging in family policy discourse is a form of family policy practice. Thus, when friends and families talk about the need for neighborhood traffic signs to ensure the physical safety of their children or about the policy constructions of presidential candidates to family problems, they are engaging not only in family policy discourse but also in family policy practice. Using Allison's (1971) concept of concentric circles of policy elites consisting of interested and disinterested publics, readers may recall from earlier discussion that I said I hoped to transform readers into a public interested and conceptually informed about the problems families confront in society.

Official Policy Roles

Some positions in the policy structure, however, are more centrally located than others to effect the development, enactment, implementation, and evaluation of family policy, as Allison's concentric circles of policy elites suggests. These include elected and appointed government officials, administrators, lobbyists, and advocates whose job descriptions in fact include family policy practice (Jansson, 1994), regardless of domain—health, education, social services, housing, income security, employment and manpower, taxes, and family law. It also includes researchers who investigate policy problems and their solutions. Elected officials who want to be reelected are particularly sensitive to public opinion polls and constituent mail with regard to policy issues in the different family policy domains. Because they want to be reelected, they also are sensitive to the preferences of those organizations, groups, and individuals likely to support them with financial contributions in their political campaigns. For a similar reason, they are sensitive to the political ramifications of certain policy constructions with regard, for example, to abortion, marriage rights for gays, and gun control laws.

Nonpolicy Positions
That Involve Family Policy Practice

Although policy practice that is part of one's job is distinguishable from that which is separate from it, those holding nonpolicy positions can still engage in family policy practice by serving on committees in their work settings that are concerned about policy issues pertaining to families and what can be done about them. Examples include serving on a committee to consider the effects of differential foster care rates on the availability of foster homes for abused children, or serving on a committee that evaluates proposals for the funding of foster parent education programs for foster parents caring for children with disabilities of different ages, and/or serving as agency liaison to create a coalition of agencies or groups to effect the enactment of a given family policy.

When staff in nonpolicy positions try to change a work-setting policy that works to undermine family well-being (e.g., clinic or agency hours that prevent working parents from obtaining services they or their children need), they also are engaging in a form of family policy practice. Indeed, family policy practice probably is an unrecognized part of most jobs in all settings that serve families.

Just as they are likely to engage in some form of family policy practice in their work settings, persons working in nonpolicy positions also can engage in such practice outside their work settings, during nonworking hours, by participating in political campaigns, contributing to the discourse on family policy issues at community and political meetings, acquiring access to networks of people with information and power within specific settings, and using power assertively and skillfully themselves (Jansson, 1994) to effect the enactment of a family policy that has the potential of advancing or supporting the goal of family well-being.

Here, findings from a survey of 177 Republican and Democratic state legislative leaders in all 50 states and 167 child and family organizations that participate in state-based legislative activities conducted by the State Legislative Leaders Foundation in 1994 (State Legislative Leaders, 1995) are pertinent. Based on their observations and experience, leaders offered the following suggestions for child and family advocates and advocacy groups interested in advancing a family policy agenda:

1. Establish consistent visibility and ongoing relationships with legislative leaders, legislators, and staff
2. Build consensus around a realistic and manageable agenda that recognizes the importance of compromise in the legislative process
3. Develop grassroots support for child and family issues on a district-by-district basis
4. Expand the base of support for such issues by involving new voices and leaders from other sectors
5. Employ bipartisan strategies
6. Become active in political campaigns
7. Provide factual and compelling information about children and families in usable form
8. Become actively involved in the state budget process early and stay involved during the entire process, working with key legislators

Underscoring what has been said before, these findings suggest that family policy practitioners cannot succeed in achieving their objectives on the basis of their family policy agenda alone, even though research findings may support it. They must be actively engaged in the process. Family policy advocates, educators, and researchers have distinctive roles to play: advocates in pleading their cause and defending a family policy agenda that seeks to promote the well-being of families; educators in imparting knowledge about the issues involved in such an agenda; and researchers in investigating such issues to establish their factual basis and the factors that underlie and account for them.

Because state- and local-level family policy issues—such as child and family welfare and child and domestic abuse—involve governmental responses that transcend political jurisdictional boundaries, family policy advocates, educators, and researchers are required to understand the connections between the different levels of family policy—local, state, and national—and broaden their efforts accordingly. Moreover, because many policy issues, though pertaining to families, are not commonly viewed as being within the domain of family policy, family policy practitioners are required to be sensitive to the family dimensions of such issues—wage and income disparities being but one example—and call them to the attention of others, if they indeed are to effect higher levels of well-being for families.

The Social Critic/Advocate Role

Relevant here is Seidman's (1994) reference to the role of the social critic, who, he says, has a responsibility to critique current realities not only in some abstract way but as specifically as possible. For this task, he advises the critic to outline the social change desired in detail and the consequences that might be expected to follow from such change. Seidman goes on to advise that critics' arguments should be informed by *conceptual* understandings that allow for *conceptual* analysis of the impact of such change on society, which extends to family policy practitioners in terms of the conceptual analysis of change on families. Although Seidman uses feminist theory to demonstrate what a gendered order of equality in specific domains would be like and what its social impact would be, the same approach could be taken in analyzing impacts of different policies on families, using other family frameworks: family systems theory, exchange and choice theory, symbolic interactionism, family stress theory, conflict theory, and cultural theory—in addition to feminist theory.

In Seidman's view, theorists as agents of social change would become advocates of family policy. However, unlike the advocacy of social activists or public officials, which typically takes the form of rhetorical or moral appeals, he writes, or appeals to particular interests accompanied by the presentation of documents and data, theory-based advocacy takes the form of elaborated social and moral arguments about the consequences of alternative courses of action for different social values such as family well-being. Theory-based advocates, he says, would encourage public discussion and be catalysts for moral and social debate involving family policy issues. In contrast to adherents of particular measures who, he says, repeatedly act to restrict elaborated discourse, theory-based advocates would provide socially informed analyses that would be useful not only to adherents of particular policy solutions but also for open public discussion about such issues. The basic postmodern concepts guiding the family policy practitioner as social critic/advocate would revolve around the notion of self, with multiple identities and group affiliations, entangled in heterogeneous struggles with multiple possibilities for empowerment.

The Family Policy Educator Role

Seidman's description of the role of the social critic as a form of family policy practice is compatible with the role of the family policy educator, a role crucial to the creation of a public interested in and informed about family policy issues and the development and enactment of family policy—and for increasing civic engagement in problems related to families in need of solutions. As another form of family policy practice, family policy education enables citizens to become better informed about the family issues embedded in public policies (McKenzie, 1991). It is based on a Jeffersonian view of the importance of education in the democratic political process. Although not all family policy issues are amenable to rational or factual analysis, they are all amenable to the analysis of different constructions of family problems and solutions to them in terms of the ways such problems are perceived and defined and by whom—and the values such constructions represent.

The family policy educator role takes on an advocacy function when educators examine a family policy issue and, in light of their professional knowledge and values, identify the policy alternative they believe to be best for families and society. Then, based on scientific evidence and their interpretation of it, they argue for their position or the policy they think would be best for a group to support. Another variation of family policy education takes a more participatory and less hierarchical approach based on the notion of participatory democracy and the assumption that if affected groups are included in the process and have access to the same information about an issue, they will be able to arrive at their own decision about the policy they think would be best to support—and be more committed to it. Here the educator serves as moderator and group facilitator. In short, McKenzie says, the family policy educator/practitioner is either an advocate for a particular policy choice in relation to families or an advocate for an open and inclusive democratic process that minimizes informational disparities among individuals and groups and empowers them to arrive at their own decisions about such choices.

The National Issues Forums that civic and educational organizations around the country have initiated at the local level are illustrative of the latter version of family policy education (Roe, 1998) and similar to many of the forums sponsored by university extension programs around the county. The forums provide opportunities for citizens to deliberate on challenging public policy issues having to do, for example, with the economy, education, health care, and violent crime. Varying in size and the issues discussed, the forums are different from everyday policy discourse and adversarial policy debates in that they present each issue or problem in a neutral, nonpartisan way and encourage participants to reflect on the issue or problem in light of their own values and beliefs when examining alternative policy solutions. Analyzing each alternative in light of the values they hold, participants present arguments for and against each alternative solution and discuss the tradeoffs of each.

The forums are useful for leading to shared understandings of a particular problem, and they also often lead to sufficient consensus for participants to consider policy solutions that would best address the problem. Generally, Roe says, a public voice emerges, sending a signal to lawmakers about the direction forum participants want government to take with regard to particular issues. Each year, forum results are shared with people in public office, and in this way, participants help to set the government's policy agenda. Forums also can lead to complementary actions as individuals and groups decide which portions of a public problem they themselves can help remedy. By enabling widely diverse citizens to come together to determine the kinds of action and legislation they favor and the kinds of action and legislation that, for their common good, they resist, the forums not only help to create interested publics engaged in public issues but, in doing so, help to increase the nation's social capital that Robert Putnam (2000) decries has declined in this country.

■ Challenges to Family Policy Education/Practice

Cultural Challenges

Relevant here are features of the American culture that stand in the way of developing an interested, attentive public that is informed and engaged in policy issues related to families. One is the cultural penchant for material success and social status and having fun in the process (McKenzie, 1991). The cultural assumption that an invisible hand produces individual, family, and societal well-being from the sum of our individual, not collective, pursuits runs counter to engagement in public and family policy issues, McKenzie says.

Another challenge that family policy practitioners have to confront is the general tendency to regard public policy only in terms of what government does or does not do, rather than what individuals in society do or do not do to support or not support what government does. Illustrative here is George W. Bush's assertion in the 2000 presidential campaign with regard to his tax cut plan, namely that he wanted to empower people to make their own decisions about how they spent their money rather than have government make those decisions for them, projecting the view that government in the United States is separate from the people and that the people are separate from government.

Institutional Challenges

Another challenge to developing an interested public has to do with institutional competition, whereby family policy practice/education competes with religious institutions, voluntary associations, print and electronic media, neighborhood, and community in transmitting civic and social values. Also at odds with such engagement and the consensus required for it is the American model of adversarial politics and policy. Big policy agenda items, McKenzie (1991) says, are addressed only when there is sufficient consensus to do so, which raises such questions as: Whose views are to become part of the consensus? and How is that consensus to be reached—by crisis, political force, manipulation, political maneuvering, or civic engagement and participation?

Scholars who focus on political institutions—the relatively permanent, routinized arrangements that organize formal political activity—point to institutional factors that stand in the way of civic engagement in family policy issues. To understand and explain what government does and does not do in relation to family policy, Noble (1997) suggests that special attention should be paid to historically specific sequences in state formation, the structural properties of states, and their "policy legacies." Like the National Issues Forums, Noble advises that preconditions for advancing a family policy agenda includes a high level of political organization on the part of those who would benefit from policy changes, agreement among potential beneficiaries of the elements of a common political agenda, a strategy for achieving it, and a political structure that does not overly burden those working to overcome such challenges—which here pertains to family policy practice.

In referring to legacies from the past that have served to establish the direction that policy has taken in the United States, Noble cites, in particular, strategic choices that have led the country to rely more heavily on market actors and market processes than the public sector. Such choices, he says, have restricted the kinds of policy solutions that can be constructed to adequately confront the problems that families experience in society (e.g., affordable housing, affordable health insurance, and quality public education). Such constraints, as noted earlier, have led to a vicious circle, whereby policy inadequacies and perceptions of unfairness in public programs have led to the erosion of popular support for government and public policies and programs; declining support in turn has made such programs vulnerable to retrenchment; and retrenchment has further eroded the government's ability to adequately address the problems families experience in American society. Creating the perception that government cannot work for them, such constraints also have hampered efforts to restructure institutional arrangements in relation to the public and private sectors.

Indeed, some attribute the decline in civic engagement to the blurring of private sector and public sector roles, which in recent years has become increasingly pronounced, making efforts to increase government's effectiveness even more difficult (Sanger, 1999). Consider, for example, all the "noncommercials" on public television that with each passing year seem to turn into longer and longer promotions for corporate sponsors and interests. Although the public sector is supposed to rein in the private, the blurring of the two sectors has resulted in the shrinkage of the public sector and the expansion of the private sector, resulting in and reflecting a sea change in traditional political constituencies. Whether or not the public good has suffered as a result depends on what people think government is all about, Sanger advises. According to Robert Putnam's analysis (2000) of the Organization of European Community Development (OECD) countries, the size of government is positively related to civic engagement and social capital. By social capital, Putnam means certain features of social life—namely networks, norms, and basic trust—that enable people to act together to pursue shared objectives more effectively—such as different family policies that aim to enhance family well-being. By civic engagement, he means people's connections with the life of their communities, like those facilitated by small-scale, face-to-face associations. When citizens become actively engaged in public life, it rejuvenates their communities, culturally and economically (Roe, 1998). In short, it increases the social capital that makes solutions possible.

Social and Technological Challenges

Putnam's (2000) observations about the strange disappearance of civic engagement in United States are pertinent. Identifying television as the culprit in analyzing the effects of age on civic engagement, Putnam observed that whereas older people have consistently been more engaged and trusting than younger people, people do not become more engaged and trusting as they age. Generational effects show up in disparities among age groups at a single point in time, he says, producing real social change as successive generations, enduringly imprinted with divergent views, enter and leave the population. With generational effects, he says, individuals do not change, but society does.

The visible effects of generational disengagement, which began in the 1940s and 1950s, were delayed in part because of the postwar boom in college enrollments, which raised levels of civic engagement and offset generational trends and the time it takes for such effects for a given generation to become numerically dominant in the adult population. According to Putnam, television watching per household was more than 50% higher in 1995 than in the 1950s, resulting in a massive change in the way Americans spend their time and occurring precisely during the years of generational civic disengagement. Although finding television viewing to be associated with low social capital and newspaper reading with high social capital, Putnam observed that newspaper circulation per household in 1996 dropped by more than half from its peak in 1947. Not sure as to how the tie between newspaper reading and civic involvement worked, the two, he said, were clearly linked. Television viewing, Putnam said, privatizes leisure time and comes at the expense of nearly every social activity outside the home, especially social gatherings, community meetings, and informal conversations, the very venues of family policy discourse and family policy practice.

■ Family Policy Practice:
A Venue for Increasing Civic Engagement and Social Capital

Then what is the meaning of such challenges for family policy practice? Although most Americans believe that government is not working as it should, Roe (1998) maintains that the problem does not lie with government but with citizens who have neglected their citizenship responsibilities and whose participation and engagement are key to making our democracy live up to its promise. What is needed, he says, are new relationships with government and each other and new ways of making decisions and acting together. Government, he says, is about the collaborative efforts of all citizens and elected and appointed officials to meet common needs. Improving civic education for adults as well as for children, he says—which here includes family policy education—would strengthen the bridge to civic engagement and give citizens the skills to tackle problems effectively. Citizenship, he continues, involves much more than paying taxes and voting. For democracy to function as it should, citizens must be actively engaged in community organizations, election campaigns, deliberative forums, and a range of other activities associated with family policy practice. Thus, despite the challenges that confront family policy practice—cultural, institutional, and social/technological—it appears that family policy practitioners are strategically positioned to encourage and increase public engagement not only in the construction of policy solutions to family problems but the nation's social capital as well.

■ Concluding Comments

Before closing the chapter and ending the discussion that constitutes this book, I would like to say a word about the role of government in the social and economic life of the country and in family life too, topics about which people hold widely divergent views, and as readers, if they did not know before, know now. On this particular topic, I agree with those who view our political system as a relational network for fostering political and social integration and our collective well-being—and family well-being as well. Based on feelings of solidarity, obligation, and mutual trust, governments, as political arrangements, are our primary instruments for countering incentives to pursue narrow self-interests (Mansbridge, 1994). Governments also are mechanisms for connecting micro- and macro-level concerns—that is, the concerns of individuals and families with the concerns of the larger society via family policies as outputs of the political system (MacRae, 1985; Zimmerman, 1992a). From this point of view, government can be seen as a form of social capital that family policy practice needs for constructing policy solutions to family problems that enhance family well-being, a view I hope many readers share.

If readers are still confused about the meaning of *postmodernism*, they have only to consider the 2000 presidential election, the ambiguity, uncertainty, and ambivalence characterizing its results being the very hallmarks of postmodernism. Although Al Gore had won the popular vote, it was the electoral vote that mattered, as, we all learned, it does in all presidential elections. The difference between the 2000 presidential election and most other such elections was the closeness of the electoral vote and the ambiguities surrounding the election process itself, particularly in the state of Florida, where the outcome of the election remained highly uncertain long after the election was over. In the end, George W. Bush prevailed and became the next and 43rd president of the United States.

As to what George W. Bush's presidency might mean for families and family policy, you, the readers, will have to judge for yourselves, ideally by assessing the family implications of his proposals and the legislation he signs off on and using one of the family frameworks presented in this book to do so. We can assume, given earlier discussion about the processes involved in the making of family policy, that radical departures from existing policies are highly unlikely, especially in the context of the closeness of the election, the 50/50 party split in the Senate, and the almost 50/50 party split in the House. On the basis of his speeches during the presidential campaign, however, George W. Bush's policy approach to families is likely to be more implicit than explicit, especially when compared to what Al Gore's approach might have been had he prevailed in the election. Whereas Gore mentioned family and family-related words 29 times in his acceptance speech for his party's nomination for president, Bush used such words only 11 times in his acceptance speech for his nomination for president, not counting references to his family of origin and family of procreation.

389

That language is important in mirroring and shaping people's cognitive structures, that is, how they think and what they do in terms of family policy, was illustrated in a December 2000 discussion about a highly controversial issue, school vouchers. Indeed, Senator Trent Lott, Senate majority leader, ventured to remark in that discussion that the word *voucher* was part of the problem in addressing problems related to the education of the nation's children (Wilgoren, 2000). A linguistic cue, vouchers involve the use of public money for private school tuition. As a consequence of the strong emotional responses the term evokes, school voucher advocates considered changing their strategy to stage a broader philosophical attack on the way public education has been run in this country for a century and avoiding use of the term *voucher,* which they said was loaded. Thus far, studies on the effects of vouchers on student performance— and their impact on local public schools—have produced mixed results (which, parenthetically, like the election, is also in keeping with postmodernism).

Armed with knowledge of the family and policy frameworks and the history of American social and family policy in the United States and the values that policy choices such as school vouchers and similar changes would reflect, you, the readers, will understand what is at stake in issues advocates would like to obscure, and act accordingly.

January 2001

REFERENCES

Aaron, H. J., Mann, T. E., & Taylor, T. (1994). Introduction. In H. J. Aaron, T. E. Mann, & T. Taylor (Eds.), *Values and public policy* (pp. 1-15). Washington, DC: Brookings Institution.

Aaron, H., & Reischauer, R. (1999, Winter). Should we retire Social Security? *Brookings Review*, 6-11.

Aboud, F. E. (1987). The development of ethnic self-identification and attitudes. In J. S. Phinney & M. J. Rotheram (Eds.), *Children's ethnic socialization: Pluralism and development* (pp. 32-55). Newbury Park, CA: Sage.

Adams v. Howerton, 486 F. Supp. 1119 (C.D. Cal. 1980).

Allison, G. (1971). *The essence of decision: Explaining the Cuban Missile Crisis.* Boston: Little, Brown.

Almond, G., & Verba, S. (1963). *The civic culture.* Princeton, NJ: Princeton University Press.

Almond, G., & Verba, S. (1989). *The civic culture: Political attitudes and democracy in five nations.* Newbury Park, CA: Sage.

Alvarez, L. (1998, February 12). A conservative battles corporate health care. *New York Times,* p. A10.

The American ethnic experience as it stands in the nineties (1998, February-March). *Public Perspective, 9*(2), 50-65.

Americans on parenting (1999, October-November). *Public Perspective, 10*(6), 18.

Anderson, E. A., & Skinner, D. A. (1995, Spring). The components of family policy education. *Journal of Family and Economic Issues, 16*(1), 65-77.

Anderson, J. Z., & White, G. D. (1986). Dysfunctional intact families and stepfamilies. *Family Process, 25,* 407-422.

Andrews, E. L. (1999, October 8). A new Swedish prosperity even with a welfare state. *New York Times,* p. A1.

Andrews, F. M., & Withey, S. B. (1976). *Social indicators of well-being: American's perceptions of life quality.* New York: Plenum.

Angier, N. (2000, August 22). Do races differ? Not really, genes show. *New York Times,* p. D1.

Applebome, P. (1994, June 23). Anti-gay act splits family of an official. *New York Times,* p. A11.

Applebome, P. (1999, July 11). For better or worse, poverty's poster child. *New York Times,* p. Wk. 3.

Arac, J. (1989). *Postmodernism and politics.* Minneapolis: University of Minnesota Press.

Baehr v. Lewin, 852 P 2d 44 (Ha Sup Ct 1993).

Bahr, H. M., & Bahr, K. S. (1996, August). A paradigm of family transcendence. *Journal of Marriage and the Family, 58,* 541-555.

Bailyn, B. (Ed.). (1993). *The Debate on the Constitution.* New York: Library of America.

391

Baker v. Nelson, 191 NW 2d 185 (Minn 1971).

Baldwin, W. (1905, April 15) Family desertion and non-support laws. *Charities, 14*(3), 650-655.

Ball, R. (1996, November-December). A secure system. *The American Prospect,* 34-35.

Barone, M., & Ujifusa, G. (1989). *The almanac of American politics 1989.* Washington, DC: National Journal.

Barone, M., & Ujifusa, G. (1997). *The almanac of American politics 1998.* Washington, DC: National Journal.

Barone, M. ,& Ujifusa, G. (1999). *The almanac of American politics 2000.* Washington, DC: National Journal.

Barringer, F. (1992, November 16). Hillary Clinton's new role: A spouse or policy leader? *New York Times,* p. A1.

Behind a 15 year old's decision to forego medical treatment (1994, June 13). *New York Times,* p. A7.

Belief in America's Promise (1996, February-March). *Public Perspective, 7*(2), 34-35.

Berg, S. (1994, May 9). Graduates confront shifting definition of success. *Star Tribune,* p. A1.

Berke, R. (1994, February 20). Tides that brought Democrats to GOP have turned. *New York Times,* p. E3.

Berke, R. (1995. January 1). Epic political realignments often aren't. *New York Times.* p. E3.

Beutler, I. F., Burr, W. R., Bahr, K. S., & Herrin, D. A. (1989, November). The family realm: Theoretical contributions for understanding its uniqueness. *Journal of Marriage and the Family. 51,* 805-816.

Blake, L. (1993, May 10). Like citizens, officials often tear their hair. *Star Tribune,* p. 8A.

Blau, P. (1964). *Exchange and power in social life.* New York: John Wiley.

Boss, P. (1999). *Ambiguous loss.* Cambridge, MA: Harvard University Press.

Bowman, K. (1999, April-May). Living happily ever after: Marriage under the microscope. *Public Perspective, 10*(3), 35-40.

Bragg, R. (1995, August 13). All she has, $150,000, is going to a university. *New York Times,* p. A1.

Brandt, L. (1905, April 15). Broken families. *Charities, 14*(3), 665-670.

Bray, J. H., & Berger, S. H. (1993). Development issues in Stepfamilies Research Project: Family relationships and parent-child interactions. *Journal of Family Psychology, 7*(1), 7-17.

Brennan, T. (1996, October 20). American democratic institutions and social values. Paper presented at a conference on Social Values and Public Policy, Washington, DC, George Washington University.

Broder, J. (1999, July 6). A pledge of federal help for the economic byways. *New York Times,* p. A10.

Broderick, C. B. (1993). *Understanding family process.* Newbury Park, CA: Sage.

Brody, J. (2000, March 15). Earlier work with children steers them from crime. *New York Times,* p. A16.

Bronfenbrenner, U. (1986). Ecology of the family as a context for human development: Research perspectives. *Developmental Psychology, 22*(6), 723-742.

Brunswick, M. (1998, May 22). One-time welfare recipient leaves $5,000 to county. *Minneapolis Star Tribune,* p. B1

Bryson, K., & Casper, L. (1998, March). *Current population reports: special studies,* Coresident grandparents and grandchildren. Washington, DC: Population Division, U.S. Bureau of the Census.

Bubolz, M.. & Sontag, M. S. (1993). Human ecology theory. In P. Boss, W. Doherty, R. LaRossa, W. Schumm, & S. Steinmetz (Eds.), *Sourcebook of family theories and methods* (pp. 419-447). New York: Plenum.

Bumps in the road. (1999, October-November). *Public Perspective, 10*(6), 23.

Burgess, E. W. (1926). The family as a unity of interacting personalities. *Family, 7,* 3-9.

Burr, W. R., Leigh, G. K., Day, R. D., & Constantine, J. (1979). Symbolic interaction and the family. In W. R. Burr, R. Hill, I. Nye, & I. Reiss (Eds.), *Contemporary theories about the family* (Vol. 2, pp. 42-111). New York: Free Press.

Bush, G. (1989, January 21). Nation stands ready to push on [Transcript of Bush's inaugural address]. *New York Times,* p. Y10.

Bush, G. W., Jr. (1999, June 20). Bush: "No turning back" from race for presidency. *New York Times,* p. Y16.

Byrne, C., Benidt, B., & Hudgins, C. (1980, June 20). Family feud. *Star Tribune,* p. 1A.

Califano, J., Jr. (1976, September 17). American families: Trends, pressures, and recommendations. A Preliminary Report to Governor Jimmy Carter (Mimeo.) Washington, DC: U.S. Government Printing Office.

Campbell, A., Converse, P. E., & Rodgers, W. L. (1976). *The quality of American life: Perceptions, evaluations, and satisfactions.* New York: Russell Sage.

Capizzano, J., Adams, G., & Sonenstein, F. (2000, March). Child care arrangements for children under five: Variation across states. *National Survey of American's Families,* Series B, No. B-7. Urban Institute.

Caroli, B. (1987). *First ladies.* New York: Oxford University Press.

Casper, L. M. (1996, March). *Who's minding our preschoolers?* [Current Population Reports P70-53]. Washington, DC: U.S. Bureau of the Census.

Casper, L. M. (1997a, November). *Who's minding our preschoolers? Fall 1994 update.* [Current Population Reports P70-62]. Washington DC: U.S. Bureau of the Census.

Casper, L. M. (1997b, September). *My daddy takes care of me! Fathers as care providers.* [Current Population Reports P70-59]. Washington DC: U.S. Bureau of the Census.

Casper, L., & Bryson, K. (1998a, March). *Household and family characteristics: March 1998 Update.* [Current Population Reports P29-515]. Washington DC: U.S. Bureau of the Census.

Casper, L., & Bryson, K. (1998b, March). *Co-resident grandparents and their grandchildren: Grandparent maintained families.* [Population Division Working Paper No. 26]. Washington DC: U.S. Bureau of the Census.

Cavan, R., & Ranck, K. R. (1938). *The family and the Depression.* Chicago: University of Chicago Press.

Cherlin, A. (1996). *Public and private families.* New York: McGraw Hill.

Chilman, C. (1973). Public social policy and families in the 1970s. *Social Casework, 54,* 575-585.

Chira, S. (1993a, October 20). Elizabeth Dole: Power player, playing cautiously. *New York Times,* p. B7.

Chira, S. (1993b, October 21). Obstacles for men who want family time. *New York Times,* p. B4.

Christian group keeps to right and old time. (1993, September 12). *New York Times,* p. Y20.

Clark, E. (1999, November 1). Why it pays to quit. *U.S. News and World Report,* 74-86.

Clinton applies health plan to citizens' personal lives. (1993, September 27). *Star Tribune,* p. A2.

Clinton, B. (1992, July 17). [Text of address by President Clinton accepting the Democratic nomination]. *New York Times,* p. A12.

Clinton, B. (1994, January 27). [Transcript of President Clinton's message on the State of the Union]. *New York Times,* p. A10.

Clinton, B. (2000, January 28). [Text of President Clinton's State of the Union Address to Congress]. *New York Times,* p. A16.

Clinton job ratings. (1993, July-August). *Public Perspective, 4*(5), 82-84.

Clymer, A. (1993a, January 27). Voices of new women resound in the Senate. *New York Times,* p. A16.

Clymer, A. (1993b, March 8). After three decades working in Senate, Kennedy gets a turn for his agenda. *New York Times,* p. A8.

Clymer, A. (1993c, July 27). A top GOP couple splits on National Service bill. *New York Times,* p. A8.

Clymer, A. (1993d, October 13). Many health plans, one political goal. *New York Times,* p. 14.

Clymer, A. (1994a, February 11). Senator outlines three alternatives to Clinton plan. *New York Times,* p. A1.

Clymer, A. (1994b, June 9). Health bills making gains in committees. *New York Times,* p. A12.

Clymer, A., & Seelye, K. (2000, January 4). Bradley and Gore renew the battle. *New York Times,* p. A1.

Cohen, N. E., & Connery, M. F. (1967). Government policy and the family. *Journal of Marriage and the Family, 29,* 6-17.

Collins, R. (1975). *Conflict sociology: Toward an explanatory science.* San Diego: Academic Press.

Converse, P. (1964). The nature of belief systems among mass publics. In D. Apter (Ed.), *Ideology and discontent* (pp. 206-261). New York: Free Press.

Cooley, C. H. (1902). *Human nature and the social order.* New York: Scribner.

Coombs, R. H. (1991, January). Marital status and personal well-being: A literature review. *Family Relations, 40*(1), 97-102.

Couple who left 2 daughters at home give them up for adoption (1993, July 12). *New York Times,* p. A7.

Crispell, D. (1999, October-November). The new materialism. *Public Perspective, 10*(6), 29-31.

Cummins, H. (1999a, July 20). Parents' anti-marijuana stand not getting across. *Star Tribune,* p. A1.

Cummins, H. (1999b, October 21). A child at a crossroads. *Star Tribune,* p. A1.

Cummins, H. (2000, June 28). It's time for parents to reclaim family time. *Star Tribune,* p. B1.

Cuomo, M. (1984, July 17) [Transcript of keynote address by Cuomo to Convention]. *New York Times,* p. 16.

Dao, J. (1999, July 24). Short on tax-cut bill: Gain or loss for moderates. *New York Times,* p. A9.

Dawson, D. (1991). Family structure and children's health: United States, 1988. National Center for Health Statistics, *Vital Health Statistics, 10* 178.

Defense of Marriage Act of 1996, Pub. L. No. 104-199.

DeFlebre, C. (1998, February 17). Legislation aims to help nursing mothers at work. *Star Tribune,* p. B1.

Dempsey, J. J. (1981). *The family and public policy.* Baltimore: Paul H. Brookes.

DeParle, J. (1994a, May 22). Proposal for welfare cutoff is dividing Clinton officials. *New York Times,* p. A17.

DeParle, J. (1994b, April 22). Scrap welfare? Surprisingly, the notion is now a cause. *New York Times,* p. A10.

Devine, D. (1972). *The political culture of the United States.* Boston: Little, Brown.

Devroy, A. (1993, November 9). White House runs and stumbles: Agenda is huge but authority is diffuse. *Washington Post,* p. A1.

Dilworth-Anderson, P., Burton, L., & Johnson, I. (1993). Reframing theories for understanding race, ethnicity, and families. In P. Boss, W. Doherty, R. LaRossa, W. Schumm, & S. Steinmetz (Eds.), *Sourcebook of family theories and methods* (pp. 627-646). New York: Plenum.

Disney's maid bequeaths $4.5 million to aid children (1994, October 28). *Star Tribune,* p. 7A.

Doherty, W. (1997). *Postmodernism and family theory.* [Mimeo]. St. Paul, MN: University of Minnesota, Family Social Science.

Doron, G. (1992, Autumn-Winter). Rational choice and the policy sciences. *Policy Studies Review, 11*(3/4), 359-369.

Dowd, M. (1994, September 29). Amid debate on her role, Hillary Clinton pushes on. *New York Times,* p. A1.

Draper, N. (1999, March 12). Schools enlist parents in quest for funds. *Minneapolis Star Tribune,* p. B1.

Draper, T. (1993, October 10). A review of the book, The Constitution was made, not born. *New York Times Book Review,* p. 3.

Dreble, D. (1999, March 8). Paul Weyrich: Crank or prophet? *Washington Post National Weekly Edition,* p. 10.

Duchschere, K. (1993, June 3). Algerian convicted in Dakota County of depriving ex-wife of parental rights. *Star Tribune,* p. 20B.

Dugger, C. (1995, May 12). Budget cuts imperil efforts to save families. *New York Times,* p. A1.

Dumon, W., & Aldous, J. (1979). European and United States political contexts for family policy research. *Journal of Marriage and the Family, 41,* 497-505.

Dupuis, M. D. (1995). The impact of culture, society, and history on the legal process: An analysis of the legal status of same-sex relationships in the United States and Denmark. *International Journal of Law and the Family, 9,* 86-118.

Dye, T. (1975). *Understanding public policy.* Englewood Cliffs, N.J.: Prentice Hall.

Easton, D. (1979). *A framework for policy analysis,* Chicago: University of Chicago Press.

Eckholm, E. (1994, July 11). Frayed nerves of people without health coverage. *New York Times,* p. A1.

Edelman, M. (1968), *Constructing the political spectacle.* Chicago: University of Chicago Press.

Edelman, M. (1975, July-August). Language, myths and rhetoric, *Society,* 14-21.

Edelman, M. (1985). *The symbolic uses of politics.* Chicago: University of Chicago Press.

Ehrlich, Paul (2000). Membership recruitment letter. Zero Population Growth.

Ekeh, P. (1974). *Social Exchange Theory.* Cambridge, MA: Harvard University Press.

Elazar, D. (1972). *American federalism: A view from the states* (2nd ed.). New York: Crowell.

Elazar, D. (1984). *American federalism: A view from the states* (3rd ed.). New York: Harper & Row.

Elazar, D. (1986). Marketplace and the commonwealth and the three political cultures. In M. Gittell (Ed.), *State politics and the new federalism* (pp. 172-178). New York: Longman.

Elkind, D. (1994). *Ties that stress: The new family imbalance.* Cambridge, MA: Harvard University Press.

Ellperin, J. (1999, August 30). A diatribal tradition: Town hall meetings draw fewer voters. *Washington Post National Weekly Edition,* p. 14.

Engleberg, S., & Seelye, K. (1994, December 20). Gingrich: Man in spotlight and organization in shadow. *New York Times,* p. A1.

Erikson, R. S., Wright, G. C., & McIver, J. P. (1993). *Statehouse democracy: Public opinion and policy in the American States.* New York: Cambridge University Press.

Eskridge, W. N. (1996). *The case for same-sex marriage.* New York: Free Press.

Esping-Anderson, G. (1996). After the golden age? Welfare state dilemmas in a global economy. In G. Esping-Anderson (Ed.), *The welfare state in transition: National adaptations in global economies.* Thousand Oaks, CA: Sage.

Ethnicity in black and white. (1998, February-March). *Public Perspective, 9*(2), 58-65.

Even governments can get high marks. (1993, July-August). *Public Perspective, 4*(5), 91.

The family (1998, February-March). *Public Perspective, 9*(2), 17-24.

Family delegates rank issues.(1980, July 14). *Minneapolis Sunday Tribune,* p. A8.

Farrington, K., & Chertok, E. (1993). Social conflict theories of family. In P. Boss, W. Doherty, R. LaRossa, W. R. Schumm, & S. Steinmetz (Eds.), *Sourcebook of family theories and methods.* (pp. 357-381). New York: Plenum.

Firestone, D. (2000, January 11). South Carolina GOP limits black voters, suit says. *New York Times,* p. A12.

Fitzpatrick, J. L., & Hero, R. E. (1988). Political cultures and political characteristics of the American states. *Western Political Quarterly, 41,* 45-53.

Fox-Genovese, E. (1999, April-May). Women's status: A century of enormous change, *Public Perspective, 10*(3), 26-28.

Friedman, T. (1999, March 28). From supercharged financial markets to Osama bin Laden, the emerging global order demands an enforcer. That's American's new burden. *New York Times Magazine,* 40-97.

Frohock, F. (1979). *Public policy: Scope and logic.* Englewood Cliffs, N.J.: Prentice Hall.

Galinsky, E. (1999). *Ask the children: What America's children really think about working parents.* New York: Morrow.

Geertz, C. (1973). *The interpretation of cultures.* New York: Basic.

Gelfand, D. E., & Barresi, C. M. (Eds.). (1987). *Ethnic dimensions of aging.* New York: Springer.

Gergen, K. J. (1999). *An invitation to social construction.* Thousand Oaks, CA: Sage.

Giele, J. Z. (1976). Social policy and the family. *Annual Review of Sociology, 5,* 275-302.

Gilbert, S. (1998, July 28). Raising grandchildren, rising stress. *New York Times,* p. B8.

Gillis, J. R. (1996). *A world of their own making: Myth, ritual and the quest for family values.* New York: Basic.

Glaser, B. G., & Straus, A. L. (1967). *The discovery of grounded theory.* Chicago: Aldine.

Goldberg, C. (1999a, June 30). Insurance for Viagra spurs coverage for birth control. *New York Times,* p. A1.

Goldberg, C. (1999b, October 23). On web, models auction their eggs to bidders for beautiful children. *New York Times,* p. A10.

Goldberg, C., & Connelly, M. (1999, October 20). Fear and violence have declined among teenagers, poll shows. *New York Times,* p. A1.

Goode, W. J. (1963). *World revolution and family patterns.* New York: Free Press.

Goode, W. J. (1971); Force and violence in the family. *Journal of Marriage and the Family, 33,* 624-636.

Gordon, R., & Chase-Lansdale, L. (1995). *Resource guide to careers in child an family policy.* Chicago: Irving B. Harris Graduate School of Public Policy Studies and the Chapin Hall Center for Children.

Gore, A. (1999, June 20). Gore: 'Within a generation's journey is a new horizon.' *New York Times,* p. Y16.

Gossett, T. (1965). *Race and the history of an idea in America.* New York: Schocken.

Gouldner, A. W. (1960). The norm of reciprocity. *American Sociological Review, 25,* 161-178.

Gov. Sundlun settles lawsuit on paternity (1993, June 18). *New York Times,* p. A1.

Greenfield, M. (1996, September 9). The family values party. *Newsweek*, 82.

Griffin, J. (1986). *Well-being: Its meaning, measurement and moral importance.* Oxford, UK: Clarendon.

Grimsley, K., & Salmon, J. (1999, October 4). A few surprises for working parents. *Washington Post National Weekly Edition*, p. 29.

Gross, J. (1993, December 11). Second wave of AIDS feared by officials in San Francisco. *New York Times*, p. 1.

Gubrium, J. F., & Holstein, J. A. (1990). *What is family?* Mountain View, CA: Mayfield.

Hafen, B. (1990). Individualism in family law. In D. Blankenhorn, S. Bayme & J. Elshtain (Eds.), *Rebuilding the nest* (pp. 161-178). Milwaukee: Family Service America.

Hall, R. (1972). *Organizations: Structure and process.* Englewood Cliffs, NJ: Prentice Hall.

Hamburger, T. (1999, May 18). Health plan group is waging its own campaign for 2000. *Minneapolis Star Tribune*, p. A3.

Hamburger, T., & Meyers, M. (1993, October 25). Seeking a cure: Looking for answers to America's health care woes. *Star Tribune*, pp. 5H-7H, 9H-10H.

Hanley, R. (1993a, October 17). Shoplift arrest leads police to children in attic. *New York Times*, p. Y16.

Hanley, R. (1993b, November 8). Use of curfews growing against youths at night. *New York Times*, p. A13.

The harm in family welfare caps (1994, June 9). *New York Times*, p. A18.

Hawaii slams door on gay marriages: Eyes turn to Vermont (1999, December 11). Retrieved from the World Wide Web: http://www.startribune.com.

Health care: Clinton's plan and the alternatives. (1993, October 17). *New York Times*, p. A14.

Health care: The public reacts. (1993, November-December). *Public Perspective*, 5(1), 74-75.

Health care update. (1994, July-August). *Public Perspective*, 5(5), 84.

The heart stands still. (1999, October-November). *Public Perspective*, 10(6), 20.

Heath, A. (1976). *Rational choice and social exchange.* Cambridge, UK: Cambridge University Press.

Helping hands. (1999, October-November). *Public Perspective*, 10(6), 24.

Henson, D. M. (1993). Will same-sex marriages be recognized in sister states? Full faith and credit and due process limitations on states' choice of law regarding the status and incidents of homosexual marriages following Hawaii's Baehr v. Lewin. *University of Louisville Journal of Family Law, 32*(3), 551-600.

Herbert, W. (1999, November 29). When strangers become family. *U.S. News and World Report,* 59-67.

Herzog, A. R., Rodgers, W. L., & Woodsworth, J. (1982). *Subjective well-being among different age groups.* Ann Arbor: University of Michigan, Institute for Social Research.

Hetherington, E. M.. & Jodl, K. M. (1993). Stepfamilies as setting for child development (mimeo). University of Virginia.

Hill, R. (1949). *Families under stress.* New York: Harpers.

Hill, R. (1958). Generic features of families under stress. *Social Casework, 49*, 139-150.

Hill, R. (1971). Modern systems theory and the family: A confrontation. *Social Science Information, 10*, 7-26.

Hill, R. (1980). Status of research on families. In *The Status of Children, Youth and Families, 1979.* Administration for Children, Youth and Families, U.S. Department of Health and Human Services. [DHHS Publication No. (OHDS) 80-30274]. Washington, DC: U.S. Department of Health and Human Services.

Hill, R., & Hansen, D. (1960). The identification of conceptual frameworks utilized in family study. *Marriage and Family Living, 22*, 299-311.

Hillbery, R. (1994), June 26). Family leave laws mark is minimal on working world. *Star Tribune*, p. A1.

Holloway, L. (1993, December 12). A grandmother fights for her second generation. *New York Times*, p. 20.

Hopfensperger, J. (1994, June 24). Welfare doesn't foster out-of-wedlock births, researchers declare. *Star Tribune*, p. A8.

Hopfensperger, J. (2000, June 2). Senate candidates debate social problems. *Star Tribune*, p. A16.

House health debate: Forensics medicine. (1994, March 17). *Star Tribune*, p. A7.

Howe, P. (1993, October 15). "Citizens' jury" supports Wellstone's health care proposal over Clinton plan. *Star Tribune,* p. A10.

Ibrahim, Y. (1995, December 20). To French, solidarity outweighs balanced budget. *New York Times,* p. A1.

Ibrahim, Y. (1996, December 13). Welfare's snug coat cuts Norwegian cold. *New York Times,* p. A1.

Ifill, G. (1993, September 28). Making deals, not waves in strategy for health plan. *New York Times,* p. A10.

Inglehart, R. (1990). *Culture shift in advanced society.* Princeton, NJ: Princeton University Press.

Iovine, J. (1996, November 7). When parents decide to take charge again. *New York Times,* p. A13.

Jansson, B. (1994). *Social policy: From theory to practice.* Belmont, CA: Brooks-Cole.

Jay, S. (1995, December 25). Woman works toward a career and reunites with daughter. *New York Times,* p. A10.

Jehl, D. (1994, July 20). Coverage of 95 percent might be enough, Clinton concedes. *New York Times,* p. A1.

Jernegan, M. (1931). *Laboring and dependent classes in Colonial America: 1607-1783.* Chicago: University of Chicago Press.

Johnson, C. (1976). Political culture in the United States: Elazar's formulation examined. *American Journal of Political Science, 20,* 491-509.

Johnson, D. (1997a, October 13). She smoked and he sued; she quit and they won. *New York Times,* p. A1.

Johnson, D. (1997b, January 22). Father who won custody of boy moves out. *New York Times,* p. A8.

Johnston, D. (1997, May 5). Paralyzed since fall in 1962, man is still seeking benefits. *New York Times,* p. A1.

Johnston, D. (1999, September 5). Gap between rich and poor found substantially wider. *New York Times,* p. Y14.

Jones v. Hallahan, 501 SW 2d 588 (Ky App 1973).

Just what is the WTO and how does it operate? (1999, November 30). *Minneapolis Star Tribune,* p. A16. [First appeared in the Washington Post].

Kahn, A. J. (1969). *Studies in social policy and social planning.* New York: Russell Sage.

Kahn, A., Kamerman, S., & Dowling, M. (1979). *Government structure versus family policy.* New York: Columbia University Press.

Kamerman, S. (1976). *Developing a family impact statement.* New York: Foundation for Child Development.

Kamerman, S., & Kahn, A. (1976). Explorations in family policy. *Social Work, 21,* 181-186.

Kamerman, S., & Kahn, A. (Eds). (1978). *Family policy: Government and families in fourteen countries.* New York: Columbia University Press.

Kantor, D., & Lehr, W. (1975). *Inside the family.* Harper & Row.

King, E., & Hill, M. A. (Eds.) (1993). *Women's education in developing countries: Barriers, benefits and policies.* Baltimore: Johns Hopkins University Press (for the World Bank).

Klauda, P. (1980, June 27). Conference on families filled Carter campaign pledge. *Star Tribune,* p. A1.

Kleinfield, N. R. (1993, June 8). Immigrant dream of heaven chokes in journey of misery. *New York Times,* p. A1.

Koepke, L. (1999, November 10). Academic programs in family policy. Presentation at annual meeting of the National Council on Family Relations, Irvine, CA.

Kohler, J., & Zimmerman, S. L. (1999). The congressional debate over the Defense of Marriage Act (DOMA): An examination of competing perceptions. [Mimeo]. St. Paul, MN: University of Minnesota, Family Social Science.

Kolata, G. (1993, October 17). Will U.S. be healthier? Not so easy, experts say. *New York Times,* p. A1.

Kolbert, E. (1995, August 6). Whose family values are they anyway? *New York Times,* p. E1.

Koos, E. L. (1946). *Families in trouble.* New York: Kings Crown.

Kozol, J. (2000, August 22). Losing my father one day at a time. *New York Times,* p. A27.

Kristof, N. D. (1996, September 10). Welfare as Japan knows it: A family affair. *New York Times,* p. A1.

Krugman, P. (2000, March 29). Pursuing happiness. *New York Times,* p. A29.

Labation, S. (1999, September 6). Anti-federalism measures have bipartisan support. *New York Times,* p. A8.

Lacey, M. (2000, August 6). President vetoes marriage-tax cut he calls reckless. *New York Times,* p. Y1.

Ladd, E. (1999, April-May). Everyday life: How are we doing? *Public Perspective, 10*(3), 1-20.

Lambda Legal Defense and Education Fund (1997-1998). *About Lambda* Retrieved from the World Wide Web: http://www.lamdalegal.org/egi-bin/pages/about.

Lang, J. (2000, February 14). Young workers value lifestyle over cash, surveys say. *Star Tribune,* p. E5.

Langdon, S. (1994, December 31). Clinton's high victory rate conceals disappointments. *Congressional Weekly,* 3619-3623.

LaRossa, R., & Reitzes, D. (1993). Symbolic interactionism and family studies. In P. Boss, W. Doherty, R. LaRossa, W. Schumm, & S. Steinmetz (Eds.), *Sourcebook of family theories and methods* (pp. 135-162). New York: Plenum.

Lasswell, H. (1968). The policy orientation. In D. Lerner & H. Lasswell (Eds.), *Policy sciences* (pp. 3-15). Stanford, CA: Stanford University Press.

Legitimacy: Americans continue to believe their society extends real opportunity to advance. (1999, April-May). *Public Perspective, 10*(3), 9.

Leiby, J. (1987). History of social welfare. In A. Minahan, R. Becerra, S. Briar, C. Coulton, L. Ginsberg, J. Hopps, J. Longres, R. Patti, W. Reid, T. Tripodi, & S. K. Khinduka (Eds.), *Encyclopedia of Social Work* (Vol. 2, pp. 755-588). Silver Spring, MD: National Association of Social Workers.

Leik, R. (1979, July 1), A program for training family impact analysts. [Mimeo]. St. Paul, MN: University of Minnesota.

Leik, R., & Hill, R. (1979). What price national policy for families? *Journal of Marriage and the Family, 41,* 457-459.

Leonard, P. (1997). *Postmodern welfare: Reconstructing an emancipatory project.* London: Sage.

Levi-Strauss, C. (1966). *The Savage Mind.* Chicago: University of Chicago Press.

Levy, C. (2000, March 26). Citing a crisis, Bush proposes literacy effort. *New York Times,* p. A1.

Lewin, T. (1993, November 8). Conflict for working couples: When he retires, must she? *New York Times,* p. A1.

Lewin, T. (1998, June 7). Report tying abortion to welfare is rejected. *New York Times,* p. A10.

Lighthizer, R. (1999, December 3). Conceding free trade's flaws. *New York Times,* p. A29.

Lindblom, C. (1959). The science of "muddling through." *Public Administration Review, 19,* 79-88.

Lipset, S. M. (1996). *American exceptionalism: A double-edged sword.* New York: Norton.

Litwak, E. (1985). *Helping the elderly: The complementary roles of informal and formal networks.* New York: Guilford.

Lomax, A. (1968). *Folk song style and culture.* Washington, DC: American Academy for the Advancement of Science.

Ludwig, J. (1999, April-May). Economic status: Americans assess opportunity, fairness and responsibility. *Public Perspective, 10*(3), 2-13.

Lugaila, T. A. (1998, March). *Marital status and living arrangements: An update.* [Current Population Reports P20-514]. U.S. Bureau of the Census. Retrieved from the World Wide Web: http://www.census.gov/population/socdemo/ms-la/tabad-2txt.

MacRae, D. (1985). *Policy indicators: Links between social science and public debate.* Chapel Hill: University of North Carolina Press.

Making sense of Social Security: A discussion starter. (1998). Washington, DC: *Americans discuss Social Security,* a project funded by the Pew Charitable Trusts.

Man sentenced to 24 years in prison for withholding child support (1999, August 20). *St. Paul Pioneer Press.,* p. B2.

Manegold, C. (1993, February 7). After 2 failed nominations, many women are seething. *New York Times,* p. A1.

Manegold, C. (1994, March 15). A meeting a Labor Secretary can't help but love. *New York Times,* p. C5.

Mann. T. (1998, February-March). Is the era of big government over? *Public Perspective, 9*(2), 27-29.

Mansbridge, J. (1994). Public spirit in political systems. In H. J. Aaron, T. E. Mann, & T. Taylor (Eds.), *Values and public policy* (pp. 146-172). Washington, DC: Brookings Institution.

Marin, R., & Broder, D. (1998, September 21). Worried about morals but reluctant to judge. *Washington Post National Weekly Edition*, p. 10.

Marriage license discount. (2000, March 10). *Session Weekly, 17*(6), 10.

Mashaw, J. L., & Marmor, T. (1996, November-December). The great Social Security scare. *The American Prospect*, 30-37.

"Material status" is more than economic: Children raised in one-parent families have more than doubled in last quarter-century.(1999, April-May). *Public Perspective, 10*(3), 14.

Mattessich, P. (1976a). *Writing of state level family impact statements: A preliminary report.* [Family Impact Series Report No. 1]. St. Paul, MN: University of Minnesota, Family Study Center.

Mattessich, P. (1976b). *An annotated bibliography for family impact analysis.* [Family Impact Series Report No. 3]. St. Paul, MN: University of Minnesota, Family Study Center.

McCall, G. J., & Simmons, J. L. (1978). *Identities and interactions: An examination of human associations in everyday life* (Rev. ed.). New York: Free Press.

McClosky, H., & Zaller, J. (1984). *The American ethos.* Cambridge, MA: Harvard University Press.

McCubbin, H., & Patterson, J. (1981). *Systematic assessment of family stress, resources, and coping: Tools for research, education and clinical intervention.* St. Paul, MN: University of Minnesota, Family Social Science.

McDonald, G. (1979). Family well-being and quality of life. *Family Coordinator, 28,* 313-320.

McKenzie, R. H. (1991, Spring). Consensual public policy in an adversarial culture. *National Forum* (The Phi Kappa Phi Journal). 20-21.

McLean, S. (1999, April-May). Land that I love: Feelings toward country at century's end. *Public Perspective 10*(2), 21-25.

McTavish, D. G., & Pirro, E. B. (1990). Contextual content analysis. *Quality and Quantity, 24,* 245-265.

Mead, G. (1934). *Mind, self, and society: From the standpoint of a social behaviorist.* Chicago: University of Chicago Press.

Measuring up to the past. (1999, October-November). *Public Perspective, 10*(6), 22.

Merida, K. (1993, July 15). A House and Senate divided. *Star Tribune*, p. A4. [Reprinted from the *Washington Post*].

Meyers, M. (1994, December 11). No reform, no cost Rx. *Star Tribune*, p. D1.

Miles, M. B., & Huberman, A. M. (1984). *Qualitative data analysis: A sourcebook of new methods.* Beverly Hills, CA: Sage.

Mintz, S., & Kellogg, S. (1988). *Domestic revolutions: A social history of American family life.* New York: Free Press.

Mitchell, A. (1999a, July 14). On patients' bill, Republicans defeat Democrats' provisions. *New York Times*, p. A16.

Mitchell, A. (1999b, July 24). Tax-cut bill could well revive a thing of the past: The "three martini lunch." *New York Times*, p. A9.

Mitchell, A., & Lacey, M. (1999, October 16). Lawmaker amasses power, and uses it. *New York Times*, p. A1.

Mom fights for baby's life (1993, September 25). *Star Tribune*, p. A5.

Moroney, R. (1976). *The family and the state: Considerations for social policy.* London: Longman.

Morris, R. (1987). Social welfare policy: Trends and Issues. In A. Minahan, R. Becerra, S. Briar, C. Coulton, L. Ginsberg, J. Hopps, J. Longres, R. Patti, W. Reid, T. Tripodi, & S. K. Khinduka (Eds.), *Encyclopedia of Social Work* (Vol. 2, pp. 664-681). Silver Spring, MD: National Association of Social Workers.

Moynihan, D. P. (1965, September 18). A family policy for the nation. *America.* 280-283. [Cited in Family and Nation, The Godkin Lectures, Harvard University, April 8-9, 1985].

Mydans, S. (1994, June 21). Laotian's arrest in killing bares a generation gap. *New York Times*, p. A8.

Myrdal, A. (1941). *Nation and family: The Swedish experiment in democratic family and population policy.* New York: Harper.

Myrdal, A. (1968). *Nation and Family.* Cambridge: MIT Press.

National Center for Health Statistics (1991, August 28). *Annual summary of births, marriages, divorces, and deaths: United States, 1990.* [Monthly Vital Statistics Report 39(13)]. Hyattsville, MD: Public Health Service.

A new framework for health care (1993, September 23). *New York Times*, p. A10.

Nieves, E. (2000, June 25). In San Francisco, more live alone, and die alone, too. *New York Times,* p. Y10.

NIMH post doctoral training program in national policy and the family (1976). [Mimeo]. Institute of Policy Science.

Noble, C. (1997). *Welfare as we knew it: A political history of the American welfare state.* New York: Oxford University Press.

Nossiter, A. (1993, December 18). As boot camps for criminals multiply, skepticism grow. *New York Times,* p. 1.

NPG statement on population (1994, March-April). *Sierra, 79*(2), 17.

Nye, I. (1979). Choice, exchange, and the family. In W. Burr, R. Hill, I. Nye, & I. Reiss (Eds.), *Contemporary theories about the family* (Vol. 2, pp. 1-41). New York: Free Press.

Ojito, M. (1997, June 29). Culture clash: Foreign parents, American children. *New York Times,* p. E3.

Olson, D., Sprenkle, D., & Russell, C. (1979). Circumplex model of marital and family systems: Cohesion and adaptability dimensions, family types, and clinical application. *Family Process,* 3-27.

Olson, M. (1974). *The logic of collective action.* Cambridge, MA: Harvard University Press.

O'Neill, M. (1993, December 21). When holiday styles are generations apart. *New York Times,* p. A1.

Osmond, M., & Thorne, B. (1993). Feminist theories: The social construction of gender in families and society. In P. Boss, W. Doherty, R. LaRossa, W. Schumm, & S. Steinmetz (Eds.), *Sourcebook of family theories and methods* (pp. 591-622). New York: Plenum.

Parents can be charged. (1993, July 3). *Star Tribune,* p. A7.

Parker, I. (1992). Discourse: Social psychology and postmodernity. In J. Doherty, E. Graham, & M. Malak (Eds.), *Postmodernism and the social sciences* (p. 83). New York: St. Martins Press.

Partners Task Force for Gay and Lesbian Couples (1998), *Hawaii marriage suit timeline.* Retrieved from the World Wide Web: http://www.buddybuddy.com/t-line-3.html.

Peacock, J. (1996, October 26). The Well-Springs of Social Values. Paper presented at a conference on Social Values and Public Policy, George Washington University.

Pear, R. (1991, May 11). Focusing on welfare. *New York Times,* p. 5.

Pear, R. (1993a, October 5). Poverty in U.S. grew faster than population last year. *New York Times,* p. A10.

Pear, R. (1993b, October 10). Poverty 1993: Bigger, younger, getting worse. *New York Times,* p. E5.

Pear, R. (1994, June 14). Panel on benefits spending see storm brewing on costs. *New York Times,* p. A6.

Pear, R. (1996, April 20). Health legislation: Gradualism wins the day, for now, but doubts persist. *New York Times,* p. Y32.

Pear, R. (1997, June 1). Groups are lining up to defend interest in Medicare debate. *New York Times,* p. A24.

Pear, R. (1999a, October 4). House bills diverge over a patient's right to sue. *New York Times,* p. A24.

Pear, R. (1999b, October 9). Stung by defeat in house, HMOs seek compromise. *New York Times,* p. A9.

Pear, R. (1999c, March 23). Reports of abuse of elderly are ignored, panel is told. *New York Times,* p. A20.

Pear, R. (2000. August 14). How one county cleared the welfare rolls. *New York Times,* p. A1.

Peterson, D. (1999, October 22). Good old days weren't so great, demographic report says. *Star Tribune,* p. B1.

Phillips R. (1988). *Putting asunder: A history of divorce in Western society.* New York: Cambridge University Press.

Pinker, S. (1997). *How the mind works.* New York: Norton.

Polity Watch—of the people, by the people (1999, October-November). *Public Perspective, 10*(3), 39.

Poll reveals another sign of changing U.S. family. (1999, November 26). *New York Times,* p. A22.

Preston, J. (1998, November 3). With New Jersey family cap, births fall and abortions rise. *New York Times,* p. A29.

Profiling the Clinton presidency (2000, January-February). *Public Perspective, 11*(1), 8.

Public perceptions of Social Security: Public supports using the budget surplus (1999, February). Princeton, N.J.: Princeton Survey Research Associates. Retrieved from the World Wide Web: http://www.adss.org/poll_data/poll_budgetsurplus.cfm.

Putnam, R. (2000). *Bowling alone: The collapse and revival of American community.* New York: Simon & Schuster.

Quoss, B. (1992). Teaching family policy through advocacy and empowerment. *Family Relations, 41,* 39-43.

Reilly, K. (1999, October 27). State Sen. Steve Kelley announces candidacy. *St. Louis Park Sun Sailor,* p. A1.

Reno, R. (1999, July 17). Republican family is split on what to do about marriage-tax issue. *Star Tribune,* p. A18.

Rettig, K., & Bubolz, M. (1983). Perceptual indicators of family life quality. *Social Indicators Research, 12*(4), 417-438.

Rettig, K., Danes, S., & Bauer, J. (1991). Family life quality: Theory and assessment in economically stressed farm families. *Social Indicators Research, 24,* 269-299.

Rice, R. (1977). *Family policy: Content and context.* New York: Family Service Association.

Rimer, S., (1994, June 18). Prosecution in '89 on domestic violence charges is called "a terrible joke." *New York Times,* p. 8.

Roe, J. (1998) *Governing America: Our choices, our challenge.* Dayton, OH: National Issues Forums Research.

Roe v. Wade, 410 U.S. 113, 93 S. Ct. 705 (1973).

Role of government in good times. (1999, October-November). *Public Perspective, 10*(6), 39.

Rosenbaum, D. E. (1994, June 1). A giant voice in Congress: Rostenkowski is one of a vanishing breed. *New York Times,* p. A1.

Rosenbaum, D. E. (1999, January 28). Social Security: The basics, with a tally sheet. *New York Times,* p. A19.

Rossi, P., & Wright, S. (1977). Evaluation research: An assessment of theory, practice and politics. *Evaluation Quarterly, 1,* 5-52.

Rules change: "It's a whole Newt world." (1995, January 5). *Star Tribune,* p. A1.

Sabatelli, R., & Shehan, C. (1993). Exchange and resource theories. In P. Boss, W. Doherty, R. LaRossa, W. Schumm, & S. Steinmetz (Eds.), *Sourcebook of family theories and methods* (pp. 385-411). New York: Plenum.

Sanger, D. (1999, December 3). Clinton criticizes free trade body in stormy Seattle. *New York Times,* p. A1.

Schaar, K. (1978, August). Seminar urges caution in family impact area. *APA Monitor, 9*(6), 1.

Schimke, D. (1995, January 4-10). The carrot and the club. *Twin Cities Reader,* 8-11.

Schmitt, E. (1999, October 28). Helms orders 10 women from House out of Senate hearing. *New York Times,* p. A17.

Schorr, A. (1968). *Explorations in social policy.* New York: Basic.

Schorr. A. (1972, January). Family values and public policy: A venture in prediction and prescription. *Journal of Social Policy, 1*(1), 33-43.

Schorr, A. (1984, May 18). Change the definition in poverty decline. *Star Tribune,* p. A25.

Schram, S. (1995). *Words of welfare: The poverty of social science and the social science of poverty.* St. Paul, MN: University of Minnesota Press.

Seeking a cure: Looking for answers to America's health care woes. (1993, October 25). *Star Tribune* (Supplement), pp. 1H-35H.

Seelye, K. Q. (1994, March 6). Leader on Senate: Not a lifetime job. *New York Times,* p. 11.

Seelye, K. Q. (1997, January 16). House rule may rein in liberal advocacy groups. *New York Times,* p. A12.

Seelye, K. Q. (1998, May 30). Vote set for prayer and marriage penalty bills. *New York Times,* p. A2.

Seidman, S. (1994). *The postmodern turn: New perspectives on social theory.* New York: Cambridge University Press.

Sen, A. (1980). Description as choice. *Oxford Economic Papers, 32.*

Sen, A. (1985). Well being, agency, and freedom. The Dewey Lectures 1984. *Journal of Philosophy, 82.*

Sexton, J. (1997, March 24). Working and welfare parents compete for day care slots. *New York Times,* p. A12.

Shapiro, I., & Greenstein, R. (1999, September 6). *The widening income gulf*. Washington, DC: Center on Budget and Policy Priorities.

Sheffield, A. (1915, July 24). The influence of Mothers' Aid on family life. *Survey, 34*(17), 378-379.

Shellencharger, S. (1998, March 15). More execs resigning for family time. *Star Tribune*, p. D5.

Shogren, E. (1997, January 3). Fewer chums in the cabinet. *Star Tribune*, p. A7.

Simon, H. (1957). *Models of man*. New York: Wiley.

Singer v. Hara, 522 P 2d 1187, 11 Wash. App. 247 (1974).

Six-month study shows that working families are moving out of poverty. (2000, March-April). *Minnesota Investment*, 1.

Skolnick, A., & Skolnick, J. (1977). *Family in transition: Rethinking marriage, sexuality, child rearing, and family organization*. (2nd ed.). Boston: Little, Brown.

Slovut, G. (1994, March 15). Study: Elderly poor happy with HMOs. *Star Tribune*, p. 1B.

Smelser, N., & Halpern, N. J. (1978). The historical triangulation of family, economy, and education. In J. Demos & S. S. Boocock (Eds.), *Turning points: Historical and sociological essays in the family* (pp. S288-S315). Chicago: University of Chicago Press.

Smith, D. (1999, July 31). Evolving answers to the why of suicide. *New York Times*, p. A15.

Smith, L. (1997, November 16). Group aims to improve family-values debate. *Star Tribune*, p. E10.

Smith, M. (1999, September 9). Ramsey county increases spending for kids. *Star Tribune*, p. B1.

Smothers, R. (1994, April 18). Schools are taking parents to court on truancy. *New York Times*, p. A1.

Snyder, S., & Boyce, S. (1994). *Sources of health insurance: Characteristics of the uninsured*. Washington, DC: Employee Benefits Research Institute.

Sontag, D. (1993, September 27). Women asking U.S. asylum expand definition of abuse. *New York Times*, p. A1.

Spousal assault trial cast as cautionary tale for men and women. (1993, November 8). *New York Times*, p. A8.

Sprey, J. (1979). Conflict theory and the study of the family. In W. Burr, R. Hill, I. Nye, & I. Reiss (Eds.), *Contemporary theories about the family* (Vol. 2, pp. 130-159). New York: Free Press.

Stacey. J. (1996). *In the name of the family: Rethinking family values in the postmodern age*. Boston: Beacon.

Stack, C. (1974). *All our kin: Strategies for survival in a black community*. New York: Harper & Row.

Stack, S., & Eshleman, J. R. (1998, May). Marital status and happiness: A 17-Nation Study. *Journal of Marriage and Family, 60*(2), 527-536.

Stanley, B. (1999, October 10). Europeans living the good life Americans find little time for. *Star Tribune*, p. A22.

State Legislative Leaders Foundation (1995). *Keys to effective legislation for children and families*. Centerville, MA: Author.

Stein, H. (1995, September 5). On families and values. *Congressional Record*. Retrieved from the World Wide Web: http://thomas.loc.gov.

Steiner, G. (1981). *The futility of family policy*. Washington, DC: Brookings Institution.

Stevenson, R. (1999a, July 23). Republicans pass big tax cut to set stage for debate. *New York Times*, p. A1.

Stevenson, R. (1999b, February 2). Seeking the high ground on spending surpluses. *New York Times*, p. A16.

Stevenson, R. (1999c, July 30). Senate GOP moves ahead on tax plan. *New York Times*, p. A16.

Stevenson, R. (1999d, September 24). Clinton vetoes GOP tax cut but seeks compromise. *New York Times*, p. A20.

Stokes, R., & Hewitt, J. P. (1976). Aligning actions. *American Sociological Review, 41*, 838-849.

Stolberg, S. G. (1997, May 26). Women's issues and wariness in Congress. *New York Times*, p. A7.

Stone, L. (1977). *The family, sex, and marriage in England, 1500-1800*. New York: Harper & Row.

Straus, A., & Corbin, J. (1990). *Basics of qualitative research: Grounded theory procedures and techniques*. Newbury Park, CA: Sage.

Stryker, S. (1964). The interactional and situational approaches. In H. Christensen (Ed.), *Handbook of marriage and the family* (pp. 125-170). Chicago: Rand McNally.

Study: Earth population outpacing resources (1994, February 22). *Star Tribune*, p. A7.

Swarns, R. (1998, May 27). Despite abuse, a boy wants home back, and may get it. *New York Times*, p. A1.

Taffel, R. (1999, September-October). Discovering our children. *Networker*, 24-35.

Tallman, I. (1979). Implementation of a national family policy: The role of the social scientist. *Journal of Marriage and the Family*, 41, 469-472.

Teenager says parents deprived him of food (1999, April 19). *New York Times*, p. A14.

Teixeira, R. A. (1992, Fall). Voter turnout in America. *Brookings Review*, 10(4), 28-31.

Terreberry, S. (1972). The evolution of organizational environments. In K. Azumi & J. Hage (Eds.), *Organizational Systems* (pp. 75-91) Lexington, MA: D.C. Health.

Theodorson, G., & Theodorson, A. (1969). *A modern dictionary of sociology*. New York: Thomas Crowell.

Thibaut, J. W., & Kelley, H. H. (1959). *The social psychology of groups*. New York: Wiley.

Things have always gone up and down. (1993, July-August). *Public Perspective*, 4(5), 93.

Thomas, W. I., & Thomas, D. S. (1928). *The child in America*. New York: Knopf.

Thompson, G. (1999, April 18). Battered and unprotected. *New York Times*, p. Y31.

Time to retire the filibuster (1995, January 1). *New York Times*, p. E8.

Toner, R. (1993, October 22). Abortion and the health plan: Hard questions in both camps. *New York Times*, p. A10.

Toner, R. (1994, August 18). House action of health measure may wait till after Labor Day. *New York Times*, p. A1.

Toner, R. (1999a, October 4). House is set to take up debate on patients' rights. *New York Times*, p. A24.

Toner, R. (1999b, October 9). Fevered issue, second opinion. *New York Times*, p. A1.

Toner, R. (1999c). July 28). Long term care merges political with personal. *New York Times*, p. A1.

Toogood, M. (1997, February 23). Behind door of privacy, kids pay a terrible price. *Star Tribune*, p. A21.

Trattner, W. (1974). *From poor law to welfare state: A history of social welfare in the United States*. New York: Free Press.

Truman, D. (1971). *The Government Process*. New York: Knopf.

Tully, C. T. (1994). To boldly go where no one has gone before. The legalization of lesbian and gay marriages. *Journal of Gay & Lesbian Social Services*, 1(1), 73-87.

Uchitelle, L. (1999, October 18). Devising new math to define poverty. *New York Times*, p. A1.

U.S. Bureau of the Census (1983). *Statistical abstracts of the United States, 1984* (104th ed.). Washington, DC: U.S. Government Printing Office.

U.S. Bureau of the Census (1986). *Statistical abstracts of the United States, 1987* (107th ed.). Washington, DC: U.S. Government Printing Office.

U.S. Bureau of the Census (1990). *Statistical abstracts of the United States, 1990* (111th ed.) Washington, DC: U.S. Government Printing Office.

U.S. Bureau of the Census (1993). *Statistical abstracts of the United States, 1993* (113th ed.). Washington, DC: U.S. Government Printing Office.

U.S. Bureau of the Census (1994). *Statistical abstracts of the United States, 1994* (114th ed.). Washington, D.C.: U.S. Government Printing Office.

U.S. Bureau of the Census (1996). *Statistical abstracts of the United States, 1996* (116th ed.). Washington, DC: U.S. Government Printing Office.

U.S. Bureau of the Census (1997). *State government finances, 1995* (117th ed.). Washington, DC: U.S. Government Printing Office.

U.S. Bureau of the Census (1998). *Statistical abstracts of the United States, 1998* (118th ed.). Washington, DC: U.S. Government Printing Office.

Use of "ma'am" or "sir" may soon be law in Louisiana (1999, June 16). *Star Tribune*, p. A5.

Verhovek, S. H. (1995, August 30). Mother scolded by judge for speaking in Spanish. *New York Times*, p. A9.

Von Sternberg, B. (2000, July 24). Many say death to the "death tax." *Star Tribune*, p. A1.

Wade, F. (1905, April 22). Family desertion and non-support laws. *Charities*, 14(4), 682-684.

Wayne, L. (1996, December 20). Interest groups prepare for huge fight on Social Security. *New York Times*, p. A9.

Weber, R. P. (1985). *Basic content analysis*. Beverly Hills, CA: Sage.

Weiner, T. (1997, December 27). Many Laotians in U.S. find their hopes betrayed. *New York Times*, p. A1.

Westendorp, K. (1994, April 30). Aaron needs family, not this cruel policy. *Star Tribune*, p. A21.

White House Conference. (1977-78, December-January). *The American family: National action overview.*

Who cares? Minnesotans do. (2000, January 20). *Star Tribune,* p. A22.

Wilgoren, J. (1999, October 21). Quality day care, early, is tied to achievements as adults. *New York Times* p. A16.

Wilgoren, J. (2000). School vouchers: A rose by any other name? *New York Times,* p. A1.

Wilkerson, I. (1993, April 4). First born, fast grown: The manful life of Nicholas, 10. *New York Times,* p. A1.

Will, G. (1999, June 28). Social disease to social policy. *Star Tribune,* p. A11.

Wilson, J. Q. (1993, April). The family values debate. *Commentary, 95*(4), 24-31.

Wines, M. (1992, March 10). President focuses on "family values." *New York Times,* p. A15.

Wines, M. (1993, November 25). Moynihan and Kennedy tangle over handling of health bill. *New York Times,* p. A12.

Wines, M. (1994, December 18). Republicans seek sweeping changes in House rules. *New York Times,* p. A1.

Wisconsin woman is jailed after her daughter, 15, dies weighing 15 pounds (1998, November 28). *Star Tribune,* p. A8.

With wit and reflection, Dee Dee Myers bows out. (1994, December 23). *Star Tribune,* p. A9.

Wolf, C. P. (1976, Spring). Social impact assessment: The state of the art restated. *Sociological Practice, 1,* 56-69.

Wolfe, A. (1998). *One nation, after all.* New York: Penguin.

Wolfe, W. (2000, March 15). Tears, fear, and anxiety cloud days as nursing homes close. *Star Tribune,* p. B1.

Woodward, B. (1994). *The agenda: Inside the Clinton White House.* New York: Simon & Schuster.

Yankelovich, D. (1994). How changes in the economy are reshaping American values. In H. Aaron, T. Mann, & T. Taylor (Eds.), *Values and Public Policy* (pp. 16-54). Washington, DC: Brookings Institution.

Yankelovich. D. (1998, February-March). How American individualism is evolving: American opinion in the 1990s. *Public Perspective, 9*(2), 3-6.

Zack, M., & Klauda, P. (1980, June 20). Unity plea opens family meeting. *Star Tribune,* p. A1.

Zaltman, G., Duncan, R., & Holbeck, J. (1973). *Organizations and innovations.* New York: Wiley.

Ziegler, H., & Huelshoff, M. (1980). Interest groups and public policy. *Policy Studies Journal, 9*(3), 439-448.

Zill, N., Morrison, D. R., & Coiro, M. J. (1993). Long-term effects of parental divorce on parent-child relationships, adjustment, and achievement in young adulthood. *Journal of Family Psychology, 7*(6), 1-13.

Zimmerman, S. L. (1976). The family and its relevance for social policy. *Social Casework, 57,* 547-554.

Zimmerman, S. L. (1979). Policy, social policy, family policy: Concepts, concerns, and analytic tools. *Journal of Marriage and the Family, 41*(3), 487-496.

Zimmerman, S. L. (1982). Confusions and contradictions in family policy developments: Applications of a model. *Family Relations, 31*(3), 445-455.

Zimmerman, S. L. (1988a). *Understanding family policy: Theoretical approaches.* Newbury Park, CA: Sage.

Zimmerman, S. L. (1988b). State level public policies as predictors of state teenage birthrates. *Family Relations, 37*(3), 315-321.

Zimmerman, S. L. (1992a). *Family policies and family well-being: The role of political culture.* Newbury Park, CA: Sage.

Zimmerman, S. L. (1992b). Family trends: What implications for family policy? *Family Relations, 41*(4), 423-429.

Zimmerman, S. L. (1993a, November 6-9). Congressional votes on key family legislation 1976, 1985, 1990: Political culture, political party, or gender? In B. Settles and J. Trost (Eds.), *Gender and Families: Choices, challenges, and changing policy.* [Working papers]. Seminar, Committee on Family Research, International Sociological Association. Annapolis, MD.

Zimmerman, S. L. (1993b). Political culture, policy choices, and unmet needs. In A. Leenaars (Ed.), *Suicidology: Essays in honor of Edwin Shneidman* (pp. 42-60). Northvale, NJ: Jason Aronson.

Zimmerman, S. L. (1994). The role of the state in family life: States' AFDC payments and their divorce rates. *International Journal of Sociology and Social Policy, 14,* 14-29.

Zimmerman, S. L. (1995a). *Understanding family policy: Theories and applications.* Thousand Oaks, CA.: Sage.

Zimmerman, S. L. (1995b). Psychache in context: States' spending for public welfare and their suicide rates. *Journal of Nervous and Mental Disease, 183,* 425-434.

Zimmerman, S. L. (1997a). Educational policy and the role of advocacy. In M. L. Fuller & G. Olsen (Eds.), *Home-school relations: Working successfully with parents and families* (pp. 332-554). Boston: Allyn & Bacon.

Zimmerman, S. L. (1997b). A potential case of social bankruptcy: States' AFDC payments and their teen birth rates. *Policy Studies Review, 25*(1), 109-123.

Zimmerman, S. L. (1999, May). Family policy research: A system's view. *Family Science Review, 12*(2), 113-130.

Zimmerman, S. L. (2000). States' political cultures and their family policies in the 1990s. In J. Mercier, S. Garasky, and M. Shelley II (Eds.), *Redefining Family Policy: Implications for the 21st Century* (pp. 21-41). Ames, IA: Iowa University Press.

Zimmerman, S. L., & Gager, C. (1997). *The gender factor in policy choices relations to families: Congressional votes, 1985, 1990, 1993, 1995.* [Mimeo]. St. Paul, MN: University of Minnesota, Family Social Science.

Zimmerman, S. L., Mattessich, P., & Leik, R. (1979). Legislators' attitudes toward family policy. *Journal of Marriage and the Family, 41*(2), 507-517.

Zimmerman, S. L., & Owens, P. (1989). Comparing the family policies of three states: A content analysis. *Family Relations, 38,* 190-196.

Zimmerman, S. L., & Sterne, R. (1978, Fall). The use of I&R data in social planning. In V. Doyle (Ed.), *Proceedings of an I&R Roundtable* (pp. 60-69). Phoenix, AZ: I&R Alliance.

NAME INDEX

407

☐ Shirley L. Zimmerman is Professor-Emeritus, Family Social Science, at the University of Minnesota, where she taught courses on family policy, family policy research, and family policy from an international perspective. She is the author of *Understanding Family Policy: Theoretical Approaches* (1988, 1st ed.; 1995, 2nd ed.) and *Family Policies and Family Well-Being: The Role of Political Culture* (1992). She also is the author of numerous articles dealing with family policy and related issues appearing in academic and professional journals. Her research focuses on policy choices related to families, the factors that influence such choices, and the outcomes of such choices for families.

She has served as consultant to state and local social agencies in the planning and development of educational programs for professional staff, and she has served in a leadership capacity on numerous local, state, and national task forces and committees. Earlier in her professional career, she was actively engaged in child advocacy and in advocating programs to meet the needs of children and their families. She is a former chair of the Minnesota Governor's Council on Families and Children. She was a postdoctoral fellow in the Family Impact Analysis Training program sponsored by the Minnesota Family Study Center at the University of Minnesota.

She is married, has three sons, one daughter, three daughters-in-law, one son-in-law, six grandsons, and one granddaughter.